THE UN
WIN

D1627607

2005

THE ROMAN VILLA IN BRITAIN

THE ROMAN VILLA
IN BRITAIN

edited by

A. L. F. RIVET

Routledge & Kegan Paul
LONDON

First published 1969
by Routledge & Kegan Paul Limited
Broadway House, 68–74 Carter Lane
London, E.C.4
Reprinted 1970
Printed in Great Britain
by W. & J. Mackay & Co Ltd, Chatham
© Routledge & Kegan Paul Limited 1969
No part of this book may be reproduced
in any form without permission from
the publisher, except for the quotation
of brief passages in criticism

SBN 7100 1657 3

Contents

List of Illustrations $page$ vii

Preface and Acknowledgments xiii

Abbreviations xv

I   The Celtic Background 1

         H. C. BOWEN, M.A., F.S.A.
         Royal Commission on Historical Monuments (England)

II   The Plans of Roman Villas in Britain 49

         THE LATE SIR IAN RICHMOND, C.B.E., M.A., D.LITT., LITT.D.,
         F.B.A., F.S.A.
         Late Professor of the Archaeology of the Roman Empire, University of Oxford

III   The Mosaic Pavements 71

         D. J. SMITH, PH.D., F.S.A.
         Keeper and Secretary of the Museum of Antiquities of the University of New-
         castle upon Tyne and the Society of Antiquaries of Newcastle upon Tyne

IV   Furniture and Interior Decoration 127

         JOAN LIVERSIDGE, M.LITT., F.S.A.
         Honorary Keeper of the Roman Collections, Museum of Archaeology and
         Ethnology, University of Cambridge

V   Social and Economic Aspects 173

         A. L. F. RIVET, M.A., F.S.A.
         Reader in Romano-British Studies, University of Keele

VI   The Future of Villa Studies 217

         GRAHAM WEBSTER, M.A., PH.D., F.S.A.
         Staff Tutor in Archaeology, Extra-Mural Department,
         University of Birmingham

CONTENTS

Ancient Authorities Cited   *page*   251

Modern Authorities Cited   253

Bibliography of Individual Villas and Similar Buildings   265

Index of Places   281

General Index   291

List of Illustrations

CHAPTER ONE: THE CELTIC BACKGROUND

ILLUSTRATIONS IN THE TEXT

page

1.1 Some Iron Age Settlements and Enclosures in southern
England   5
1.2 Some Iron Age and Romano-British house sites   6
1.3 Some features of the 'Little Woodbury' economy   14
1.4 'Celtic' fields and Strip-lynchets   27
1.5 Plan of settlement on Meriden Down, Winterbourne
Houghton, Dorset   36
1.6 Romano-British farm implements   39
1.7 Reconstruction of the 'vallus'   40
1.8 Plan of 'Celtic' fields on Brading Down, Isle of Wight, in
relation to Brading villa   43
1.9 Interpretation of Plate 1.3 (Cuckoo Bridge, Lincs.)   46

PLATES

Between pages 8 and 9

1.1 Air photograph of Fosbury hill-fort, Wiltshire
1.2 Replica of a prehistoric light plough pulled by cattle comparable in
size with the ancient British shorthorn
1.3 Vertical air photograph of the area east of Cuckoo Bridge, south-
west of Spalding, Lincolnshire

CHAPTER TWO: THE PLANS OF ROMAN VILLAS IN BRITAIN

ILLUSTRATIONS IN THE TEXT

page

2.1	Plans of cottage-houses and winged corridor houses	54
2.2	Elaboration of the winged corridor plan	57
2.3	Block plans of villas	58
2.4	Plan of the courtyard villa at North Leigh, Oxon.	61
2.5	Plan of the courtyard villa at Chedworth, Glos.	63
2.6	Plans of aisled houses and a 'farm-house'	66
2.7	The fourth-century plan of the house at Lullingstone, Kent	70

PLATE

2.1	Air photograph of the Ditchley villa, Oxon.	*facing page* 49

CHAPTER THREE: THE MOSAIC PAVEMENTS

ILLUSTRATIONS IN THE TEXT

3.1	Distribution of villas with mosaics	73
3.2	Horkstow, Lincs.	89
3.3	East Coker, Som.	92
3.4	Fourth-century schools of Mosaic (map)	96

PLATES

Between pages 112 *and* 113

3.1	Eccles, Kent: mosaic of *c.* A.D. 65	
3.2	Fishbourne, Sussex, *c.* A.D. 150–200	
3.3	Pitney, Som.: Gods and Seasons	
3.4	Bramdean, Hants: the Gods of the Week	
3.5	Low Ham, Som.: Dido and Aeneas	
3.6	Codex Vaticanus Latinus 3225: Aeneas at the court of Dido	
3.7	Lullingstone, Kent: the rape of Europe	
3.8	Brading, Isle of Wight	
3.9	Thruxton, Hants: Bacchus and (?) the Seasons	

3.10 Newton St Loe, Som.: Orpheus
3.11 Withington, Glos.
3.12 Barton Farm, Cirencester, Glos.: Orpheus
3.13 Woodchester, Glos.: Orpheus
3.14 Woodchester, Glos.: mosaic in Room 10
3.15 Stonesfield, Oxon.: three mosaics
3.16 Littlecote Park, Wilts.: Orpheus and the Seasons
3.17 Winterton, Lincs.: Orpheus and (?) Ceres
3.18 Winterton, Lincs.: (?) Providentia
3.19 Brantingham, E. Yorks.: *tyche* and water-nymphs
3.20 Rudston, E. Yorks.: Venus and scenes from the amphitheatre
3.21 Great Weldon, Northants.: plan showing disposition and patterns of mosaics
3.22 Scampton, Lincs.: geometric corridor mosaic
3.23 Mansfield Woodhouse, Notts.: geometric mosaic
3.24 Mill Hill, Castor, Northants.: geometric mosaic
3.25 Great Staughton, Hunts.: geometric mosaic
3.26 Denton, Lincs.: geometric mosaic, *c.* A.D. 370
3.27 Frampton, Dorset: mosaic of the Chi-Rho
3.28 Frampton, Dorset: mosaic of the river-god and Winds
3.29 Hinton St Mary, Dorset: mosaics of Christ and Bellerophon
3.30 Fifehead Neville, Dorset: (?) Christian mosaic
3.31 Lenthay Green, Sherborne, Dorset: Apollo and Marsyas
3.32 Woodchester, Glos., and Trier, Germany

COLOUR PLATES

facing page 116

3.1 Bignor, Sussex: head of Venus
3.2 Hinton St Mary, Dorset: head of Christ

CHAPTER FOUR: FURNITURE AND INTERIOR DECORATION

ILLUSTRATIONS IN THE TEXT

		page
4.1	Imitation marbling and tessellated designs	131
4.2	Imitation marbling	132

ix

page

4.3   Beaded lines from panel frameworks   135
4.4   Curvilinear designs   136
4.5   Curvilinear designs   138
4.6   Designs from Harpham, Yorks.   140
4.7   Foliate motifs   142
4.8   Decorated wall, Witcombe, Glos.   143
4.9   Carved sandstone slab, Ashtead, Surrey   156
4.10 Column capital, Warleigh, Bathford, Som.   157
4.11 Cupids playing at shoemakers, Herculaneum   160
4.12 Folding stool, Bartlow, Cambs.   161
4.13 Reconstruction of a Roman bronze tripod, Baltimore   163
4.14 Marble table, Pompeii   164
4.15 Marble table support, Pompeii   166
4.16 Bronze table, Pompeii   167

PLATES

between pages 144 and 145

4.1   South-west angle of the 'painted room', Iwerne, Dorset
4.2   Bignor, Sussex, Room 33
4.3   Carisbrooke, Isle of Wight
4.4   Wall-painting, Comb End, Glos.
4.5   Wall-painting, Brading, Isle of Wight
4.6   Wall-painting, Otford, Kent
4.7   Wall-painting, Otford, Kent
4.8   Motifs from wall-painting at Greetwell, Lincs.
4.9   Wall-painting, Farningham, Kent
4.10 *Graffito* on plaster, Hucclecote, Glos.
4.11 Relief, Wellow, Som.
4.12 Statue of Luna, Woodchester, Glos.
4.13 Statue of Bacchus, Spoonley Wood, Glos.
4.14 Statue of Venus (?), Froxfield, Wilts.
4.15 Detail of marble bust, Lullingstone, Kent
4.16 Pipeclay statuette of Mother-Goddess, London
4.17 Wall-painting, Trier
4.18 Tombstone of Julia Velva, York
4.19 Tombstone of Aelia Aeliana, York
4.20 Reconstruction of roof with finial, Llantwit Major, Glam.
4.21 Shale table-foot, Upper Langridge Farm, Bath

4.22 Bronze foot, Stanton Low, Bucks.
4.23 Bronze foot, Caerwent, Mon.
4.24 Shale table-leg, Dorchester, Dorset
4.25 Shale table-leg, Frampton, Dorset
4.26 Shale table-leg, Preston, Dorset
4.27 Shale table-leg, Rothley, Leics.
4.28 Shale table-leg, Norden, Dorset
4.29 Top of shale table-leg, Foscott, Bucks.
4.30 Sarcophagus, Simpelveld, Netherlands

COLOUR PLATES

between pages 168 *and* 169

4.1 Wall-painting, Ickleton, Cambs.
4.2 Wall-painting, Ickleton, Cambs.
4.3 Wall-painting, Brading Isle of Wight
4.4 Wall-painting, Box, Wilts.
4.5 Wall-painting, Ickleton, Cambs.
4.6 Wall-painting, Ickleton, Cambs.

CHAPTER FIVE: SOCIAL ECONOMIC ASPECTS

ILLUSTRATIONS IN THE TEXT

		page
5.1	Distribution of villas in relation to towns and roads	178
5.2	Pre-Roman economic development: (a) Highland and Lowland Zones. (b) Approximate tribal areas, showing known coin mints. (c) Distribution of Celtic coins, (d) Distribution of Continental imports, excluding coins, from 100 B.C. to the Roman conquest	187
5.3	The military occupation of Britain	191
5.4	(a) Hill-forts and other defended enclosures of less than 3 acres. (b) Open farms and other undefended settlements in the Iron Age	193
5.5	Producing and consuming areas in Britain and Gaul	194
5.6	Total distribution of villas in Britain	211
5.7	Distribution of 3rd-4th century villas of classes A and B	213

CHAPTER SIX: THE FUTURE OF VILLA STUDIES

ILLUSTRATIONS IN THE TEXT

		page
6.1	Villas where occupation ceased before A.D. 360	229
6.2	Villas occupied after A.D. 367	230
6.3	Section QR, Llantwit, Glam.	239

Preface and Acknowledgments

'Roman villas are so well-established in Romano-British archaeology as to require, paradoxically, some explanation.' So the late Sir Ian Richmond began his chapter on the countryside in the first volume of *The Pelican History of England*. Some of the questions to which they give rise are discussed in the several chapters of this book, but it does not pretend to offer a full explanation, for it is not designed as a coherent whole. The degree of co-ordination is simply that which is natural between friends and colleagues working in closely related fields, and each author has treated of his topic as he thought best. We hope nevertheless that its wide coverage and the provision of common bibliographies and indexes will make it not useless as a work of reference.

It has been a sad book to edit, for two reasons. First, while it is in no sense a 'conference report', it owed its origin to the last of the summer schools in archaeology organised by the late Dr Frederick Wainwright: he had died before the meeting took place. Second, as recorded on page 49, the writing of a chapter for this book was one of the too many tasks on which Sir Ian Richmond was engaged at the time of his death. Beyond this, it has been subject to all the vicissitudes which beset a composite work, and staff changes at the publishers have imposed further long delays.

For permission to use or to reproduce material for illustrations we are greatly indebted to the following individuals and institutions: Messrs J. Anstee, D. Baker, S. Brown, J. Christiansen, Mrs E. Clifford, Mr D. B. Connah, Dr F. L. M. Dawson, Messrs O. Fein, J. Gardner, E. Greenfield, Dr D. K. Hill, Mr A. W. G. Lowther, Lieut.-Col. G. W. Meates, Messrs H. J. Mellon, E. Mellor, Dr J. Mertens, Mrs E. Minter, Messrs L. P. Morley, A. T. Morley-Hewitt, D. S. Neal, the late Major D. Oglander, Mr A. Pacitto, Dr K. Parlasca, Mr M. Parsons, Dr J. K. S. St Joseph,

Professor J. M. C. Toynbee and Capt. H. Tupper; the Society of Anti-quaries of London, Bristol City Museum, the British Association for the Advancement of Science, the Trustees of the British Museum, the Cambrian Archaeological Association, the University of Cambridge, Cambridge University Museum of Archaeology and Ethnology, Cheltenham Museum, Chichester Civic Society, Devizes Museum, Dorset County Museum, the Fishbourne Excavation Committee, Hull City Museums, the Rijksmuseum van Oudheden te Leiden, Letchworth Museum, Lincoln City Museum, the Trustees of the London Museum, the Ministry of Defence, the Ministry of Public Building and Works, the Museo Nazionale, Naples, the Ash-molean Museum, Oxford, Eastgate House Museum, Rochester, the Vatican Library, Rome, the Römisch-Germanische Kommission des Deutschen Archäologischen Instituts, the Royal Commission on Historical Monu-ments (England), the *Salisbury Times*, Surrey Archaeological Society, the Castle Museum, Taunton, the Landesmuseum, Trier, the National Museum of Wales, the Walters Art Gallery, Baltimore, the Warburg Institute, the Wiltshire Archaeological and Natural History Society, the Yorkshire Museum; and above all to Lady Richmond and to Messrs Methuen and Company Ltd for permission to print as Chapter II the text and illustrations of the chapter on villas from Sir Ian's revision of Colling-wood's *Archaeology of Roman Britain*.

Keele, 1969   A.L.F.R.

Abbreviations

used in the Notes and Bibliography

Ag. H.R.	*Agricultural History Review*
Ant.	*Antiquity*
Ant. J.	*Antiquaries Journal*
Arch.	*Archaeologia*
Arch. Ael.	*Archaeologia Aeliana*
Arch. Camb.	*Archaeologia Cambrensis*
Arch. Cant.	*Archaeologia Cantiana*
Arch. J.	*Archaeological Journal*
B.B.C.S.	*Bulletin of the Board of Celtic Studies*
Berks. A.J.	*Berkshire Archaeological Journal*
B.M.	British Museum
C.A.H.	*Cambridge Ancient History*
CBA	Council for British Archaeology
C.I.L.	*Corpus Inscriptionum Latinarum*
Gents. Mag.	*The Gentleman's Magazine*
J.B.A.A.	*Journal of the British Archaeological Association*
J.R.S.	*Journal of Roman Studies*
P.C.A.S.	*Proceedings of the Cambridge Antiquarian Society*
P.D.N.H.A.F.C.	*Proceedings of the Dorset Natural History and Archaeological Field Club*
P.P.H.F.C.	*Papers and Proceedings of the Hampshire Field Club*
P.P.S.	*Proceedings of the Prehistoric Society*
P.S.A.L.	*Proceedings of the Society of Antiquaries of London*
P.S.A.N.H.S.	*Proceedings of the Somerset Archaeological and Natural History Society*
RAI	Royal Archaeological Institute
RCHM	Royal Commission on Historical Monuments (England)
R.I.B.	R. G. Collingwood and R. P. Wright, *The Roman Inscriptions of Britain*, vol. i, Oxford, 1965

ABBREVIATIONS

Sx A.C.	*Sussex Archaeological Collections*
Sy A.C.	*Surrey Archaeological Collections*
T.B.G.A.S.	*Transactions of the Bristol and Gloucester Archaeological Society*
T.C.W.A.A.S.	*Transactions of the Cumberland and Westmorland Antiquarian and Archaeological Society*
VCH	*The Victoria History of the Counties of England*
W.A.M.	*Wiltshire Archaeological Magazine*
Y.A.J.	*Yorkshire Archaeological Journal*

In the footnotes, references to the list of Modern Authorities Cited are expressed in the form

Aberg (1957);

references to the Bibliography of Individual Villas are expressed in the form

Abbotts Ann (1900)

CHAPTER ONE

The Celtic Background

H. C. BOWEN

THE NATIVE CELTS supplied more than the background to Roman villas in Britain. It seems likely that they actually owned most of them. It will be the aim of this essay to consider, firstly, something of Celtic social structure; secondly, the types of settlement so far known to have existed in the pre-Roman Iron Age; thirdly, above all, the farming economy which the term 'villa' demands; and, lastly, the changes observed in it during the Roman period. Because villas are generally found in the lowland zone of Britain, which was also where native arable farming was concentrated, most attention will be given to this zone. Because there was a large degree of continuity from the Iron Age into the Roman period and because without excavation we can sometimes not be sure whether a native site belongs to the Iron Age or the Romano-British period or both, our headings for discussion will tend to be subjects rather than periods. There are other warnings and qualifications. Our information is scattered and generally scanty. We have firstly a few documented facts,[1] although tantalisingly few in view of their apparent accuracy. Secondly, there are the results from a very small number of large-scale excavations and a larger number of minor ones, the total affecting only a small fraction of even the

[1] Rivet (1964), 16–23

1

known sites. Thirdly, there is still a considerable number of earthworks, though suffering rapid destruction, and a growing host of air photographs showing the crop or soil marks of sites otherwise destroyed.

Because our information is so scattered we have to accept evidence, some of it not precisely dated, from anywhere within a total period that spans a thousand years. The British Iron Age itself lasted longer than the time which separates us today from the Wars of the Roses. Forms of settlement and practice varied within regions and between different regions. There were advances and changes within the period. Others followed throughout the nearly 400 years of Roman government, made possible or accelerated by the fact of conquest. Finally, it must be emphasised that, where evidence is limited, more than one conjecture is often possible. Where theories are advanced below, they must be regarded as working hypotheses that seem reasonable to the writer at the moment. Conversely, some attempt will be made to indicate what are undeniable facts.

Descriptions of the Celts are found in the writings of classical contemporaries.[1] Some of these relate to the Celts of Gaul, but there are many indications of a community of culture with Britain. Thus Tacitus, writing at the end of the 1st century A.D., says that certain Britons had lost their valour with their liberty, but that the rest were still what the Gauls used to be.[2] A recent analysis of the oldest Irish traditions, little affected by Rome, shows considerable parallels between the heroic structure depicted therein and that in Gaul described by the Romans.[3] Celtic culture was widespread and deep-rooted. Scholars today are striving to use the early Welsh Laws to throw light on the structure of society in Roman Britain and earlier. Reference to this will be made again, but another warning must be sounded. Archaeologically attested differences are perhaps even more striking because of the Celtic connection. As an example, round houses were normal in Iron Age Britain, while on the Continent the rectangular form was well known. This is particularly odd in view of the fact, for instance, that we usually accept the arguments for the use of rectangular stilted granaries in this country. Within Britain there was the broad economic division, largely determined by geology and climate, between the highland and lowland zone;[4] and there was a multitude of small differ-

[1] Tierney (1960) discusses the statements of, and provides relevant translations from, Athenaeus, Diodorus Siculus, Strabo, and Caesar.

[2] Tacitus, *Agr.*, xi

[3] Jackson (1964), 29

[4] S. Piggott, in Richmond (1958)

2

ences, some of which will be mentioned in due course. A tendency to fierce 'parochialism' was certainly exploited by the Romans and was not dead even amongst recent Celts. When George Borrow, some hundred years ago in the central Welsh valley of the Ystwyth, was mistaken for a north Welshman he was told to 'go back to your goats in Anglesey; you are not wanted here'. It is surely the echo of a reason for hill-forts.[1]

The Ancient Britons were, however, much more than warriors daubed in woad. It is true that they were on occasion colourful in this and other ways, that they did often fight naked, but trousers were probably normal male peacetime wear and we know that they were capable not only of a vigorous and attractive art form but that they were excellent smiths and carpenters as well. Classical contemporaries saw the Celts as big, blue-eyed, fair-haired, and extravagant in their ways. Wild bravery and carelessness of death had its sinister aspect in human sacrifice and the display of enemy heads. 'To the frankness and high-spiritedness of their temperament must be added the traits of childish boastfulness and love of decoration.'[2] Their chief people affected gold ornaments and brightly coloured clothes. They paid much attention to their hair, often plastering the drawn-back locks with whitewash. Their characteristic moustaches were less tractable and dignified, the clean-shaven Romans marvelling how they became 'entangled in the food' and served as 'a sort of strainer for what they drank'.[3] One suspects it would not have been safe to make such a comment face to face. There was a vigour to all they did. It shone in their art, where their spirit was matched by their craftsmanship. Stop their fighting and there was talent in abundance to use. They were in Britain tempted, and many of them ready, to settle down. The recent find of a sailing-barge in the Thames, carvel-built of native oak, dated to c. A.D. 100, smacks of peace and the readiness and ability to profit from it.[4]

The Britons had long traded with the Continent and were said to have exported 'corn, cattle, gold, silver and iron . . . and also skins, slaves and dogs sagacious in the hunt'.[5] In the century before the Roman Conquest imports of pottery, in particular, were made into the Belgic south-east, but finds of amphora sherds indicate that foreign wine was appreciated outside these areas as well (see p. 20 below). Their society was clearly divided

[1] G. Borrow, *Wild Wales*, World's Classics edn (1920), 501
[2] Strabo, IV, iv, 5 (C 197)
[3] Diodorus Siculus, V, xxviii, 2–3
[4] P. Marsden, 'The Blackfriars Ship', *Mariners' Mirror*, li (Feb. 1965), 59–62
[5] Strabo, IV, v, 2 (C 199)

into classes. Caesar called the aristocrats in Gaul 'equites'. Professor
Tierney has shown that his descriptions were not entirely trustworthy and
that he, like other authors, drew largely but not always accurately on a lost
'ethnography' of Posidonius.[1] Whatever the precise meaning of *equites* in
such a context, there can be no doubt that men of rank existed who could
call on the services of dependants, *clientes*. Most of the common people
tended, said Caesar, to 'bind themselves to serve men of rank'.[2] There is
an inference of mutual duty and mutual privilege. Support for the existence
of the relationship is found in the fact that it was a Celtic institution attested in the customary law of the Irish Celts.[3] In medieval Wales, moreover, the picture may be filled in by descriptions of the lord in his *llys*, or
court, 'maintained by a network of appendant hamlets'.[4] The discovery
within the north Welsh hill-fort of Dinorben of the post-holes of a very
large round building, 65 feet in diameter, dated to the 3rd or 4th centuries
A.D., has been taken as evidence for such a *llys* in a hill-fort on elevated
ground with a *bond village* below, the connection being partly suggested by
the finding in the hill-fort of the winged ploughshare of a heavy plough
suitable for low-lying heavy land.[5] Whatever the merits of this, there can
be no doubt that the archaeologist is justified in looking for the evidence of
social distinction in the character of the settlements as well as in the small
objects of the Iron Age.

The larger hill-forts, with interiors of up to, but rarely over, 50 acres,
with massive defences, must surely represent the most important focal
points of local power and some of them contain the largest community
settlements.[6] A hint of the respect with which they were regarded is given
by the temples built inside the hill-forts of Maiden Castle, Dorset, and
Lydney, Glos., even after 300 years of Roman rule. They most often originated in an early phase of the Iron Age, though contemporary houses are
rarely found; subsequent enlargement of the original enclosure as well as
of the defences frequently followed. It may be imagined that they were
intended to hold people and herds from outside when trouble threatened.
In the later Iron Age, however, numbers of them, such as Maiden Castle

[1] Tierney (1960), 197–201
[2] Caesar, *B.G.*, vi, 13; trans. S. A. Handford, p. 31; *cf.* Tacitus, *Agr.*, xii, 1
[3] Powell (1958), 75–79
[4] G. Jones (1960), 78
[5] Savory (1959); G. Jones (1960), 76–77
[6] Plate 1.1 shows untested hollows and platforms covering 26 acres inside a
dominantly sited hill-fort.

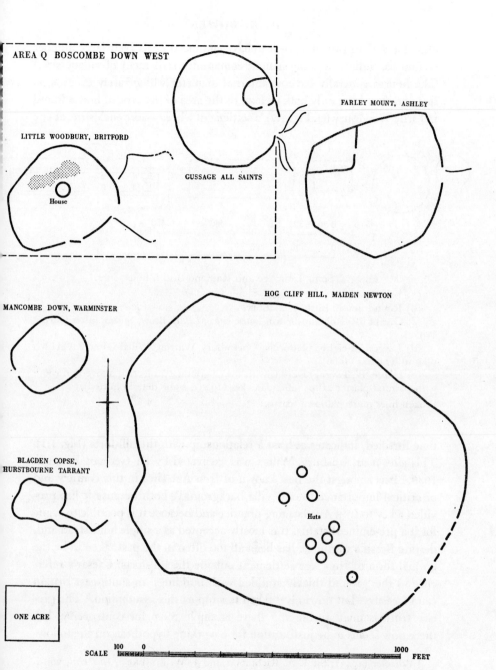

AREA Q BOSCOMBE DOWN WEST

FARLEY MOUNT, ASHLEY

LITTLE WOODBURY, BRITFORD

GUSSAGE ALL SAINTS

House

MANCOMBE DOWN, WARMINSTER

HOG CLIFF HILL, MAIDEN NEWTON

BLAGDEN COPSE,
HURSTBOURNE TARRANT

Huts

ONE ACRE

SCALE 100 0   1000
            ⊢⊢⊢⊢⊢⊣   FEET

Fig. 1.1. Some Iron Age Settlements and Enclosures in southern England.

5

and Hod Hill in Dorset, appear to have embraced a relatively large number of houses, indicating a permanent community settlement of village size.[1] The houses generally have an internal diameter which rarely exceeds 30 feet and thus have only half, or less, of the area of the type of house found in Little Woodbury (*cf.* Fig. 1.2), a settlement whose 4-acre enclosure, at one

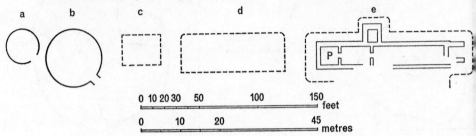

Fig. 1.2. Some Iron Age and Romano-British house sites.

(a) Iron Age hut, 30 ft. across.
(b) Round house, Little Woodbury.
(c) One of five Romano-British house sites at Park Brow, Sussex (after Garnet Wolseley).
(d) Largest of eighty platforms, Chisenbury Warren, Wilts. (after R.C.H.M. plan in Thomas (1966)).
(e) House 'B', Iwerne, Dorset, with tower granary projecting above and room with painted plaster at 'p' (after Hawkes (1947); some detail omitted).
Broken lines mark platform scarps.

time fortified, indicates at least a relationship with the hill-forts (Fig. 1.1). This site, near Salisbury, Wilts., was excavated by Dr Gerhard Bersu in 1938.[2] It is amongst the best known of Iron Age sites in this country and of critical importance to our 'villa background', both because it has provided a key to Iron Age farming practice and because it is possible to argue for it a pre-eminent status. It is mostly accepted as a single homestead and, despite Bersu's warnings, has been all too often in the past taken to be the normal form of Iron Age settlement outside the hill-forts. Caesar's reference to the 'ground thickly studded with buildings' in south-east Britain can be easily—but unwisely—taken to support this assumption.[3] The precise truth is unattainable and there is ample room for controversy, but there now seems to be justification for a working hypothesis on the follow-

[1] Wheeler (1943); Sir I. A. Richmond and J. W. Brailsford, *Hod Hill*, vol. ii
[2] Bersu (1940)
[3] Caesar, *B.G.*, v, 12

ing lines. Settlements in the lowland zone in the Iron Age include: village-sized communities in some hill-forts; community settlements of generally lesser size in other enclosures; settlements, larger than single homesteads, unenclosed by any traceable ditch; establishments of *Little Woodbury* type (to be allowed the same status as the smaller hill-forts); and smaller enclosed establishments each credibly belonging to a single family or family group. Whether and just how these should be seen as the equivalent of the documented Celtic institutions such as *llys*, *tref*, *taeogtref*, and *tyddyn* it would be rash to say, but the idea of a uniform pattern of single farms outside the hill-forts can no longer stand for the country as a whole. It can be stated just as firmly that in the Roman period there were community settlements of village size as well as smaller establishments, hamlets and single farms. Most Romano-British lowland sites were unenclosed by any defensive work.

As has been said, Little Woodbury is of vital consequence. Firstly, thanks to Bersu's pioneer and invaluable reconstruction of farming practice there, it has given its name to the mixed-farm economy of the British Iron Age. Secondly, it deserves separate consideration as a particular type of settlement. Thirdly, selected features of the 'Little Woodbury complex' have been taken to represent a native cultural tradition. Fourthly, Bersu's authoritative and generally accepted interpretation of the deep pits as for storage not only illuminated farming practice but also removed the idea that they could be pit dwellings. It is now time to examine these matters in some detail, to note an amendment to Bersu's original calculations about the pits, and to consider recent archaeological work which supports the generalisations made above.

The site of Little Woodbury was discovered from the air, the earthworks and any occupation layers on the surface having been long destroyed under strip cultivation. It consisted of an irregular rounded enclosure, at first palisaded and then ditched, with an area of about 4 acres. It had a gap entrance at the east and 'antenna' ditches, at one time splaying outwards from points near this. Far from being the cosy little farmyard which photographs of a reconstruction sometimes suggest, its perimeter was a quarter of a mile in length and within it there was ample space for thirty small modern houses and their gardens—or for one very large Roman villa. Owing, doubtless, to the most difficult circumstances in which it was produced, the Little Woodbury report has no plan of the whole site. Fig. 1.1 does a little to remedy this, but it must be said immediately that only one-third of the interior was excavated. A single large round house 45 feet across lies dwarfed in the middle of its big enclosure (there were traces of a second), the total 'working hollows' of the occupation lie behind the house away from the entrance, and the pits, though scattered, are generally clear of the entrance. There can be little doubt that the ditch dug around the already existing farm was intended to make of it, defensively, a 'hill-fort', though the situation, on a sheltered tongue of land below and east of 'Great Woodbury', was surely chosen for its advantages as a farm site.

A brief look at reasonably comparable sites in Wessex indicates that the character of the enclosure and situation make of it a valid and recognisable type. The settlement on Meon Hill, 15 miles east of Little Woodbury, near Stockbridge, Hants, was of similar size and shape and acquired massive defences.[1] It is tempting to consider Spettisbury, Dorset, too. This site, 20 miles south-west of Little Woodbury, is a 5-acre enclosure with a probably unfinished single rampart of hill-fort scale in a sloping, sheltered position. There is no information about its interior, but an apparently Iron Age 'A' twisted torc has been found. The site was almost certainly attacked by the Second Legion Augusta in A.D. 44 and mass burials in the ditch suggest that at least a hundred defenders were killed.[2] Two other sites with comparable characteristics to Little Woodbury have an additional feature—a small compound set against the inside of the larger. The first is by Farley Mount, west of Winchester, and the second is west of Gussage All Saints, in Dorset[3] (Fig. 1.1). The antenna ditches flaring outwards from the entrance of the Gussage site are clear indication that those at Little Woodbury were similar, and not, as Bersu wondered, part of an unfinished second enclosure. Traces of narrow-set antennae at Farley Mount open on to what appears at one time to have been pasture land. It might be guessed that a house or houses lay inside the small compounds, fenced off like the supposedly superior establishment in the otherwise quite different Swiss Halstatt site on the Goldberg.[4] The contemporary houses at West Harling, Norfolk, were each inside their own circular enclosures.[5]

Almost all known houses in Iron Age Britain were round, but it is perhaps important to remember that the Little Woodbury type was both

[1] Liddell (1934) and (1937)
[2] Gresham (1939)
[3] H. C. Bowen and P. J. Fowler, in Thomas (1966), 44 and pl. VI. The Gussage site will appear in RCHM, *Dorset*, vol. V (forthcoming).
[4] Childe (1950), 224
[5] G. Clark and Fell (1953)

1. 1 Air photograph of Fosbury hill-fort, Wiltshire, showing probable settlement features inside and 'Celtic' fields outside. Photo J. K. St Joseph, copyright Cambridge University

1. 2 Replica of a prehistoric light plough pulled by cattle comparable in size with the ancient British shorthorn. Dexters owned by Dr F. L. M. Dawson; Donneruplund ard replica by Mr J. Anstee. Photo *Salisbury Times*, copyright

1. 3   Vertical air photograph by R.A.F. of the area east of Cuckoo Bridge, south-west of Spalding, Lincolnshire (TF 2020). For interpretation see figure 9. Ministry of Defence (Air Force Department), crown copyright

much larger than the preceding Bronze Age forms, and larger than some contemporary houses, as well as larger than most of the known forms in the lowland zone during the later part of the Iron Age. Its size is its most notable characteristic. With a diameter of about 50 feet it had a floor area of some 1,900 square feet and was nearly three times as big as a house 30 feet in diameter. It probably had a conical thatched or earth-covered roof. Its entrance, as in almost all Iron Age houses, was to the east or south-east, away from the prevalent south-west or cold north winds. It had a porch. Such a house is sometimes found in enclosures larger than Little Woodbury, as on Longbridge Deverill Cow Down, Wilts.,[1] and occasionally on sites apparently different from Little Woodbury, as in the 11-acre enclosure on Pimperne Down, Dorset, where no pits have been found,[2] or at West Harling, already mentioned, where there was no overall enclosure or associated storage pits. It also occurs in some highland zone sites. Bersu seems to have come to regard it, in the Isle of Man, as a type of house appropriate to the Celtic aristocracy.[3] A large round house of the 2nd century A.D., 52 feet in diameter, with features recalling the Little Woodbury house, has now been found under a Roman villa at Winterton, Lincs.[4] This might suggest it was the villa-owner's previous dwelling and thus indicate his substantial status. Other considerations can be mentioned. There is the possibility that the size was used to accommodate animals as well as people, since there is very little evidence for Iron Age byres in lowland Britain, though growing evidence for the rectangular byre-house in the Roman period. Comparison with traditional types in the Far East indicates that large houses there may just be for large families, but that they may also be the symbol of rank, serving on occasion as general meeting-places.[5]

The argument that there were no 'rich' small finds at Little Woodbury is scarcely enough to disqualify it, as house or establishment, from a position of relative pre-eminence. It has sometimes been compared unfavourably with All Cannings Cross, the classic Iron Age 'A' type site in north Wiltshire, where within a similar area of about 4 acres there were copious small finds from occupational levels remarkably preserved under soil-slip but, as at Little Woodbury, little of value in the pits.[6] Little Woodbury

[1] S. Chadwick, in Frere (1960), 18–20
[2] Harding and Blake (1963)
[3] Bersu (1946)
[4] *Winterton* (1966), 83
[5] Forde (1948), 133–5, 183
[6] Cunnington (1923), 60

was for long under an arable *open field* of medieval type and finds of value
may have been picked up by cultivators (as, in recent years, were the
Snettisham torcs).[1] It may be remembered, too, that even at Maiden Castle,
Dorset, few metal objects of any sort belonged to Iron Age 'A'.[2] Alternatively, the lord's wealth was disposed of elsewhere or lay in perishables
such as cattle. A more telling criticism is that, since only one-third of the
internal area of Little Woodbury was excavated and since neither the big
house nor traces of a second house appear on air photographs, it is impossible to say whether further houses existed. This is true and it is highly
desirable that the excavation should be completed to resolve the issue, but
the evidence at present available shows the big house isolated and the
working hollows, which preclude houses in part of the unexcavated area,
too, set behind it away from the enclosure entrance. It might be added that
more structures should be expected. A hut in a farm is not necessarily a
dwelling and a small cluster of huts might well mark a single homestead.
In sum, Little Woodbury is regarded as a recognisable type of settlement,
plausibly of the status of a lord's establishment because of its size (3 acres
or more), because of the number of examples which were converted into
hill-forts (presumably by dependants but a manifest of the lord's *duty* to
protect), and possibly because of the large house. The head man there was
presumably of a class which the Romans would have drawn into the towns,
perhaps as *decuriones*, eventually to be amongst the villa-builders.[3] If this
is so, it is necessary to look for settlements, apart from hill-forts, appropriate to other elements in the social or economic structure. These now
seem to be appearing in a variety of forms (Fig. 1.1).

At the lower end of the size scale there is the enclosed establishment
with one to three huts, one of which may be larger than the others, as at
Draughton, Northants., where a hut 34 feet in diameter was accompanied
by two huts 20 feet in diameter in an enclosure of one-fifth of an acre, the
excavator regarding it as a settlement of iron workers. At Colsterworth,
Lincs., a Belgic enclosure of about 1 acre contained one round hut, 44 feet
in diameter, as well as a number of smaller huts. The excavator suggested
some reflection of social grading here.[4] The river-gravels have numbers of
Iron Age enclosures under an acre in size, not all necessarily settlements.[5] A

[1] R. Clarke (1954), 28
[2] Wheeler (1943), 270
[3] *cf.* Tacitus, *Agr.*, xxi
[4] W. F. Grimes, in Frere (1960), 21–27
[5] RCHM (1960), 14–15

simple rounded enclosure of almost 1 acre on Mancombe Down, Wilts., is now known to be an Iron Age 'A' settlement[1] (Fig. 1.1). By contrast, in the later Iron Age there is still the site at Glastonbury where a total of sixty huts within 2 acres, even if not all contemporary, suggests that its usual description of 'village' is a valid one.[2] At Heath Row, Middlesex,[3] an enclosure of the same size as Little Woodbury held at least eleven huts, concentrated in one half of the enclosure, as well as a square structure interpreted as a temple with *cella* and peristyle remarkably anticipating the common Romano-Celtic form. Largest of all so far found is the 26-acre enclosure on Hog Cliff Hill, Maiden Newton, Dorset,[4] inside which a dozen or so contemporary smallish round houses, mostly clustered together, all belonged to Iron Age 'A'. The enclosure was not a hill-fort, since its tactical siting was poor and its single ditch was generally inside the bank, perhaps suggesting an intention to enclose stock. There were no pits. In contrast to this, but with pits in numbers to suggest much more than a single homestead, was the area of settlements on Boscombe Down West, Wilts.[5] This extended over 76 acres, chronologically spanning the whole Iron Age and part of the Roman period. The 20 acres of Iron Age 'A' pits spread over one area (site Q), which were not enclosed by any visible ditch, might suggest either a settlement of five times the size of Little Woodbury or an occupation five times as long, which would be absurd. The fact that the existence of this widespread site would have been unsuspected but for wartime clearance shows how great is the need for care in dogmatising from known facts. By citing specific examples it is thus possible within the Iron Age to point to small single establishments, to community settlements, possibly villages—though whether 'bond' or not, archaeology cannot tell— and to establishments plausibly attributable to the lesser lords. It seems likely that many of the community settlements also housed people of eminence.

We have noted how Bersu's basic reinterpretation of pits revolutionised the view of native settlements where pits occur, but we have also seen how subsequent excavations and fieldwork have indicated that, despite the elimination of 'pit dwellings', community settlements did exist in the Iron Age. There is a further consequence, deriving from a revision of Bersu's

[1] Fowler, Musty, and Taylor (1965), 52–54
[2] Bulleid and Gray (1911)
[3] W. F. Grimes, in Frere (1960), 25–28
[4] RCHM (1963), 14–15
[5] Richardson (1951)

calculation of pit capacity, which should be briefly considered, since it affects any view of the amount of land in arable use and, we may suppose, the population that this reflects. Recent calculations made necessary by the need to get corn for a practical experiment—and confirmed by the amounts actually used—show that Bersu greatly underestimated the storage capacity of the pits. In making the conversion from cubic metres to bushels he reached a figure about one-ninth that of the true capacity.[1] His estimate of the population of Little Woodbury was, at most, 'several families'. This is usually thought of as a 'family group'. It is tempting but scarcely possible to do a straight multiplication by nine. In particular, not all suitable pits would have held grain, and those that did may have held corn in the ear. Guessing an allowance for this and assuming that *most* of the pits would have held grain, it is still reasonable to consider that the amount of grain stored at Little Woodbury was three times that formerly envisaged. Unfortunately, we can still not be sure that this means a population of correspondingly bigger size. The reason for this is that Bersu worked out his estimate of population by dividing his calculated figure of capacity of the pits in use at any one time by an average *modern* annual consumption of corn per head, namely, $4\frac{1}{2}$ bushels. This is less than half of that allowed a Roman slave in Cato's time[2] and only a third of a German farm labourer's in the 18th century A.D.[3] However, Athenaeus[4] does mention that it was Celtic practice at feasts to eat much meat and few loaves, and it is perhaps permissible to feel that there *was* a larger Iron Age population than has hitherto been allowed. It seems possible that corn was stored for people who lived outside Little Woodbury and this might reinforce its interpretation as an establishment of local pre-eminence. Certainly, the proportion of pits to houses (180:1, allowing the contemporary existence of the second house found) is vastly greater than in hill-forts where such a calculation can be made. On Hod Hill, Dorset, for instance, there appear to be only three or four pits for every recognisable hut. The occupation was undoubtedly shorter, but the statistic is an important challenge to interpretation. In considering the lowland-zone population as a whole, however, it is also wise to remember that some arable farmers, apart from the Belgae, who

[1] The experiments were conducted by the Research Committee on Ancient Fields and Agriculture of the British Association for the Advancement of Science. A preliminary report has appeared in *Ant*, xli (1967), 214–15

[2] Cato, *Agr.*, lvi. I am grateful to Prof. L. A. Moritz for this observation.

[3] van Bath (1963), 86

[4] Athenaeus, iv, 151

always seem to have favoured storage in jars, probably did not make use of pits. Not a great deal is known about Belgic settlements, but it would be unwise to assume, until it is demonstrated, that any were like Little Woodbury. The type site must be clearly distinguished from the economy, and the economy itself seems to have been as variable as possible within the rather narrow Iron Age technical limits (Fig. 1.3).

The Little Woodbury type sites (Fig. 1.1) are only found with certainty in Wessex, though they may well have existed beyond. The Caburn, south-east of Lewes in Sussex, is a settlement of the right size practising a 'Little Woodbury economy' whose first phase produced Iron Age 'A' pottery suggesting Wessex connections.[1] The War Ditches at Cherry Hinton near Cambridge was also akin to Little Woodbury in plan and size and had what may have been antennae flaring out from its entrance.[2] The 'Little Woodbury economy', however, is found in most areas south-east of the Jurassic Way. This fact as well as the diversity of Iron Age settlement types indicates that it must be thought of as a way of farming not confined to sites of the Little Woodbury type, but one which was practised, with many variations, in diverse establishments. At Tallington, Lincs., for instance, there has now been found a late Iron Age farm within an enclosure, the largest single one in the Welland Valley, not much short of Little Woodbury in size, but near-rectangular in form. The site, like others in the area, was probably a single farm, and all the Little Woodbury structures were reported except the large house (though one of 43 feet in diameter was found at a near-by site) and pits.[3] This omission scarcely affects the farming practice, in so far as corn was grown and stored, but it is a matter of opinion whether the description of 'Little Woodbury economy' can, strictly speaking, be applied. It was a mixed cattle-corn economy utilising pits extensively, particularly for storage, and probably predominated in the lowland zone, though there is considerable evidence, to which it will be necessary to return, that mainly pastoral establishments also existed.

Apart from the long-recognised objects such as grinding-stones for corn, spindle-whorls that denoted wool-spinning and so on, the techniques of farming practised at Little Woodbury were deduced from a consideration of pits, hollows, arrangements of post-holes, and the finding of large numbers of 'pot-boilers' (heat-crackled flints) and fragments of cob (chalk and clay

[1] Curwen (1939), 214–16
[2] RCHM (1959), 1–2
[3] W. G. Simpson, in Thomas (1966), 18

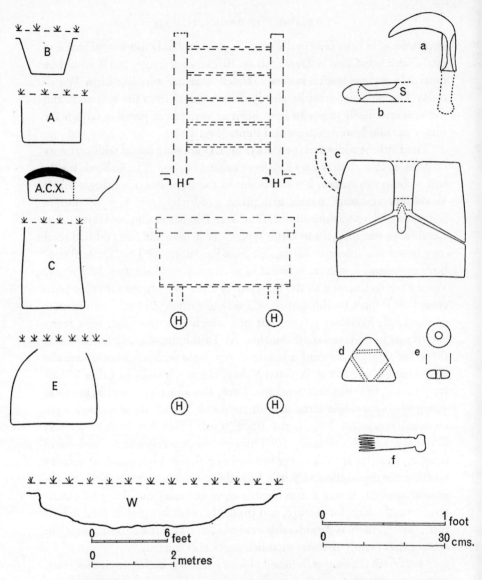

Fig. 1.3. Some features of the 'Little Woodbury' economy.

Left: Bersu pit types (B) and (A) (non-storage); pit with baked 'cob' lid from All Cannings Cross (Cunnington (1923) No. 39); Bersu storage pits (C) and (E); section across 'working hollow' (W).

Centre: Suggested drying rack (Bersu), based on pairs of post-holes (H); side elevation of granary on four 'stilts'—the form of the superstructure is quite uncertain.

Right: (a) 'Angle' sickle with conjectural handle; (b) Iron flanged share attached to conjectural plough-sole (S); (c) Rotary quern (with suggested handle, *rynd* and spindle based on E. C. Curwen, *Ant XV* (1941), 15–32); (d) clay loom-weight; (e) spindle-whorl; (f) weaving comb of antler.

daub) from gently domed structures, some pierced by holes[1] (*cf.* Fig. 1.3). Although 120 'deeper' pits were found and 360, in all, were thought to have existed, it was demonstrated that only a small number could have been open at a time. Pits put out of use were filled with rubbish, including much burnt matter, most of it assumed to be the residue from corn-drying ovens. The very large number of post-holes was thought to be due to renewals and replacements. Considering these features, together with others whose interpretation was not in doubt, and allowing for the existence of 'Celtic' fields probably destroyed in the Middle Ages, a convincing general picture of Iron Age mixed farming was reconstructed for the first time. Corn was sown in the fields which were already manured.[2] It was harvested, possibly before it was entirely ripe, with very small-bladed sickles, and dried on massive double-posted racks. An alternative, though rejected by Dr Bersu, is that these racks were for hay or other fodder, since it is likely that the corn was cut short just below the ear. The grain intended for consumption was parched in temporary ovens, probably roofed by cob. Other post-harvest activities, such as threshing and winnowing, were probably carried out in an area of shallow working hollows associated with deeper pits. The consumption corn was then stored in the beehive, barrel-shaped, or cylindrical pits, generally more than 4 feet deep. Seed corn, an arbitrarily estimated one-third of the harvest, was kept in granaries whose presence was deduced from arrangements of substantial post-holes at each corner of a small square with sides of about 6 feet. Cattle, sheep, and other animals were kept, but 'husbandry stood absolutely in the foreground'. This statement was based largely on the assumed 'water deficiency', the only immediate source being eaves' drips, though some shallow pits were probably used to hold water-butts. It could, on the other hand, be argued that the possible fodder racks, the existence of riverside meadows, noted by Dr Bersu, three-quarters of a mile away, and the antennae ditches funnelling towards the entrance, suggest a greater concern for animals than was allowed.

This view of Little Woodbury gives a general idea of how mixed farming might be carried on in the Iron Age. As occasionally noted above, not all sites of the period produce similar clues to the economy. There are variations both of omission and addition, some of which, notably the use of pits, are important to assessments of population and distribution as well as

---

[1] Brailsford (1949), 159
[2] Plate I.I. shows 'Celtic' fields in process of destruction by modern ploughing over their boundaries.

of farming usage. Some evidence suggests that certain pits might themselves be connected with the process of corn-drying. In the Late Bronze Age site of Itford Hill, Sussex, for instance, there were no deep pits, but one pit (no. 26) of Bersu's type A, not a storage type, held on its floor a litre of hulled barley and emmer. Dr Helbaek's suggestion that it was connected with a corn-drying device seems reasonable.[1] In Cyprus corn was 'fumigated by heat' in much deeper pits until recent years.[2] Little is known about Iron Age corn-driers except that they existed, but the cob domes remarkably preserved at All Cannings Cross, sitting like dustbin lids on pits with single ramped vents or flues, suggest a possible form and indicate that pits could form an integral part of their structure. Lack of evidence for oven heat in these pits at All Cannings Cross is not surprising, since corn-driers must depend on a relatively gentle heat and the corn has to be insulated from flame; but, conversely, it may be noted that pit 7 there was floored with clay baked *in situ*.[3]

Bersu first emphasised that there were pits of different sorts. The shallower pits, his types A and B (mostly less than a metre deep), generally wider than deep, were allotted miscellaneous functions such as holding tubs upright in the ground. The 'deeper' were usually deeper than wide, cylindrical, or narrower at the top than the bottom, often beehive-shaped and usually with flat bottoms. About 51 per cent were between 1 and 2 metres deep. Only one was more than $2\frac{1}{2}$ metres (say, 8 feet). None at Little Woodbury was seen to have lining, but Bersu thought basketry would have been employed, and traces of this and other linings have occasionally been noted elsewhere. It is worth stressing that these deeper pits probably had very varied functions, too, while noting that on sites in the river-gravels the depths even of storage pits are generally much less than on the chalk and limestone.[4] In the Welland Valley sites already referred to it has been suggested that a high water table made pit storage impracticable. Most were doubtless used for corn as well as for foods such as fruits and berries, possibly for a harvest of leaves,[5] and for meat. Even in recent years armies in the field have been instructed to dig pits for the short-term storage of meat. In modern jargon, the people were 'pit-minded'. A partial motive for this may perhaps be seen in Tacitus's reference to the Germans' habit of

[1] Burstow and Holleyman (1957), 178, 206
[2] Wheeler (1956)
[3] Cunnington (1923), 61, 63, 73
[4] *cf.* Bradford (1942)
[5] Steensberg (1943), 179–90

hollowing out cavities (*specus*) underground as a store-place for produce, and piling refuse on top, presumably above a suitable lid. The method not only gave protection from the winter but allowed a chance of concealing the buried stores from any invader.[1] At Maiden Castle, Dorset, 'hoards' of sling-stones found in deep, narrow pits[2] can surely only mean that these were magazines, since the sling-stones (brought some miles from Chesil Beach and all the more important because of the apparent insignificance of the bow and arrow in the Iron Age) were hardly regarded as rubbish. On this site and others, certain pits were carefully lined, and sometimes floored, with limestone, even though this had to be brought from a distance. How far this might reflect an individual's wealth or fastidiousness we shall never know, but it does suggest a particular function. Perhaps it greatly lengthened the life of a pit. The Iron Age or Romano-British 'Portland beehives',[3] for instance, comparable structures dug into limestone and clay, with narrow mouths closed with single stones, were also lined; of some twenty found, none seems to have been filled with rubbish, though one had a quantity of carbonised grain. When pits are found inside huts and are apparently contemporary it is tempting to regard them as general store cupboards. A very few pits, as at Maiden Castle, Dorset, were dug to a depth of 12 feet. Many have held human as well as animal skeletons amongst the rubbish. A few, shallow and irregular, have been stained in a way that suggests they held manure.[4] Columella advocated manure-pits, built to shelve like ponds, and also said: 'they can gather . . . not only the waste matter from their own bodies, but . . . the dirt which the yard and . . . buildings produce'.[5] Certainly the peoples of the Iron Age—and earlier— manured their fields, and it is because folds or byres were mucked out on to middens used as general rubbish dumps that potsherds were eventually spread on 'Celtic' fields in sufficient quantities to make this interpretation certain. Some, even of the deeper pits, seem to have held water-butts[6] fed by ditches leading into them, if not from eaves' drips. No ponds of Iron

[1] Tacitus, *Germ.*, xvi, 4. Iron Age pits similar to those at Little Woodbury have been found in Germany, *e.g.* near Halle; see 'Früheisenzeitliche Vorratsgrube auf der Bösenburg': *Ausgrabungen u. Funde* **10** (1965), 29–31; and near Mackenberg; see 'Eine Siedlung der vorrömischen Eisenzeit bei Sünninghausen', *Heimatkalender Kreis Beckum* (1967), 33–39

[2] Wheeler (1943), 91 (pit B 12)

[3] Holmes (1885); RCHM, *South-East Dorset* (forthcoming).

[4] Cra'ster (1961), 30

[5] Columella, *R.R.*, II, xiv, 7–8; *cf.* I, vi, 21

[6] Wheeler (1943), 54, 91; *cf.* Brewster (1963), 41–43

Age date have been recognised for certain. The absence of 'pot-boilers' on some sites demonstrates an interesting difference of detail. In fact, of course, only a few features bearing on the economy are usually found on any one site; the others are perhaps assumed, allowing for an unknown number of variations, but also incurring the danger that a whole economy may be wished on a site with very slender evidence.

Information about implements and crops has to be supplied from a variety of sites (cf. Fig. 1.3). The ploughs of the period were light and manœuvrable, made of wood with narrow or broad iron-tipped shares but without coulters or mould-boards, and probably pulled, in most instances, by two oxen[1] (Pl. 1.2). Although many shares have been found in the lowland zone, the only wooden parts so far discovered in this country are from Scotland. They are from a 'beam' or 'bow' *ard*, a type of light plough now thought to have been developed, in the Roman period, into a coultered form. Other types, probably simpler, may have existed. Only in rare circumstances could the Iron Age form of such ploughs break up virgin turf, so we have to allow for the use of other methods. Wooden tools were undoubtedly used, though they rarely survive. Ladles, mallets, tubs, a 'spade handle' and other objects found at Glastonbury demonstrate the high quality of native woodworking and show how desirable it is to locate and excavate other sites where conditions have allowed such survival. Imprints of a wooden shovel at the headlands of small fields have been found, by meticulous excavation, even in the Bronze Age.[2]

It has often been suggested in the past that the Belgae introduced a heavy, wheeled plough. There is no evidence whatsoever to support this, although it is important to remember that they appear to have been very skilled smiths and to have made and used iron tools in a way which anticipates development in the Roman period. No wheels have ever been found, but these are not necessary to a heavy plough. The evidence has generally been based on a small tanged, gently curved blade from Bigbury, Kent, called a coulter, but now better thought of as a bill-hook, and also on the findings from a site at Twyford Down, Winchester.[3] Here was found a broken heavy blade, perhaps a coulter, within the area of a Belgic settlement. Although its associations are now considered Romano-British, it was

[1] For ploughs of the prehistoric and Roman periods, see especially Glob (1951); Payne (1947) and (1957); Aberg (1957); and Manning (1964b)

[2] Megaw, Thomas, and Wailes (1961)

[3] Stuart and Birkbeck (1936), 190–1

originally thought to belong to a Belgic heavy plough which had been used to plough a strip field on a slope a quarter of a mile away from the settlement. This strip field, long destroyed, had in published plan all the characteristics of what may now be recognised as a common secondary phenomenon, the cutting of a medieval or later strip field across pre-existing and probably unrecognised 'Celtic' fields. There was no sign of strip cultivation on the flatter ground adjacent to the settlement, where such an alteration in the field pattern could have been made much more easily than where the strip was found.

Carts were used. As in the Roman period, they could have had solid or spoked iron-tyred wooden wheels of a form that was traditional until recent years.[1] Such vehicles could have transported manure from domestic middens on to the fields. The recognition of broken household pottery and other rubbish spread with such manure is one way in which the fields may be independently dated and shows that manuring continued in many places throughout the Roman period. It seems likely that chalk from those pits that were eventually filled with rubbish also went out to be spread on the fields. Reaping was generally done with very small iron angled sickles, usually less than 6 inches along the blade. There was very little variety in the crops grown; only hulled barley, and two forms of wheat, *emmer* and *spelt*, are known in any quantity. The evidence generally comes from grain preserved by charring, often perhaps the result of overdrying. There can be little doubt that corn-drying was a general necessity, probably because of the unfavourable climate, but it seems that *spelt* in particular required parching before it could be threshed.[2] Oddly, no complete Iron Age ovens of a likely kind have ever been found, but it is certain that the practice was continued in Roman times, when corn-driers, as will be seen, are commonly found in a great variety of rural sites as well as villas, although again it has to be confessed that the readily recognisable forms do not occur before the 3rd century A.D. Oats are rarely found before the Roman period, and then mostly in a mixed crop. There may have been regional differences in what was grown. Up to 1952 rye had been noted only in two adjacent sites in south Wiltshire and the 'Celtic bean' only in north Somerset.[3]

[1] Fox (1946), 65. An axle-box was found at Glastonbury. At Maiden Castle, Dorset, wheel ruts were 5 feet apart.

[2] Helbaek (1952), 233

[3] Helbaek (1952), 210–11

The Celts had a reputation for appreciating their food and drink. Both barley and wheat were used for beer, with or without honey. Imported wine was also much liked by the upper classes. Meal or flour was produced by rotary querns in the later Iron Age, the tall thick 'beehive' form becoming in time flatter and thinner, particularly amongst the Belgae, anticipating Romano-British forms (*cf*. Figs. 1.3 and 1.6). The ground corn would doubtless be used as gruel, such as was found in the stomach of an Iron Age man in Denmark, or made into bread. Carbonised buns have been found which show no evidence for leavening, though the fact that those from Glastonbury are 'largely insoluble even in powerful chemicals'[1] is due to carbonisation and age and not, it is to be hoped, to their original character. 'Their food', said Athenaeus of the Celts, quoting Posidonius, 'consists of a small number of loaves of bread together with a large amount of meat.'[2] It is a timely reminder that they did not live by bread alone.

The Little Woodbury economy was, as already noted, a mixed one. In pre-Roman times the cattle were of very small 'Celtic shorthorn' type (*bos longifrons*), about the size of Kerry or Dexter cows (Pl. 1.2) and including a polled variety.[3] It has recently been shown that there is no good evidence for the killing off of most of the stock each autumn.[4] Preservation of meat by drying and salting must, on the other hand, have been widespread and may one day result in the identification of means used, such as brine tubs. Salt also became the more necessary a part of diet as cereal foods grew in importance. Extensive traces of salt working have been found in Lincolnshire, East Anglia, and in the Isle of Purbeck, Dorset. Though much is Roman, it started at least in the early part of the Iron Age. The salt was sometimes packaged in pottery moulds.[5] Whether cheese was made is uncertain. Strabo thought not,[6] but pottery jars with pierced bases like colanders, frequently found, have been regarded as strainers to take off the whey. This sort of vessel could also have strained honey. There was probably much permanent pasture, and meadowland by stream and river was likely to have been used. The value of river pastures must have been early appreciated and the need for them stressed by the very limited feeding value of stubble and the considerable areas of grass required by

[1] Helbaek (1952), 212
[2] Athenaeus, iv, 151
[3] *cf*. W. Jackson, in Cunnington (1923), 44
[4] Higgs and White (1963)
[5] Riehm (1961), 185–8
[6] Strabo, IV, v, 2 (C 200)

oxen. It has been calculated that 25 acres of rough pasture might be the need of one ox.[1] We have to allow for small oxen and low standards, but even if we divided this figure by five it is a reminder that the actual area available to Little Woodbury must, for this reason alone, have been greater than the 20 or so acres arable of the original calculation. That dwellers in downland settlements were familiar with the river banks is indicated by the bones of water-vole occasionally found in pits on such sites.[2] A romantic might think of small neat-herds passing away the time in trapping, while their charges, by browsing amongst the trees, were thinning or eliminating the natural forest and unwittingly preparing the ground for valley settlement. Next to cattle, sheep were most numerous— a 'Soay' type that gave point to the ancient difficulty of distinguishing them from the goats that are also found. Apart from meat they provided manure on the fields, perhaps milk, and certainly a coarse wool which, it seems, could be plucked off them.[3] Shears are not found until the Roman period. Spindle-whorls of shale, bone, pottery, or stone were used in spinning wool. It was woven on upright frame looms with the warp suspended taut by stone or baked clay loom-weights that were generally triangular—though cylindrical ones, as a further reminder of links with the Bronze Age, have also been found. Objects generally thought to be weaving combs or 'beaters' were used to keep the weft tight (and one of these, also emphasising early native origins, has now been found in a Bronze Age pastoral site, on Shearplace Hill, Dorset).[4] The prevalence of sheep, as close-cropping animals, suggests extensive open land, which would include the arable fields lying fallow, if sufficiently re-covered, as well as their unploughed lynchet faces, and recalls the key position of sheep as makers of fertility on downland in historic times. It is generally thought that the rabbits which have kept so much modern land cropped and free of scrub were not introduced into this country until the 12th century A.D.[5] Ponies, small animals, were mainly used to pull vehicles. If we are to believe Caesar, Cassivellaunus must have had at least 8,000 to draw his chariots.[6] There is no doubt, however, that oxen were the farmers' main draught animals, though ox-shoes are not found. Caesar

[1] Stamp (1955), 40
[2] *e.g.* Clay (1924), 469
[3] Boyd, Doney, Gunn, and Jewell (1964), 146
[4] Rahtz (1962), 323
[5] Veale (1957)
[6] Caesar, *B.G.*, v, 19

said that hares, fowl, and geese were reared for amusement only. Bones of the domestic fowl have been found on four sites only.[1] Dogs have been found on numerous settlements and were undoubtedly useful scavengers and herd dogs as well as sagacious in the hunt, as Strabo suggested. Bones of wild animals are, however, not common (though varying use was made of shed deer antlers) and this is perhaps to be associated with the surprising fact, already noted, that there is no sure evidence for any archers amongst Iron Age farmers.[2]

The evidence that, even in the lowland zone, animals were sometimes kept in numbers larger than the term 'mixed farming' suggests is indicated both in Strabo's note of Iron Age exports and in the existence of boundaries probably delimiting pasture. The so-called 'ranch boundaries' of Wessex, commencing in the Bronze Age and occasionally surviving in some form into the Romano-British period, are an example. They consist of long runs of bank and ditch, making enclosures which may be each of 50 acres or much more. Frequently they divide 'Celtic' fields from land that was not cultivated. The earliest are sometimes associated with small, rather irregular enclosures of between about a quarter of an acre and 2 acres in area.[3] Their distribution is limited to a zone, including Wiltshire and Hampshire but not Sussex, marked sharply, at least on the west, in the region of Blandford, Dorset. Whether by coincidence or not, this is much the same boundary as that recently defined by Mr J. B. Calkin for his barrel urns, which are regarded as a mark of cultural infiltration in the Bronze Age.[4] On Quarley Hill, Hants, some linear ditches were shown to precede, and others to continue into, Iron Age 'A'.[5] It has been plausibly suggested that large enclosures may have been used to protect winter-sown spelt, though this is almost impossible to prove.[6] On the other hand, there are instances, as on Milston Down, Wilts.,[7] or Martin Down, Hants,[8] where stretches of the long ditches have cut across 'Celtic' fields in such a way as to put them out of arable use. This must be regarded as

---

[1] Clifford (1961), 270

[2] A bowman on a Belgic coin is of doubtful import. Allen (1958), 58

[3] C. M. Piggott (1942)

[4] Calkin (1962), especially fig. 9

[5] Hawkes (1940), 153–69

[6] Applebaum (1954a), 111. It has now been possible to check the Figheldean Down earthworks on the ground, as Dr Applebaum could not. Fieldwork by Mr P. J. Fowler and the author shows that the 'ellipse' does not exist.

[7] Crawford (1953), 91

[8] Bowen (1961), 24, 33, 35

local rearrangement and not as a general trend, but the same sort of thing occurs in the late Roman period, as seen at Soldier's Ring, a pentagonal enclosure of 28 acres, at Damerham, Hants.[1] Another type of earthwork to suggest stock-keeping is becoming recognisable. This is the small, roughly circular enclosure defined by a bank with inner ditch and having a long, parallel-sided entrance track, the whole making a 'flask' or 'banjo' shape. It has a distribution in Wessex very similar to the 'ranch boundaries'.[2] Two, at Blagden Copse, Hurstbourne Tarrant (Fig. 1.1), and by the Roman villa of Bramdean also in Hampshire, have recently been excavated.[3] At most of these sites long ditched banks run from either side of the mouth of the 'funnel'. The enclosure size is variable, the limits being from about 150 feet to 250 feet in diameter.

Even outside the 'ranch boundary area', but still within the lowland zone, it is apparent that certain earthwork arrangements were meant primarily for stock. In West Dorset the enclosure of 26 acres by a bank with inner ditch on Hog Cliff Hill suggests, as already noted, an intention to keep animals in rather than out. An apparently pastoral settlement, also of Iron Age 'A', on Knowle Hill in the Isle of Purbeck, was set between a pair of probably contemporary cross-ridge dykes with outlying dykes perhaps connected with ranching.[4] Other Iron Age land divisions, some associated with small and some with large, possibly tribal, units, are now claimed in various downland areas.[5] Whether for stock or not, clearly marked blocks must have eventually made it easier for people to deal in land. The size of actual farms is difficult to determine and virtually impossible to declare with certainty. There seems little doubt, however, as we have hinted, that the Little Woodbury type settlement had at least three times the 20 or so acres of arable land formerly suggested on the basis of storage-pit capacity. Some confirmation for this comes from an actual minimum of 60 acres of 'Celtic' fields recognisable around the comparable site on Farley Mount near Winchester.[6] This was probably augmented by at least as much pasture or land only sporadically tilled.

---

[1] Crawford and Keiller (1928), 252

[2] B. Perry, in Thomas (1966), 39

[3] Information kindly given by the excavators, Dr I. M. Stead and Mr B. Perry respectively, who show that both these examples belong to the later phase of the Iron Age.

[4] Forde-Johnston (1957) and RCHM, *South-East Dorset* (forthcoming).

[5] *e.g.* Dyer (1961) and Fowler (1964)

[6] *cf.* Thomas (1966), pl. VI

The actual requirement due to poor corn yields, the inadequacies of stubble as feed, and indifferent grass, may have been much more. The assumed density of 'rounds' in Roman Dumnonia allows over 1 square mile of land per round and within this Mr A. C. Thomas has suggested upwards of 40 or more acres of arable.[1] On the much richer soils of the Welland Valley in the late Iron Age or Roman periods, blocks of land apparently associated with two different farms have been estimated at 140 and 55 acres.[2] The Romano-British village of Chisenbury had up to 200 acres of 'Celtic' fields around it.[3] The large villas of the 4th century A.D., in particular, will have had vastly greater acreages than these, but they are extremely difficult to calculate. On the basis of ox stalls, granary capacity, and 'natural' boundaries, for instance, Dr Applebaum has, however, suggested 1,900 acres for Bignor, Sussex.[4]

There were undoubted advances in the later part of the Iron Age and much remains to be learned about the settlements of the period. The Belgae who moved into the south-east of Britain in the 1st century B.C. were technically amongst the most advanced of the pre-Conquest peoples. This may be connected with the fact that they were most closely associated with Continental influences. They made lavish use of iron and had heavy axes to facilitate their occasional settlement on heavy soils. Belgic settlement in Prae Wood, near St Albans—partly on glacial clays—was, as Sir Mortimer Wheeler noted, the sort of wooded settlement that Caesar may have seen elsewhere.[5] It is now known, too, that the area around the Park Street Roman villa (also at St Albans) immediately adjacent to the River Ver was intensively occupied in the Belgic period, probably for the first time.[6] Some Belgic establishments seem to have been primarily concerned with pastoral farming. If we allow this attribution to the hill-fort of Casterley, Wilts., with an interior of 60 acres bounded by a single bank and ditch and partly subdivided into ditched compounds, it may be an example.[7] Of quite different type is Robin Hood's Arbour, a subrectangular enclosure of three-quarters of an acre on clay loam by the Thames in Berkshire, recently shown to have had within it a sunken paved yard

[1] Thomas (1966), 96
[2] W. G. Simpson, in Thomas (1966), 18
[3] H. C. Bowen and P. J. Fowler, in Thomas (1966), 50–51
[4] Applebaum (1958), 61
[5] Wheeler (1936), 13–14
[6] *Park Street* (1961), 120
[7] Cunnington (1913), 61

probably for stock.[1] Iron Age as well as Roman sites are well known on the gravels of the Thames Valley. In recent years air photographs have brought to light a very large number of crop marks of enclosures, ditch lines, and pits in other river valleys, even including some north of the Jurassic ridge where such density of settlement had scarcely been suspected. Such are the Severn and the Warwickshire Avon. Research planned here will indicate how much of it is pre-Roman.[2] In the Welland Valley, already referred to, on the border of Northamptonshire and Lincolnshire, immediately north of the Jurassic Way, excavation has now proved the existence of settlements with Iron Age origins. These appear to be associated with ditched roads and a system of land blocks, mostly marked by 'pit alignments', rows of holes about 6 feet across and 3 feet deep with a gap between each hole. The picture here is of a thoroughly organised landscape suggesting sophistication unknown to Little Woodbury.[3]

We do not yet know how many sites of Little Woodbury type lasted up to the Conquest. The Caburn near Lewes, already mentioned, may be one such. It is an enclosure of much the same size as Little Woodbury which was given hill-fort-type defences, and had storage pits in use until about A.D. 100. We do know that a large number of other types of site continued in occupation into Roman times. These included Pitt-Rivers's Cranborne Chase settlements[4] and the small settlement on Woodhouse Hill, Studland, also in Dorset.[5] Most so far known seem to originate in the late Iron Age, but settlement *areas* do tend to continue in use over long periods, even though there is sometimes doubt whether this means unbroken continuity of settlement or not. The site, already mentioned, on Boscombe Down West, is an example of this in Wessex. Great Woodbury, too (immediately west of Little Woodbury), produced finds which suggested occupation from Iron Age 'AB' (Hawkes Southern Second 'A') to the 4th century A.D., but the later finds came from near the top of the silted ditch of the hill-fort.[6] As elsewhere, the defensive nature of the settlement had changed in character. Thundersbarrow Hill in Sussex provides a good example of an 'open' Romano-British settlement just

---

[1] Cotton (1961), 7–8, 17
[2] Webster and Hobley (1965)
[3] RCHM (1960), 33–42; W. G. Simpson, in Thomas (1966), 15–25
[4] Analysed by Prof. C. F. C. Hawkes (1948)
[5] Field (1966)
[6] C. W. Phillips, in Bersu (1940), 107–10

outside the limits of an Iron Age defended one.[1] At War Ditches near Cherry Hinton, Cambridge, the later settlement sprawled over the filled-in ditch of the small hill-fort. At Wangford, Suffolk, on the Breckland, a surface spread of finds led to small-scale excavations which showed Iron Age 'A', a little Belgic, and much Romano-British material.[2] Here the excavator argued that the natural situation, close to the 20-foot contour line south of the river Little Ouse, on dry sandy soil, had attracted so much early settlement that coincident siting may have been pure chance. The Iron Age settlement was the sixth that had been discovered along a 3-mile stretch in three years. Settlement on the downland, river-gravels, and other well-drained farmable areas seems therefore to have continued and expanded.

Just how much of the lowland zone had been cleared for arable or pastoral use by the time of the Roman Conquest it is difficult to say. We have seen that the tradition of dividing land into large blocks goes back at least to the Bronze Age. We now know that 'Celtic' fields also originate at least in the Middle Bronze Age. In this chapter it is probably important to stress that 'Celtic' in this usage is a misnomer. It has been recognised for a long time that these small squarish fields, of about one-third of an acre to $1\frac{1}{2}$ acres each, are not certainly to be associated with Celtic peoples alone. The term, in inverted commas, is kept because most people understand in general what is meant by it. There is no change in shape which can be certainly attributed to the Roman period, though 'long fields' with parallel sides perhaps up to seven times as long as broad, with square ends, seem more likely to be Roman than earlier[3] (Fig. 1.4). 'Celtic' fields survive now only on areas that have not been heavily ploughed in historic times. They are infrequently detectable in the river-gravels, probably because deep-ditched boundaries, the only sort that would be visible today as crop marks, were rarely needed. They are rare, too, on the Cotswolds[4] and Chilterns, but there is little doubt that they were once much more widespread in both areas. It is interesting to note that almost the only group still to be seen on the Chilterns is at Knocking Hoe, near Hitchin, within a Nature Reserve so designated for the interest of its old turf. Outside the lowland zone 'Celtic' fields of quite 'normal' type are found to

[1] Curwen (1933), 113

[2] Briscoe (1958), 27

[3] Bowen (1961), 24, 41, 44

[4] Remains have been identified in current investigations by staff of RCHM (England).

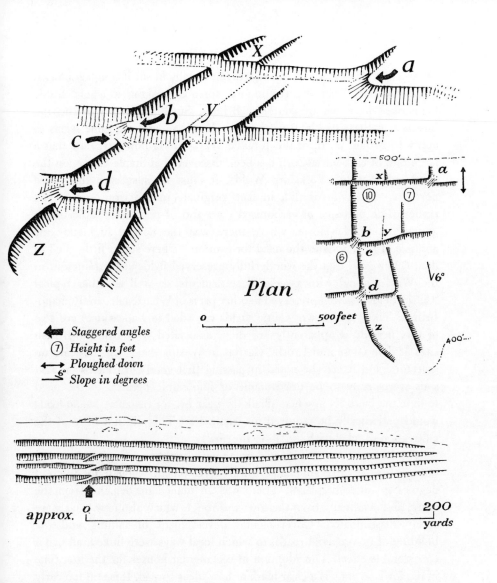

Plan

← Staggered angles
⑦ Height in feet
↔ Ploughed down
∠6° Slope in degrees

approx.

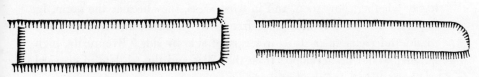

Fig. 1.4. 'Celtic' fields and Strip-lynchets.

Top: 'Celtic' fields, three-quarter view, with plan for comparison.

Centre: Strip-lynchets of medieval date, showing characteristic proportions and 'open' ends.

Bottom: 'Celtic' long-fields.

(With acknowledgments to the British Association for the Advancement of Science.)

the west on Dartmoor and elsewhere, but usually in small compact blocks, quite different from the continuous spreads—making a whole arable landscape—in much of southern Britain. Stock farming was the big business in these highland parts in the Iron Age, and the same seems to apply to Britain north of the Jurassic Way.[1] Here, however, now that a large find of carbonised corn has been discovered at Staple Howe, on the north edge of the Yorkshire Wolds, it must be suspected that some northern 'Celtic' fields did, in fact, originate in the Iron Age, if not earlier. The presence of carbonised corn and of post-holes indicating a granary at Staple Howe, where there was the normal highland-zone absence of pits, adds to the need for caution.[2] There seems little need to doubt, however, that the wonderfully preserved fields at Grassington, in the West Riding, with associated settlements, as well as other typical 'Celtic' fields less well preserved in other parts of Wharfedale, are Romano-British. The only known 'Celtic' fields recorded in Lancashire[3] are also of this period, as apparently are those associated with Romano-British sites at Ewe Close and Crosby Garrett in Westmorland. All these are on limestone and it may be noted in passing that good corn yields on acid soils were likely to be uneconomic or impossible because of the need to lime the land. Even where chalk lay near by, for instance, 30–80 loads would periodically be required for each acre.[4] This did not prevent the cultivation of 'clay-with-flints' on the chalk.

The Roman Conquest opened up a new situation tending to peace and order which greatly stimulated rural development, though to different degrees in different places. There was an immediate demand from the army, and eventually from the towns, through which also new ways were surely disseminated. Governmental development of mining and the building of new arterial roads, to which local ways were linked, all had a considerable effect. The adoption of rectangular houses for the first time in the lowland zone is a clear mark of how ideas spread. It is still too early to say whether, how soon, and in what areas, they became the norm. In highland areas the round house frequently persisted and in some sites round and rectangular structures existed side by side.[5] Eventually, high farming would be developed from the villas and the wisdom of classical

[1] Lady A. Fox, in Frere (1960), 49, 54–55
[2] Brewster (1963), 47, 52
[3] Lowndes (1963)
[4] Fream (1955), 166
[5] Hogg, in Thomas (1966), 33

farming books, *mutatis mutandis*, would be taken to heart. The much closer link with the Continent also seems to have allowed the introduction of tools hitherto only used by the Celts there. Nevertheless, although civilisation had arrived, it cannot be supposed that new methods were brought in and imposed. It is significant that the heavy plough, as Pliny noted, originated north of the Alps. The demand, the official encouragement, the peace, must be seen as accelerating the potential of development that already existed.

Apart from the occupying legions and auxiliaries, the actual number of new-comers was probably small. Britain was to be exploited for her resources. First, though, the troops had to be fed. Mr Rivet argues (p. 196) that they needed something like 530,000 bushels a year. A hundred years previously Caesar came without corn and had to forage. In the earliest years of the Claudian invasion it seems that some of the need was met by imports.[1] But this could have been only a temporary measure. There can be no doubt that the area of farm land was considerably extended. Ultimately, the most striking example of this was to be in the Fens. Here half a million acres of rich land was taken into use, which in later times was renowned for both corn and pasture. Cobbett's descriptions of 1830 remind us of its great virtues: in the Thorney area 'twenty thousand acres . . . covered with fat sheep or bearing six quarters of wheat or ten of oats to the acre, without any manure'. Around Crowland the larger fields, 'covered with beautiful grass,' looked like 'immense bowling-greens separated by ditches'.[2] The whole area was probably an Imperial estate.[3] A rapid scanning of vertical air photographs alone, however, suggests to the writer that the dramatic pattern of crop marks and earthworks shows very considerable differences, in this almost entirely Romano-British layout, from what is usually detectable in the field remains accumulated since perhaps 1500 B.C. on the downland of south Britain. A sense of order is given by straight boundary lines, an elaborate road and track system and a 'Roman' angularity, but most striking is the paucity of 'Celtic' fields in the northern Fens. The enclosures so often shown on air photographs and sometimes referred to as 'Celtic' fields generally occur in small blocks which usually include features that can only be regarded as belonging to settlements, not to field systems. These enclosures

[1] *Fishbourne* (1963), 13–14
[2] *Rural Rides* (Everyman edn, 1957), ii, 238–9
[3] Rivet (1964), 117

may be house plots, yards, gardens, or paddocks, and doubtless some were arable, as could be the crofts around medieval settlements, but the main fields must have lain in the areas between these isolated blocks. Pl. 1.3 is a remarkable air photograph of an area near Cuckoo Bridge, south-west of Spalding, Lincs. (about TF 205205), showing all the main ditches that ever existed over 200 acres. It is suggested that the clusters of small enclosures mark settlement concentrations. There are one or two closes whose size and proportions recall 'Celtic long fields', but it is the relatively very large enclosures in the areas between the assumed settlements which are the most remarkable. We cannot know what temporary subdivisions may have existed here, but the surviving pattern is certainly not of 'Celtic' fields as they are generally known. Conversely, nowhere in the Fens is there any good evidence for strip cultivation that could be compared with the medieval. Comparison of the drawing of crop marks 4 miles east-south-east of Crowland, near Gothic House, published by Crawford,[1] with R.A.F. vertical air photographs, shows that the strip divisions at that site are immediately by a settlement. The strips shown are all that existed there, and this area is not big enough for a normal group of arable fields. The plots are, moreover, defined by substantial ditches. They vary in width, and half of them are completely enclosed by ditches. Though all are narrow, some are short. Like the large fields and the blocks of parallel ditched banks sometimes referred to as lazy beds,[2] they represent the appearance of something new to the old Iron Age pattern and their eventual interpretation is a matter of great interest.

However it might have been in the Fens, the demand for corn must have given a general boost to production. Some sign of an organised increase may be detectable on the Grovely ridge west of Salisbury. Here one hill-fort, Bilbury, received special treatment. It was the only hill-fort on the ridge not to be destroyed. In it was a quite separate enclosure with irregular 'stepped' outline defined by a ditch 8 feet deep with a bank outside it. In this was a settlement, perhaps originating before the Conquest, that was certainly developed and maintained in the Roman period. Finds of brooches and horse trappings are compatible with Roman military connections, though there is nothing to suggest that this was a military site as such, and have specific parallels at the Roman fort on Hod

[1] Crawford (1953), 206
[2] G. Clark (1949), 147

Hill 15 miles away.[1] The surrounding 'Celtic' fields are contemporary, of interesting but not unusual form except in so far as they are divided by parallel but irregularly spaced banks in a way not so far known elsewhere on the downland. There appear, however, to be air-photographic traces of a 'chessboard' grid containing normal 'Celtic' fields, probably to be associated with an aisled villa building near West Blatchington, Sussex.[2] It may be remarked that air photographs of the Cottenham area of Cambridgeshire, south of the Fens, also suggest the bounding of normal 'Celtic' fields within long, straight boundaries, but there is no question of centuriation, a Roman method of dividing land into precise squares with sides of 776 yards, nor has any convincing example been adduced in an area where actual fields have survived. The postulated existence of former centuriation elsewhere has been based on fossilisation assumed in modern roads and other boundaries.[3]

The form of settlement, as already noted, generally tends to change. In the more persistently 'native' sites, whose total number may be very large—we do not know—this may take the form of piecemeal and untidy expansion. Prof. Hawkes has given the best example of this in his analysis of Woodcuts and Rotherley, both of which he thought were established shortly before the Conquest. At the latter site a round ditched enclosure about one-third the size of Little Woodbury was in Roman times added to by angular enclosures. The settlement as a whole was not apparently enclosed. The road leading into the settlement belonged to the Iron Age 'C' phase. 'Celtic' fields lay close to the settlement. Pits were used in the Roman as in the earlier period. There were other features of the 'Little Woodbury economy' such as rectangular patterns of post-holes suggesting granaries above ground, but also interesting innovations, particularly the floor of a small rectangular structure. At both Rotherley and Woodcuts there were also T-shaped corn-drying ovens, and at Woodcuts there were deep wells, one 180 feet deep. Leaving the details of the economy to one side, however, what was the nature of these settlements? Although both eventually covered about 4 acres of ground, they may have been 'homesteads', perhaps akin to Little Woodbury in status, but certainly not in

---

[1] R. Colt Hoare (1810), 108. The site has been recently excavated by the Rev. E. S. Steele, but most of the metalwork was found previously. I am indebted to Mrs P. J. Fowler and Dr G. Webster for comments on it.

[2] Applebaum (1958), 72

[3] Nightingale (1952), 150–9

form. Apart from the rectangular floor at Rotherley, there is no sure indication of house type and no indication of the number of houses. In the days before Bersu the pits and other sinkings, regarded as dwellings, could have made villages of both these Cranborne Chase settlements, though the excavator certainly did not think the pits were lived in. The current *Oxford History of Roman Britain,* written in 1937, depends on such a view, applied to Salisbury Plain, for a well-known analysis of dichotomy between Roman *villas* and native *villages*.[1] This is generally discredited, because of Little Woodbury, but must be re-examined because of more recent discoveries.

First, it may be wise to look at the word 'village'. In modern terms this has been very recently defined as 'a nucleated rural settlement of twenty or more homesteads, a large village being distinguishable from a small market town by its paucity of services'. A hamlet, on the other hand, 'is taken to be a nucleated settlement, with or without a parish church, having from three to nineteen homesteads'.[2] It is impossible to use this definition in a *precise* sense in our present context, because we can almost never make a safe count of houses. None the less the use of the term to distinguish an organised and apparently nucleated settlement, incorporating many houses, from one which may be no more than a large farm with workers' cottages and outbuildings seems to be justified. To use the undifferentiated term 'settlement' when a distinction can be seen is to cloud the issue. It is only necessary to remember that 'village' has no tenurial significance and must not be taken to include the necessary existence of public services such as shop or smithy. R. G. Collingwood, in the *Oxford History* referred to, thought of native villages as untidy collections of small round huts ('sometimes pit dwellings') presenting the most marked contrast with villas—'the distinction between these two types of settlement is of fundamental importance'. He went on to say that 'certain regions . . . were exclusively occupied by villas, others exclusively by villages'. His interpretation can no longer stand. Native settlement sites are much more widespread than was then appreciated and occur in areas both without and with villas and surely in many instances were closely connected with them. Pits are rarely found on the more Romanised sites. Fieldwork in the Fens and in Wessex has, however, produced new reasons for talking of the existence of villages, and these sites, although not yet

[1] Collingwood and Myres (1937), 209
[2] Thorpe (1964), 359

examined closely, appear to represent an organisation and way of life much superior to those formerly envisaged.

It is interesting—and no more—to see that the claim to reinstate the village has been raised on behalf of the Salisbury Plain region and of the Fens, two areas otherwise only linked by the suggestion of their being Imperial Estates. To take Wessex first, it will be seen that the term can as yet be used only for what appears to be the more sophisticated forms, based on 'streets', where an extremely rough assessment of the numbers of houses can be made.[1] One of the most remarkable is on Knook Down, near Warminster, Wilts. On the west wide of the Down is one village, covering at least 20 acres, joined to another settlement of 8 acres by roads, part of an elaborate local system. Although the earthworks are relatively well preserved, it is not possible to say how many houses were involved, but if we can accept the platforms as evidence there were certainly many more than twenty rectangular buildings along a street the main part of which stretches for some 700 yards. The form of these platforms and of the rectangular closes bounding the 'street' call to mind the earthwork remains in some deserted medieval villages, but the abundant finds reported in the past make the Roman date absolutely certain. It is one of a number of Roman sites on which coal has been found.[2] A rather smaller village, but with about eighty platforms along a street over a quarter of a mile long, has also been recognised on Chisenbury Warren, in north-east Wiltshire. Here again the Roman date cannot be in doubt. The rectangular platforms vary in size, but none so far found are longer than 90 feet. The smaller ones may be comparable with the house sites on Woodhouse Hill, Studland, Dorset, described later, or with five adjacent platforms, none longer than about 40 feet, cut into the chalk on Park Brow, Sussex. These had supported Romano-British rectangular wood-framed cottages with Roman tiled roofs. Coloured plaster, window-glass, and a door-key were also found.[3] Conversely, it should be noted that none of the platforms suggest a structure anything like the size of the Iwerne building excavated by Pitt-Rivers, where the platform was 150 feet long—and, even so, often only grudgingly called 'villa' (Fig. 1.2e).

A striking feature of Knook Down West, found also in other sites, is a

[1] H. C. Bowen and P. J. Fowler, in Thomas (1966), 43–53, for discussion of Wessex examples, including those cited here.
[2] Webster (1955), 214, site 38
[3] Wolseley, Smith, and Hawley (1927), 8

triangular 'open space' of half an acre which the street enters from the south, at the apex of the triangle, and leaves by the north. Another road leaves the triangle at the north-west corner. On other parts of Knook Down the local roads tend to splay in funnel shapes at junctions, but the resultant open space is much smaller. It is at the junction of roads on the edge of settlements that the 'open spaces' are usually found. Where the date is known it is Roman. Their small size contrasts with that of 'greens' in later periods, but since there is usually only one even in a certain community settlement there is a strong suggestion that the open space is connected with the settlement as a whole and not with the nearest house. A rare feature, possibly comparable in intention but different in form, is the 'broad way', of 30 feet or more across, which is considerably wider than the very widest 'normal' local road, in Wessex, of about 24 feet. The road south of the triangular open space on Knook Down West takes this form, and by the Iron Age/Romano-British settlement of Ebsbury near Salisbury there is a stretch 100 feet wide between slight banks at least 300 yards long. There is a comparable broad way approaching the settlement on Thundersbarrow Hill, Sussex.[1] 'Celtic' fields lie adjacent to all these settlements.

Destruction has immeasurably reduced the possibility of earthwork examination such as described above, but it is clear that there were other types of settlements, of unknown status, where new features—including some already noted—seem to appear. Without excavation we can never be quite sure of the nature of such features or their date in any particular instance. We should not be too surprised to find pre-Roman antecedents. The rectangular form of enclosure, for instance, so characteristic of the shape in the Roman and later periods, though acknowledged in some areas to be an introduction of the later Iron Age, has recently been demonstrated in the Middle Bronze Age on Shearplace Hill in Dorset, where also there seemed already to be a road system.[2] Much more curiously, perhaps, the wells that first appear on settlement sites in the Roman period are now shown to be a technical possibility in the Middle Bronze Age too, by the radioactive carbon dating of wood found at the bottom of a circular shaft sunk 100 feet into the chalk near Stonehenge.[3] In Dorset the 'open spaces' have been noted in settlements both with and without rectangular plat-

[1] Curwen (1933), pl. XVI
[2] Rahtz (1962), 293
[3] Ashbee (1963)

forms. In two instances, in Frampton parish by Westminstone Down, and on West Hill, Plush, Piddletrenthide, the settlements largely consist of irregular platforms undoubtedly levelled for structures, but of any shape, spread over an area of 3 or 4 acres. Both settlements had roads leading in from two directions and both lacked any visible remains of an overall enclosure, though the former existence of fences must always be considered. A larger site, also in Dorset, with open space, elaborate road systems and some rectangular platforms, is here illustrated because of its remarkable state of preservation, which incidentally shows its relationship to a largely undisturbed group of 'Celtic' fields indistinguishable in form from the prehistoric (Fig. 1.5). It is on Meriden Down, 4 miles south of Hod Hill near Blandford, Dorset. The only datable find is a single sherd of a Romano-British flanged bowl, but there can be no doubt of the Roman date of the settlement in its present form. By the time an early medieval park pale was built across it its former existence as a settlement was ignored and probably not recognised. The apparent nucleus of the settlement, of about $3\frac{1}{2}$ acres, is bounded for the greater part by a slight bank and ditch. It is covered by a number of platforms, some of them rectangular and quite unlike the rounded form associated with Iron Age settlements. North of this is an open space bounded partly by the ditch of the nucleus and partly by another slight bank and ditch, the continuation of one side of road (a), whose other side has terminated somewhere near the park pale. Within the open space are four small low round mounds of unknown purpose. Three of four roads running into the settlement come into this open space. These roads are well marked either by banks or by lynchets, demonstrating their general contemporaneity with the fields. Road (d) is, however, demonstrably laid out along the edge of fields that had been in use, and then continued in use, for a long time. Some of the field lynchets above Park Bottom, where the natural slope contributes to their apparent height, are over 15 feet high. There is another contemporary settlement less than half a mile to the south, and signs of others on this ridge where an ancient way led towards Hod Hill to the north, and south towards a possible junction with the Roman road to Dorchester, Dorset. Such fragments help to show that in Wessex, and over most of the chalk downland, there was, for at least most of the Roman period, permanent occupation wherein settlements of different status were connected to each other by roads. In many instances these made together a network of communication ancillary to the main, perhaps military-inspired, Roman

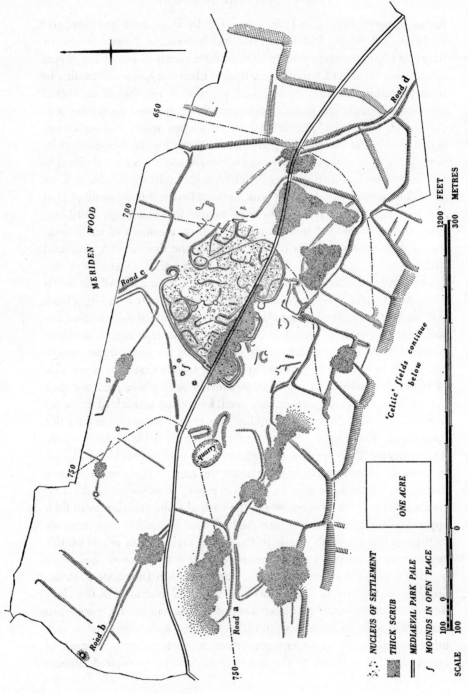

Fig. 1.5. Plan of settlement on Meriden Down, Winterbourne Houghton, Dorset (Crown Copyright).

roads. It also seems certain enough that there was an increasing development of the lower lands, but proof of this, in areas other than open river valleys, lies largely in isolated finds in areas of intensive later development. This can be quickly seen by reference to the Third Edition of the Ordnance Survey Map of Roman Britain. The ability to open new land requiring an elaborate drainage system has been referred to in describing the Fens. Widespread use of tools such as iron-shod spades must have greatly facilitated such development. A detailed report giving the result of many years of research is shortly to appear and some of the results have been anticipated in occasional articles.[1] One of these has recently demonstrated the existence there of a variety of settlement types, some convincingly described as 'nucleated' villages.

This particular investigation has been conducted mostly by meticulous field observation combined with the use of air photographs. It showed that in south Lincolnshire early-phase settlements, started in the 1st century A.D., are mostly single farms or loosely knit collections of houses. Although there are no upstanding remains, the occupation areas exposed by the plough suggest rectangular houses similar to those indicated by earthworks and excavated remains in Wiltshire and Dorset, and some that were larger and nearer in size to the Iwerne villa. There was a development towards much greater nucleation in the later periods, though in south Lincolnshire the farmsteads do not appear to have exceeded eleven in a group. There were 'loose clusters' stretching along waterways for almost a mile in places.

In the higher, lighter silts around the Wash estuary the settlements are larger, more concentrated and longer-lived than in south Lincolnshire. 'There is complete and continuous graduation up to aggregates like that which Dr Salway [the excavator] has described as a "town" at Hockwold on the eastern fen-edge. . . . It would be perverse to deny that the range includes nucleated rural settlements.'

It is, fortunately, no purpose of this chapter to make technical distinctions between cottages, small farmhouses and villas, but it has to be noted once more that a considerable number of rectangular houses is now recognised and there are clear indications that many were relatively humble, like the well-known example at Catsgore, north of Ilchester, Somerset.[2]

[1] P. Salway, in Thomas (1966), 26–27, general account; Mrs S. J. Hallam (1964) for villages.

[2] *Catsgore* (1951)

Here a round house 33 feet across was replaced, near the beginning of the 1st century A.D., by a rectangular building. In the 2nd century there were two blocks, one 46 feet by 24 feet and the other 40 feet by 22 feet, separated by a passage 4 feet wide. The establishment was of 'humble nature'. In Dorset, on Woodhouse Hill, Studland, within a half-acre investigated, small round huts were being replaced by rectangular forms platformed into the slope as early as the second half of the 1st century A.D. These were followed in the 2nd century and onwards by substantial rectangular cottages, one reaching some 50 feet in length, with cob walls on stone footings. They were probably thatched. Like the Iwerne building in phase B (Fig. 1.2), they were divided into dwelling-quarters for humans at one end and for housing animals at the other. There were in addition 'work-rooms' in the Studland cottages and a tower granary to the Iwerne building. It will be interesting to see, in the course of time, how far, with what variations, and how soon in this lowly context, the change-over from round to rectangular houses was effected.

It is time to consider briefly the evidence for development or changes in farming practices, methods, crops and stock. By the 4th century technological advances were very impressive (*cf.* Fig. 1.6), although it is difficult to say when new devices were introduced or how widespread was their use. Most are associated with villas and towns. There is ample proof that new tools and methods eventually led, in places, to efficiency such as the Iron Age never knew. Ironworking grew in skill and volume. Hoards found in the towns of Silchester, Hants,[1] or Great Chesterford, Essex,[2] or at the villa of Brading in the Isle of Wight[3] are themselves dramatic lessons in the history of technology. Tools assume shapes quite familiar to modern eyes. They include hammers, nails of all sorts, bow saws, a diversity of axes and knives, chisels, spokeshaves, and even jack-planes. Although finds are very rare, it is certain enough that wooden implements increased in numbers and quality. It is not surprising that implements could be and were built to meet particular conditions. Amongst the most significant innovations are the two-handed scythe and field anvil for sharpening it, enabling hay to be harvested so much more easily—with consequent effect on winter feed for cattle; the balanced sickle to speed the corn harvest; the iron hoe, turf-cutter, and iron-shod spade. Surface

[1] Boon (1957), 186–7
[2] Neville (1856)
[3] Cleere (1958)

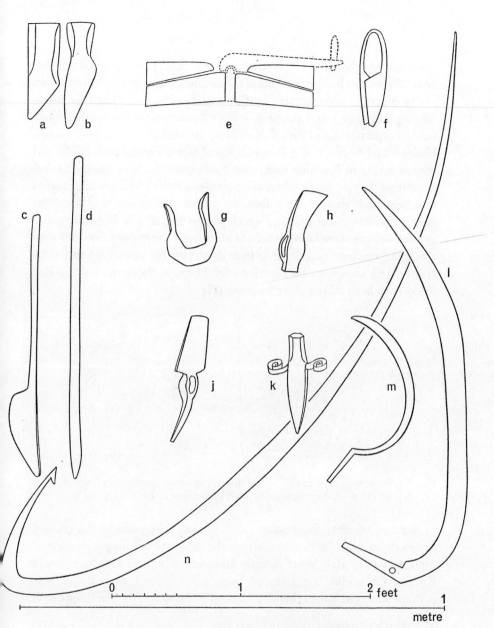

Fig. 1.6. Romano-British farm implements.

(a) and (b) Asymmetric iron plough-shares (a) from Brading (after Cleere (1958), (b) from Folkestone (after Aberg (1956)). (c) Coulter and (d) Iron fore-share from probable coultered *ard* (after Manning (1964)). (e) Quern (after Curwen). (f) Cropping shears (after Boon (1957)). (g) Iron spade-shoe (based on 111 a.4 in *Antiquities of Roman Britain* (B.M. 1951). (h) Iron axe-head of common form (after Collingwood (1930)). (j) Iron mattock (after Collingwood (1930)). (k) Mower's anvil (after Collingwood (1930)). (l) Scythe blade (slightly longer than the longest quoted in recent modern catalogue). (m) Balance sickle. (n) 'Scythe' blade from Great Chesterford (after Neville (1856)).

granaries and barns seem in time to have superseded pits for storage generally, but we have few details of the decline of this marked cultural trait.

Machinery is demonstrated by the remains of geared wheels for transmitting animal or water power to mills.[1] Refinement of technique, readiness to experiment and diffusion of ideas are shown by very long narrow blades found in pits in the Roman town of Great Chesterford, Essex, and now at a villa in Barnsley Park, near Cirencester.[2] These blades, $5\frac{1}{2}$ feet or so from pointed tip to where their gentle curve is suddenly accentuated and bent back sharply for 1 foot, are usually called scythes, but differ greatly from the normal type, which is also found. We know that new cutting devices were being tried out elsewhere. Experiment in Gaul with a reaping machine called the *vallus*, illustrated on bas-reliefs and sufficiently well known to be described by Pliny, is the sort of thing that could have been taking place here too (Fig. 1.7).[3]

Fig. 1.7. Reconstruction of the 'vallus' from fragments of sculpture from Buzenol (*left*) and Arlon (*right*). (By kind permission of Dr J. Mertens.)

Some of the most interesting developments took place in the craft of the ploughwright. In this connection the progressive thought of agricultural writers in Italy must directly and indirectly have had its effect in Britain. Columella, a provincial from Cádiz settled near Rome, was perhaps the most comprehensive of such writers. An analytical approach

[1] Manning (1964a)

[2] Information kindly given by the excavator, Dr G. Webster. I am indebted to Mr John Anstee of the Museum of English Rural Life, Reading, for information, received after this text was finished, concerning experiments he is currently carrying out on reconstructed forms of this type of implement. He is sure that it is a practicable, specialised scythe.

[3] Mertens (1958)

is well seen in his consideration of soils. There were six characters: 'fat or lean, loose or compact, wet or dry'. Failing the ideal of 'rich and mellow' the next best was 'rich and dense, a soil which rewards the expense of toil of the husbandman with rich increase . . .' British ploughs to meet diverse conditions include the old beam (or bow) ard and a development fitted with ground wrests or ears. These ears were for clearing the furrow and burying seed broadcast, but they also allow the possibility of turning the furrow to one side or the other, a 'one-way' practice. It has recently been shown by Mr W. H. Manning that a coultered form of beam ard was also developed, with the wooden foreshare of the pre-Roman type replaced by an iron bar share and a heavy knife coulter added to cut a slice vertically.[1] The assumption depends on the identification of iron bars of the right type found with a dozen out of the thirteen coulters found in this country. It greatly reduces the weight of evidence for the existence of a true heavy plough, but does not remove it. The evidence remains in three shares with 'wings' on one side only, showing that they belonged to a plough intended to turn a furrow consistently to one side[2] (cf. Fig. 1.6). This plough would have had a mould-board, as well as knife coulter, and would have been of the same type and effectiveness as many of medieval and later date.

Such a plough was clearly developed to deal with heavy soils, but the claim has also been made in the past that its existence led to the introduction of strip fields. The argument runs as follows: because turning at the headland is a cumbersome business, a heavy plough is most economically employed in making a long furrow; and since, as Pliny says, a field should be of a size which can properly be ploughed in one day, a long narrow plot is the result. Whether owing to this or not, long 'Celtic' fields do occur. Going further, however, it has occasionally been suggested that *strip lynchets* of the type so commonly seen in most hilly areas of England were first introduced in this period. There is no reputable evidence to support this.[3] It must be emphasised, however, that strip lynchets are not just any long fields. They have definite characteristics. They are almost always 200 yards or more in length and more than ten times as long as broad. They never have square ends, but may have curved ones. Usually they are open-ended so that the plough could turn on a headland or other

[1] Manning (1964b), 62
[2] Aberg (1957), 174
[3] Bowen (1961), 44; Taylor (1966)

adjacent land. They usually survive along the contour, but not infrequently lie up and down or athwart the slope. Strip lynchets, so defined, are in innumerable instances seen to be part of the medieval system, and whenever in known contact with Roman remains they are demonstrably later. Examples excavated in north Wiltshire lie over a Romano-British ditched earthwork which must have been levelled before the strips were laid out.[1] The same applies to those which lie over the *vicus* outside the Roman fort at Housesteads, on Hadrian's Wall. Countless others impinge unconformably on 'Celtic' fields. The strip lynchets are, moreover, only the counterpart of the strips, ridged or flat, which form the furlongs of the *open fields* on less steep ground. The few ditched strips in the Fens (p. 30) remain a curiosity. Claims have been made for the survival of ridge-and-furrow from the Roman period. It is perfectly possible that ridged fields did exist, because the mould-board ploughs—even the coultered ards—could have built them, but it seems unlikely that any will ever be proved of Roman date. There was until recently, for example, a considerable area of ridged fields near the Roman villa at Great Witcombe, Glos., where a massive coulter was found. Similar ridged fields also existed close to the late Romano-British corn-drying establishment on Rockbourne Down, Hants,[2] but mere contiguity is not enough. Areas of strip cultivation on the high downland are common, particularly in Wessex, although the strip lynchets on Thundersbarrow Hill in Sussex are perhaps a better-known example, while the writer has examined others over 'Celtic' fields on New Timber Hill, near Lewes. Recent fieldwork and excavation on Fyfield Down, north Wilts., together with documentary evidence, have demonstrated that ridged fields and low strip lynchets over 'Celtic' fields there (where Iron Age and Romano-British settlements certainly existed) mostly belong to the 13th century A.D.[3] We have seen that 'Celtic' fields, used on the downland throughout the Roman period, were generally little different from those tilled in the prehistoric period. It has already been suggested that some fields, rather longer and narrower than usual and dubbed 'Celtic long fields', may have been developed in the Roman period, but they are still enclosed plots with squared ends and are quite different from the much longer and normally open-ended medieval strips

[1] Wood and Whittington (1959), 166

[2] Sumner (1914). Annotation on plan opp. p. 15 suggests he excavated ridge-and-furrow south-west of 'hypocausts' (2) and (3)

[3] Bowen and Fowler (1962), 104

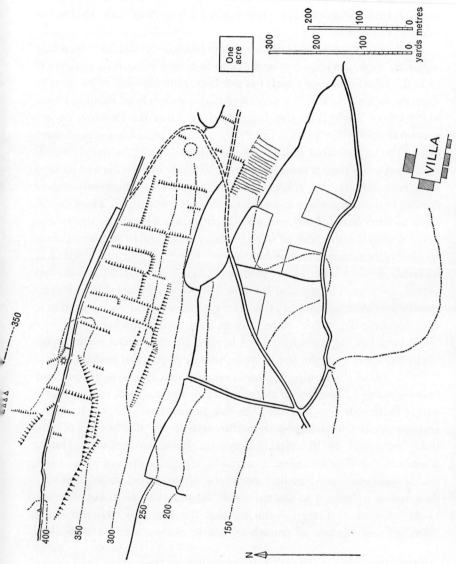

Fig. 1.8. Plan of 'Celtic' fields on Brading Down, Isle of Wight, in relation to the Brading villa.

(Fig. 1.5.). Occasionally, ditched plots of long narrow form like the 'Celtic long fields' are found adjacent to Roman villas, or near settlements of Roman date but unproven type, as at Kirk Sink, Gargrave, Yorks.,[1] or near Worthing, Sussex,[2] but these could be 'paddocks' akin to those in Fenland settlements.

On the other hand, fields, almost always much disturbed but apparently of 'Celtic' type, are known to occur close to certain villas. The problem is to find a significant area which has not been radically altered by farmers since the Roman period. It is suggested that one such is on Brading Down in the Isle of Wight (Fig. 1.8). Immediately south of the Down is an important Roman villa which has yielded what is most probably a winged share of a type to be associated with a fixed mould-board plough, as already noted. In Roman times the sea came close to the east side of the villa and its land must have included the ridge just above it, as well as the gently rolling ground to the west, where any evidence has been destroyed. There are no signs of strip fields of any sort and the ridge top adjacent to the villa is covered with 'Celtic' fields of quite ordinary form, and including lynchets 10 feet high as a measure of long usage. Excavation of the lynchets is desirable, to show whether the fields were first laid out in the pre-Roman period, as is most likely, and for how long they continued in use. The possibility remains, however, that *new* ground was laid out quite differently from the old 'Celtic' pattern, as we have seen in the Fens.

Pastoral farming must have been boosted by the general introduction of the hay-cutting scythe and of wells, already noted, and perhaps by the introduction of the turnip. Columella remarks that it served 'as food, not only for mankind but also for cattle, especially in Gaul', where it 'provides winter fodder for . . . animals'.[3] By late Roman times, large-scale stock-keeping could match large-scale arable agriculture, the two apparently being combined in the establishment on Rockbourne Down, Hants, where remains of ox and horse occurred in large numbers and where there was a stockaded and ditched enclosure of 96 acres, so impressively designed as to suggest to the excavator the influence of Roman farming books.[4] Elsewhere there is evidence that the breed of cow was being improved and remains of animals of nearly modern size are sometimes

[1] I am grateful to Mr H. G. Ramm for the note on Gargrave.
[2] Lewis (1960)
[3] Columella, *R.R.*, II, x, 22
[4] Sumner (1914), 27

found.[1] Other beasts were exploited on a large scale. The *birrus Britannicus*, probably of goat's hair, and the *tapete Britannicum*, of wool, had an international reputation;[2] the names are curiously recalled by the modern 'British warm'. Dr Applebaum has made the interesting suggestion that the relative scarcity of loom-weights on Romano-British sites indicates the importance of state weaving mills. Pigs were kept in sufficient numbers to indicate pig-farms. Cats were introduced.

Crops of different sorts must have embellished the countryside as well as improved the larder. There is recent evidence for the existence of formal gardens in the great Roman villa at Fishbourne, established in the 1st century A.D., and Tacitus, writing at this time, seems to imply experiment and the introduction of new plants, and praises the fertility of the soil when he says 'it can bear all produce except the olive, vine and other natives of warmer climates . . .'. There is little doubt that his information on the climate was reliable; he said it was foul.[3] Dr Helbaek has indicated that spelt became the principal corn crop, but that rye, oats, and flax were also grown deliberately and in quantity for the first time. The use of wheat for malting has been proved by carbonised finds from Wales.[4] Amongst crops new to Britain, Dr Applebaum lists cabbage, broad bean, parsnip, pea, radish, celery, carrot, mustard, vetch, tare and corn spurry, as well as rape and turnip. Fruits included cherry, medlar, plum, damson, bullace, apple and mulberry; amongst flowers the rose and (on philological evidence) the lily, violet and pansy.[5]

The large-scale development of corn-growing is shown not least in the history of the corn-drying oven. Elaborate types with channelled flues are known in a number of villas, but the more common form which spread into rural settlements is the T-shaped oven. It was first recognised in what is still the most impressive collection of such ovens in a villa at Hambleden in Buckinghamshire.[6] No less than fifteen of this type were concentrated in and around a yard, suggesting 'factory' methods that give a feeling of sympathy with the period until the account tells of ninety-seven infants buried in the yard. This form of oven is associated particularly with the

---

[1] Jewell (1962), 163; *cf.* Green (1959), 27
[2] Rivet (1964), 123–4
[3] Tacitus, *Agr.*, xii; Fishbourne (1965b). Evidence for vines in Roman Britain (*cf.* Applebaum (1958), 71) scarcely affects the generalisation.
[4] Helbaek (1964)
[5] Applebaum (1958), 70–71
[6] *Hambleden* (1921)

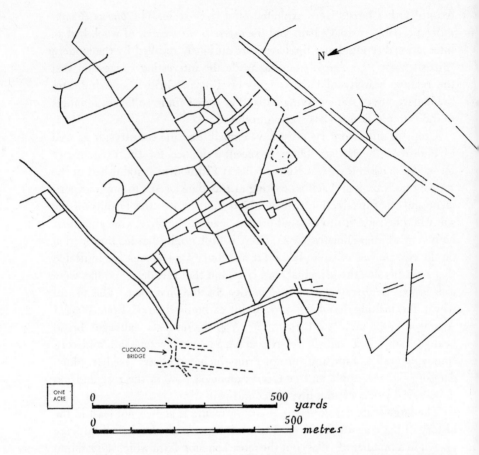

ONE
ACRE

0   500
                                          yards
0   500
                                        metres

Fig. 1.9. An interpretation of Plate 1.3. Dark lines on light-coloured corn fields, photographed on 8 May 1947, represent greater growth over ancient ditches. Sinuous lines are old water channels and only some are apparently contemporary with the fields. Successive phases of field and track arrangement are clear in places. Division of the land into major blocks by running boundary lines is also suggested. Settlements, represented probably by clusters of small closes, are surrounded by very large fields (see p. 30).

4th century, when agricultural production and the display of rural wealth in villas seem to have been at a peak. To what extent their general use was due to direction or stimulus by villa-owners is uncertain, and is connected with the whole problem of how far other rural settlements had become dependent on villas.

The difficulty of determining tenurial relationships is one that can only be resolved on grounds of probability—and then after excavation. It has been suggested, for instance, that the Roman establishment at Tarrant Hinton in Dorset, found by chance over a hundred years ago and never planned or adequately described, was the headquarters of an estate including a number of farms, amongst which might be the unexcavated site at Chettle.[1] The present writer once made a similar suggestion, rashly putting forward the unusual enclosures on Tarrant Hinton and Pimperne Down as his examples. One of those on Pimperne Down has since been proved to belong to Iron Age 'A', without any secondary use. It is still desirable to find genuine contemporary associations and there are many likely places for considering this aspect further. At Rockbourne, Hants, for example, adjacent to the present village, is a large and rich villa which existed at least through the 4th century.[2] So far there is little evidence for agricultural operations in the villa area itself, but 1½ miles to the north is the carefully built enclosure, already referred to, taking in some 96 acres of low downland dropping to a large pond. Associated with this enclosure were three T-shaped corn-drying ovens called hypocausts by the excavator. There was a large number of querns as well as animal bones, including cattle and horse. Almost certainly people lived on the site, but a connection with the villa is strongly suggested not only by the sophisticated form of the earthwork but also by the fact that the flues of the well-built corn-drying ovens included combed box-tiles and Purbeck stone roofing slabs. A Purbeck stone roof over its corridor is one of the proud features of the villa. The excavator has suggested an estate running beyond the bounds of the enclosure just noted. It is possible to infer that we have here an example of intensive stock and arable farming at some distance from, but dependent upon, a villa.

How far the old ways continued unchanged in the multitude of sites now revealed by air survey it is much too early to say, but it is certain that by the end of the Roman occupation, establishments, agricultural tools, and techniques were in places notably sophisticated in comparison with those of the Celtic Iron Age. Virtually all the implements known in the Middle Ages were in common use; the lower and richer lands were being exploited and 'high' farming was being practised. There can, at the least, be no great technical contrast between the resources of the late

[1] Applebaum (1954b)
[2] *Rockbourne* (1962)

Roman and those of the full Saxon period and certainly none to the disadvantage of the Roman.[1]

[1] I am grateful to Prof. S. S. Frere, Mr R. A. H. Farrar and the Editor for reading and commenting on drafts of this chapter in typescript.

2. 1   Air photograph of the Ditchley villa. Photo Major G. W. G. Allen, copyright Ashmolean Museum

CHAPTER TWO

The Plans of Roman Villas in Britain

THE LATE SIR IAN RICHMOND

EDITOR'S NOTE: *A consideration of their plans must clearly be central to any discussion of villas, and it was therefore fitting that this chapter, which was to form the keystone of the book, should have been undertaken by our greatest authority on Roman Britain, Sir Ian Richmond. He was working on it at his untimely death in October 1965, and his draft for the opening paragraphs, which was found among his papers, gives some idea of the approach he intended to adopt.*

This fragment is printed below, as he left it. For the rest, by the very great kindness of Lady Richmond and of the publishers, Messrs Methuen and Company Ltd, we are able to use the chapter on villas which is appearing in Sir Ian's revision of Collingwood's Archaeology of Roman Britain. *Although the approach is slightly different, it has seemed best not to amend it to fit its new context, and apart from some minor changes in the system of reference it is reproduced here unaltered.* A.L.F.R.

WHEN A SERIES of plans is available, and these of varying kind, size and aspect, it is tempting to arrange them according to type, and tempting, further, to apply time to type and so to construct a chronology. This is specious. On the whole too little is known about the dating of types. But it is at least clear that one of the simplest and most primitive of types was in fact one of the most lasting, and that, although it is characteristic of the earliest 1st-century stage in the development of many villas, it can also be found newly built in its simplest form as late as the 4th century. It is wiser, then, to categorise the houses according to the economic needs which they seem to satisfy than to suppose that the one type necessarily grew out of another, or that any one style was typical of a given age.

The simplest style of house, from which a start may be made, is represented by such a villa as Park Street I, in which two or more rooms are arranged in a row while a through passage from back to front lies off centre. This closely resembles the simplest form of farm-house in later England. There is, however, no reason to suppose that this implies a connexion between them. The type arises in both cases out of the simple function of the family farm related to the provision of rooms. The existence of doors between rooms is seldom demonstrable, since only the foundations of such structures are normally found, but they seem demanded by the fact that no linking corridor is provided, and it may be assumed that, as in the medieval examples, there were communicating doorways between each room and that access to and through the building was obtained by the through passage. Houses of this kind are not uncommon, and often mark the first stage in a villa that developed into something grander. Park Street I, Lockleys I, Ditchley I and Hambleden I provide examples, and in each this stage marks a beginning. At Little Milton, however, where the plan is known through air-photography, it is clear that no enlargement ever took place. Whether such houses had an upper storey is unknown, but it should be noted that by modern standards their foundations are sufficiently solid to have supported one. If, moreover, the upper fabric of the building was of timber-framing, as seems likely, and this framing was itself erected upon a sill-beam, as would then seem certain, then later analogy would support the expectation that the roof-space could be used for sleeping accommodation. Occasionally, as at Park Street, the accommodation is improved by the provision of a room with special function, in this case a half-underground stable.

The simplest general improvement upon so simple a design is the addition of an external corridor, obviating the use of all but the end rooms as passageways. This is seen at Chedworth I, the corridor being furnished with doorways at the ends and in the centre. There too the principal room had thicker front and back walls, as if the building had here carried an upper storey of more pretension, perhaps one which had full headroom as opposed to a cock-loft. It has been thought that Ditchley I also had a front portico, carried on wooden posts, but this does not run the full length of the building and seems disproportionately narrow. It is probably better explained as going with the remains of a primary timber house of which the post-holes were traced sporadically below the earliest stone building.

Both of the foregoing types of building must undoubtedly be regarded as farm-houses. . . .

*　　*　　*　　*　　*

General Features

The Latin word *villa* means a farm. It is primarily an economic term, indicating that the place so designated is an agricultural establishment. There was in antiquity, and there still is today, a tendency to restrict application of the term to country houses of the rich, with their luxurious accessories and ambitious plan; but this restriction narrows down the term from its broader application, which covered the establishment of any folk who farmed the land and were able to build upon it a house of Romanised style. The contrast is with a town house on the one hand and a native hut on the other.[1] Most Romano-British farms were viable economic units. Their lands might support other occupations than farming; and the man-power of the establishment, whether slave or free, might therefore be employed not only in agriculture but in skilled production of saleable objects, made from materials produced by the estate. Such deviations from purely agricultural or pastoral farming are essentially rare, if mainstays of the economy, and were normally concerned with by-products which scarcely altered the general tone of the picture.

Architecturally considered, the Romano-British villa has a character of its own. Its construction and materials varied according to the building materials available in the district and the wealth and taste of the owner; but the average villa seems to have been a single-storey, half-timbered building standing on foundations of stone, for these foundations are too slight, as a rule, to carry anything either high or heavy in their own material. The timbering itself was strong enough to carry a tiled or slated roof, and its in-filling was clay-daub, applied to a panel of wattle-work inserted between the framing and rendered seemly and waterproof by a coating of lime-wash or plaster. Tessellated or mosaic floors were common; in every villa except the poorest or least civilised there were rooms heated by hypocausts, and generally a suite of baths.

Since the villas are primarily connected with agriculture, their distribution not unnaturally coincides with the good arable lowland areas of

[1] Cato, *Agr.*, iii; xiv; Varro, *R.R.*, I, 11–13; II, i; *Digest.*, L, 16, 211

Britain. The majority of them thus lie south-east of a straight line between Exeter and the mouth of the Trent. Beyond that, they occur more sparsely, as in the Vale of York and the Welsh marches; but examples, isolated so far as present knowledge goes, are also found as far north as County Durham and as far south-west as the toe of Cornwall.[1]

The Romano-British villa shows variety in general planning, and many varieties in detail; but comparative study reveals four basic types: the cottage house, the corridor house, the courtyard house, and the aisled house.

The lineage of these types is somewhat obscure. It is evident that from the first their structure, in the Roman style, was profoundly different from that of native buildings: as different as are buildings in European style from indigenous native structures of Africa or North America. What is quite uncertain is the type of British chieftain's hall which some must have succeeded. The earliest and simplest type of Romano-British farm-house comprises a single row of rooms divided by a passage or lobby opening from back to front, and these are known sometimes to overlie primitive native huts, round or subrectangular. One of the commonest developments is to add to such a building a front corridor or veranda, serving large projecting rooms at either end. This is a pattern common throughout north-western Europe in Roman days, and was termed by Swoboda the 'Eckrisaliten-villa', that is, the 'villa with corner projections'.[2] But while in Britain the development is as described, in the Rhineland such a façade commonly masks a large open hall, with a cellar; and these are features that certainly belong to the native building tradition of Gallia Belgica. There is, on the other hand, no certainty that the British pattern derived from native prototypes, and it may well represent imported skills rather than native tradition.

The Cottage House

Whatever its origin, the simplest type of Romano-British house is undoubtedly the cottage type, already described, with through passage flanked by one or more rooms on each side. The division into rooms is based upon functional requirements as opposed to social distinctions. In

[1] *OSRB* (1956)
[2] Swoboda (1919), 77

short, the plan serves the simple needs of a family farm. As for date, some examples are as early as the sixties of the 1st century, but the type continues and even reappears, with cow-house attached, at Iwerne (Dorset: Fig. 2.6j) in the 3rd and 4th centuries. There is no evidence for an upper storey in such houses and their walls are normally so thin and slight that they must have served as the sill for a wooden frame. Examples are Lockleys and Park Street (Herts: Fig. 2.1a, b), Little Milton (Oxon.: Fig. 2.1c), Bignor I (Sussex), Cox Green near Maidenhead (Berks.), and Hambleden (Bucks.: Fig. 2.2a). All, except Little Milton which survived unaltered, illustrate very well the development of the cottage type of villa into the winged corridor house.

The Winged Corridor House

In the winged corridor house a corridor or veranda runs along the front of the building, while projecting principal rooms are provided at either end. These represent social developments, as significant in their way as the separation of the parlour or the solar in the medieval house; and they have the same meaning, that a distinction is made between the heads of the family and the other members of the household. The design is not an abstract creation, but a practical answer to a social development itself arising naturally out of growing prosperity.

As already observed, the winged corridor house is the standard type of small Romano-British country house: a type not confined to Britain, but very common in France, Belgium and Germany,[1] and ultimately derived, so far as treatment of the main façade is concerned, from the Mediterranean houses depicted in Pompeian wall-paintings[2] and found in actuality. In Britain and Gaul the main body of the house tends to be planned as a row of rooms; whereas in Germany there is a large central room, often with smaller rooms grouped round it. It has been demonstrated by excavation at Mayen in the Eifel, west of Coblenz,[3] and at Müngersdorf, outside Cologne,[4] that the area behind the corridor was originally a one-roomed house to which the corridor and wings were added. Thus, the development in Britain and Belgica is parallel rather

[1] Swoboda (1919), 89, 95
[2] Rostovtzeff (1957), pl. VIII, IX
[3] *Mayen* (1928)
[4] *Müngersdorf* (1933)

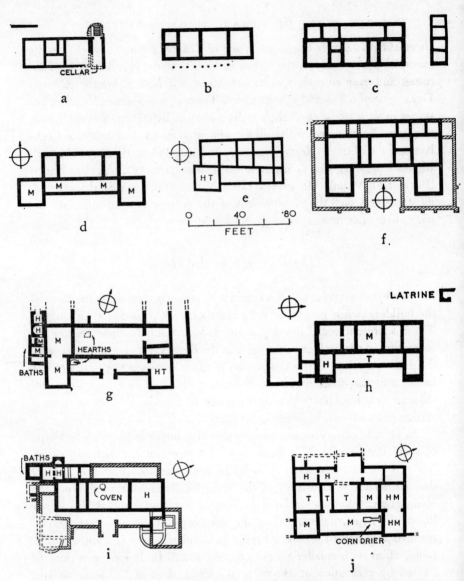

Fig. 2.1. Plans of cottage-houses and winged corridor houses (a) Park Street I, Herts, after O'Neil, *Arch. J.* cii, fig. 3; (b) Lockleys I, Herts, after Ward-Perkins, *Ant. J.* xviii, pl. lxx; (c) Little Milton, Oxon, sketch from St. Joseph, *JRS* xl, pl. vi, 24; (d) Great Staughton I, Hunts, after Greenfield, *JRS* xlix, fig. 15; (e) Frilford, Berks, after Haverfield and Macdonald (1924) fig. 52; (f) Ditchley, Oxon, after Radford, *Oxoniensia* i, fig. 9; (g) Kings Weston, Bristol, after Boon, *TBGAS* lxix, 48, plan; (h) Mansfield Woodhouse, Notts, after Haverfield and Macdonald (1924), fig. 57; (i) Engleton, Staffs, after Monroe, *JRS* xxviii, pl. xxxv; (j) Brading, I.o.W., after Mayhew, *JBAA*, xxxvi, 364, plan, and Price, *Remains . . . at Morton, near Brading*, plan.

H = Hypocaust; M = Mosaic pavement; T = Tessellated floor.

than connected. As for date, the winged corridor house appears to have come into existence in Britain about A.D. 100, whether as a single design, as at Ditchley, or as an addition, as at Park Street. This harmonises with Swoboda's conclusion that on the Continent the type came into general favour in the early 2nd century.[1]

An example of the simple winged corridor house is Great Staughton I (Hunts.), which is, as it happens, of 4th-century date, like its counterpart at Frocester (Glos.). Great Staughton (Fig. 2.1*d*) is a simple oblong block, with a very large central room and a kitchen, and was divided into three rooms fronted by a corridor, which opened at each end into a spacious projecting wing room. Corridor and wing room were embellished with mosaic pavements of geometric pattern. This fundamentally simple plan has, however, even simpler forms, suited to poorer purses. A typical example is Frilford (Berks.: Fig. 2.1*e*), which has one wing only, as is often seen in Germany, with hypocaust and mosaic pavement. The house measures 73 by 40 feet over all. Somewhat more elaborate, though still simple, is Mansfield Woodhouse (Notts.: Fig. 2.1*h*), where, apart from out-buildings, the villa consists of a front corridor or veranda, backed by five rooms and flanked by wing rooms. The central room, for dining, has a mosaic pavement; one wing, heated by a hypocaust, is connected by a pas-sage with an additional outbuilding. Another large and comfortable ver-sion of the simple form is Engleton (Staffs.: Fig. 2.1*i*), which has deep wings with bow fronts, in Mediterranean manner, later modified as rectangular rooms. A more workaday establishment, which contrasts with Engleton, is Ditchley (Oxon.), where the stone-built villa (Fig. 2.1*f*) was designed as a winged corridor house, superseding a timber house of rectangular plan. It was contained within a rectangular, ditched and walled enclosure (Pl. 2.1) (not of defensive type) and never seems to have received a bathing establishment. Its developed winged form belongs to the early 2nd century, and it was much enhanced by the addition of an elaborate colonnaded front in a 4th-century rebuilding. Ditchley may be compared with Ely near Cardiff (Glam.), which seems to date from the early 2nd century, and is bounded by non-defensive earthworks. Its wings are unusually large in proportion to the house as a whole; and a central offshoot at the back is a later addition, as is the bath building at the south-west corner.

An exceptional variation of the simple plan is Kings Weston, near Bristol, built in the late 3rd century. This (Fig. 2.1*g*) has large wing rooms,

[1] Swoboda (1919), 87

a front corridor and porch; but the back wall of the corridor is an arcade looking on to a gravelled area, presumably roofed, round which rooms are grouped. The full plan of the rearward range could not be recovered, but it is much more reminiscent of Roman Germany, whence indeed it could well have been derived.

Winged houses of originally simple form were often modified by additions, as at Cox Green near Maidenhead (Berks.), or Park Street (Herts.). The modifications usually take the form of extra rooms or a small suite of baths. Enlargement by adding a rearward range of rooms is well exemplified at Brading (Isle of Wight: Fig. 2.1j). In front is a corridor with a wing at either end, behind which are set four rooms and a lobby; and at the back of these come at least five more rooms, including a large dining-room, reached from the front of the house through the lobby. There are large outbuildings, indicating clearly the function of the establishment as a farm; and a corn-drying kiln inserted into the front corridor of the main house shows that utility ultimately drove out elegance, here exemplified by remarkable mosaic pavements illustrating philosophical subjects inspired by late-Roman eclecticism (see pp. 91–4). Here, as in other examples of the type, the central rooms may have been higher than the others in order to allow for lighting by clerestory windows, as suggested at Mayen.[1]

A further elaboration, neat and compact, is to equip the house with winged corridors at both front and back. Several examples of this fashion of planning, whether original or resulting from modification, are known. At Great Chesterford (Essex)[2] a central range of rooms is flanked by a corridor at each side, and at each end is a wing projecting front and back. This is matched at High Wycombe (Bucks.), where, however, the villa stands in a walled enclosure with gatehouse and has a detached bath-house of some size. At Hambleden (Bucks.: Fig. 2.2a) the main front of the house in its final form exhibits a porch in the middle of the corridor, indicating that the principal façade was not on the workaday side of the house. The house, however, began as a cottage like Park Street, which was next enlarged by a room at one end and a tiny bath-house at the other. Corridors with wing rooms were then added on each front, one of the rearward wing rooms containing a new and somewhat larger bath suite.

Much more elaborate additions are, however, possible. At Spoonley

[1] *Mayen* (1928)
[2] VCH, Essex, iii (1963), 78

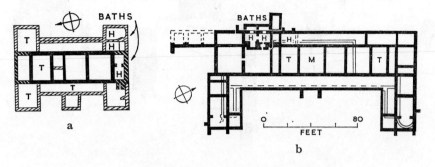

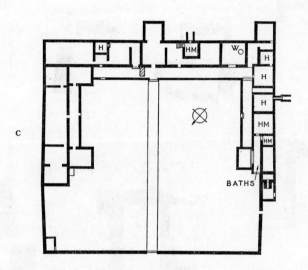

Fig. 2.2. Elaboration of the winged corridor plan (a) Hambleden, Bucks, after Cocks, *Arch.* lxxi, pl. xiii; (b) Folkestone, Kent, after *VCH Kent* iii, pl. xxi; (c) Spoonley Wood, Glos., after Middleton, *Arch*, lii, pl. xvii.
H = Hypocaust; M = Mosaic pavement; T = Tessellated floor; W = Well.

Wood (Glos.: Fig. 2.2c) a winged house came to form the side of a much larger villa with three wings, in which the principal rooms were transferred to the middle block: in short, the winged villa became a courtyard villa, as at Bignor (p. 62). At Folkestone (Kent) only the secondary plan (Fig. 2.2b) is known in detail, though the earlier wing rooms appear to have been bow-fronted, as at Engleton. The house commanded a wide prospect of the Channel, and is a good example of a villa related to seascape. The range of eleven rooms between the wings has front and back corridors,

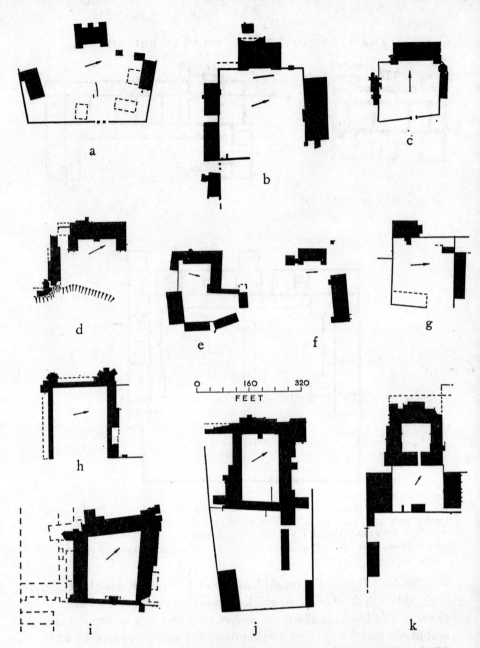

Fig. 2.3. Block plans of villas (a) Hambleden, Bucks, after Cocks, *Arch.* lxxi; (b) Brading, I.o.W., after Mayhew, *JBAA* xxxvi, 364 and Price, *Remains . . . at Morton, near Brading*; (c) Stroud, Hants, after Williams, *Arch. J.* lxvi, 33; (d) Folkestone, Kent, after *VCH Kent* iii, pl. xxi; (e) Llantwit Major, Glam, after Nash-Williams, *Arch. Camb.* cii, fig. 20; (f) Mansfield Woodhouse, Notts, after Haverfield and Macdonald (1924), fig. 57; (g) Clanville, Hants, after Lyell, *Arch.* lvi, pl. i; (h) Keynsham, Som, after Bulleid, *Arch.* lxxv, 111, fig. 1; (i) North Leigh, Oxon, (drawn by D. R. Wilson, based on excavations and on air photographs by D. N. Riley, and J. K. St Joseph); (j) Bignor, Sussex, after Winbolt and Herbert, *The Roman Villa at Bignor*, plan; (k) Woodchester, Glos, after Ward (1911), fig. 47, with additions from Lysons.

the latter in due course converted into a series of rooms and a bath suite. The central dining-room, 21 feet by 20, has a mosaic pavement. But the main house, with its secondary set of baths, is matched by a very large detached wing with its own bath-house, perhaps once serving the whole establishment.

The fact that these corridor houses in Britain do not in general belong to very large estates is emphasised by a comparison with the much larger examples associated with landed wealth on the Continent. Folkestone, for example, is small indeed compared with Hosté (Belgium)[1] or Nennig (Germany),[2] both of which have at least forty rooms. There is, however, one quite exceptional villa in Britain, which in early date, large size and elaborate plan stands by itself. This is at Fishbourne (Sussex), 1 mile west of Chichester (Noviomagus Regnensium), at the head of a sea-creek. The building, with contemporary mosaics in black and white, belongs to the last quarter of the 1st century. It could be classified as a winged corridor house, but the portico which is the connecting unit forms also the front side of two colonnaded courts round which blocks of rooms are recessed. The east wing contains the entrance hall and bath-house, as well as two larger colonnaded courts; the west wing, with apsed audience-chamber at the centre, dominates the scheme from a higher level. The whole villa, occupying $5\frac{1}{2}$ acres, is of palatial scale, in harmony with its marble decoration in wall-veneering and patterned floor inlays (*opus sectile*); and this emphasises its wholly exceptional character, which might well accord with the senatorial status of the royal house of Cogidumnus, though the building seems a little late for the King-Legate. It is, however, the sole villa in Britain which can be recognised immediately as an imported Italian type, and may be compared in this respect, though not in date or plan, with the Herodian villa in Wadi Qelt, outside Jericho.

The Courtyard House

The largest and richest Romano-British villas are a provincial type of courtyard house, built round a more or less rectangular courtyard usually entered by a front gateway. Some kind of yard-space, often a farmyard, is indeed normal in any villa; and convenience will tend to group the various

[1] Cumont (1914), 41
[2] *Nennig* (1908), 83

buildings of the villa round it. An L-shaped grouping occurs at Mansfield Woodhouse and Folkestone (Fig. 2.3*f*, *d*); at Brading, Hambleden, and Stroud (Fig. 2.3*b*, *a*, *c*) the house stands at the far end of a yard flanked by detached out-buildings; while at Clanville (Hants.: Fig. 2.3*g*) the buildings lie on three sides of a yard, entered at the corner diagonally opposite to the house, rather as at Llantwit Major (Glam.: Fig. 2.3*e*). But miscellaneous buildings grouped round a farmyard, even if contained by a continuous enclosure wall, as at Ditchley, do not constitute a courtyard villa. The true courtyard villa is one in which the court is completely surrounded by buildings forming a connected architectural whole.

The essential features of the type are strikingly seen at North Leigh, Oxon. (Figs. 2.3*i*, 2.4) where the main house, measuring almost 300 feet square, is ranged round a court some 200 by 160 feet in size. All round the court runs a corridor, punctuated by steps and doorways, but broken only by the main gate with porter's lodge. This unity was the result of complicated growth, not yet completely elucidated. A small main house at first occupied the middle position at the back, and was accompanied by a little detached bath-house to the north-east. This house was presently extended south-westwards, the old and new being united by a niched pavilion, the focal point in their joint façade, and by mosaic pavements in the two-colour style of the 2nd century. Short wings were next added, one of them screening the baths; and their extension, in several stages, must somehow coincide, first, with the joining of the baths to the main house, and, later, with a total reconstruction of that house, introducing new three-colour mosaics and more elaborate baths, themselves in due course twice remodelled and extended. A new dining-room was inserted in the west corner, and was later on equipped with heated walls and vaulted ceiling, all painted with panels enclosing olive branches. Another late addition is the small bath suite, in the south corner, whose cramped planning, as if to fit the aisle of an aisled structure, contrasts with the succession of spacious bath suites in the east corner, which are comparable with the later *laconicum* suite at Chedworth.

The North Leigh courtyard probably contained the entire household. Aerial photography,[1] however, has revealed traces of an enclosing wall and also many buildings to south-west. Through the latter a metalled track led to contemporary quarries 200 yards to the south. Such subsidiary blocks no doubt often existed in large villas; but exploration tends to concentrate

[1] *North Leigh* (1944)

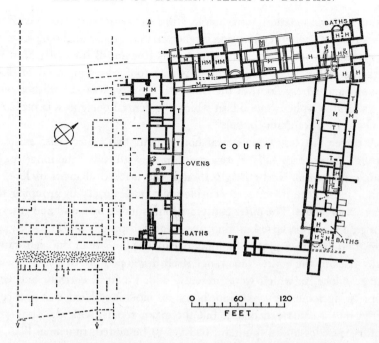

Fig. 2.4. Plan of the courtyard villa at North Leigh (drawing by D. R. Wilson based on published and unpublished excavation and on air photographs by D. N. Riley and J. K. S. St. Joseph).

H = Hypocaust; M = Mosaic pavement; T = Tessellated floor.

upon the main house, treating it as an isolated antiquarian curiosity instead of an integral part of an important social and economic unit. Yet North Leigh, for all its final unity, has not an impressive plan. Other villas less completely known as a whole, such as Southwick (Sussex) and Keynsham (Som.: Fig. 2.3*h*), reveal in their parts very much more imaginative unitary planning. The special interest of North Leigh is rather its long and highly complicated development.

Detailed knowledge is also lacking of the magnificent Cotswold villa at Woodchester (Glos.: Fig. 2.3*k*). Here so striking is the nucleus, and so coherent its planning, that it is often assumed to be complete as recorded. The original magnificent account by Lysons[1] makes it clear, however, that the innermost court, with its splendid mansion, and the middle court, with farm buildings, are only part of an even more extensive establishment.

[1] *Woodchester* (1797)

Bathing accommodation, for example, still awaits discovery. The luxurious character of the whole conception is reflected in the individual rooms, which are perhaps the most splendid known in any Romano-British villa. Most remarkable is the great dining-room, whose roof was supported on four columns and whose floor, of the early 4th century, was embellished with an elaborate Orpheus mosaic, in which the central octagon was probably occupied by a fountain (p. 99).

A larger but less symmetrical house, with two courtyards, exists at Bignor (Sussex: Fig. 2.3j). Here a corridor runs all round the inner courtyard, rather as at North Leigh, though the marked changes of level at Bignor must have introduced considerably more variety in grouping the different elements. The outer courtyard, surrounded by a wall and entered by a gate, contains farm buildings irregularly disposed. But in its original form the villa was a timber building occupying the site of the main range at the back of the court. This range itself developed out of a five-roomed cottage house, to which were presently added a front corridor and very simple wing rooms. The corridor house, of modest comfort, was next converted into a courtyard house; but the major rooms, with elaborate 4th-century mosaics and a fountain, had yet to be added, in a final blaze of splendour.

The villa at Chedworth (Glos.: Fig. 2.5) presents yet another variety of complicated development. The inner courtyard, probably developed as a formal garden, had a walk, part corridor and part veranda, all round it with rooms on three sides, thus resembling North Leigh; but outside this is a second courtyard, whose sides are formed not by separate buildings, as at Woodchester or Bignor, but by prolongations of the wings, not known on the south in full.

Originally, however, the villa did, in fact, comprise blocks of independent buildings. The main house extended less far south; the south wing, at first half-timbered, ended less far west, while the north wing, less long towards the east, terminated near the main house in a large bath-house. The visible and later arrangement belongs to the 4th century, when the whole establishment was united by corridors or porticoes, and received a great dining-room and two sets of baths, a 'Turkish' suite at the north end of the main wing and a 'Swedish' suite on the site of the earlier bath-house. The 'Swedish' baths were equipped with large cold plunges, long mistaken for a fullery or laundry. An industrial explanation has also been erroneously offered for iron bars, now known to be boiler supports discarded

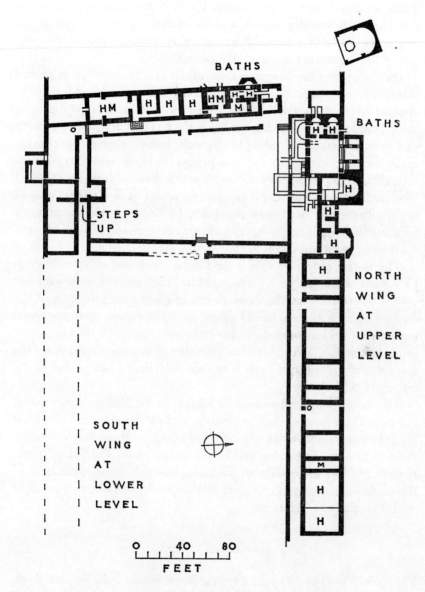

Fig. 2.5. Plan of the courtyard villa at Chedworth (after Richmond, *Chedworth Roman Villa*, plan, with additions).
H = Hypocaust; M = Mosaic pavement.

63

during alterations to the earlier baths. The villa thus takes its place among the other large country houses, and its relationship to a great estate is emphasised by further outbuildings recognised some distance in continuation of the south wing of the visible establishment.

On the basis of the foregoing examples, it may be observed in general that, while courtyards of some kind are among the commonest features of classical architecture, the Romano-British courtyard villa is not a copy of any classical house. The difference lies in the fact that in Britain the courtyard is a thoroughfare leading to the main house, whereas the classical courtyard is a garden-court within or behind the house, and away from the main entrance, as exemplified at Pompeii or at Italianate Fishbourne (p. 59).[1] The garden-court, with the house ranged round it, is a feature only of larger villas in the north-west provinces. In Britain, while containing a main entrance path or drive, it is clearly recognisable at Woodchester, Southwick, and Chedworth, to cite striking examples.

The British courtyard villa is thus to be recognised either as the improvement of the farmyard, surrounded by buildings, into an elegant and unified structure or as the development in more grandiose style of the corridor house with deep lateral wings, as at Folkestone. Spoonley Wood is simply a corridor house which has been extended and walled to make a courtyard; and at North Leigh the extension of the wings right down the two sides of the courtyard seems to date only from a late period in the history of the building.

This development, when seen in relation to the Mediterranean world, produces a new type of courtyard house, in which the courtyard is in front of the hall and chief living-rooms, instead of behind them. It is a development well known in Britain, and not unknown on the Continent. It was not the product of pre-Roman tradition, but rather the application of Roman building and gardening practice to provincial fashion, a result of wealth applied to rural needs.

The Aisled House[2]

This term is used to designate a type of house which, in its simplest form, is a rectangular building divided along its length by two rows of posts into nave and aisles. The type is fairly common in Britain, but appears to be

[1] Mau (1899), figs. 139, 145
[2] Ward (1911), 174; Haverfield and Macdonald (1924), 227; J. T. Smith (1963)

rare on the Continent, where, however, examples occur at Királyudvar (Königshof) and Šmarje-Grobelce[1] in Hungary, at Kastell Larga,[2] and also at Maulévrier in Normandy.[3] As to the form of the house, there is no doubt that the nave was roofed and was not an open courtyard, for no arrangement for draining off rain-water is ever found to exist. The entrance is sometimes, though not always, in the middle of one side. In the more developed form of the building, internal partitions are added, mostly in the aisles, but not infrequently in the nave also, cutting off the space into individual rooms. Light was presumably found for rooms cut out of the nave, as for example at Clanville, by clerestory windows. This is suggested by two models of houses from Kreuznach,[4] one representing a small rectangular house with a kind of lean-to corridor or veranda running along each of its two long sides, while the other represents a house with a lean-to on one side only, like a corridor house without wings. On the other hand, in the original house at Mayen,[5] restored as a rectangular hall, with an entrance in the middle of one side and a continuous pitched roof, two internal rows of posts served merely to facilitate spanning.

As for the origin of the aisled house, Ward pointed out a general resemblance between it and an early type of Frisian and Saxon farmhouse, now known to derive from prototypes contemporary with the Roman world and indeed also much older. Further, it may be remarked that in Britain the type is very frequently associated with houses of more advanced pattern in the guise of a barn, or *villa rustica*, where farm-workers, stock and tackle might all be assembled under the same roof. It may thus be recognised as a more primitive type of establishment which belongs to a lower grade of society, represented either by the less wealthy farmer or by the workers dependent upon a wealthier master. Its relative frequency in Roman Britain is only one of the facts which show that Romano-British rural society included many primitive elements.

Most of the examples of the aisled house in Roman Britain are late in date. But an early dated example is at Exning (Suffolk), where an aisled house wholly built in timber was associated with early 2nd-century pottery and succeeded Flavian huts. The whole house was rebuilt in stone (Fig. 2.6f) in the early 3rd century, with a large dining-room at one end and many

[1] Swoboda (1919), 115, 344
[2] *Kastell Larga* (1907), 273
[3] *Maulévrier* (1934), 805
[4] *Bonner Jahrbücher*, cxxxiii (1928), 124
[5] *ibid.*, 141

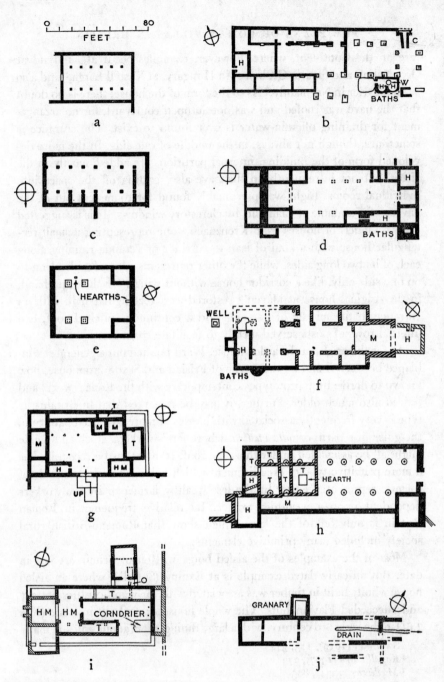

Fig. 2.6. Plans of aisled houses and a 'farm-house' (a) Spoonley Wood, Glos, after Middleton, *Arch.* lii, pl. xvii; (b) Brading, I.o.W., after Price, *Remains . . . at Morton, near Brading*, plan; (c) Ickleton, Cambs, after Neville, *Arch. J.* vi, 15, fig.; (d) Mansfield Woodhouse, Notts, after Rooke, *Arch.* viii, pl. xxii; (e) Holbury, East Dean, Hants, after *VCH Hants*. i, fig. 20; (f) Exning, Suffolk, after Greenfield, *JRS* 1, fig. 29; (g) Clanville, Hants, after Lyell *Arch.* lvi, pl. i; (h) Stroud, Hants, after Williams, *Arch. J.* lxvi, 33, pl. i; (i) Great Casterton, Rutland, after *Great Casterton* ii, pl. v, and iii, fig. 21; (j) Iwerne, Dorset, after Piggott. *Arch J.* civ, fig. 10b H = Hypocaust; M = Mosaic pavement; T = Tessellated floor; W = Well.

rooms in the residual aisles. One of the best examples of the elaborately modified aisled house is, however, Clanville, near Andover (Hants: Fig. 2.6g). A rectangular building, 96 by 52 feet over all, lying north and south, here forms the main house of a farm; its door, in the middle of its eastern side, gives on to a courtyard, on the north and east sides of which are out-buildings. Two rows of stone bases divide it into a nave and aisles, and beyond the western aisle lies a narrow corridor. The south end, cut off by a thick partition, is divided into three rooms: the central room has a mosaic pavement, and one of the others appears to be a bath. Six other rooms have been made by inserting partitions; two are heated with hypo-causts, and others have tessellated pavements. The central space has a dirt floor. Abundant window-glass and painted wall-plaster showed that parts of the house at least had some comfort and elegance. In other words, the owner of the farm was living under one roof with his workers and stock, as in Friesland today. At Clanville the planning of the end rooms is related to an earlier and more spacious version of the house. Similar rows of rooms at Mansfield Woodhouse (Fig. 2.6d), added to the ends of the main hall, do not reflect the division of its aisles. By contrast, at North Warnborough (Hants) projecting end rooms in similar position are integrated and contemporary with the hall, but convert it into a much more pretentious dwelling.

Simpler examples occur in the same county at Castlefield and Holbury. The former is a rectangle 66 by 41 feet, at one end of which is a projecting chamber, 22 by 14 feet externally. Apart from this the whole building is a single room, in which coins were found dating from A.D. 238 to 378. Holbury (Fig. 2.6e), 59 by 49 feet internally, is walled off into small cham-bers at two corners, the rest of the house being divided into nave and aisles, by four massive bases, while a hearth occupies the middle of each end.

A most interesting aisled house at Stroud, near Petersfield (Hants: Fig. 2.6h) is a rectangle 140 by 52 feet, with projecting wing rooms at two cor-ners. The main block had been divided at first by two rows of wooden columns, but rooms had been later partitioned off at its west end, using the front aisle as a corridor. The easternmost room in the nave contained a hearth, while the door at the east end was an addition, the original entrance occurring in the middle of the south side. Here the aisled and corridor plans are combined.

Buildings of the aisled type are, as already observed, frequently found serving as outbuildings in farms where the main house was of more ad-vanced type. Thus, at Spoonley Wood (Fig. 2.6a) there is a barn or byre 60 by 40 feet, while at Ickleton (Cambs.: Fig. 2.6c) one 78 by 36 feet was found, with partitions as if for stalls. Elsewhere, at Brading (Figs. 2.3b, 2.6b), West Dean (Hants), Mansfield Woodhouse (Figs. 2.3f, 2.6d) and Woodchester, large buildings of aisled plan were not only barns or stables, but also quarters for farm-workers, as shown by inserted rooms, hypocausts, suites of baths and so forth. The fact that a socially lower class lives in a building of native type, is not without bearing on the Romanisation of the Celtic provinces. In this respect the example of Llantwit Major is particularly instructive. For while in the most prosperous phase of the villa the main house and the aisled workers' quarters existed side by side, the final century of its existence saw the main house deserted and the workers' quarters still occupied, indicating that the destinies of the estate were in the hands of an absentee landlord. The late date at which such buildings not only continued to exist, as at Great Casterton (Rutland: Fig. 2.6i), but were newly erected, as at Denton (Lincs.), is also highly significant. Once established, the type was found to suit the needs and ambitions of a certain social class: and here the modern parallels from Friesland and Saxony are of the greatest value as comparisons.

Outbuildings

All villas, even the very humblest, possessed buildings other than the dwelling-house proper. Quite often these are bath-houses, which danger of fire made it desirable to separate from the main building, especially if this was half-timbered.

An example has already been noted at High Wycombe, but the earlier houses at North Leigh and Chedworth were both associated with bath-houses, the former isolated and small, the latter from the first luxurious. Chedworth, indeed, provides in its latest phase the interesting arrangement of two bath-houses. A suite of Turkish type comprising a gently heated *apodyterium*, a *frigidarium* with cold plunge, a *tepidarium* and a *caldarium* with hot bath, was built into the north end of the main, west wing. At the adjacent west end of the north wing, covering a large part of the primary bath-house, a second bath suite offered the more rigorous Swedish type of bath. Here, behind an external colonnade, lay a large *frigidarium* or *apodyterium*, out of which opened on the west a double *laconicum* of graded heat, while the north side was occupied by cold plunge-baths, comprising a large rectangular basin between a pair of small D-shaped baths designed for the elderly or less venturesome. The plunge-baths were covered by a clerestory roof, carried upon a row of columns on either side of the rectangular bath, an elaborate architectural composition not without parallel. The great Somersetshire villas at Low Ham and Lufton have both yielded impressive bath-houses, the latter centred round a large octagonal plunge-bath; but both are imperfectly recorded, and it is not clear how they were related to the main house. Chedworth remains the outstanding example, with its water supply still running and visible in a sacred well-house that housed an octagonal pool, ultimately Christianised by at least three chrisms carved on the stonework of its rim.

Other buildings associated with villas are less imposing, though perhaps economically more important. They usually comprise cottages, barns, stables, and so forth. It is noteworthy that such buildings, even when they were undoubtedly dwellings, very rarely match the architectural type of the main house and usually show a more primitive plan. The winged corridor house at Gayton Thorpe (Norfolk), with a similar house as an outbuilding, is an exception. An aisled villa like Clanville has barn-like outbuildings; a corridor villa like Mansfield Woodhouse has an aisled outbuilding, as has also the winged villa at Spoonley Wood.

A very frequent accessory of the outbuildings is the corn-drying kiln, often in the past mistaken for a primitive hypocaust and so described. In fact, such structures form a link between the native type of farm and the Romanised villa, since they are found in both and belonged to the pre-Roman economy. In essence they comprise a furnace flue, containing the fire, and a double floor above it. Vents drew a stream of warm air into the interspace between the floors, heating the top floor to a gentle heat only, so as to dry the corn without roasting it or destroying its goodness. Thresh-ing floors, as at Ditchley, Langton (E. Yorks.), and Old Durham, are not unknown and must have been common. Granaries are less common. The later phase at Ditchley had a large one and a fine example is at Lullingstone (Kent). Small, square, silo-like granaries, probably for storing seed-corn, are known at Stroud (Hants) and Iwerne (Dorset).

Other Types of Villa

Nearly all villas in Britain fall into one of the four classes already described, and it may be suspected that most supposed exceptions, if better known, would conform to the stock types. For example, at Holcombe (Devon) rooms of various shapes radiate from an octagonal hall or court. This is probably a suite of apartments attached to a large villa, comparable with the hexagonal hall and adjoining rooms in the courtyard villa at Keynsham (Som.). Lullingstone (Kent: Fig. 2.7) is a house of which the dining-room is accompanied by so few other rooms as to suggest that it may have been predominantly a pleasure-house. Yet in the 4th century, when the great dining-room was built, it was primarily the centre of an estate associated with a large granary. Earlier, when the house was much more modest, it

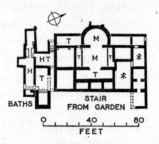

Fig. 2.7. The fourth-century plan of the house at Lullingstone (after Meates, *Lullingstone Roman Villa*, fig. 3).
H = Hypocaust; M = Mosaic pavement; T = Tessellated floor; chi-rhos indicate rooms with Christian wall paintings.

had been graced by marble busts of senators, and was associated with a large family tomb-temple. Finally, in the second half of the 4th century one corner of the Lullingstone villa was converted into a small house-church or chapel, richly decorated with paintings of the Chi-Rho within a wreath of victory and of *orantes*, dead and living, standing between columns (p. 150).

The 4th-century house at Iwerne (Dorset: Fig. 2.6*j*), which took the place of an aisled villa, is, however, a significant link between the villa and the purely native farmhouse. It comprises a long rectangular building divided into three compartments. The end compartment is a living-room with plastered walls, the middle is a long farm kitchen, while the farther end is a byre, with central drain. The farming folk here lived under one roof with their animals, as in a West Highland long-house.

CHAPTER THREE

The Mosaic Pavements

D. J. SMITH

THIS CHAPTER IS concerned with the decorated mosaic floors of Roman villas in Britain, though it will, of course, be necessary to refer in discussion to mosaics of urban sites, as well as to mosaics of rural sites apart from villas, not only in Britain but also in other lands. Consideration will be given first to the number and distribution of Romano-British villa-mosaics, and secondly to the question of their dating. Then follows a résumé of the most common themes and subjects of the figured mosaics and a brief attempt to assess their significance. Finally there is a summary of the evidence for a number of schools of mosaicists in Britain, for which the villa-mosaics provide almost the whole of the available material.

Number and Distribution (Fig. 3.1)

Some 600 known or suspected villas are indicated on the Map of Roman Britain.[1] About a quarter of them have produced decorated mosaic pavements or evidence of their former existence.[2] That is to say, each had at

---

[1] *OSRB* (1956); see General Introduction, pp. 10–11, for the term 'villa' as defined for the purposes of the Map.

[2] *i.e.* loose tesserae of different colours and of appropriate size and materials; evidence for wall mosaic is rare.

least one, though less than ninety—15 per cent[1] of the total—appear to have had no more than one. Woodchester in Gloucestershire, with twenty, and Fishbourne in Sussex, with an even greater number, are in this respect so far in a class by themselves, but there are other reasons for regarding the 'villa' at Fishbourne as exceptional.[2]

The number of villa-mosaics that have survived, or for which there is evidence, is approaching 400, and it can safely be said that decorated pavements must have been considered *de rigueur* in the houses of the Romano-British landed gentry. In so far as they represented surplus wealth[3] as well as Romanisation, or a desire to appear Romanised, it is not unlikely that they were at least something of a 'status symbol'. At any rate, it is noticeable that the single, or as the case may be, the best mosaic was generally laid in the principal room. In many villa-plans, if not in most, this room is readily recognisable by its size and often also by an axial position and an apsidal extension. It has been plausibly identified as the *triclinium* or dining-room.[4]

Where there is more than one mosaic, the second-best can be taken as indicating the family's private living-room or rooms, while any others will generally be found in ante-rooms and corridors—occasionally also in rooms which seem probably to have been servants' quarters.[5] In other words, just as the number and quality of the mosaics in any villa must have a bearing on its proprietor's economic status, so must their disposition and degrees of elaboration within the house be related to the sociological aspect of villa life.

[1] If sites of proved villas only are counted, and all which are uncertain strictly excluded, this figure would be appreciably higher. But there are many border-line cases in which, although there seems little or no reason for doubt, the evidence at present does not amount to certainty.

[2] In order to minimise the number of footnotes, a select bibliography for every villa with mosaics mentioned in this chapter is given in an Appendix, pp. 119–25. References to mosaics of urban sites, of rural sites other than villas, and also when desirable to specific villa-mosaics, are given in the footnotes as and when they are mentioned.

[3] *cf. OSRB* (1956), Introduction, 11

[4] Richmond (1963), 113, 122

[5] *e.g.* at Great Weldon (Northants.), where the family's living-room, with channelled hypocaust, is clearly indicated by the most elaborate of the mosaics recorded there, while the pattern in the room which may have been the servants' hall was very much simpler even than that in the corridor. See VCH, Northants., i (1902), fig. 22, opp. 192, but also, for an accurate plan of this range of rooms, *J.R.S.*, xliv (1954), 95, fig. 15. Presumably there was a decorated mosaic in the principal, apsidal room, which had been destroyed before the villa was first uncovered in 1738. See Pl. 3.21

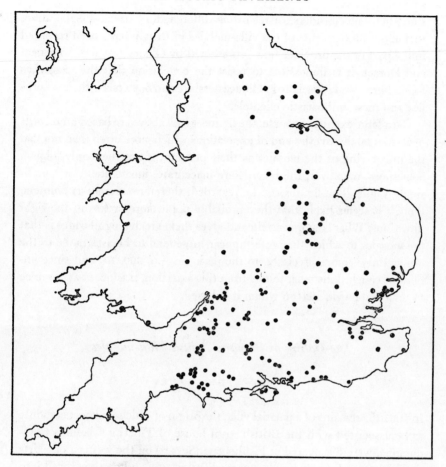

Fig. 3.1. Villas with Mosaics.

Unfortunately it is impossible at present to convert these generalities into more meaningful terms, since nothing is known or can be safely inferred concerning the cost of mosaic paving in any period of antiquity.[1]

[1] Except that, from certain tessellated inscriptions in mosaics, it seems that the cost of such pavements was calculated by the foot or its equivalent. This must mean per square foot or, as a firm of flooring contractors would quote today, 'per foot super'. Moreover, in modern practice, and doubtless also in Roman times, this would apply only to all-over or repeating patterns, borders being costed 'per foot run' and figured panels as separate items. For the inscriptions, see *Jahresheft des Öst. Arch. Inst.*, i (1898), Beiblatt, cols. 29–36; Blanchet (1928), 49

But when one considers, disregarding differences of size and elaboration, that about 50 per cent[1] of the villa-mosaics in Britain have been recorded in the part of the province now represented by Gloucestershire, Somerset, and Dorset, it is impossible to resist the conclusion that the mosaicists found here—and especially in Gloucestershire and Somerset—their wealthiest and most enthusiastic clientele.

To a large extent, of course, the figures given above are based on records of accidental discoveries and of excavations which more often than not had the uncovering of the mosaics as their primary, if not their only, object. Sometimes, moreover, the records are inaccurate, inconsistent, or tantalisingly vague. The figures can be regarded, therefore, merely as pointers, though it seems likely that they probably point more or less in the right directions. What is more certain and gives them greater significance is that the mosaics to which they refer appear in general to be assignable to the 4th century—more precisely, to the period *c.* A.D. 300–70; and since important conclusions must follow from this assertion, it is necessary at once to review the evidence on which it is based.

The Dating of Romano-British Villa-mosaics

A. PRE-4TH CENTURY

In 1961 the remains of a palatial villa, the origin of which is almost certainly to be associated with the British royal house of Tiberius Claudius Cogidumnus, were discovered at Fishbourne (Sussex) on the western outskirts of Chichester. Founded *c.* 75–80, modified *c.* 100, and occupied well into the 3rd century, it was ultimately demolished after a fire *c.* 270–80. Excavations[2] have so far brought to light a score of mosaics in varying states of preservation and evidence for others which have not survived. They were of four periods: *c.* 75–80, *c.* 100, *c.* 150–200, and *c.* 200.

The majority date from *c.* 75–80. Pre-eminent amongst them is a group of neatly executed mosaics in black and white, of which four consist of lozenge-diaper patterns with square or cruciform motifs inset at regular

[1] See p. 72, note 1
[2] Still in progress at the time of writing (1965). I am indebted to Chichester Civic Society Excavations Committee, to Prof. B. Cunliffe and to Mr D. Baker for photographs of the mosaics.

intervals. One of these is matched exactly at Besançon,[1] in a mosaic for which stratified samian indicates an early Flavian *terminus post quem*. But there are near-parallels in later mosaics at Besançon[2] for other patterns dated to *c.* 75–80 at Fishbourne, and in general the black and white mosaics at Fishbourne seem ahead of their time by several decades.[3] This implies that their designer was a leading mosaicist, presumably from Italy, and the implication is borne out by four other mosaics[4] laid at the same time and doubtless under the same direction. One of these had been executed in $\frac{1}{4}$-inch tesserae—an instance of the fine and costly Hellenistic technique known as *opus vermiculatum*, perhaps unparalleled outside the Mediterranean provinces, and all employed colour—itself a novelty with few contemporary parallels north of the Alps. One of the two best-preserved incorporates representational motifs—two amphorae between scrolls and two canthari between pairs of confronted fish and dolphins respectively—which are sufficiently distinctive to encourage a hope that they may eventually be matched elsewhere.

The outburst of Romanisation represented by the discoveries at Fishbourne was not confined to that site. At Eccles in Kent another villa of 'palatial' dimensions has produced fragments of a figured and partly coloured mosaic of *c.* A.D. 65 (Pl. 3.1), even earlier than any of the pavements of Fishbourne, while at Angmering in Sussex grey and white tesserae from a destroyed mosaic have been found in a late 1st-century context. Angmering lies only a dozen miles east of Fishbourne and it seems probable

---

[1] *pace* J. M. C. Toynbee (1964), 237. See *Ant.*, xxxix, no. 155 (Sept. 1965), 180, pl. xxxvb; *cf.* Stern (1963), ii, no. 297A, pl. XII–XIV

[2] Stern (1963), nos. 297C, 297D, pl. XII, XVI, XVII; for a slightly later, almost identical pattern at Aquileia, and on the pattern generally, *cf.* M. E. Blake, *Memoirs of the American Academy in Rome*, xiii (1936), 5, 187, pl. 16, no. 3. Stern assigns the second period at Besançon to 'probably about a century later' than the first; but see note 3 below.

[3] *e.g. cf.* Becatti (1961), no. 14, pl. XXXII (assigned to *c.* 128–38); no. 170, fig. 29 (*c.* 110–20); no. 257, pl. XXXIII (*c.* 130); no. 261, pl. XXIII (*c.* 130); no. 267, pl. XIII (*c.* 130); no. 285, pl. XVIII (*c.* 127); no. 305, pl. XXXVI (*c.* 150); no. 307, pl. XVI (*c.* 150); von Gonzenbach (1961), no. 120, pl. 4 (*c.* 100–25 or *c.* 100–50). In the light of these examples, Stern's dating of *Recueil*, nos. 297C and 297D, and also no. 427A, to perhaps *c.* 175–200 seems unnecessarily late. On the other hand, for the simple mosaics of Rooms 60 and 70 at Fishbourne there are close Domitianic parallels, also in association, in Rome; see M. E. Blake, *Memoirs of the American Academy in Rome*, viii (1930), 102, pl. 47

[4] *Ant. J.*, xlii (1962), 20, pl. XIb, XIIb (= Toynbee (1964), pl. LVIb); xliv (1964), 4–5, pl. IIIb

that craftsmen who had worked at Fishbourne also laid the pavement or pavements at Angmering. This suggests that the workshop (*officina*) which must have been specially set up for the work at Fishbourne may have stimulated sufficient local demand to prolong its existence when that work came to an end. But if so, the mosaic laid at Fishbourne *c*. 100—a polychrome patchwork of motifs with a central medallion portraying the head of Medusa[1]—reveals either the supervention of a new local firm or a marked degeneration of standards on the part of the old.

The mosaic of *c*. 100 had been laid over one of the black and white pavements of *c*. 75–80 and its date is derived from that of the little-worn fragments of South Gaulish samian liberally employed in it as red tesserae. Similarly, a considerable quantity of samian 'tesserae', predominantly from Antonine vessels, suggests a date *c*. 150–200 for one of two contemporary polychrome mosaics assignable to the next structural phase. Its design[2] (Pl. 3.2)—a central medallion supported by four semicircular panels or lunettes, with four quarter-circular panels in the angles of the enclosing square—is one especially common in Britain. The medallion portrays Cupid bearing a trident and riding on a dolphin. Two of the lunettes contain winged sea-horses in black on a white ground—an echo of 2nd-century fashions in Italy,[3] winged sea-panthers in colour occupying the other two. Radial fluting fills the quarter-circular panels in the angles[4] and somewhat misshapen canthari stand in the four interstitial spaces. Each side of the square frame is decorated with a foliate scroll proceeding from

[1] *ibid.*, xlii (1962), 29, pl. xɪɪa; xliv (1964), 5–6

[2] *ibid.*, xlii (1962), 22; xliv (1964), 5–7, pl. v; *Ant.*, xxxix (1965), 181, frontispiece.

[3] *cf.* Becatti (1961), nos. 70, 71, pl. ccɪvff. (*c*. 115, *c*. 139)

[4] For the origin of this motif, perhaps in a representation of an open fan rather than a scallop shell, *cf.* Pernice (1938), pl. 50, no. 2. For its employment in quarter-circular panels in the angles of mosaics of the same design as at Fishbourne, *cf.* von Gonzenbach (1961), no. 127–I (Unterlunkhofen), pl. 21, also with sea-creatures in the lunettes (assigned to 175–225), and Parlasca (1959), 95–96 (Laufenburg, Westhalle), pl. 13, no. 3. Parlasca finds it difficult, however, to date the Unterlunkhofen mosaic later than 150, preferring to assign it, with that of Laufenburg, to *c*. 125–50. It must be noted that possibly important details of the Laufenburg mosaic appear not to have survived, but there can be no doubt that it was more or less contemporary with that of Unterlunkhofen or that the date of both falls between that of the mosaic of the same design and similar details (aquatic creatures, guilloche knots, though no radial fluting) in the House of the Tragic Poet at Pompeii (VI, 8, 5; Pernice (1938), pl. 44, no. 6) and that of the Fishbourne pavement.

a central cantharus, a single small bird being perched on a leaf of the scroll on one side.

This mosaic is the most immediately attractive of all those so far uncovered at Fishbourne. In striking contrast, its contemporary is an ill-considered and clumsily executed attempt, obviously by a semi-skilled assistant, to produce a design[1] based largely upon the radial fluting in the angles of Cupid's pavement. This same motif, together with the roundel of chain pattern which frames the central medallion in Cupid's pavement, and the lozenges in oblongs of the assistant's work, reappear in the latest mosaic at Fishbourne—that of *c*. 200,[2] suggesting that all three pavements may actually have been laid within a relatively short period.

These three mosaics can, in fact, be regarded as late products of the boom which mosaicists throughout southern Britain enjoyed from the time of Hadrian until *c*. 200. The demand appears, however, to have come almost entirely from the towns[3] and to have been especially heavy during the years 160–90. Although other villas are known to have originated in this period, and many more may have done so, only three[4] so far have yielded

[1] *Fishbourne* (1964), 5–7, pl. VI

[2] *Fishbourne* (1962), 22; (1964), 5–7, pl. VIA. A date *c*. 200 seems implied by the condition of the *denarius* of 196–7, giving a *terminus post quem* for the structural phase in which this mosaic was laid.

[3] The best-known examples are those of Verulamium: Wheeler (1936), 142–8, 1, 2, 6, 7, 8, 9, 10, pl. XXXIX, XLI, XLII, XLIVB, XLVA, B, XLVIA; *Ant. J.*, xxxix (1959), 13, pl. IVA; xl (1960), 16–18, pl. I, IIIB; Toynbee (1963), nos. 177–80, pl. 206–9; Toynbee (1964), 275–7, pl. LXIIIA, b. To the mosaicists who laid Mosaic 7, also the mosaic depicting a lion with a stag's head in its mouth, and others of the second half of the 2nd century at Verulamium, can be attributed the group discovered at Colchester in February 1965 and, through them, others previously known there; see *Vetusta Monumenta*, iii (1796), pl. xxxix, Hull (1958), 78, 209, pl. xv, xvi, xxxiii and *Arch. J.* cxxiii (1967), 40–43. For 2nd-century mosaics in Silchester, see *Arch.*, xlvi (1881) pl. xiii; lv (1896), pl. xii–xiv; lviii (1902), pl. iii. Even small and distant Caerwent has yielded a Hadrianic mosaic, *Arch.*, lix (1905), pl. LXVIII; *cf.* Becatti (1961), no. 261, pl. xxiii (assigned to *c*. 130). The list could be extended further, but these examples will suffice to illustrate the point.

[4] *pace* V. E. Nash-Williams, a 2nd-century date for the mosaic of the villa at Llantwit Major (Glam.) cannot be entertained. The only parallel in Britain for the arrangement of the square and octagonal panels forming its design is to be found in the mosaic recovered in 1914 from the 'Bon Marché' site in Gloucester and now in the City Museum. For this there was external evidence suggesting a date in the 4th century; see *T.B.G.A.S.*, lvi (1935), 73–76. The details and degree of elaboration of the Llantwit Major design stamp it not only as 4th century but also as later than the Gloucester pavement. *Cf.* G. Webster, below, pp. 238–43

remains of decorated mosaics to which so early a date can be assigned on external evidence. They are High Wycombe (Bucks.), Winterton (Lincs.) and Well (Yorks., N. Riding). At High Wycombe, again, many fragments of samian, including little-worn sherds assignable to *c.* 150–75, had been used as red tesserae. Unfortunately the mosaic had been largely defaced, but sufficient survived to show that the design included four square panels portraying busts.[1] At Winterton, however, a fragment of scroll was all that remained, while at Well the patterns were only of the simplest kind.

Employment of samian 'tesserae' in quantity has been noted at Fishbourne as well as at High Wycombe. It is, however, relatively rare and may or may not be taken as in itself a reliable criterion of date. Many fragments from both plain and figured vessels have been observed in only one other pavement, probably of a villa, at Walton Heath (Surrey). It is the more regrettable, therefore, that no details were recorded or specimens preserved. But apart from this the design included a cantharus which appears to have been of a form very unlike that generally found in late mosaics, and it is conceivable that here also was a villa-mosaic of the second half of the 2nd century.

By *c.* 200, or soon after, the boom was over and the mosaic-working industry in Britain appears to have entered a period of recession which lasted until perhaps just before 300, when it revived with surprising suddenness and vigour. Now the demand for new pavements came not only from the towns[2] but also, and apparently to an even greater degree, from the many country houses which seem to have been built or enlarged and embellished in the early decades of the 4th century. Indeed, it is from the villa-pavements of the 4th century that the student of Romano-British mosaics has at present most to learn, and it is to these that the remainder of this chapter must be devoted.

[1] Only one bust survived. Toynbee (1964), 274–5, has suggested that it may have been a portrait, but actual portraits in mosaic pavements are rare, and, in a 2nd-century mosaic, almost out of the question. My own suggestion—that it was a bust of one of the Seasons—though not entirely satisfactory, is probable; see *Records of Bucks.*, xvi (1959), 249–53, pl. IX. It is easier to accept as possible portraits the busts without attributes in the 4th-century pavements at Bramdean (Hants.), Fullerton (Hants.), Horkstow (Lincs.), and Lufton (Som.): Toynbee (1964), 247, 258–9, 281

[2] The evidence, though largely fragmentary, is best established at Verulamium; see Wheeler (1936), 142–8, Mosaics 3, 4, 5, 9, 11, 13, pl. XLII, XLIII, XLIVA, XLVIB, XLVIIIB

B. DATED VILLA-MOSAICS OF THE 4TH CENTURY

Some of the dated pavements have been described by their excavators simply as '4th-century', others more precisely as 'Constantinian', but for a considerable number it is possible to cite a definite *terminus post quem*. It may be noted at the outset that the earliest of these are not confined to any one part of the province, though in the midlands and north the seeds sown at the beginning of the century blossomed later and less luxuriantly than those in the south-west. At Verulamium, at the villa of Denton in Lincolnshire (Pl. 3.26), and at the temple-establishment of Lydney Park in Gloucestershire west of the Severn, mosaicists were still active *c*. 370,[1] while a worn coin of 395 (Theodosius) in the mortar bedding of a pavement of the villa at Hucclecote (Glos.) shows that in the vicinity of Gloucester they were still at work at the very end of the 4th century—or even perhaps in the early 5th.[2]

Most of the dated 4th-century mosaics will be at least briefly described in the sections that follow. They can therefore merely be listed here. The length of the list may come as a surprise to many. It must, however, be divided into two categories:

(*a*) mosaics with a *terminus post quem* established on external evidence;

(*b*) mosaics assigned by their excavators, on general but reliable grounds, to the Constantinian period or simply to the 4th century.

(*a*) Mosaics with a terminus post quem c. A.D. 300 or later

This is a list based on dates. Logically, therefore, it must be chronological in order. But it will be remembered that a *terminus post quem* is no more than the earliest possible date as determined by external, sealed evidence. For example, though a coin of Marcus Aurelius recovered from the make-up of Mosaic 1 in the villa at Great Weldon (Northants.) is sufficient to indicate that that pavement could not have been laid before the later 2nd century, it does not necessarily follow that the pavement must date from that period: in fact, its pattern (Pl. 3.21) was almost identical with that of Mosaic 2 in the near-by villa at Great Casterton (Rutland), for which numismatic evidence has afforded a *terminus post quem c*. 350–65, so that a date

---

[1] Verulamium: *Ant. J.*, xxxix (1959), 10; xl (1960), 20, pl. v; Denton: *J.R.S.*, xl (1950), 100, and *Denton* (1964); Lydney Park: Wheeler (1932), 65–67, frontispiece and pl. xix–xxii

[2] *Hucclecote* (1933), 328, 366, pl. x

in the later 4th century rather than the later 2nd is to be preferred for the pavement at Great Weldon. On the other hand, in the absence of evidence to the contrary it is reasonable to conclude that the date of a mosaic may be not much later than that of any common coin in mint condition sealed beneath it, provided it be demonstrably neither a survival nor one of a hoard: thus, a chessboard-pattern mosaic in the villa at Harpham (E. Yorks.) can quite probably be assigned to 305 or soon after on the evidence of the bronze coin of that year (Constantius) in 'almost mint condition' reported to have been found below it in 1950. Next to a coin in mint condition comes the evidence of pottery, particularly samian ware until its manufacture ceased about the middle of the 3rd century, but in the following list the *terminus post quem* in nearly every case depends primarily on numismatic evidence. All the sites listed are those of proved or probable villas and, as will be seen later, the evidence from some of them bears directly upon the dating of many mosaics of other villas.

c. 270–300   *Kings Weston, Bristol* Three curious and poorly executed geometric mosaics, all laid when the villa was built, *i.e. c.* 270 at the earliest but possibly as late as *c.* 300.

c. 305   *Harpham (E. Yorks.)* Chessboard pattern. A coin of 305 (Constantius) in 'almost mint condition' was found beneath it in 1950. Five other geometric mosaics and one destroyed, possibly contemporary.

c. 330+   *Low Ham (Som.)* (Pl. 3.5) Mosaic with scenes illustrating episodes in the *Aeneid* and accompanying geometric mosaics. On being taken up for removal to Somerset County Museum in 1953 the figured mosaic was found to have been laid over a cold plunge-bath which had been constructed *c.* 330, used for an unknown period of time, and then packed with debris to form a foundation for this pavement. Its actual date must therefore be later than 330.

c. 330–5   *Brantingham (E. Yorks.)* Two geometric mosaics discovered in 1941. One may possibly have been laid some time after the other.

c. 330–7   *Whittington Court (Glos.)* Eight geometric mosaics. In the opinion of their excavator they could have been laid at any time up to thirty years after 330–7. If indeed so much later they would have been contemporary with the mosaics of Lydney

Park (Glos.), and comparison of drawings and photographs suggests that they may, in fact, have been produced by the same mosaicists.

c. 340   *Lullingstone (Kent)* (Pl. 3.7) Two figured mosaics in one room, one depicting the Rape of Europa, the other Bellerophon killing the Chimaera.

c. 340+   *Winterton (Lincs.)* (Pls. 3.17, 18) One mosaic depicting Orpheus and animals, one portraying Ceres and one a figure (bust) bearing a *cornucopiae* (? Providentia).

c. 350/65+ *Great Casterton (Rutland)* Three geometric mosaics, of which two were later than the third.

c. 370   *Denton (Lincs.)* (Pl. 3.26) Three geometric mosaics.

c. 395+   *Hucclecote (Glos.)* Destroyed.

(b) Mosaics assigned to the Constantinian period or to the 4th century in general

It must be noted here that when excavators have used the term 'Constantinian' without further definition they presumably expected it to be understood, as it normally is, to mean the period of the reign of Constantine I (Constantine the Great), *i.e.* 306–37; but the possibility that those who first excavated the villa at Rudston used it less precisely for the much longer period of rule of the Constantinian House, 306–61, cannot be entirely excluded and should be borne in mind. The mosaics in this list are those of the following villas, which are given in alphabetical order:

Downton (Wilts.). Geometric mosaic.
Frocester Court (Glos.). Geometric mosaic.
Great Staughton (Hunts.). Two geometric mosaics (Pl. 3.25).
Hinton St Mary (Dorset). Two figured mosaics (Pl. 3.29).
Hucclecote (Glos.). At least five simple geometric mosaics.
Lufton (Som.). Three mosaics, figured and geometric.
Rudston (E. Yorks.). One mosaic portraying Venus and hunting scenes (Pl. 3.20), one depicting sea creatures, one geometric. 'Constantinian.'

To sum up so far, some fifty mosaics of nearly twenty villas as far apart as Kent, Somerset, and Yorkshire have at present been firmly dated on external evidence to the 4th century. This is a fair proportion of a total approaching 400. Moreover, as will become evident in the course of the next two sections, among those for which no external evidence of date is available a great many are sufficiently similar to one or more of the dated mosaics for their contemporaneity to be beyond serious doubt.[1] The volume of material for study is thus considerable and two of the questions that it raises are especially germane to a chapter on mosaics in a book devoted to the Roman villa in Britain. They are: what do the mosaics reveal concerning the villa-proprietors for whom they were made, and what do they tell of the mosaicists who made them?

Subjects and Themes of the Villa-mosaics

The fact that the villa-mosaics of Britain can with few exceptions be assigned to the 4th century endows them with a peculiar importance, in that they can be treated as expressive of the taste and interests of a particular social class in a particular period. This applies even to the geometric mosaics, which understandably tend to attract less notice than those with figured scenes; but the latter are undeniably the more informative as well as more intriguing. Admittedly, most of them appear at first glance to consist of conventional representations of gods, goddesses, and mythical heroes, or of personified phenomena, or of favourite episodes in mythology. At the same time, there are others which clearly cannot be so easily dismissed and some of these raise far-reaching questions. Whatever the theme or subject may be, however, it must be assumed as a general principle that it was not chosen without thought. In other words, it implies a preference for that theme or subject as opposed to any other, for there is evidence that the mosaicists' repertory of stock motifs was not always or even necessarily a factor limiting choice: special requests can be recognised with certainty in Britain as in other provinces.

Before discussing the more significant of the figured villa-mosaics it is essential to indicate something of the range and variety of their themes and subjects. They can be classified and listed as follows:

(a) Individual gods and goddesses

Bacchus (Pls. 3.27, 15, 9)	Frampton (Dorset), Stonesfield (Oxon.), Thruxton (Hants.)
? Ceres (Pl. 3.17)	Winterton (Lincs.)
Cupid (Pl. 3.27)	Frampton

[1] cf. Toynbee (1964), 238-9; but these words will apply to the geometric as well as to the figured mosaics.

Days of the Week (Pl. 3.4) (*i.e.* the internundinal week of eight days)	Bramdean (Hants.), as busts of Sol, Luna, Mars, Mercury, Jupiter, Venus; two destroyed, viz. Saturn and Bonus Eventus or Fortuna
Mars	Frampton
Mercury (Pls. 3.3, 20)	Pitney (Som.), Rudston (E. Yorks.)
Neptune (Pls. 3.27, 3, 15, 11, 13)	Frampton (figure and mask), Pitney, Rudston (mask), Stonesfield (Oxon., mask), Withington (Glos., bust), Woodchester (Glos., mask)
Venus (Colour Pl. 3.1, Pls. 3.5, 20)	Bignor (Sussex, bust), Hemsworth (Dorset), Low Ham (Som.), Rudston
? (Pl. 3.3)	Pitney (several)

(b) *Mythological creatures and episodes*

Aeneas and Dido (Pl. 3.5)	Low Ham (Som.)
Apollo and Marsyas (Pl. 3.31)	Lenthay Green (Dorset)
Bacchus, birth of (Fig. 3.3)	East Coker (Som.)
Bellerophon and Chimaera (Pl. 3.29)	Hinton St Mary (Dorset), Lullingstone (Kent)
Ceres and Triptolemus (Pl. 3.8)	Brading (I. of Wight)
Europa, rape of (Pl. 3.7)	Keynsham (Som.), Lullingstone
Ganymede, rape of	Bignor (Sussex)
Hercules and Antaeus	Bramdean (Hants.)
? Hercules and Hydra	Pitney (Som.)
Lycurgus and Ambrosia (Pl. 3.8)	Brading
Medusa, mask of (Pls. 4.2, 3.8)	Bignor (twice), Brading, Bramdean
Perseus and Andromeda	Brading

83

Theseus and Minotaur ? (Pls. 3.8, 27; Fig. 3.2)	Oldcoates (Notts.) Brading, Frampton (Dorset), Horkstow (Lincs.), Keynsham

(c) *Orpheus*

Orpheus and animals (Pls. 3.10, 17)	Newton St Loe (Som.), ? Pit Meads (Wilts.), Winterton (Lincs.)
Orpheus, animals, birds (Fig. 3.2; Pls. 3.11, 13)	Brading (I. of Wight), Horkstow (Lincs.), Withington (Glos.), Woodchester (Glos.)
Orpheus and Seasons (Pl. 3.16)	Littlecote Park (Wilts.)

(d) *Christian, Dionysiac and Gnostic imagery*

Abraxas	Brading (I. of Wight)
cantharus alone	a common filling motif, perhaps not especially significant except where it prominently occupies a central position
cantharus between confronted dolphins, fish, panthers or peacocks (Pls. 3.16, 11)	Littlecote Park (Wilts.), Wellow (Som.), Withington (Glos.)
cantharus encircled by dolphins and fish (Pl. 3.30)	Fifehead Neville (Dorset)
Chi-Rho ☧ with cantharus (Pl. 3.27)	Frampton (Dorset)
Christ (? and evangelists) (Pl. 3.29)	Hinton St Mary (Dorset)
doves pecking at fruit or holding a twig (Pls. 3.20, 15)	Chedworth (Glos.), Keynsham (Som.), Rudston (E. Yorks.), Stonesfield (Oxon.)
grapes between confronted peacocks (Fig. 3.2)	Horkstow (Lincs.)

(e) *Personifications*

Astronomy (Pl. 3.8) ? Providence (Providentia) (Pl. 3.18)	Brading (I. of Wight) Winterton (Lincs.)

River (? Stour)	Hemsworth (Dorset)
Seasons (Pls. 4.2, 3.16, 3, 9)	Bignor (Sussex, twice as busts), Brading (as busts), Chedworth (Glos., as cupids), Itchen Abbas (Hants., bust of Spring or Summer), Littlecote Park (Wilts., as mounted female figures), Lullingstone (Kent, as busts), Pitney (Som., as cupids), Spoonley Wood (Glos., bust of Winter), ? Thruxton (Hants., as busts)
spring of water (Pls. 3.19, 13)	Brantingham (E. Yorks.), Woodchester (Glos.)
tyche (Pl. 3.19)	Brantingham (E. Yorks.), Whatley (Som.)
virtus	Fullerton (Hants.)
winds (Pls. 3.8, 28, 3)	Brading, Frampton (Dorset, twice), Pitney

(*f*) *Cupids, maenads, nereids, nymphs, satyrs, shepherds, tritons*

cupids as attendants (Pls. 3.5, 7)	Low Ham (Som.), Lullingstone (Kent)
cupids as gladiators	Bignor (Sussex)
cupids as the Seasons (Pl. 3.3)	Chedworth (Glos.), Pitney (Som.)
cupids making garlands? (Fig. 3.2)	Horkstow (Lincs.)
maenads	Bignor
nereids and tritons (Pl. 3.8; Fig. 3.2)	Brading (I. of Wight), Horkstow
satyrs and maenads (Pl. 3.8; Fig. 3.2)	Brading, Chedworth, Fullerton (Hants.), ? Horkstow
shepherd and nymph (Pl. 3.8)	Brading, ? Rudge (Wilts.)
?triton as attendant (Pl. 3.20)	Rudston (E. Yorks.)

(*g*) *Sporting scenes*

amphitheatre	Bignor (Sussex, cupids as gladiators), Brading (I. of Wight, gladiators in combat)

85

circus (Fig. 3.2)	Colerne (Wilts., charioteer with four-horse chariot), Horkstow (Lincs., chariot race)
hunting (Pls. 3.27, 29, 20, 11; Fig. 3.2)	East Coker (Som.), Frampton (Dorset), Hinton St Mary (Dorset), Horkstow, Rudston (E. Yorks.), ? Withington (Glos.)

(h) *Compositions of aquatic creatures*

dolphins, fish, etc. (Pls. 3.30, 27, 11)	Bromham (Wilts.), Fifehead Neville (Dorset), Frampton (Dorset), Great Witcombe (Glos.), Hemsworth (Dorset), Llanfrynach (Brecon), Lufton (Som.), Rudston (E. Yorks.), Whatley (Som.), Withington (Glos.), Woodchester (Glos.)

To begin with the last, freely composed patterns of aquatic creatures, suggesting a natural pool,[1] probably reflected not so much an interest in fishing as the universal habit of bathing. At any rate, it was in bath suites that they were found at Llanfrynach, Lufton, Rudston, and Witcombe, and at Rudston the suggestion was heightened by the choice of a border of lotuses and enlivened by a head of Neptune[2] emerging, as it were, from the water. In short, except perhaps in a relatively formal design such as that at Fifehead Neville (see p. 87, below), these compositions can in general be regarded as purely decorative.

Again, despite Britain's early reputation for hunting-dogs[3] and chariot-driving,[4] and the evident popularity of scenes from circus and amphitheatre

---

[1] It is worth mentioning, because little known (*e.g.* not mentioned in Toynbee (1963), 198, no. 186, or Toynbee (1964), 272–3), that the octagonal centrepiece of the Orpheus pavement at Woodchester is said to have been treated in this way; see the note in the margin of the drawing in the B.M. by R. Bradley, dated 31 July 1722 (Add. MSS. 5238, folio 3)

[2] The late Sir Ian Richmond recognised the head from the part of it that remains and drew my attention to it in 1963. The idea has parallels elsewhere.

[3] Strabo, IV, v, 2 (C 199)

[4] Cicero, *ad Fam.*, vii, 7; Caesar, *B.G.*, iv, 33; Tacitus, *Agr.*, xii, 1

on 4th-century British pottery, representations of hunting, chariot-racing and gladiatorial contest—the 'sporting prints' of the Roman world—are so few as to suggest that the villa-owners, at least, were not greatly preoccupied with such diversions. Rather, if the number of personifications of the Seasons has any significance, it would seem that their interests lay much more in the annual round of rural life.[1]

The significance of representations of individual gods and goddesses, which are even more numerous than those of the Seasons, is less easy to surmise. It might be thought that just as the portrait of Christ at Hinton St Mary (Colour Pl. 3.2) is indicative of a villa-proprietor who had embraced Christianity, so the portraits of pagan deities in the homes of his contemporaries ought equally to imply that, though perhaps not actively opposed to the new faith, these still preferred the gods of their fathers. But at Frampton (Pl. 3.27), to take the first example that springs to mind, an inscription in praise of Cupid and the portrayal of pagan deities and mythological scenes in association with a prominently placed Chi-Rho is a warning, if one be needed, that subjects and motifs in the art of the 4th century demand exceptionally close scrutiny. Most of them do, indeed, seem to betoken continued adherence to paganism, however conventional and uninspired, but some which had long been established in the repertory of pre-Christian art can now be viewed in certain contexts as, probably at least, symbols or allegories open to interpretation in Christian terms. One of the commonest of such motifs is the cantharus, originally symbolic of the mystic communion between Dionysus (Bacchus) and those initiated into his cult, yet equally capable of representing the Christian chalice, symbol of the Eucharist, as the wine of the Eucharist is itself symbolic of Christ's blood.[2] Other common and well-known early Christian symbols were fish and dolphins.[3] It is almost impossible, therefore, not to interpret the cantharus encircled by dolphins and fish at Fifehead Neville in Dorset (Pl. 3.30) as evidence that the proprietor of this villa, too, numbered himself among the faithful; and here the interpretation is supported by the discovery on the same site of two finger-rings bearing the Chi-Rho

[1] I am, of course, well aware of the eschatological significance of personifications of the Seasons in funerary art. But outside such a context other interpretations become possible and seem more plausible, and that implied here has at least the virtue of simplicity.

[2] Matthew 26: 27–29; Mark 14: 23–25; Luke 22: 20

[3] cf. Cabrol/Leclercq, s.v. Dauphin, Poisson; G. Brusin, *Due nuovi sacelli cristiani di Aquileia* (1961), 12 and note 14

monogram.[1] At Frampton the association of a cantharus with the Chi-Rho compels the same conclusion, and the cycle of pagan themes in the same mosaic is a reminder that the early Christian was still so steeped in the repertory of pagan art and literature that he saw nothing incongruous in the juxtaposition of Christian symbols and even apparently un-Christian motifs. At Hinton St Mary, also in Dorset, the Chi-Rho monogram appears again in a British mosaic (Pl. 3.29):[2] here, however, as a means of indicating the identity of the male figure whose head and shoulders are portrayed in the central medallion of the larger of the two pavements. This is the earliest known portrait of Christ in a floor-mosaic, and there is reason to think that the four male figures (amended versions of the wind gods of two of the mosaics at Frampton, Pl. 3.28), whose busts occupy the angles of the same pavement may have been intended to represent the four evangelists.[3]

In the light of these mosaics one is bound to consider whether Christian influence may have been responsible for the exceptional number of British pavements which in the first half of the 4th century depicted Orpheus subduing earth's wild creatures by the charm of his voice. Altogether eight are known, or nine if that of Pit Meads can be included (see below, pp. 98–100), all but two being villa-mosaics. In no other province have so many representations of this theme in mosaic been recorded.[4] Although apparently never common in Christian art, the subject

[1] *cf.* Toynbee (1953), 19

[2] *Hinton St Mary* (1964a) and (1964b). For another mosaic in Dorset, at Halstock, in which the Chi-Rho may have appeared, see *Gents. Mag.*, 1818, i, 5. There were four small medallions, 'each containing the head of a warrior in his helmet, the back of which is represented having a double cross in an oblique position from right to left, extending far above the shoulder . . .' Although it is difficult to visualise precisely what was portrayed, it does seem possible that this is a garbled description of four busts, each having a Chi-Rho behind the head. If so, the heads were most probably intended to portray the four evangelists (*cf.* note 3 below). From the rest of the account it is clear that the geometric basis of the design was the same as that of the Christ mosaic at Hinton St Mary and of mosaics at Fifehead Neville and Lufton.

[3] As early as *c.* 185 St Irenaeus had linked the number of the Gospels with that of the winds: *Contra Haereses*, III, xi, 8. I owe this reference to Mr G. N. Drinkwater; *cf.* J. M. C. Toynbee, *J.R.S.*, liv (1964), 14. But the germ of the idea may be seen still earlier, in Revelation 7: 1

[4] *cf.* H. Stern, *Gallia*, xiii (1955), 41ff.; additional examples cited by R. M. Harrison, *J.R.S.*, lii (1962), 13ff. I take this opportunity to thank Mr Harrison for kindly reading and commenting upon this chapter in typescript; responsibility for any errors of fact or interpretation which remain is, however, entirely my own.

Fig. 3.2 Horkstow (*Lincs*). Reconstruction drawing, from R. Hinks, *Cat. of the Greek, Etruscan and Roman Paintings and Mosaics in the British Museum* (1933), fig. 112. By permission.

had been adopted by the Church at least as early as the second century, the pagan hero having the attributes of a type or prototype of the Good Shepherd; and in the period of Constantine I (306–37) the panegyrist Eusebius (*c.* 260–*c.* 340) expressly likened the Saviour of men to 'Orpheus of the Greeks who tamed and subdued the wild beasts'.[1] It may be worth noting, therefore, that two of the British Orpheus mosaics, at Horkstow (Lincs., Fig. 3.2) and Withington (Glos., Pl. 3.11), incorporate other motifs possibly of Christian significance—respectively, a cluster of grapes between confronted peacocks and a cantharus between confronted peacocks. Yet although it is tempting to attribute the propagation of the Orpheus theme in Britain to Christian influence[2] it would probably be unwise as yet to regard these mosaics as positive evidence for the extent of Christianity in the province in the period to which they can be assigned.

Numerous other pavements owe their choice of theme not to Christian inspiration but to that of some celebrated episode in classical literature. The mosaic of Low Ham (Som., Pl. 3.5), which has in its central panel a figure of Venus with attendant symbolic cupids, was certainly inspired by the famous love story of Aeneas and Dido as related by Virgil in the first and fourth books of the *Aeneid*.[3] Moreover, one of the scenes depicting successive events in the tale seems almost as certainly to have been derived at first hand from an illuminated manuscript of the *Aeneid* such as that of *c.* A.D. 400 in the Vatican (Pl. 3.6):[4] so much so that whoever conceived this unique mosaic most surely have possessed, and been proud to possess, a very similar manuscript. Furthermore, in devotion to Rome's greatest poet he was not alone among his peers. A contemporary at Lullingstone (Kent) was so captivated by a jocular reference to events recounted in the first book of the *Aeneid*[5] that he commissioned a mosaic to illustrate and commemorate it, with the actual words[6]—in tolerably good

[1] *de Laudibus Constantini*, xiv; *cf.* Northcote and Brownlow (1879), ii, 30–32; Cabrol/Leclercq, *s.v.* Orphée; R. M. Harrison, *loc. cit.*, 17–18

[2] *cf.* Cabrol/Leclercq, *s.v.* Bretagne (Grande), col. 1182, fig. 1634 (Horkstow); Richmond (1963), 122–3; Toynbee (1963), 14

[3] *cf.* Toynbee (1963), 15, 203, no. 200, pl. 235; (1964), 241–6, pl. LVIII

[4] *Codex Vaticanus Latinus* 3225; *cf.* J. de Wit, *Die Miniaturen des Vergilius Vaticanus* (1959), pl. 7, no. 1 (Pictura II), and Toynbee (1963), pl. 260. The relevant illustration in *Codex Vaticanus Latinus* 3865 'Romanus' seems to me hardly comparable; *cf.* Toynbee (1963), 205, pl. 261; (1964), 245

[5] *cf.* Toynbee (1963), 200, no. 192, pl. 229; (1964), 262–5, pl. LXA

[6] How such a couplet might have originated in impromptu versification during a meal is well illustrated by the account of the Emperor Majorian's dinner party

Virgilian hexameters—preserved in a tessellated inscription (Pl. 3.7); and it was perhaps at much the same time that the proprietor of the neighbouring villa of Otford (Kent) commissioned a wall-painting depicting an episode in the *Aeneid* with a painted caption taken from the poem itself (see below, p. 145).

Examples such as these arouse a suspicion that other mosaics with narrative scenes may have been inspired by illustrations in a favourite manuscript rather than produced from the models available in the local mosaicists' pattern-books. This applies particularly to scenes for which parallels are exceptionally rare or even do not appear to exist in the thousands of mosaics known from the Empire at large. The Low Ham pavement is one such. Another is the scene at East Coker (Som.) which depicted, most probably, the miraculous birth of Bacchus (Fig. 3.3).[1] For this scene there seem to be only two parallels, one in the frieze of a sculptured sarcophagus and the other in a figured textile from Antinoë in Egypt;[2] so that, in the light of the evidence from Low Ham, it can be suggested that at East Coker the source of inspiration was quite possibly an illustration of the birth in a manuscript of Ovid's *Metamorphoses*.[3] Indeed, it is perhaps to the influence of this work above all others that we owe the innumerable scenes portraying the transformation of gods, heroes, nymphs and human beings into other forms.

Of all the mosaics of this period in Britain, however, none better reflect the intellectual and spiritual cross-currents of the times than do those of the villa at Brading (I. of Wight). In addition to separate and probably not contemporary pavements portraying respectively Orpheus and the Gnostic deity Abraxas with other scenes there is a suite of four connected panels with themes which appear at first sight to be unrelated (Pl. 3.8). One depicts tritons and nereids. The second has a central head of Medusa, personifications of the Winds, and male and female figures in

[1] This identification was suggested to me by the late Sir Ian Richmond; *cf.* Richmond (1963), 123; Toynbee (1964), 240. For the nurse, Ino, missing from the drawing, see *Gents. Mag.*, 1753, 293

[2] Both are illustrated in Richmond (1950), pl. III, VIA

[3] *Metam.*, iii, 273ff.; *cf.* Richmond (1963), 123

at Arles in A.D. 461; see C. E. Stevens, *Sidonius Apollinaris and his Age* (Oxford, 1933), 54–55. I owe this suggestion and the reference to the late Sir Ian Richmond. It is tempting to think that an especially fine piece of table silver with a centrepiece like that of the Neptune Dish of the Mildenhall Treasure may have prompted the verse in the border of the Neptune and Cupid mosaic at Frampton (Dorset); *cf.* p. 112 and note 2

Fig. 3.3 East Coker (*Som.*): the Birth of Bacchus. From a drawing in the Haverfield Library, Ashmolean Museum. By permission.

four pairs who are identifiable as Ceres and Triptolemus, Lycurgus and Ambrosia (the latter in process of transformation into a vine), a satyr pursuing a maenad, and a shepherd with another maenad dancing, as her crossed feet signify, to the music of the shepherd's pan-pipes and the accompaniment of her own tambourine. In the third panel a seated, bearded male figure, with gnomon and sphere, is perhaps a personification of astronomy. The fourth panel is extremely fragmentary, but preserves busts of three of the four Seasons and part of a scene illustrating the liberation of Andromeda by Perseus.

Two of the major subjects of this suite might have been inspired by the *Metamorphoses*, if not actually derived from an illustrated manuscript of the poem: the myths of Ceres and Triptolemus and of the adventures of Perseus are both related in Ovid's work.[1] But it is the minor subjects which first suggest that there may be more in these mosaics than meets the eye, for it is possible to see in them a deliberate choice of complementary themes such as philosophical minds in the ancient world were accustomed to dwell upon: the heavens (personified by the astronomer) and earth (personified by the Seasons), air (personified by the Winds) and water (represented by the tritons and nereids). Then, if the themes of the two major panels are considered together, a most interesting relationship appears possible, shedding light not only on this intriguing and hitherto somewhat puzzling set of scenes but also on the culture of the man for whom they were composed. The relationship, though not the actual design, is paralleled in the mosaic of the Corridor of Perseus and Andromeda in the House of Dionysus and Ariadne at Antioch, which has been assigned to the period 193–235.[2] No one who knows the Brading mosaics can fail to recall them when reading Levi's commentary on this pavement at Antioch, or to feel that this appreciation of the one must apply equally to both. His concluding paragraph might, in fact, have been penned with the mosaics of Brading rather than that of Antioch in mind, and is the more striking in that those of Brading seem to have been unknown to him. It is necessary to quote him almost in full:

> In regard to the presence of these panels of Dionysiac character on our floor in association with Perseus' labors, we may think in this case of something more than mere decorative additions. It must not be forgotten that the third great episode of Perseus' legend is indeed his fight with Dionysus and the Dionysiac thiasos. The tale has very ancient origins, and artistic representations much earlier than the first literary mention, provided by a poet otherwise unknown, Deinarchos, who extolled the deeds of Dionysus, including his expedition to India, and who must consequently be at least later than Alexander the Great. In

[1] *Metam.*, v, 642ff., iv, 663ff.
[2] Levi (1947), i, 141ff., 625

Deinarchos' version, as well as in other literary sources, Perseus is described as the victor and killer of Dionysus, having brought havoc to his thiasos. . . . From this connection of Perseus' myth with the Dionysiac cycle derives the transformation, mentioned before, of Perseus and Andromeda into a couple of Bacchic dancers.[1]

Abounding in allegory, allusion and symbols which have never been intensively studied and are still far from being properly understood, figured mosaics such as those of Brading constitute a body of evidence for the intellectual culture of late Roman Britain which is second only to the linguistic evidence so brilliantly interpreted by Professor K. H. Jackson.[2] Though even more difficult to evaluate, it can be seen that the evidence of the mosaics is entirely in accord with his view of the villa-proprietors as completely Romanised, educated in accordance with the standards of their class and time, and revealing through the conservatism and purity of their Latin speech the imprint of a thorough schooling in Latin literature.

This aspect of the villa-mosaics can, indeed, most appropriately be concluded with a note on those in which tessellated inscriptions afford actual evidence of literacy. Altogether eight are known, as against four, including one in Greek, in towns.[3] Two, the metrical inscriptions of Frampton (Dorset) and Lullingstone (Kent), have already been mentioned. The others are less notable, but not uninteresting. One, at Bignor (Sussex), appears to be the abbreviated 'signature' of the master mosaicist.[4] Another seems to have given the name of the charioteer portrayed at Colerne (Wilts.).[5] At Littleton (Som.) only three letters survived,[6] but the incomplete inscription at Thruxton (Hants., Pl. 3.9) may have preserved the name of the owner of the villa,[7] and that at Woodchester (Glos., Pl. 3.14)

---

[1] *ibid.*, i, 156

[2] Jackson (1953), 109–10; *cf.* I. A. Richmond, in Wacher (1966), 19

[3] For those in towns, see H. E. Smith (1852), 41, pl. xviii (Aldborough, Yorks., in Greek); Watkins (1886), 192–4 (Chester); RCHM (1928), 134, 176, fig. 88 (no. 60, Billingsgate, Monument Yard, 1887) and 139 (Bishopsgate Street, Little St Helen's, 1733). To complete the list of inscribed mosaics in Britain, that of the pavement in the temple at Lydney Park must be added; see Wheeler (1932), 102–3, pl. xixA

[4] Lysons (1817), pl. xiv

[5] *Colerne* (1856), 329

[6] *Littleton* (1827), 113

[7] *Arch. J.*, Salisbury vol. (1849), 241ff., with plate; Hinks (1933), 101, no. 35, fig. 111

possibly exhorted the spectator to worship Bonus Eventus,[1] the god whose function was to bring to good issue and who was perhaps portrayed in the missing central medallion. Most curious of all, however, because the characters clearly were meaningless to the mosaicist and even the draft that he was given to copy must have been ungrammatical, were the inscriptions naming two animals at Rudston (E. Yorks., Pl. 3.20).[2] But this pavement, with its equally naïve figures, is an exception which, while it may or may not be held to prove the rule, certainly contrasts with the relatively good standards of most 4th-century mosaics in Britain.

Fourth-century Schools of Mosaic in Britain[3] (Fig. 3.4)

In the foregoing section an attempt, admittedly sketchy, has been made to suggest what the villa-mosaics may reveal concerning the villa-proprietors. Now the question is: what have they to tell of the men who made them, of their methods and of the way in which their craft was organised? This is a threefold question to which the answer lies largely in a consideration of the third part, that of the organisation of the mosaic-working industry.

To begin with, one has only to examine the lists at the beginning of the previous section to become aware of a tendency for certain subjects and themes to appear more or less localised. Indeed, this is immediately obvious in the case of the Orpheus mosaics and almost equally true of representations of Neptune, other aquatic deities and creatures, and hunting scenes. When the urban mosaics are also taken into account, this tendency is seen to be confirmed and a significant pattern emerges. In Dorset, in Gloucestershire and adjacent counties, in the east and northeast midlands, on either side of the Humber and in other parts of the country, there are groups of interrelated mosaics and each group is characterised by features which are not found, or are found significantly less often or in a significantly different form, elsewhere. This implies the

[1] *Woodchester* (1797), pl. xix; Lysons (1813), part i, pl. xxiii. This interpretation was suggested to me by the late Sir Ian Richmond; for an alternative, treating the inscriptions in the two panels not as two parts of an exhortation but as separate, and to be read as greetings, see Toynbee (1964), 274

[2] J. M. C. Toynbee, *Papers of the British School at Rome*, xvi (1948), 36, pl. xi, 31

[3] For a more detailed treatment of subsections A, B and D of this section, see my paper, 'Three Fourth-Century Schools of Mosaic in Roman Britain', in *La Mosaïque Gréco-Romaine* (D. J. Smith, 1965); for A also *Ant. J.* forthcoming (1969)

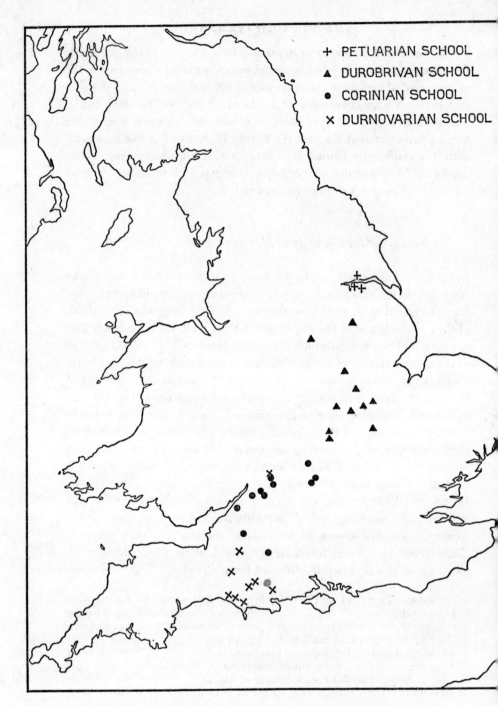

Fig. 3.4. Fourth-Century Schools of Mosaic.

existence of what can most conveniently be called 'schools' of mosaicists who had worked out their own repertory of designs and motifs. The products of four such schools, for which the evidence consists almost entirely of villa-mosaics, is sufficiently ample to justify discussion. Moreover, the distribution of the mosaics attributable to these four schools suggests that the workshops (*officinae*) were located respectively in the towns of Corinium–Cirencester (Glos.), Petuaria–Brough (E. Yorks.), Durobrivae–Water Newton (Hunts.), and Durnovaria–Dorchester (Dorset), and they will be considered in that order.

A. THE CORINIAN SCHOOL

This school, the largest in Britain and one of the most important of its time in the western Empire, is represented by approximately forty mosaics. One was discovered just outside Cirencester at the Barton Farm, while the rest have been found either actually in the town or at the villas of Chedworth, Tockington Park, Withington and Woodchester in Gloucestershire, North Leigh, Stonesfield and possibly Wigginton[1] in Oxfordshire, Newton St Loe in Somerset, and probably Pit Meads in Wiltshire.

The Corinian school specialised in, and indeed appears to have invented, a distinctive and exclusive type of Orpheus mosaic. In other provinces Orpheus, normally accompanied by animals and birds, is generally portrayed in a rectangular panel designed to be viewed from

---

[1] I am indebted to Mr E. Greenfield, who has undertaken a new excavation of this site for the Ministry of Public Building and Works, and to Mr D. S. Neal, official artist of the Ministry's Inspectorate of Ancient Monuments and Historic Buildings, for sending me a preliminary drawing of one of the fragmentary mosaics uncovered here in 1965. The design of this mosaic clearly resembled that of the pavement in Room XII at Tockington Park (Glos.), attributable to the Corinian school, while the key-pattern with short lengths of guilloche inset which borders the only mosaic of Wigginton so far published is a type of border especially frequent in mosaics of the Corinian school, *e.g.* at the Barton Farm, Chedworth, Withington and Woodchester in Gloucestershire, and at Stonesfield in Oxfordshire; for the Wigginton example, see *Gents. Mag.*, 1824, ii, 359; A. Beesley, *History of Banbury* (1848), pl. XI, opp. 43; VCH, Oxon., i (1939), 309, fig. 28. It must be noted, however, that Mr Neal has pointed out to me that the technical standard of the new Wigginton pavement is appreciably inferior to the standard of the best surviving mosaics of the Corinian school, *e.g.* those of the Barton Farm, Chedworth and Woodchester, and has suggested that the Wigginton pavement must be either one of the school's latest products or even a product of a second Corinian school, for which he believes there may be evidence at both Chedworth and Tockington Park.

only one direction and suggesting derivation from a wall-painting.[1] The design of the Orpheus mosaics of the Corinian school, however, consists basically of a number of concentric circles, the number varying from one example to another, with Orpheus normally placed in the central medallion and animals and birds occupying the surrounding zones. Five such are known, at the Barton Farm (Pl. 3.12), in Dyer Street, Cirencester, at Newton St Loe, at Withington (Pl. 3.11) and Woodchester (Pl. 3.13), while the remains at Pit Meads appear to have been those of a sixth mosaic of this type.

The simplest was that of Newton St Loe (Pl. 3.10). Here a large figure of Orpheus dominated the design and seven lively animals occupied the single encircling zone. Four of the animals were arranged in confronted pairs alternating with trees. Two of the other three also formed a confronted pair, but had no tree between them. Clearly there must have been a miscalculation while the mosaic was actually being laid, for it is impossible not to believe that it had been the designer's intention to have a balanced scheme of *four* pairs of confronted animals alternating with trees. As a result of the error, one animal and three trees had to be omitted. This is precisely the kind of mischance which is liable to occur when a mosaic is being laid by the indirect or reverse process.[2] In this process, units of the mosaic are prefabricated in the workshop, secured against disintegration by the application of glue and a sheet of suitable material, and then cut up into sections of manageable size for transport to the site. There the sections are bedded in place in fresh mortar and when this has set the material is peeled off with the aid of hot water and, unless a transparent material was used, the result is now seen for the first time; the plain background is then filled in by the direct method, that is, the tesserae being set individually by hand. An error such as that at Newton St Loe is therefore of some interest, because it suggests that the mosaicists there probably employed the indirect process and miscalculated the spacing of the animals. If so, it arouses the suspicion that they were inexperienced in

[1] See p. 88, note 4; in Britain there is only one example of an Orpheus mosaic which more or less reproduces this traditional type: at Brading (Isle of Wight, Hants.); for a recent illustration, see Toynbee (1963), pl. 232

[2] On the use of this process in antiquity, *cf.* A. Ippel, *Römische Mitteilungen* (Deutsches Arch. Inst., Rome), xlv (1930), 80–110; M. E. Blake, *Memoirs of the American Academy in Rome*, xvii (1940), 105; Levi (1947), i, 9, note 44; Parlasca (1959), 136–40. And for a denial that it was used in antiquity, see R. E. M. Moore, *Bulletin of the Institute of Classical Studies* (Univ. of London), no. 11 (1964), 87–91. For a description of the process as employed today, see H. Unger (1965), 76ff.

working to a design based on concentric circles and that this mosaic may even have been the first in which they attempted to execute such a design.

At Withington (Pl. 3.11) a similar design was executed without error, but here it was simpler in that the animals, alternating with trees, faced all in the same direction. The central medallion was smaller in proportion to the design as a whole and on two opposite sides of the design were narrow panels of which one contained a procession of birds and the other a cantharus between confronted peacocks. A frame of key pattern with strips of simple guilloche inset on the axes originally surrounded the entire design, but on one side had later been removed to make room for a panel portraying Neptune.

It seems probable that the design at Pit Meads likewise comprised a central medallion and a single encircling zone of animals, but all that survived when the mosaic was discovered were the hind legs of one animal near the perimeter of the outer circle.[1] At the Barton Farm (Pl. 3.12) and in Dyer Street, Cirencester, however, a procession of birds—foreshadowed at Withington—was introduced into the concentric circular scheme to occupy a zone between the central medallion and the zone of the animals. But it must be observed that in these mosaics the animals differed in style from those of Newton St Loe and Withington, and in Dyer Street the figure of Orpheus was reduced in size so that the central medallion could accommodate a second diminutive figure whose identity is a problem.

The Orpheus mosaic at Woodchester (Pl. 3.13) was the most elaborate of all. Here an octagonal panel containing representations of fish occupied the centre[2] and Orpheus was placed, facing the main entrance to the room, in the zone of birds which surrounded this imitation aquarium. As at the Barton Farm and in Dyer Street a laurel wreath—in Britain, exclusive to these three mosaics—separated the zone of the birds from that of the animals, while the latter was encircled by a degenerate acanthus scroll proceeding from a mask of Neptune. This concentric circular design, 25 ft in diameter, was contained in a square frame consisting of twenty-four richly ornamented geometric panels, with a pair of reclining water-nymphs on a blue-black ground flanking the column base in each of its internal angles.

[1] Hoare (1819), 111–17, figure; = D. J. Smith (1965), fig. 13 (enlarged from Hoare's figure).
[2] See p. 86, note 1

The Orpheus mosaic and other pavements at Woodchester[1] are all attributable to the same craftsmen, and their repertory is of prime importance for the identification of the work of the Corinian school. In particular, their designs, geometric patterns and individual motifs are closely or even exactly paralleled at Chedworth, Newton St Loe, North Leigh, Stonesfield (Pl. 3.15), and Withington, while the mosaics of these sites are themselves related to one another and to geometric mosaics in Cirencester,[2] at North Leigh, Tockington Park, and Wigginton.[3]

So many mosaics must represent the work of a period of many years and it is natural to speculate on the order in which they may have been produced. It has already been suggested that the earliest of the Orpheus mosaics was perhaps that of Newton St Loe, and the geometric mosaics there can probably be regarded as having been laid at the same time. Then, if increasing elaboration can be taken as a criterion, the other Orpheus mosaics must have followed in the order: Withington, the Barton Farm, Dyer Street, and Woodchester. That of Pit Meads, if included in the sequence, is to be placed between those of Withington and the Barton Farm.

At Newton St Loe, Withington and Woodchester there were geometric mosaics so similar—indeed, a number at Withington and Woodchester were identical—that there can be no doubt of their attribution to the same workshop. The marked differences of style between the Orpheus pavements of Newton St Loe and Withington on the one hand and those of the Barton Farm, Dyer Street and Woodchester on the other can hardly be explained, therefore, except by assuming the advent of a new master mosaicist specialising in figured work. He it must have been who standardised the form of the later Orpheus mosaics, introducing his own fine animals, a zone of birds with delightful naturalistic touches, the laurel wreath and, at Woodchester, the acanthus scroll (Pl. 3.13).

[1] The only publication illustrating all the mosaics known to have existed at Woodchester is S. Lysons, *Roman Antiquities at Woodchester* (1797)

[2] An unfinished and unpublished pencil, ink, and water-colour drawing, (Lysons or Smirke?) in the Topographical Collections of the Society of Antiquaries of London, shows a mosaic found in Cirencester which invites comparison with that of Room IX at Tockington Park (Glos.) and with the central design of another pavement in Cirencester recently discovered (*Ant. J.*, xlv (1965), 104, pl. xxxiiiA). Furthermore, the centrepiece of the latter is an arrangement of guilloche knot with *peltae* trailing tendrils and leaves, for which the only parallel is the centrepiece of the small mosaic in a recess of Room 1 at North Leigh (Oxon.); see *North Leigh* (1826), pl. 2, fig. 1

[3] See p. 97, note 1

These novelties appear most simply, and possibly for the first time, in the mosaic of the Barton Farm, and this, as it happens, is the only one of the Orpheus pavements for which there is as yet anything approaching external evidence of date. In 1938 two coins were recovered from earth which was being removed from beneath the pavement preparatory to its transfer to the Corinium Museum.[1] The circumstances of discovery were noted at the time and the coins were deposited in the Museum, where they still are. They were later identified at the British Museum, one as worn and illegible but recognisably of late 3rd-century type, the other as of the usurper Allectus (A.D. 293–6), struck in London and in mint condition. Unfortunately, the mosaic was not intact and the precise position of the coins in relation to it was not established, so that they cannot by any means be regarded as having been sealed in the strictest sense of the term. Furthermore, from the nature of other objects extracted at the same time it is clear that the pavement had been founded in an area already previously disturbed. Yet even when all this is considered there still remains the possibility that the coins afford valid evidence of a date *c.* A.D. 300 for this mosaic. If so, and if the sequence that has been proposed for the Orpheus pavements is accepted, it follows that the same date can be taken as a *terminus ante quem* for those of Newton St Loe and Withington. The Corinian school may therefore have originated before the end of the 3rd century.

How long the school flourished is at present largely conjectural. Re-excavation at one or more of the hypothetically later sites where its products have been identified might yet throw light on this important question. Meanwhile, the only clue appears to lie in the type of cupid, distinguished by a floating stole, employed in the Bonus Eventus mosaic at Woodchester (Pl. 3.14) and for personifications of the Seasons of Spring, Summer and Autumn at Chedworth. A close parallel for the pair of such cupids at Woodchester is to be found in a pavement assigned to the late 3rd or early 4th century in the House of the Augustales at Ostia,[2] while for individual cupids such as those of Chedworth there are dated parallels in Britain at Frampton[3] (Pl. 3.27)—post-313 on the internal

[1] *Barton Farm* (1952), 51ff.

[2] Becatti (1961), i, 223; ii, pl. ccxviii; *cf.* the pair of cupids bearing a wreath between them in the celebrated Calendar of A.D. 354, most recently illustrated in Stern (1953), pl. iii, 1; this plate in turn, and *ibid.*, pl. ii, 2, offer interesting parallels for the figure of Venus between torch-bearing cupids at Low Ham.

[3] Lysons (1813), part i, pl. v; hence Toynbee (1963), pl. 234, and D. J. Smith

evidence of the Chi-Rho in the same border, and at Low Ham (Pl. 3.5)—
c. 330+,[1] in Italy in the mosaics of 326-37 of the vault of the ambulatory
of the mausoleum of Sta Costanza,[2] and in Algeria in the mosaic of the
marine Venus of Sétif, which has recently been assigned to a date as late
as A.D. 400.[3] The type is known on another pavement in Britain, in personifications of the Seasons at Pitney (Som., Pl. 3.3), but appears to be otherwise rare in floor-mosaics[4] and a motif characteristic of the 4th century.

It would be surprising if a school as vigorous as that of Corinium had
not prompted imitation of its repertory elsewhere in Britain. In fact, the
evident popularity and success of the concentric circular Orpheus mosaics
almost certainly influenced the designers of the pavements of Littlecote
Park (Wilts., Pl. 3.16), Horkstow (Lincs., Fig. 3.2) and Winterton (Lincs.,
Pl. 3.17). But in these three mosaics the idea was carried a step further by
the radial division of the single zone encircling the central medallion, thus
forming a wheel-like design, while the small size of the central medallion
in relation to the design as a whole is a further indication that these
pavements fall late in the series. But while it is at present difficult to
attribute the Littlecote Park mosaic to any particular school there can be
little doubt that those of Horkstow and Winterton must be recognised as
products of a second local workshop, most probably to be located in
Petuaria–Brough on Humber.

B. THE PETUARIAN SCHOOL

Five miles apart on the south side of the Humber and about the same
distance from the small town of Petuaria–Brough, on the north side of the

[1] *J.R.S.*, xxxvi (1946), 142, pl. XI; xliv (1954), 99–100; Toynbee (1963), 203,
no. 200, pl. 235; (1964), 241–6, pl. LVIII

[2] See H. Stern, *Dumbarton Oaks Papers*, xii (1958), 157–218, and, in particular,
fig. 36; *cf.* Cabrol/Leclercq, *s.v.* Mosaïque, fig. 8530

[3] See J. Lassus, 'Vénus marine', in Stern (1965), 175–91, fig. 3

[4] The motif appeared earlier in other media, *e.g.* in wall-paintings and mural
mosaics at Pompeii; *cf.* Mlle D. Joly, 'Quelques aspects de la mosaïque pariétale
au Ier siècle de notre ère d'après trois documents pompéiens', in Stern (1965),
57–75, figs. 1–33, *passim*; in Britain it was employed in relief on the sarcophagus of
Julia Victorina at York, generally attributed to the early 3rd century; see RCHM
(1962), 130, no. 107, pl. LVI, LIX; Toynbee (1964), 210–11, pl. L

(1965), fig. 6. Two cupids, bearing respectively a box and a basket, resembling the
personifications of Spring and Summer at Chedworth, are portrayed on the lid
of the silver bridal casket of A.D. 379–83 in the Esquiline Treasure: Volbach and
Hirmer (1961), 332–3, pl. 116, 117

estuary, lie the villas of Horkstow and Winterton in Lincolnshire. Both have produced Orpheus mosaics sufficiently similar to suggest that they were designed by the same mosaicist, while the employment of a concentric circular scheme seems further to imply that he had at least heard of those of the Corinian school. Winterton had the simpler of the two, comprising only Orpheus and animals (Pl. 3.17), but instead of the open concentric circular design of the Corinian Orpheus mosaics the zone of animals here was divided radially into eight compartments, each containing one animal with a tree behind it. The central panel, occupied by Orpheus, was octagonal, like the central panel of the Orpheus pavement at Woodchester.

This wheel-like scheme was repeated with elaboration at Horkstow (Fig. 3.2), the eight radial compartments there being each subdivided into four registers. The outermost registers were semicircular and each contained an animal with a tree behind it. The next were curved, concentrically with the outermost, and in each of these was a pair of confronted peacocks with a cluster of grapes between them. The next, again, depicted alternately a hound and a deer, and the innermost were simply fluted. The centre medallion, circular, was occupied by Orpheus. Four busts, of indeterminate sex, flanked by Maltese crosses but without any distinguishing attributes, filled the angles of the containing square.

In the adjacent panel of the same pavement was a second wheel-like design, set in a square frame of eight-strand guilloche. From a small circular centrepiece four 'spokes' radiated diagonally, intersecting a circle scribed from the centre, so that the four compartments between the 'spokes' were subdivided into outer and inner registers. Centrally in each of the outer registers and impinging slightly on the inner register was a medallion with two figures, male and female, on a blue background. On either side of these medallions, on a red background, was a group consisting of a nereid riding on the back of a sea-horse and accompanied by a triton and cupid. The inner register of each compartment seems to have contained, again on a red background, a frieze of cupids making garlands. The entire circular scheme was supported in the angles of the guilloche frame by four anguipede titans.

In a third panel of the same pavement was the well known chariot-race. This has no surviving parallel in Britain, but reproduces the essential features of such scenes wherever and in whatever medium they are found. Two features of the other two panels of this suite are, however, more especially notable in the present context. They are the wheel-like designs which, though not common, are known elsewhere in Britain,[1] while in other western provinces there are a few which offer more or less close parallels for the Orpheus panels of Horkstow and of Winterton[2] and yet

[1] At Bramdean (Hants.), Brantingham (E. Yorks.), Chedworth (Glos.),? Lincoln (Monson Street, *Arch. J.*, xvii (1860), 16), Whatley (Som., half of the design in an apse), Pitney (Som.), and Thruxton (Hants.). All of which adequate records survive were undoubtedly 4th-century.

[2] In Austria at Hemmaberg (H. Kenner, 'Römische Mosaiken aus Österreich', in Stern (1965), 91, fig. 18); in Germany at Münster-Sarmsheim (Parlasca (1959), 86ff., pl. 84, no. 2, 86, 87; see also p. 105, note 1); in Spain at Arróniz (*Ars Hispaniae*, ii, fig. 151); in Switzerland at Avenches, in a pavement dated by a tessellated inscription to 1 August in the year 209 (Blanchet and Lafaye (1909), i, no. 1389 = von Gonzenbach (1961), no. 5.1, pl. 79); and in Yugoslavia in two mosaics of Salona (D. Mano-Zissi, 'Mosaïques gréco-romaines de Yougoslavie', in Stern (1965), 289–90, figs. 4, 5). One of the Yugoslavian examples is a six-spoked wheel design, with Orpheus in the central medallion and a bird on a branch in each of the six surrounding compartments, while the other is a nine-spoked wheel with Apollo enshrined in the central medallion and standing figures of the Muses in the surrounding compartments (reproduced in colour in W. Gerber, *Forschungen in Salona*, i, 1915, pl. 1; *cf.* also E. Ceci, *I Monumenti Cristiani di Salona*, ii, 1963, pl. xix, 3). Mano-Zissi assigns the first, which is reminiscent of the Orpheus mosaic at Winterton, to the early 3rd century, and the second, which recalls the design at Horkstow, to the end of the 3rd century.

That the designs of many mosaics were influenced by the contemporary treatment of ceilings, domes, and vaults is nowhere more evident than in those of concentric circular and radial forms. The Orpheus mosaics of Horkstow, Winterton, and Salona immediately recall the wheel-like design attributed to the first half of the 3rd century, with the figure of Orpheus in the central octagonal medallion, of the painted dome-shaped vault in the catacomb of Domitilla: Northcote and Brownlow (1879), ii, fig. 4; Cabrol/Leclercq, *s.v.* Orphée, fig. 9237. Moreover, in the panel next to the Orpheus mosaic at Horkstow the concentric circular design is supported in the angles of the containing square by four anguipede titans, an idea well suited to a design for the interior of a dome, but rather pointless when applied to a floor; precisely comparable examples can be cited elsewhere, *e.g.* in Germany at Trier (Parlasca (1959), pl. 53) and in Switzerland at Avenches (von Gonzenbach (1961), no. 5.3, pl. 79). For the decoration of domes in late antiquity in general, see K. Lehman(-Hartleben), 'The dome of Heaven', *The Art Bulletin*, xxvii, no. 1 (1945), 1–27, and for a suggestion that the mosaic of Christ at Hinton St Mary 'could be regarded as the reflection of a "dome of heaven" ceiling design, with a central roundel, groins, lunettes, and squinches, projected on to the floor of the chamber', see *Hinton St Mary* (1964b), 14; cf. Toynbee (1964), 281 (Horkstow). This prompts the thought that such designs, and hence those of comparable mosaics, might have been influenced by designs of planispheres: compare, in particular, the radial designs of Horkstow with those of ancient planispheres illustrated in Stern (1963), pl. xxii–xxiv, xxxii, 5, xxxiii, 1, 3. The zodiacal mosaics of Palestine and other provinces must certainly have been adapted from such planispheres.

are almost certainly to be regarded as independent developments: all are late and most probably, in fact, of the 4th century. But the employment of a coloured background in this period is even less common, being recorded in Britain at only two sites other than that of Horkstow and equally rare on the Continent.[1] One of the British sites is that of Wood-chester (Glos.), where the water-nymphs in the angles of the Orpheus pavement are portrayed against a uniform background of dark blue tesserae. The other is Brantingham (E. Yorks.), near the site of Petuaria–Brough on Humber, and here (Pl. 3.19) this feature is associated, surely significantly, with a wheel-like design which has features recalling those of both Horkstow and Winterton. The centrepiece of this design is, as at Winterton, an octagonal panel. It is occupied, however, not by a representa-tion of Orpheus but by the nimbed head and shoulders of an enigmatic figure clad in a dalmatic, adorned with what appears to have been intended for a mural crown, and set against a red ground. Except for the absence of a *cornucopiae* the figure might be interpreted as a *tyche* or deity presiding over a particular territory or town. From the angles of the octagon radiate eight 'spokes', each terminating at a lunette based on one of the sides of an outer octagon concentric with that just described. In each lunette is a reclining water-nymph, while each of the interstitial spaces is occupied by an ungainly amphora. Here the incorporation of lunettes into an eight-spoked wheel design suggests comparison with the Orpheus panel at Horkstow, where the only difference from the point of view of the design was that the lunettes were placed *between* the 'spokes'. This octagonal design was set in a square, in at least one of the angles of which was a bi-furcated *pelta* with its central point drawn out to form a stem like that of a goblet and for which the only near-parallels are to be found in one of the mosaics at Winterton (Pl. 3.18).[2] On two opposite sides of the design was a row of four arcuate panels, each portraying the upper part of a nimbed figure without a crown, but otherwise more or less resembling that of the central octagon. Finally, panels of intersecting circles recall both Horkstow and Winterton, and the border of lozenges in oblongs outlined in red is

---

[1] In the present context perhaps the most interesting Continental example is the mosaic of Münster-Sarmsheim (see p. 104, note 2), in which the sun-god in his chariot is depicted against a dark ground in a medallion encircled by twelve radia-ting compartments containing the signs of the zodiac. Parlasca assigns it to the mid-3rd century.

[2] Fowler (1796–1818), no. 5

reminiscent of the border of lozenges in oblongs alternating with rectangles of chessboard pattern at Winterton.

Here, then, are three figured mosaics, each only a few miles from either of the other two, all with uncommon wheel-like designs and two with rarely employed coloured backgrounds. Add to these the borders of lozenges, patterns of intersecting circles, and highly individual goblet-stemmed *peltae* and it is impossible to resist the conclusion that the mosaics of Brantingham, Horkstow and Winterton are attributable to a single firm of mosaicists, for whom the obvious centre of operations would have been the small but not insignificant town of Petuaria.[1] In other words, these mosaics offer evidence for a Petuarian school serving not only the *vicus* of Petuaria itself but also villas on the south side of the Humber. It is interesting to note in this regard, since it could perhaps be significant for the dating of this school, that two geometric mosaics discovered at Brantingham in 1941 had been laid not earlier than *c*. 330–5. If they were produced by the men who laid the figured mosaic already described, their dating, taken with that of 'soon after A.D. 340' for the Orpheus and other figured mosaics at Winterton,[2] would suggest that the Petuarian school was active in the second quarter of the 4th century. It is necessary to add at once, however, that the relationship of the two geometric mosaics of 1941 to the figured mosaic of 1961 is not established.

More mosaics are needed in south Yorkshire and north Lincolnshire for the light that they might throw, not only on the dating of this putative school, but also on an important aspect of the works here attributed to it to which reference has not yet been made. This is the standard of execution of the figures. At Horkstow the horses of the chariot-race are tolerably well rendered, the charioteers themselves less so, but the animals, peacocks and mythological figures of the other two panels in the suite have a markedly primitive character[3] and the same can be said of the animals at Winterton.[4] At Brantingham, on the other hand, the standard is higher and the repertory quite unlike that either of Horkstow or of Winterton. Although at present inexplicable, these differences do not, however, obscure the relationships revealed by comparison of the basic designs and

---

[1] The town had a theatre in the 2nd century; *cf*. P. Corder and I. A. Richmond, *J.B.A.A.*, 3rd series, vii (1942), 1–30

[2] *Winterton* (1966), 79

[3] For details, see Hinks (1933), figs. 113, 114, 119, 121, 124

[4] Fowler (1796–1818), no. 1

other strictly geometric features of the figured mosaics of these three sites, or the implications that these relationships impose.

It must be noted in conclusion that primitivism is a characteristic of 4th-century figured pavements in the north. The most striking example from a villa, of course, is the 'Constantinian' mosaic of Venus from Rudston (E. Yorks., Pl. 3.20).[1] In this pavement the portrayal of the goddess is so gross that, but for the similarly inept figures of huntsmen and animals in the surrounding hunting scene, it could perhaps have been recognised simply as an amusing caricature. In fact, the ability as well as the educational level of the mosaicists here is clearly epitomised in the illiterate inscriptions, already mentioned (above, p. 95), which accompany two of the animals. But although it is tempting to think that the mosaicists may have been the same as those who produced the figured work, slightly less primitive, at Brantingham, Horkstow and Winterton, this is perhaps doubtful.[2] On the contrary it is not inconceivable that Rudston was itself the centre of operations of a group of mosaicists, for in one of the outbuildings of the villa the excavators discovered heaps of tesserae of different sizes and colours.[3] A precisely similar discovery is recorded in the probable centre of operations of the Durobrivan school, next to be described.

C. THE DUROBRIVAN SCHOOL

The existence of a Durobrivan school was first suggested in 1954, when mosaics of villas at Apethorpe, Castor (Mill Hill), Harpole, Nether Heyford and Great Weldon, all in Northamptonshire, at Medbourne in Leicestershire and Scampton in Lincolnshire were compared with those, newly excavated and dated by sealed coins to not earlier than c. 350–65, at Great Casterton in Rutland.[4] Since then studies of the mosaics at Denton (Lincs.), re-excavated in 1949 and dated by a sealed coin to not earlier than c. 370,[5] and at Great Staughton (Hunts.), excavated in 1958 and assigned to the 4th century,[6] have enabled these, and also that at Mansfield Woodhouse

[1] *Rudston* (1963a), pl. 1; *cf.* D. J. Smith (1965), fig. 3

[2] That is to say, I now share the reservations which Dr Stead as well as Mr D. S. Neal, who carefully drew the mosaics of Rudston *in situ* before their removal to Hull City Museum, have been good enough to express to me in correspondence; for my earlier view, see D. J. Smith (1965), 98–99

[3] *Rudston* (1936), 216; *cf.* p. 108, note 1

[4] D. J. Smith, 'The mosaic pavements', in *Great Casterton* (1954), 35–39

[5] Fowler (1796–1818), nos. 9, 10; *J.R.S.*, xl (1950), 100; *Denton* (1964)

[6] *J.R.S.*, xlix (1959), 118

(Notts.), which is stylistically related to them, to be added to this list. Thus, on grounds of distribution alone (Fig. 3.4) Durobrivae–Water Newton now seems even more probably to have been the centre for a flourishing school of mosaicists, and it may again be recalled that it was there that Artis excavated a building in which 'one of the rooms . . . had been a workshop still containing heaps of small sorted tessellae evidently manufactured upon the spot'.[1] It appears at present that the period of activity of this school covered at least the third quarter of the 4th century.

The works attributable to the Durobrivan school are so far entirely geometric. Considerations of space will permit mention only of the most characteristic of the patterns employed; but it must be observed that early 4th-century parallels for this can be found, again, in mosaics of the Corinian school.[2] This pattern is based on a star of eight lozenges which is repeated to form an all-over pattern with square and triangular interspaces containing guilloche knots, swastika-*peltae* or other simple filling motifs. The simplest, those of Great Casterton, Medbourne (Leics.) and Great Weldon (Pl. 3.21) are closely similar and may represent the Durobrivan school's earliest versions of the pattern. Those of Scampton (Lincs., Pl. 3.22) and Nether Heyford (Northants.) are slightly more varied and may therefore be later. The shape of the latter is not known, but the others just noted were oblong, while those remaining to be mentioned were square. The pattern at Roxby may be the earliest of these and was perhaps followed by that of Mansfield Woodhouse (Notts., Pl. 3.23). At Mill Hill (Pl. 3.24) the pattern approaches, and at Great Staughton (Pl. 3.25) arrives at, a still greater degree of elaboration and yet, paradoxically, the designer returned in these mosaics to the employment of the central octagon with frame of guilloche characteristic of the simple eight-lozenge star-pattern of two centuries earlier.[3] The ultimate degeneration of the pattern is seen

[1] C. Roach Smith, *Arch. Cant.*, xv (1883), 132. For an identical discovery at Rudston (E. Yorks.), see p. 107, note 3, and for another, also in a villa, at Pont d'Ancy (Aisne) in France, see Stern (1957), 19, 56. From these instances it seems possible to add to the list of industries associated with villas the manufacture of tesserae, if not actually the production of mosaics. Brick tesserae were certainly a by-product of the tilery near the villa at Ewhurst (Surrey): *Sy A.C.*, xlv (1937), 80

[2] Notably at the Barton Farm, in the pattern of a panel adjacent to the Orpheus mosaic (*Barton Farm* (1850), pl. viii; Toynbee (1963), pl. 221); but also, in its basic form of a square containing a single eight-lozenge star, at Newton St Loe (Som.), Stonesfield (Oxon.), and Woodchester (Glos.).

[3] *e.g.* at Colchester (Hull (1958), 78–79, pl. xvi, xviii; probably early Antonine), at Silchester (*Arch.*, xlvi (1881), 336–7, pl. xiii; thought to be late 2nd century), and at Verulamium (Wheeler (1936), 145, pl. xl, mosaic no. 6; mid-2nd century)

at Denton (Pl. 3.26) in its semi-obliteration by a chequered treatment[1] which is paralleled in one of the contemporary mosaics of Lydney Park (Glos.).[2] Perhaps by then the Durobrivan school was nearing the end of its life.

D. THE DURNOVARIAN SCHOOL

Even if there were no other mosaics related to those of Frampton (Dorset), these alone would suffice to indicate that there were craftsmen in this part of Britain with a distinctive repertory owing nothing to that of any of the three schools already identified. All were almost certainly laid at the same time and by the same mosaicists. The most important had a central medallion with a hunting scene and eight square panels depicting mythological episodes (Pl. 3.27). Its border consisted of a procession of dolphins, interrupted on one side by a figure of Cupid between two pairs of birds and on another by a mask of Neptune. On either side of the upper part of the mask was a panel containing a tessellated metrical inscription which began by calling attention to the sea-god's portrait, but proceeded, in two similar panels flanking the figure of Cupid, to extol the superior power of the god of love.[3] Immediately opposite the mask, however, at the centre of a scroll on the threshold of an apse also paved with mosaic, was a roundel in which the Chi-Rho had been worked in tesserae. In the apse itself there appears to have been a representation of a cantharus or chalice. Unfortunately this most interesting mosaic is not available for study, and may by now have perished, but there is nothing in Lysons's meticulous engraving of it to suggest that the Christian mosaic in the apse was not laid at the same time as the pavement of Cupid and Neptune.

Other mosaics at Frampton (Pl. 3.28) contained portraits of Bacchus, Neptune, a river-god, the Winds, other gods, representations of dolphins, 'sea-cows', and of more hunting scenes, a running-*pelta* pattern, and filling motifs of which twigs bearing pomegranates and eight-petalled flowers are particularly important for the establishment of the repertory of the school under discussion.

Conclusive proof of the existence of this local school came as recently as September 1963 with the discovery at Hinton St Mary (Dorset) of two

[1] Fowler (1796–1818), no. 9

[2] Wheeler (1932), 66, pl. 1 (frontispiece): 'secondary . . . and so is presumably a few years later than A.D. 367'

[3] *i.e.* as restored by F. Buecheler, *Anthologia Latina,* ii (1897): *Carmina Latina Epigraphica,* no. 1524

connected mosaics (Pl. 3.29), of dissimilar size, which afford strikingly close parallels for a number of distinctive features of the mosaics of Frampton. The centrepiece of the larger is a medallion in which is portrayed the bust of a male figure clad in tunic and pallium. Behind his head is the Chi-Rho monogram, on either side a pomegranate. Subsidiary subjects in surrounding panels comprise a tree of distinctive type, three hunting scenes and four male busts which, though without trumpets, otherwise almost exactly reproduce the portraits of the Winds at Frampton. There seems every reason to regard the central portrait as intended to represent Christ himself, and it is possible that these four subsidiary figures are to be interpreted as at least symbols of the evangelists whom St Irenaeus likened to the four winds.[1] If so, it is highly instructive to see how, to meet Christian requirements, the mosaicists could readily adapt, or de-paganise, stock figures of pagan deities; all that was necessary here was removal of the identifying attribute, the trumpet, and the awkward formation of the right arm of each figure strongly suggests that the transformation was not carried out in the workshop but on the site, perhaps at the last minute, and necessitated some makeshift recomposition.[2]

The room in which this mosaic lay was entered from a smaller anteroom, the plan of the suite—even to the threshold panel of running-*pelta* pattern between the two rooms—being almost exactly matched at Frampton.[3] Moreover, the geometric framework of the mosaic of the smaller room was identical at both sites, comprising a scroll-encircled medallion between two oblong panels. At both sites, again, these panels contained hunting scenes, but whereas at Hinton St Mary the medallion portrayed Bellerophon putting to death the Chimaera—a pagan tale but one capable of translation in Christian minds as the triumph of good over evil, at Frampton the corresponding subject was a representation of Bacchus and his sacred panther.

In the light of the Christian symbolism at Frampton and especially at Hinton St Mary, it seems more than probable, as has already been suggested (above, p. 87), that one of the mosaics of the villa at Fifehead Neville (Dorset) betrays a Christian choice of motifs (Pl. 3.30).

All these mosaics, then, as well as others in Dorset and Somerset, must

[1] See p. 88, notes 2 and 3
[2] I acknowledge here my indebtedness to discussions on the site with the excavator, Mr K. S. Painter.
[3] See *Frampton* (1813), pl. v, reproduced in full in Kendrick (1938), pl. xxi

have been produced—that is, prefabricated—in the same workshop, and it is not difficult to visualise the contents of the pattern-books from which the craftsmen worked. They comprised, besides mythological and hunting scenes, a range of portrait-busts,[1] individual figures, busts and masks of deities, particularly of those associated with the sea and rivers,[2] and representations of fish, convoluted sea-monsters and dolphins of a distinctive type,[3] while in addition to the pomegranate and eight-petalled flower the repertory of minor motifs included a foliate scroll, an ivy leaf with long, curling stem and a small square containing a guilloche knot. All these are represented in one or other of the mosaics of villas in Dorset at Fifehead Neville, Frampton, Hemsworth, Hinton St Mary and Wynford Eagle, and in Somerset at Lufton and Whatley.[4]

The distribution of these villas (Fig. 3.4) leaves little doubt that the workshop must have been established in Durnovaria–Dorchester, and details of two mosaics which have been found there tend to confirm this conclusion. One[5] exhibits four canthari, from the base of one of which spring two leaves, a curious feature matched by a cantharus with one leaf sprouting from its base at Hinton St Mary, while two of the others disgorge speckled serpents, recalling the speckled, serpent-like tail of the Chimaera in the same mosaic there. Moreover, the guilloche surrounding the circular centrepiece of the pavement in Dorchester is linked by a single strand with that of the squares both inside and outside it in a manner exactly paralleled

[1] At Fifehead Neville (Dorset, more than one), Frampton (Dorset, ten), Hemsworth (Dorset, one), Hinton St Mary (Dorset, five), Lufton (Som., probably four, but only one survived), and Whatley (Som., one).

[2] At Frampton (Neptune, river-god, winds), Hemsworth (marine Venus, river-god), and Hinton St Mary (winds, 'de-paganised').

[3] At Fifehead Neville (fish, sea-monsters), Frampton (dolphins, sea-monsters), Hemsworth (fish, sea-monsters), Wynford Eagle (Dorset, dolphins), Lufton (fish), and Whatley (dolphins, fish, sea-monsters). The dolphins of distinctive type are those of Frampton, Withington, and Wynford Eagle. It may be worth noting that a fish was preserved in an unpublished fragment of mosaic found at Low Ham (Som.), while another unpublished fragment preserved part of a scroll very reminiscent of that at Frampton; I am indebted to Mr H. S. L. Dewar for lending me photographs of these fragments.

[4] Recent study of the lithograph of the mosaic of Whatley has encouraged me to add this pavement to the list of those attributable to the Durnovarian school, not on grounds of style, because the lithograph clearly does not reproduce the mosaic with care, but on the evidence of several features characteristic of the repertory of this school. Also the mosaics of East Coker and Pitney, as well as Low Ham?

[5] From Durngate Street, 1905, now re-laid in Dorset County Museum, Dorchester. No published illustration; photograph in Dorset County Museum.

in the braiding together of the guilloche borders of the medallion and lunettes of the mosaic of Christ at Hinton St Mary and of medallions and panels at Frampton.

The other mosaic in Dorchester attributable to this workshop displays a mask of Neptune between fish and dolphins.[1] Compared with the conventionalised mask between dolphins at Frampton, the composition is more freely treated and is probably earlier. The motif was, of course, not exclusive to the works of the Durnovarian school or to the art of mosaic.[2] It appears, however, to have been one in which this school specialised over a period of some time. A representation of it in Cirencester[3] might be held to resemble in certain respects that of the Durnovarian pavement, but the resemblance is largely superficial and could be dismissed as coincidence were there not one other example in Gloucestershire which is, in fact, almost certainly attributable to the Durnovarian mosaicists. This is the bust of Neptune, as in Cirencester equipped with a trident but with dolphins swimming *out* of the god's mouth, in one of the suite of panels which includes the Orpheus mosaic at Withington (Pl. 3.11). This is the most conventionalised and therefore probably the latest of these four representations of this motif. Cirencester has already been identified as the centre of the flourishing early 4th-century Corinian school, and the Orpheus panel at Withington as one of that school's earlier products. Yet it is clear that the Orpheus panel and that of Neptune at Withington were laid at different times and by different mosaicists, those who produced the Neptune panel actually removing the key-pattern border on one side of the Orpheus panel, and the tail of a bird on another side, in order to make more room for their own work. Moreover, from a comparison of the dolphins of the Neptune panel with those of Frampton and Wynford Eagle, of its trees with those of Hinton St Mary,[4] and—most significant of

---

[1] From Fordington High Street, 1927, now re-laid in Dorset County Museum: *Ant. J.*, viii (1928), 237–8, pl. XLIII

[2] It appears, for example, in relief in the central medallion of the Neptune Dish in the Mildenhall Treasure (Brailsford (1955), pl. 1; Toynbee (1963), 169, no. 106, pl. 117; Toynbee (1964), 308–10, pl. LXXI, detail), and is recorded as having ornamented an altar, now apparently lost, found at Cramond, Scotland (Horsley (1732), 192, no. XXVIII); *cf.* p. 90, note 6. In Gaul the motif is known in a mosaic from St Rustice; Blanchet and Lafaye (1909), i, no. 376

[3] *Arch.*, lxix (1918), 176, no. 20. No published illustration; photograph in the Haverfield Library, Ashmolean Museum, Oxford.

[4] In particular, with the trunks of the trees and especially with that of the tree which occupies an entire lunette in the mosaic of Christ. An unpublished

3. 1   Eccles, Kent: mosaic of c.A.D. 65. Reconstruction drawing
by David S. Neal. Crown copyright

3. 2   Fishbourne, Sussex, c.A.D. 150-200. With acknowledgements to Chichester Civic Society and Fishbourne Excavation Committee. Photo David Baker

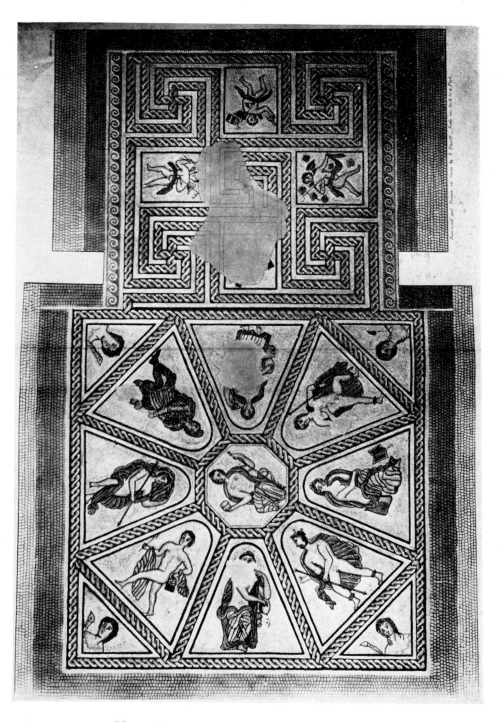

3. 3 Pitney, Som.: mosaic of Gods and Seasons. From the
coloured lithograph by Samuel Hasell, 1828

3.4 Bramdean, Hants.: the Gods of the Week. From a coloured engraving, 1839, in the Haverfield Collection, Ashmolean Museum

3. 5   Low Ham, Som.: mosaic of Dido and Aeneas.
Photo S. Brown

3. 6 Codex Vaticanus Latinus 3225: Aeneas at the court of Dido. Photo Vatican Library

3. 7 Lullingstone, Kent: the rape of Europa. With acknowledgement to Lt.-Col. G. W. Meates. Photo M. B. Cookson

3. 8 Brading, Isle of Wight: From the coloured lithograph in
J. E. and F. G. H. Price. *Remains. . . . . near Brading*, 1881

3. 9   Thruxton, Hants.: Bacchus and (?) the Seasons. From
the coloured engraving in *Arch. Jour.*, Salisbury Vol., 1851

3. 10   Newton St Loe, Som.: Orpheus. From the coloured
tracing by T. E. Marsh, 1837, preserved in Bristol City Museum

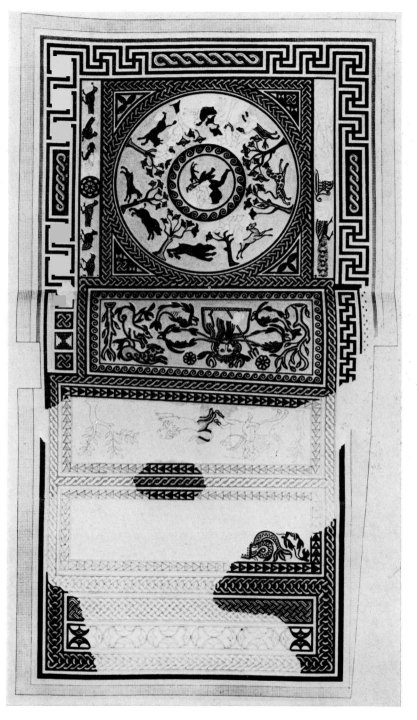

3. 11   Withington, Glos.: From the coloured engraving in S.
Lysons, *Reliquiae Britannico-Romanae* II, 1817, part i, Pl. XX

3. 12 Barton Farm, Cirencester, Glos.: Orpheus. From a coloured engraving in the Haverfield Collection, Ashmolean Museum

3. 13   Woodchester, Glos.: Orpheus mosaic. From the reconstruction (coloured engraving) by S. Lysons, *Roman Antiquities at Woodchester*, 1797, Pl. X

3. 14   Woodchester, Glos.: mosaic in Room 10. From the reconstruction (coloured engraving) by S. Lysons, *Roman Antiquities at Woodchester*, 1797, Pl. XIX

3. 15 Stonesfield, Oxon.: three mosaics. From a coloured
engraving in the Haverfield Library, Ashmolean Museum

3. 16 Littlecote Park, Wilts.: Orpheus and the Seasons. From
a coloured engraving in the Haverfield Collection, Ashmolean
Museum

3. 17 Winterton, Lincs.: mosaics of Orpheus and (?) Ceres.
From the coloured engraving by W. Fowler, 1796

A Roman tessellated Pavement discovered in the Year 1797 upon the estate of Mr. Jno. Lawrence, in the field of Winterton in Lincolnshire about three Miles from the River Humber

3. 18 Winterton, Lincs.: (?) Providentia. From the coloured engraving by W. Fowler, (?) 1799

3. 19 Brantingham, E. Yorks.: mosaic portraying a *tyche* and water-nymphs. Photo A. Pacitto, crown copyright

3. 20 Rudston, E. Yorks.: Venus and scenes from the amphitheatre. Photo Hull City Museums

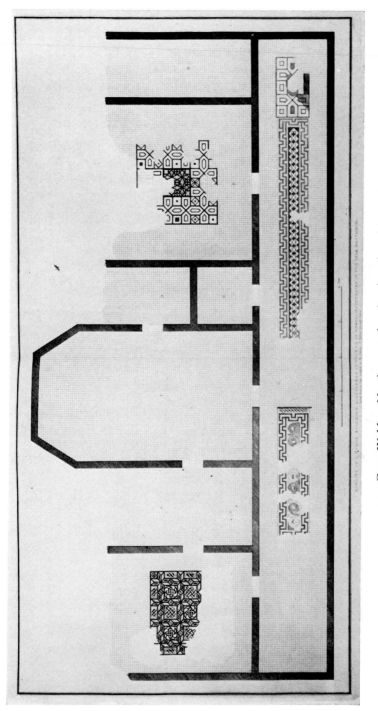

3. 21 Great Weldon, Northants.: plan showing disposition and patterns of mosaics. From the coloured engraving in S. Lysons, *Reliquiae Britannico-Romanae* I, 1813, part iv, Pl. VII.

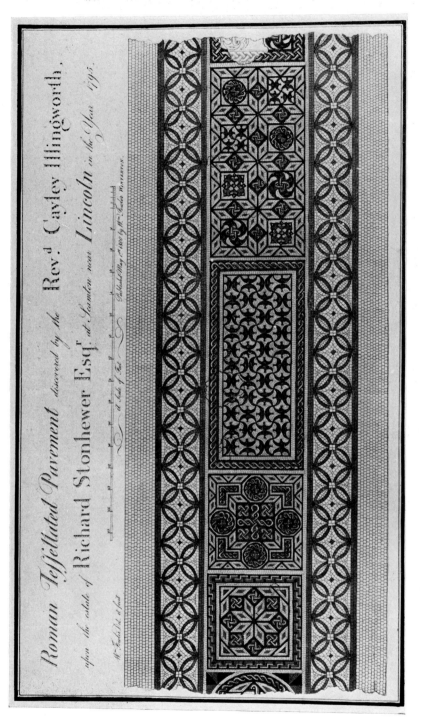

Roman Tessellated Pavement discovered by the Rev.d Cayley Illingworth. upon the estate of Richard Stonhewer Esq.r at Scampton near Lincoln in the Year 1795.

3. 22 Scampton, Lincs.: geometric corridor mosaic. From the coloured engraving by W. Fowler, 1800

3.23 Mansfield Woodhouse, Notts.: geometric mosaic. From the coloured engraving by W. Fowler, 1802

3. 24 Mill Hill, Castor, Northants.: geometric mosaic. From
the coloured engraving of 1823 in E. T. Artis, *Antiquities of the
Durobrivae* etc., 1828, Pl. XIX

Room 1

3. 25 Great Staughton, Hunts.: geometric mosaic. From a coloured scale drawing by Mrs. E. M. Minter

Roman Tessellated Pavement *discovered some years ago upon the estate of* William Gregory Williams Esq. *in the Lordship of* Denton *near* Grantham *in the County of* Lincoln.

a Scale of Feet

3. 26   Denton, Lincs.: geometric mosaic, c.A.D. 370. From the coloured engraving by W. Fowler, 1800

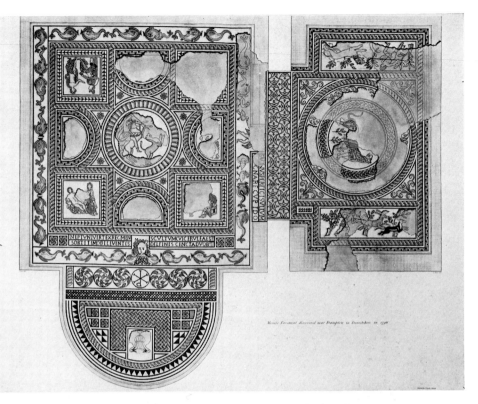

3. 27   Frampton, Dorset: mosaic of the Chi-Rho. From the
coloured engraving in S. Lysons, *Reliquiae Britannico-Romanae*
I, 1813, part iii, Pl. V

Mosaic Pavement discovered near Frampton in Dorsetshire

3. 28 Frampton, Dorset: mosaic of the river-god and Winds. From the coloured engraving in S. Lysons, *Reliquiae Britannico-Romanae* I, 1813, part iii, Pl. VII

3. 29 Hinton St. Mary, Dorset: mosaics of Christ and Bellerophon. With acknowledgements to the Trustees of the British
Museum. Photo R.C.H.M. (England), crown copyright

3. 30 Fifehead Neville, Dorset: (?) Christian mosaic. From a
water-colour by Miss E. Parker, 1800, preserved in Dorset
County Museum. Photo Dorset County Museum

3. 31   Lenthay Green, Sherborne, Dorset: Apollo and Marsyas.
Photo R.C.H.M. (England), crown copyright

3. 32   Woodchester, Glos. and Trier, Germany: from K. Parlasca, *Römische Mosaiken in Deutschland*, 1959, Pl. 50. With acknowledgements to K. Parlasca and the Römisch-Germanische Kommission des Deutschen Archäologischen Instituts

all—of the curious insertion of eight-petalled flowers on either side of the head with precisely the same feature at Hinton St Mary, it is as certain as it can be that the craftsmen who made this panel and the three others which went with it were mosaicists of the Durnovarian school. This is one of the most intriguing conclusions to emerge from recognition of the work of a number of distinct schools of mosaicists in Britain in the 4th century. The Orpheus panel at Withington has been attributed to the Corinian mosaicists, and the geometric pavements there were certainly their work. Why, then, should the proprietor of this villa have sent to Durnovaria for the craftsmen of evidently inferior ability who executed the Neptune panel? The most probable explanation is that when the Neptune panel was laid the Corinian school no longer existed. If this is so, it follows that this panel—and the three panels that went with it—must be later than the latest works attributable to the Corinian school, which appear to be among those of Chedworth or Tockington Park or perhaps Wigginton,[1] and that a northward expansion or movement of mosaicists of the Durnovarian school is a possibility worth bearing in mind.

Epilogue

What, in conclusion, is the significance of these mosaics for the study of the villa in Britain and for the economic and social history of the province at large? The first point of importance to emerge from a survey of them is that with few exceptions they can be regarded as a phenomenon of the period c. A.D. 300–70. This conclusion is supported by numismatic and other evidence. It implies that this was the optimum period for the villa estates in Britain, and the implication is of the utmost interest when compared with the contemporary situation in adjacent provinces on the Continent. There the Germanic incursions of 260–75 appear to have dealt

[1] See p. 97, note 1

---

photograph, preserved in the Dept of British and Medieval Antiquities of the B.M., shows part of a mosaic uncovered at Cherhill (Wilts.) with a tree of very similar type and a border of open triangles, placed apex to base, such as framed one of the Durnovarian mosaicists' panels at Withington; it seems probable, therefore, that this was another late product of the Durnovarian school, and if so it supports the suggestion that the school ultimately moved or extended its sphere of activity farther north.

a fatal blow to villa life, for neither in north Gaul nor in the provinces bordering the Rhine is there comparable evidence of rural prosperity in the 4th century.[1]

From this contrast of contemporary events on either side of the Channel the Romano-British villa-mosaics thus emerge with enhanced importance. For they can be regarded for practical purposes as the only substantial body of material of their kind and period north of the Alps, and one is bound to wonder to what this outburst of activity in Britain might be attributed. In particular, it is tempting to ask whether there may not have been a direct connection between the end of villa life in Gaul and Germany in the last quarter of the 3rd century and the remarkable surge of villa-building and renovation that seems to have begun in Britain just before c. A.D. 300.[2] Was there, to put it baldly, a 'flight of capital' from the troubled areas of the Continent to the relative security of this island? The idea is attractive, for this may have been at least one of the factors in the wide-spread evidence of investment in town[3] as well as country property that can be inferred from the dating of the vast majority of Romano-British mosaics.

The differential distribution of the villa-mosaics suggests that in certain parts of the province investment paid exceptionally handsome dividends. In particular, it may be recalled that some 50 per cent of them are con-centrated in what today are the counties of Gloucestershire, Somerset and Dorset. This, of course, does not necessarily mean that here was the richest part of Britain in the 4th century, though it may well have been, but it certainly indicates that many landowners in the south-west enjoyed a superfluity of wealth and that they were prepared to invest some of it in the reconstruction and embellishment of their country houses. Investment of wealth in this way is one of the surest signs of rural peace and prosperity

---

[1] cf. von Gonzenbach (1961), 336; Parlasca (1959), 49ff.; Stern (1957), 19–20, (1960), 10 and note 2, (1963), 10–11

[2] Coin-lists in which the numbers become significant with issues of c. 270 and onward are a regular feature of the literature on Romano-British villas. For an analysis of the extensive collection at Chedworth, see T.B.G.A.S., lxxviii (1960), 162–5, and for an independent attribution of the rise of the large villas of 4th-century Britain to a class of wealthy immigrants from the Continent see now S. Applebaum, in Thomas (1966), 104

[3] At Verulamium the excavation of only a small part of the site was sufficient to produce evidence of extensive rebuilding, with at least five mosaics, c. A.D. 300: Wheeler (1936), passim (for the mosaics, 142–8, nos. 3, 4, 5, 9, 11, and 13, pl. XLII, XLIIIA, XLIIIB, XLIVA, XLVIB, XLVIIIB)

and, even more important, of a settled outlook. There is, then, evidence here which should be of interest to the economic and social historian.

So far as it is possible to see at present, the mosaics of the Corinian school suggest that in the West Country the era of prosperity came in towards the end of the 3rd century, those of the Durnovarian school that in Dorset it may not have arrived before the beginning of the 4th century, and those of the Petuarian school that in south Yorkshire and north Lincolnshire it may not have come until relatively late in the reign of Constantine I (306–37). The dating of the mosaics of the Durobrivan school, on the other hand, implies that in the east midlands the wave of affluence did not break until the third quarter of the century, and this raises the question whether the basis of prosperity was everywhere the same. It is, in fact, improbable that this was so; for while the production of wool[1] might account for that of the Dorset downland,[2] the Cotswolds[3] and the Wolds of Lincolnshire and Yorkshire, it is unlikely to explain that of the east midlands, where the most obvious sources would have been cereal cultivation[4] and the thriving industry of the Water Newton and other potteries.[5]

The identification and dating[6] of these schools of mosaic are thus at least potentially of great importance for the study of Britain in the 4th century. It is probably not an exaggeration to say that there is no clearer evidence for the existence of such schools in any province.[7] What is not at present at all clear, however, is their origin and ultimate fate. As to

[1] cf. Collingwood (1932), 71; Collingwood and Myres (1937), 239–40; Richmond (1963), 131, 163; Rivet (1964), 123–4

[2] cf. Hawkes (1948), 33–45, 48, 71

[3] Though the 'fullery' at Chedworth has now been shown to be only a bath-suite; I. A. Richmond, T.B.G.A.S., lxxviii (1960), 5–23; J.R.S., l (1960), 230

[4] Mention of the shipment of corn to the Rhineland in A.D. 361 is almost certainly not unconnected with the prosperity of the Durobrivan school of mosaicists.

[5] It is interesting to recall here the mosaic of Apethorpe (Northants.), which had in its four angles what appear to have been slightly conventionalised representations of the small beakers of 'Castor' ware of a type produced in vast quantities by the Water Newton potteries during the later 3rd and 4th centuries.

[6] No problems in the study of Romano-British mosaics are more in need of elucidation than those of the origin, floruit, and fate of these schools and the dates of the individual works attributable to them. The results of the re-excavation of Denton show that much might be learnt from careful re-examination of other sites already once, or even more than once, explored.

[7] For a wide-ranging survey of schools of mosaic in the Roman Empire, see Stern (1965)

their fate, the life of any one of them will have been entirely dependent on the duration of local demand for their products.[1] But where did the master craftsmen who founded or directed them come from, and where did they go when demand had been satisfied? It might be thought that the answers to these questions should not be difficult to determine, that it should be possible to recognise elsewhere, even in other provinces, mosaics which can be regarded as precursors or successors of those of one or more of these schools. Yet while it is conceivable that the repertories of the Petuarian and of the Durobrivan schools respectively owe certain elements to that of the Corinian school, the highly distinctive motifs which characterise that of the Durnovarian school do not seem to reappear elsewhere except at Withington (Glos.), Cherhill (Wilts.) and possibly in Cirencester, while there is only one known parallel for a complete design of the Corinian school.

This single instance of the repetition of a design of the Corinian school elsewhere strikingly re-emphasises, however, this school's importance. For it amounts to almost an exact parallel between a panel in the border of the Orpheus mosaic at Woodchester and part of a mosaic uncovered in the Palastplatz in Trier (Pl. 3.32).[2] Both pavements have been assigned on grounds of style to the Constantinian period[3] and the only means of deciding which is the earlier within that period is by a comparison of details. In fact, the mosaic in Trier is slightly more evolved and may perhaps be regarded as the later of the two.[4] If so, it would appear that the master who standardised the Orpheus mosaics and designed the later geometric pavements of the Corinian school eventually moved on to the new capital of the West on the banks of the Mosel. Had his reputation preceded him, and was he perhaps invited or summoned there by some imperial official connected with the villa at Woodchester?

This leads back to the question of the class of society which provided the mosaicists' clientele in 4th-century Britain. It has been suggested above that the figured mosaics, if sympathetically interpreted, may offer a valuable guide to the intellectual and spiritual inclinations of the villa-

[1] Elsewhere I have ventured to guess that mosaicists looking for employment in any ordinary Romano-British town and its surrounding country houses could hardly have expected to have work for more than ten or twenty years; see Stern (1965), 113

[2] Parlasca (1959), 50, pl. 50; *cf.* D. J. Smith (1965), 113, fig. 18 (after Parlasca).

[3] For the dating of the mosaic in Trier, see Parlasca, *loc. cit.*

[4] *cf.* D. J. Smith (1965), 114, and notes 82, 83

3. 1 Bignor, Sussex: head of Venus. With acknowledgements to Capt. H. Tupper. Photo David Baker

3. 2 Hinton St Mary, Dorset: head of Christ. With acknowledgements to the Trustees of the British Museum. Photo D. S. Smith.

proprietors.[1] Interpretation and, still more, inference here all too often mean skating on thin ice, but these mosaics present a challenge and an opportunity which cannot be ignored. The question is, *how* are they to be interpreted: allegorically, eschatologically, as straightforward illustrations of or allusions to literary texts, with whatever that might imply, or simply as all that the local mosaicist's pattern-book had to offer and therefore not necessarily of any intrinsic significance at all? Here thought reverts at once to the mosaic of Dido and Aeneas from Low Ham (Som.), which stands not only as the most obviously 'literary' mosaic in Britain but also as a reminder that Roman mosaicists were capable of producing, if required, a work unique and quite outside the normal repertory of any known school or pattern-book.[2] Supported by the clear evidence of familiarity with the *Aeneid* afforded by this mosaic, as well as by its contemporary at Lullingstone (Kent), it is possible to contend that a choice of mythological scenes was perhaps more often than not inspired by favourite passages in the classics, and even, more frequently than one might formerly have been prepared to admit, actually copied from illustrations in manuscripts. For the intellectual culture of late Roman Britain in general, and for that of villa society in particular, these two pavements and the numerous others depicting mythological scenes may, therefore, have a real significance.

Equally important, but from a different viewpoint, is the mosaic of Hinton St Mary (Dorset). This contains, as has already been observed, the

---

[1] *cf.* Richmond (1963), 121–2; Toynbee (1963), 12

[2] As hinted on p. 111, note 3, there is reason to suspect that craftsmen of the Durnovarian school may have laid at least one pavement at Low Ham, and though there is nothing in the mosaic of Dido and Aeneas that betrays their handiwork, the possibility that this also may be attributable to them cannot be ruled out. The absence, among the several thousand mosaics recorded in North Africa, of any parallels for the Low Ham scenes seems to me to outweigh the suggestion that these were produced by an African mosaicist or from an African pattern-book; Toynbee (1963), 205, and (1964), 246. Much more suggestive of African influence in this part of Britain is the fragment from East Coker (Som.) depicting two huntsmen supporting on their shoulders a pole from which a dead deer is slung by the feet, with a small dog sitting between the huntsmen and looking up or barking at the creature. For this motif almost every parallel seems to be found in Africa or in mosaics with obvious African affinities, *i.e.* at Carthage (twice: *Mémoires de la Société Nationale des Antiquaires de France*, lxiii (1902), pl. iii, and *Dumbarton Oaks Papers*, xvii (1963), fig. 79), at Constantine, Algeria (*Dumbarton Oaks Papers*, xvii (1963), fig. 84), at Cyrene (*Arch. Anzeiger*, 1959, fig. 45), and at Piazza Armerina, Sicily (twice: G. V. Gentili, *La Villa Erculia di Piazza Armerina: I Mosaici Figurati*, figs. 4, 5, that of the latter—the Great Hunt—terminating at one end at an apse with personification of Africa in mosaic). These mosaics range in date from the 4th to the 6th century.

earliest known portrayal of Christ in a floor-mosaic, accompanied by 'de-paganised' personifications of the four winds, a representation of a tree which was clearly intended to be regarded as of special importance, hunting scenes, canthari, and a medallion depicting Bellerophon killing the Chimaera. Here, then, are a number of motifs which, excepting the Chi-Rho, would not individually or even in association necessarily have suggested Christian influence. But the presence of the Chi-Rho lays each and every one of them open to interpretation in terms of Christian symbol and allegory. Thus, Bellerophon killing the Chimaera can here be seen allegorically as the triumph of good over evil, and the other motifs as each having likewise a special meaning for the early Christian.[1] Much emphasis has lately been laid on the interpretation in allegorical or eschatological terms, pagan or Christian, of figured scenes and representational motifs in Roman art;[2] yet it is surely necessary to discriminate between the possible significance of a given scene or motif in one context and that of the same scene or motif in quite a different context. At Lullingstone (Kent), for example, the reason for the choice of a representation of the rape of Europa is implicit in the accompanying metrical inscription and suggests that the portrayal of Bellerophon's victory over the Chimaera in the associated mosaic might likewise be attributable to the inspiration of a literary account of this hero's adventures. In short, if there is any universal rule to be followed in questions of interpretation it is that each mosaic, every scene and motif, can legitimately be analysed only with due regard for its context.

Finally, it seems necessary to stress the essential *Romanitas* of the villa-mosaics of 4th-century Britain. True, they have a distinctive, provincial character of their own, but so have those of every other province. It may confidently be said, however, that there is no element in them which can be attributed to conscious derivation from the alien repertory of Celtic art[3] or to the influence of Celtic religion. And only in singularly few instances, such as the exploitation of colour, primitive features of the figures, treatment of Venus's hair, and illiterate inscriptions at Rudston

---

[1] *cf.* J. M. C. Toynbee, *J.R.S.*, liv (1964), 14

[2] Toynbee (1963), *passim*; (1964), *passim*; *J.R.S.*, liv (1964), 11

[3] *cf.* Toynbee (1963), 11. It is even more difficult, *pace* Kendrick (1938), 32–36, to see a 'possible immediate connexion' between the designs of 4th-century mosaics in south-west Britain and those of decorative pages in Hiberno-Saxon manuscripts, unless it be that both derive from late antique developments in the art of manuscript illustration. This is, however, only one of several thought-provoking ideas in Kendrick's brief but shrewd review of Romano-British mosaics.

(E. Yorks., Pl. 3. 20), or the lentoid form of the eyes of Apollo and Marsyas at Lenthay Green (Dorset, Pl. 3.31), and possibly the introduction of chequering—normally a minor feature, but in one of the mosaics of Denton (Lincs., Pl. 3.26) almost obliterating the design[1]—do the sublimated aesthetic instincts of the native craftsman supervene. In other words, with exceptions so few as to be insignificant in number, the villa-mosaics owe nothing to the late La Tène tradition of pre-Roman lowland Britain and everything, however modified or even debased, to the art of the Graeco-Roman world.

SELECT BIBLIOGRAPHY OF VILLAS WITH MOSAICS

BRECONSHIRE

Llanfrynach   *Arch.*, vii (1785), 205–10, pl. xvii; *B.B.C.S.*, xiii (1949), 106–7, fig. 1

BUCKINGHAMSHIRE

High Wycombe *Records of Bucks.*, xvi (1959), 222–57 (note on the mosaics by D. J. Smith, 249–53, pl. ix); Toynbee (1964), 274

DORSET

Fifehead Neville V. L. Oliver, 'Roman tessellated pavements in Dorset' (MS.), and water-colour drawings in Dorset County Museum; *P.D.N.H.A.F.C.*, xxiv (1903), lxxiv–lxxvi, 172–7, figures; D. J. Smith (1965), 95–116, fig. 9

Frampton   Lysons (1813), 1–6, pl. i–vii; Kendrick (1938), pl. xx, 1, xxi; Toynbee (1963), 202, no. 199, pl. 234; (1964), 250–2; D. J. Smith (1965), 95–116, figs. 6, 7

Hemsworth   Hinks (1933), 99, no. 33, pl. xxx; Toynbee (1964), 252, pl. lixa; D. J. Smith (1965), 95–116

Hinton St Mary *P.D.N.H.A.F.C.*, lxxxv (1964), 5–10, plate; *J.R.S.*, liv (1964), 7–14, fig. 1, frontispiece, pl. i–vii; D. J. Smith (1965), 95–116, fig. 5; *B.M. Quarterly* xxxii (1967), 15–31

[1] Fowler (1796–1818), no. 9; *cf.* the similar treatment of a running-*pelta* pattern in a contemporary pavement at Lydney Park (Glos.), where the presence of native British *tesserarii* is certainly indicated by the form of the heads of the entwined sea-monsters in the dedicatory mosaic in the temple: Wheeler (1932), pl. i (frontispiece, running-*pelta* pattern), xixA (dedicatory mosaic). For the Celtic character of these heads, *cf.* especially a small bronze head from Ham Hill, Somerset (VCH, Som., i (1906), fig. 63, opp. 296, no. 12); and on chequerwork as a feature of late Romano-British mosaics, see Kendrick (1938), 40

Lenthay Green RCHM, *Dorset*, i (1952), 199, pl. 127, 2; Toynbee (1964), 252

Wynford Eagle Photographs in Dorset County Museum; D. J. Smith (1965), 95–116

GLAMORGAN

Llantwit Major Coloured lithograph by J. John (1888); *Arch. Camb.*, cii (1953), 89–163

GLOUCESTERSHIRE

Barton Farm, Cirencester
J. Buckman and C. H. Newmarch, *Remains of Roman Art in . . . Corinium* (1850), 32, pl. VIII; *J.B.A.A.*, xxv (1869), 101–4, pl. 2–6; *T.B.G.A.S.*, xxxiii (1910), 67–77; lxx (1952), 51–53, pl. I, II; Toynbee (1963), 198, no. 185, pl. 221; (1964), 268, pl. LXIa; D. J. Smith (1965), 95–116

Chedworth
J.B.A.A., xxiv (1868), 129–35, pl. 10, 11; *Arch. J.*, xliv (1887), 322–36; *T.B.G.A.S.*, lxxviii (1960), 162–5 (coin list); Toynbee (1963), 199, no. 187, pl. 214–17; (1964), 266–8, pl. LXIIa; D. J. Smith (1965), 95–116, fig. 14

Comb End
Arch., ix (1789), 319–22; xviii (1817), 112–13

Frocester Court
J.R.S., l (1960), 230; lii (1962), 182; liii (1963), 143, fig. 26

Great Witcombe
Coloured engravings of a geometric and an aquatic mosaic by S. Lysons and (? his) pen and water-colour sketch-plan of another geometric mosaic are preserved in the Gloucestershire volume of the Topographical Collections of the Society of Antiquaries of London; *Arch.*, xix (1821), 178–83

Hucclecote
T.B.G.A.S., lv (1933), 323–76

Kings Weston Park
T.B.G.A.S., lxix (1950), 5–58, pl. I–VII

Rodmarton
Arch., xviii (1817), 113–16

Spoonley Wood
An engraving illustrating three geometric mosaics is preserved in the 'Brown Portfolios' of the Society of Antiquaries of London (Durham, Essex and Gloucestershire vol, p. 88); *J.B.A.A.*, xxxviii (1882), 215; *T.B.G.A.S.*, xiv (1889–90), 208; *Arch.*, lii (1890), 651–68

Tockington Park
T.B.G.A.S., xii (1888), 159–69, pl. V–VIII, XIII; D. J. Smith (1965), 95–116

Whittington Court
T.B.G.A.S., lxxi (1953), 13–87, plate facing p. 13, pl. I–XIV

Withington   *Arch.*, xviii (1817), 118–21; Lysons II (1817), part i, pl. xviii–xxi; Hinks (1933), 111, no. 37, figs. 125–8; Toynbee (1964), 271; D. J. Smith (1965), 95–116, fig. 11

Woodchester   Pen and water-colour drawing of a segment of the Orpheus mosaic by R. Bradley, dated 31 July 1722, in the B.M. (Add. MSS. 5238, folio 3); S. Lysons, *An Account of Roman Antiquities discovered at Woodchester* (1797); Lysons II (1817), part i, pl. xxii–xxvii; *T.B.G.A.S.*, xlviii (1927), 75–96; lxxiv (1956), 172–5; Toynbee (1963), 198, no. 186, pl. 222; (1964), 272–4, pl. lxib, c, lxiib; D. J. Smith (1965), 95–116, figs. 17, 18

HAMPSHIRE AND ISLE OF WIGHT

Brading (I.W.)   J. E. and F. G. H. Price, *A Description of the Remains of Roman Buildings at Morton, near Brading, I.W.* (1881, reprinted from *Trans. of the Royal Institute of British Architects*, 1880–1, 125ff.); Morgan (1886), 234–9, plates; VCH, Hants., i (1900), 313–16, figs. 22–24; Toynbee (1963), 201–2, nos. 195–7, pl. 231–3; (1964), 254–8

Bramdean   C. R. Smith (1852), 54–64, pl. xxi, xxii; VCH, Hants., i (1900), 307–8, figs. 18, 19; Toynbee (1964), 258

Fullerton   *Athenaeum*, 25 Feb. 1905, 250; Toynbee (1964), 258; *J.R.S.*, liv (1964), 174

Itchen Abbas   *J.B.A.A.*, xxxiv (1878), 233–4, 258, plate facing p. 504; Morgan (1886), 221, plates; VCH, Hants., i (1900), 307; Toynbee (1964), 259

Thruxton   RAI, Salisbury vol. (1851), 241–5, plate; Hinks (1933), 101, no. 35, fig. 111; Toynbee (1964), 259

HUNTINGDONSHIRE

Great Staughton   *J.R.S.*, xlix (1959), 118, fig. 15; l (1960), 224, 225, fig. 26. Report on excavation by E. Greenfield in preparation, with note on the mosaics by D. J. Smith

KENT

Eccles   *Arch. Cant.*, lxxviii (1963), 125–41; lxxix (1964), 121–35; *J.R.S.*, liii (1963), 158, fig. 35; liv (1964), 177, fig. 27. Excavations by A. P. Detsicas still (1967) in progress

Lullingstone   *Arch. Cant.*, lxiii (1951), 1–49; *Lullingstone* (1955); Toynbee (1963), 200–1, nos. 192–3, pl. 228–9; (1964), 262–5, pl. lx; G. W. Meates, *Lullingstone Roman Villa* (H.M.S.O., guide-book, 1962)

LEICESTERSHIRE

Medbourne   VCH, Leics., i (1907), 214, pl. vii; Kendrick (1938), pl. xix, 2

LINCOLNSHIRE

Denton   Fowler (1796–1818), nos. 9, 10; *J.R.S.*, xl (1950), 100; l (1960), 221, 222, fig. 24; *Lincolnshire Architectural and Archaeological Society Reports and Papers*, x (1964), 75–104

Horkstow   Fowler (1796–1818), no. 2; Lysons I (1813), part i, 1–4, pl. i–vii; Hinks (1933), 101, no. 36, figs. 112–24; Toynbee (1963), 202, no. 198, pl. 227; (1964), 280–2; D. J. Smith (1965), 95–116, fig. 1

Roxby   Fowler (1796–1818), no. 3

Scampton   Fowler (1796–1818) no. 8 = plate in C. Illingworth, *A Topographical Account of the Parish of Scampton* (1808)

Sturton   Fowler (1796–1818), appendix ii, nos. 10, 11

Winterton   Society of Antiquaries of London, *Vetusta Monumenta*, ii (1789), pl. 9; Fowler (1796–1818), nos. 1, 5; *J.R.S.*, xlix (1959), 109, pl. viii, 1; l (1960), 221; Toynbee (1964), 282–3; D. J. Smith (1965), 95–116, fig. 2. Report on re-excavation by I. M. Stead in preparation, with study of the mosaics by D. J. Smith

NORTHAMPTONSHIRE

Apethorpe   VCH, Northants., i (1902), 191, figs. 19, 20

Castor, Mill Hill   Artis (1828); VCH, Northants., i (1902), 172, fig. 7

Great Weldon   Coloured engraving (1739) in the Northamptonshire volume of the Topographical Collections of the Society of Antiquaries of London; inferior copy in Lysons I (1813), part iv, 4, pl. vii; VCH, Northants., i (1902), 192, fig. 22 (after Lysons); *J.R.S.*, xliv (1954), 93, 95, fig. 15; xlv (1955), 135; xlvi (1956), 131, 133, fig. 32. Report on re-excavation by D. J. Smith, with note on the mosaics, in preparation

Harpole   VCH, Northants., i (1902), 197, fig. 25

Nether Heyford   VCH, Northants., i (1902), 196, fig. 24

NOTTINGHAMSHIRE

Mansfield Woodhouse   Fowler (1796–1818), no. 16; VCH, Notts., ii (1910), 28, fig. 12

Oldcoates (Styrrup)   *Arch. J.*, xxviii (1871), 66–67; xliii (1886), 32–34; *B.B.C.S.*, xviii (1959), 304–10

Southwell   VCH, Notts., ii (1910), 34; *J.R.S.*, l (1960), 223, fig. 25.
             Trans. Thoroton Society lxx (1966), 13–54, with note on the
             mosaics by D. J. Smith, 33–40, figs. 11–13, pls. 2–3

OXFORDSHIRE

North Leigh H. Hakewill, *An Account of the Roman Villa discovered at
             Northleigh*, etc. (1826); VCH, Oxon., i (1939), 316–18,
             fig. 33; D. J. Smith (1965), 95–116, fig. 16

Stonesfield VCH, Oxon., i (1939), 315–16, pl. xxiv; *Oxoniensia*, vi
             (1941), 1–8, pl. i, ii; Toynbee (1964), 274; D. J. Smith
             (1965), 95–116, fig. 15

Wigginton   *Gents. Mag.*, 1824, ii, 359; A. Beesley, *History of Banbury*
             (1848), 41–43, pl. xi; VCH, Oxon., i (1939), 309, fig. 28.
             Re-excavation by E. Greenfield now (1967) in progress

RUTLAND

Great Casterton P. Corder (ed.), *The Roman Town and Villa at Great
             Casterton, Rutland.* First Interim Report (1951), 15ff., pl.
             ib; Second Interim Report (1954), 1–47 (note on the
             mosaics by D. J. Smith, 35–39, pl. xii, xiii)

SOMERSET

Brislington W. R. Barker, *Account of Remains of a Roman Villa dis-
             covered at Brislington, Bristol, December 1899* (1901)

East Coker   *Gents. Mag.*, 1753, 293; hence *ibid.*, *Library of Romano-
             British Remains* (1887), i 40; C. R. Smith (1852), 51, 52,
             pl. xx; VCH, Somerset, i (1906), 329, figs. 86–88; C.
             A. Ralegh Radford and H. S. L. Dewar, *The Roman
             Mosaics from Low Ham and East Coker* (Somerset County
             Museum Publications, no. 2, 1954), 5–6; Toynbee (1964),
             239

Keynsham   *Arch.*, lxxv (1926), 109–38, figs. 2–6, pl. xi–xiii, xv–
             xviii; Toynbee (1964), 240–1, pl. lvii

Littleton   *Gents. Mag.*, 1827, ii, 113–14; hence *ibid.*, *Library of
             Romano-British Remains* (1887), i, 289

Low Ham   *J.R.S.*, xxxvi (1946), 142, pl. xi; xxxvii (1947), 173;
             xxxix (1949), 109; xliv (1954), 99–100; C. A. Ralegh
             Radford and H. S. L. Dewar, op. cit., 3–5, plate; Toyn-
             bee (1963), 203, no. 200, pl. 235; (1964), 241–6, pl. lviii

Lufton   *P.S.A.N.H.S.*, xcvii (1953), 91–112, fig. 3, pl. vi–ix;
             Toynbee (1963), 201, no. 194, pl. 230; *J.R.S.*, lii (1962),
             182; Toynbee (1964), 246; D. J. Smith (1965), 95–116

Newton St Loe MS. record of discovery and excavation (1837–8) by T.
E. Marsh and his coloured tracing of the Orpheus panel
in Bristol City Museum; W. Ll. Nichols, *Description of the
Roman Villa discovered at Newton St. Loe* (1838); *J.R.S.*,
xxvi (1936), 43–46, figs. 4–6, pl. vii–ix; Toynbee (1964),
247; D. J. Smith (1965), 95–116, fig. 10

Pitney, Roman Pen and water-colour drawings by S. Hasell in Somerset
Farm   County Museum. These were published as lithographs;
hence the illustrations in VCH, Somerset, i (1906), 326–8,
figs. 84–86; Toynbee (1964), 248

Whatley   Coloured lithograph (undated but probably *c.* 1837 or
1838), of which a print is preserved in Somerset County
Museum, published by Bedford's Lithography, Bristol;
hence the illustration in VCH, Som., i (1906), 317, fig.
77; Toynbee (1964), 249

SURREY

Walton Heath   Pen and water-colour drawing of the mosaic by J. Baber
(? Barber) in the Haverfield Library, Ashmolean
Museum, Oxford; *Sy A.C.*, ii (1849), 1–13; VCH, Surrey,
iv (1912), 369; *Sy A.C.*, li (1950), 65–81

SUSSEX

Angmering   *Sx A.C.*, lxxix (1938), 3–44
Bignor   Lysons III (1817); *Arch.*, xviii (1817), 203–21; xix (1821),
176–7; S. E. Winbolt and G. Herbert, *The Roman Villa at
Bignor* (guide-book, 1934); Toynbee (1963), 199–200,
nos. 188–91, pl. 218, 223–6; (1964), 260–2, pl. lixb;
J.R.S., liii (1963), 155, fig. 34
Fishbourne   *Ant. J.*, xlii (1962), 15–23, pl. ix–xii; xliii (1963), 1–14;
xliv (1964), 1–8, pl. i–x; xlv (1965), 1–11, figs. 1, 2, pl.
i–x; Toynbee (1964), 236–8, 262, pl. lvi; *Ant.*, xxxix,
no. 155 (Sept. 1965), 177–83, frontispiece, pl. xxxv,
xxxvi

WILTSHIRE

Bromham   Hoare (1819), 123, figure
Calne Without *Gents. Mag.*, 1796, i, 472–3
Cherhill   Photograph preserved in Dept. of British and Medieval
Antiquities, B.M.
Colerne   *Arch. J.*, xiii (1856), 328–31

Downton   *W.A.M.*, lviii (1963), 303–41 (note on the mosaic in Room I by D. J. Smith, 334–6, pl. I)

Littlecote Park   Coloured engraving by T. Vertue (1730), after (? lost) drawings by a Mr George, in the Haverfield Library, Ashmolean Museum, Oxford; hence a contemporary embroidery said to be still preserved at Littlecote Park; hence Lysons I (1813), pt iv, pl. IX, X, also Fowler (1796–1818), no. 20, also Hoare (1819), 117ff., figure, and Richmond (1947); Toynbee (1964), 253–4; D. J. Smith (1965), 95–116

Pit Meads   Hoare (1819), 111–17, figures; D. J. Smith (1965), 95–116, fig. 13 (after Hoare)

YORKSHIRE

Brantingham   *Y.A.J.*, xxxvii (1941), 514–20, figs. I–IV; *J.R.S.*, liii (1963), 131, pl. XI, XII; Toynbee (1964), 286; D. J. Smith (1965), 95–116. Report on excavations from 1961 onward, by I. M. Stead in preparation

Harpham   *Trans. of the East Riding Antiquarian Society*, xiii, pt ii (1907), 141–52, figs. 1–7; *J.R.S.*, xxxi (1941), 126; *Y.A.J.*, xxxviii (1955), 117–18; xxxix (1965), 55; *B.B.C.S.* xviii (1959), 304–10. A typescript report on the excavations in August–September 1950 is preserved by the Augustinian Society of Bridlington

Rudston   *Y.A.J.*, xxxi (1934), 332, 366–76, plates; xxxii (1936), 214–20, plates; xxxiii (1938), 81–86, 222–4, 320–38; I. A. Richmond, *The Roman Pavements from Rudston* (Hull Museum Publications, no. 215, with plates and bibliography, 1963); Toynbee (1964), 287–8; D. J. Smith (1965), 95–116, fig. 3. Report on re-excavation by I. M. Stead, following presentation of the mosaics to Hull City Museums in 1962, in preparation

Well   R. Gilyard-Beer, *The Romano-British Baths at Well* (1951). For the mosaics, see pp. 14–16, 68–69, pl. VIII, IXa

CHAPTER FOUR

Furniture and Interior Decoration[1]

JOAN LIVERSIDGE

THE HISTORY OF interior decoration in Britain may, perhaps, be said to begin in the Roman period, as the simple dwellings of the Iron Age and earlier cultures have so far produced no evidence for it. Certainly these may well have contained primitive wooden furniture and a few imported luxuries, but nothing more elaborate. Yet from the second half of the 1st century A.D. onwards abundant traces of plastered walls, decorated in various ways, have been found in town and country houses of all sizes. Unlike the mosaic floors, however, comparatively little survives of the discoveries made more than twenty-five years ago, and it is only recently that the importance of this type of evidence has been realised and some attempt made to study it. A further complication results from the fact that the material is fragile and a single painted wall can produce large quantities of fragments, so that the would-be student is faced at the outset with serious problems of excavation, transport, storage and preservation. These problems were encountered for the first time during the early days of the Lullingstone excavations when, in 1949–50, the wall-surfaces of an upper

[1] The text figures accompanying this chapter are by John Christiansen.

127

room were noted lying amidst the debris of the basement. The fragments were collected and many of them pieced together to reveal the now famous series of Christian paintings.[1]

The next major development in the study of Romano-British wall-painting occurred in 1955, when the first season of a new series of excavations at Verulamium, directed by Professor S. S. Frere, revealed sheets of fallen plaster lying on a tessellated floor, some face up, some face down. Its removal required much technical ingenuity, and the methods employed were developed further by the numerous discoveries of a similar nature made on this site during the next few years. As a result, much of a reconstructed wall nearly 7 feet high was exhibited at the 'Art in Roman Britain' exhibition in 1961, together with part of a painted ceiling and a frieze decorated with a leaf scroll with bird and animal masks.[2] In the last few years important discoveries have also been made at other sites and it is clear that this type of research is still in its infancy. Even when the material is only found on a much smaller scale and where there is no hope of restoring complete walls, much can be learnt from the study of a few patterned fragments, individual motifs can be compared with those from other sites at home and abroad, and it is sometimes possible to hazard a guess at probable schemes of decoration. Now that fragments of painted wall-plaster tend to be kept as carefully as potsherds, our knowledge of their significance is rapidly increasing, and when the more recent discoveries are considered in conjunction with the clues which survive in older excavation reports and in museum collections, we find that we already have quite an impressive corpus of material.

Generally speaking, the walls of both town and country dwellings, varying in size from mansions to the smallest farm, were finished off with layers of mortar and with a fine skimming coat on top, the whole not infrequently rendered over walls of timber and wattle and daub.[3] At Verulamium tests carried out on the wall-paintings have shown an undercoat of coarse sand and lime which was allowed to dry before a finer top coat was applied. Then the ground colours were put on while this surface was still wet.[4] When the time came to add the more detailed decoration the pigments were applied mixed, perhaps, with gum or some other binding agent,

[1] *Lullingstone* (1955)
[2] Toynbee (1963), nos. 169–72
[3] *Park Street* (1945), 104
[4] Davey (1961), 174

although the exact nature of this remains uncertain.[1] Before this was done the lines of the framework might be scratched in with a stylus. The colours used were made of various materials, including red and yellow ochres, which owe their tints to iron oxide, lamp black or powdered charcoal, copper silicate (Egyptian blue), or powdered blue frit.[2] A bluish green, made of magnesium iron silicate, was identified at Hucclecote, together with yellow (limonite or hydrated iron oxide) and red haematite (iron oxide).[3] All these colours are believed to have been imported. Room I in the Witcombe villa produced two little pots used for paint and an oyster shell with traces of red, probably used as a palette. In the pots was a pink made of haematite and chalk, and a yellow composed of white chalk and green earth, and, in fact, the staircase leading into the room was painted pink, yellow and green with pink, red, yellow and white stripes. The green or celadonite earth may have come from Cornwall.[4] At Lullingstone a small *mortarium* was found, broken in antiquity and repaired with rivets, so that it was no longer strong enough for kitchen use. It contained traces of a blue pigment which a painter may have been using to touch up the Christian paintings when the room was destroyed by fire.[5]

The scheme of decoration usually adopted in both town and country houses alike tends to divide the wall into three parts. At the bottom came a dado about $2\frac{1}{2}$–3 feet high, often splashed and streaked with several colours in order to imitate fine marble wall veneers. Next would come a series of panels probably 4–5 feet high. These panels may all be of equal width, so that sometimes they could only be fitted in by continuing them from wall to wall round the corners of the room. Usually, however, the width varies so that a series of panels could be completed on each wall, the corners being frequently marked by a vertical band of colour. Doors and window openings were also plastered and painted, often with lines and stripes to fit in with the general colour scheme, while window splays were usually white or cream to reflect the maximum amount of daylight. The panels were defined by a framework of multicoloured lines and stripes and might be divided from each other by strips of colour ornamented in various ways. Geometric, floral or foliate motifs such as concentric circles or

---

[1] The use of both techniques (*buon fresco* and *tempera*) at Roman sites in Italy and in other provinces is discussed by M. Borda (1958), 385–90

[2] Forbes (1955), iii, 205–28; Plesters (1963), 337

[3] *Hucclecote* (1933), 343

[4] *Witcombe* (1954), 17, 60

[5] *Lullingstone* (1955), 154

garlands frequently appear on the panels. The decoration of the upper-most part of the wall is uncertain, as it is the least likely to survive. Often it may have been merely painted with one of the ground colours, possibly enlivened with a few stripes; or a frieze or cornice may have been added. Verulamium has produced evidence for elaborately painted ceilings,[1] but so far little of this nature has been identified from villas.

Only a small proportion of this wall-painting is found *in situ*, but a 'Painted Room' in an unusually good state of preservation was found in the house at Iwerne Minster, Dorset.[2] This was excavated in 1897 by General Pitt-Rivers and H. St George Gray and an early photograph sur-vives recording it (Pl. 4.1). The lower parts of the panels were outlined in yellow, red and green, separated by a broader red stripe from a dado faintly flecked with small pink spots. All this was painted on a white ground and traces of a green leaf design were noted on the strips between each panel. Sketches survive showing that Room 33 at Bignor had walls striped in red, greenish blue, white and yellow above a narrow dado painted black or dark brown, a simple scheme designed perhaps to show off the rather clumsy mosaic floor with its heads of Medusa and the Four Seasons set in a border of plain red tesserae (Pl. 4.2). Carisbrooke also provides similar evidence for the decoration of a complete room with a geometric mosaic and a dado ornamented with red and green rectangles outlined in white (Pl. 4.3). Frag-ments noted from higher up the walls seem to have shown flowers, foliage and other designs.[3]

Most of the wall-plaster recovered during excavation consists of pieces painted with one colour only, or with some of the multicoloured stripes and lines which usually come from the panel frameworks, sometimes deli-cately shaded and outlined. Stippling from the dado level is frequent and colourful. The excavator at Box describes walls with large panels framed in lines of red, green and white above many different kinds of such imita-tion marbling, and he attempts to identify them as serpentine and various types of granite.[4] Lysons illustrates a fragment found in the baths at Bignor with white splashes on a red ground (Fig. 4.1a). At the bottom a white line may outline a black rectangle which perhaps also formed part of the dado decoration, and white and black lines above may edge a yellow stripe which

[1] Toynbee (1963), nos. 170, 171
[2] Hawkes (1948), 59
[3] C. Smith (1868), vi, 126
[4] *Box* (1904), 244, 263

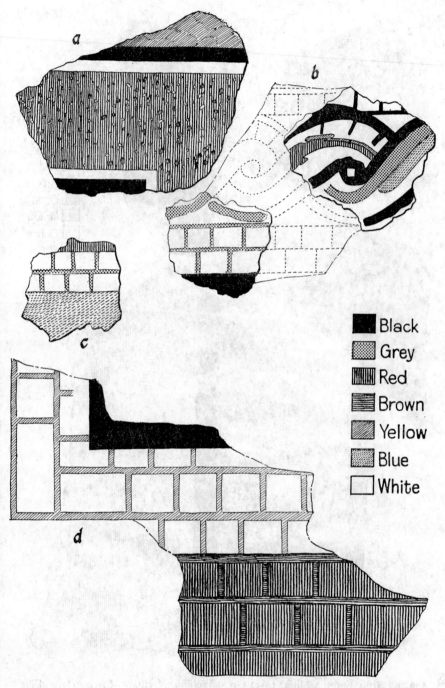

Fig. 4.1. Imitation marbling and tessellated designs; (a–c) Bignor, Sussex (after Lysons (1817), Pl. xxxii); (d) Compton Abdale, Glos. (from unpublished material, by courtesy of Cheltenham Museum). *John Christiansen.*

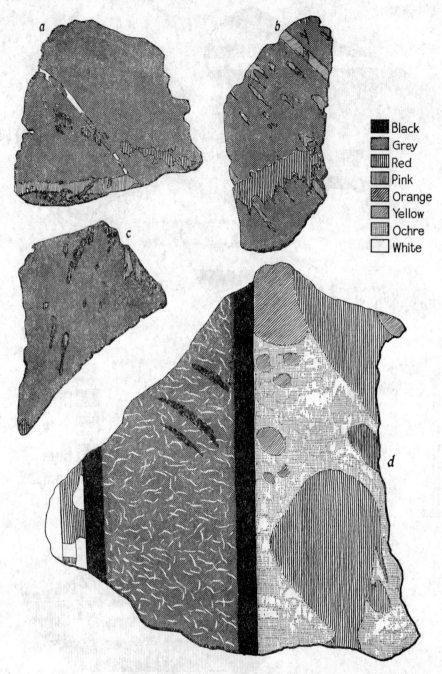

■	Black
▨	Grey
▥	Red
▥	Pink
▧	Orange
▨	Yellow
▤	Ochre
□	White

Fig. 4.2. Imitation marbling; (a–c) Great Weldon, Northants (by courtesy of Dr David Smith); (d) Darenth, Kent (by courtesy of the Eastgate House Museum Rochester). *John Christiansen.*

belongs below the panels. Dr David Smith's recent excavations at Great Weldon produced marbling of 4th-century date, with some attempt at veining in rust red, maroon and yellow on a grey ground also stippled in the same colours (Fig. 4.2, nos. *a–c*). Black and red spots and splodges on rust or yellow grounds are preserved from much the same period at Lufton.[1] Red stippling on a pink ground and also purple fragments peppered with small white spots were found in the 2nd-century house at Landwade, Exning (Suffolk), while the 3rd-century dwelling seems to have had a dado of grey flecked with red, yellow and white with occasional black and purple veining.[2] More than thirty other sites have produced similar types of decoration.

A fragment from Darenth now in the Eastgate House Museum at Rochester shows the coarser-grained type of marbling colloquially known as 'fried egg' motif (Fig. 4.2*d*). Here we have large patches of red outlined in orange and with orange blobs on a yellow ground, next to a grey stripe outlined in black. The grey is finely flecked with a turquoise blue which has had to be shown as white in the drawing. On the left of this stripe comes a scrap of some design in red and white. A sketch of another piece of plaster by Mrs Payne in the same Museum suggests that this design was more 'fried egg' in white on a red ground, and it again appears next to the grey stripe, which has a little yellow just visible to the right of the black outline. A band of yellow 'fried egg' on a red ground also survives in the National Museum of Wales (no. 88.72) from the 19th-century excavations at Llantwit Major. There wall-paintings still *in situ* are recorded in stretches up to 9 feet high, but no detailed account of them seems to have been preserved.[3] Darenth, too, obviously produced a wealth of material when excavated in 1895, but it is only briefly described. Such frustration is apt to result when the material from the older excavations is studied, although in the case of Darenth we are able to gain some information from Mrs Payne's drawings.[4]

The dado at Carisbrooke (Pl. 4.3) shows that not everyone wanted imita-

---

[1] *Lufton* (1952), 94. I am much indebted to Mr L. C. Hayward for showing me this material.

[2] Excavated for the Ministry of Public Building and Works by Mr E. Greenfield, to whom my thanks are due for enabling me to study this evidence. Report forthcoming; preliminary notice in *J.R.S.*, l (1960), 228

[3] *Llantwit* (1888), 414. For more recent wall-painting discoveries, see *Llantwit* (1953), 133, pl. XI, no. 2

[4] *Darenth* (1897), 74. I am indebted to the Curator and the Eastgate House Museum for permission to study these drawings and the surviving fragments.

tion marbling, multicoloured rectangles and probably other geometric designs being sometimes used instead or in addition. In 1948 the lower part of a wall of Flavian date at Manor Farm, Farningham, was uncovered with the painted plaster still *in situ*. The pale cerise ground is splashed all over with red, yellow, blue and white, and about a foot above ground-level a dark blue trellis appears with white dots marking the points where the lines cross (Pl. 4.9). The trellis is decorated with yellow flowers in red diamonds. Elsewhere on this site blue flowers occur.[1]

On other sites the dado occasionally seems to echo the border of a mosaic floor. Lysons records a scrap of red, black, yellow and blue guilloche, and two pieces showing white tesserae outlined in grey or black, all from Bignor (Fig. 4.1*b, c*). Unpublished material from the Compton Abdale villa (Glos.), excavated by Mr C. E. Key in 1931 and now in Cheltenham Museum, shows quite an elaborate design of red tesserae outlined in brown next to white tesserae outlined in yellow, apparently a border for some black panel or pattern (Fig. 4.1*d*).[2] Lufton also has some fascinating fragments probably depicting guilloche in yellow, red and black on white, marked out with deeply incised guide-lines and with the spaces between the tesserae heavily accented in black. A piece of black and white Greek fret at Chedworth may also continue the design of a mosaic floor.

Blobs or beads of colour sometimes embellish the fine lines which usually appear on the inner side of the framework of individual panels. A red line on a white ground at Sapcote has the corner marked in this way, and more beads apparently occupy the space between it and the next line of the border (Fig. 4.3*a*).[3] Fragments from Great Staughton also show such beaded corners, this time in purple on white (Fig. 4.3*b*).[4] A red line on a white ground at Rockbourne seems to have outsize beads (Fig. 4.3*d*), while other material from this site shows a white line more delicately ornamented (Fig. 4.3*c*).[5] Some painters elaborated the idea of the beaded line a little more, and at North Warnborough a purple line seems to be ornamented at

[1] My warmest thanks are due to Lt.-Col. G. W. Meates for showing me the Farningham material and for the photograph, pl. II

[2] I am indebted to the Curator and the Cheltenham Museum for permission to use this material for fig. 4.1*d*

[3] *Sapcote* (1935), colour pl. opp. 194

[4] For this my thanks are due to the Ministry of Public Building and Works and to Mr Greenfield. Report forthcoming; preliminary notice in *J.R.S.*, xlix (1959), 118

[5] I am greatly indebted to Mr A. Morley Hewitt for showing me the Rockbourne material. Preliminary notices in *J.R.S.*, li (1961), 189; lii (1962), 185

Fig. 4.3. Beaded lines from panel frameworks; (a) Sapcote, Leics. (after A. J. Pickering, *Sapcote* (1935), colour plate opp. p. 194); (b) Great Staughton, Hunts. (by courtesy of E. Greenfield); (c, d) Rockbourne, Hants. (by courtesy of A. T. Morley Hewitt); (e–g) Kintbury, Berks. (by courtesy of D. B. Connah). *John Christiansen.*

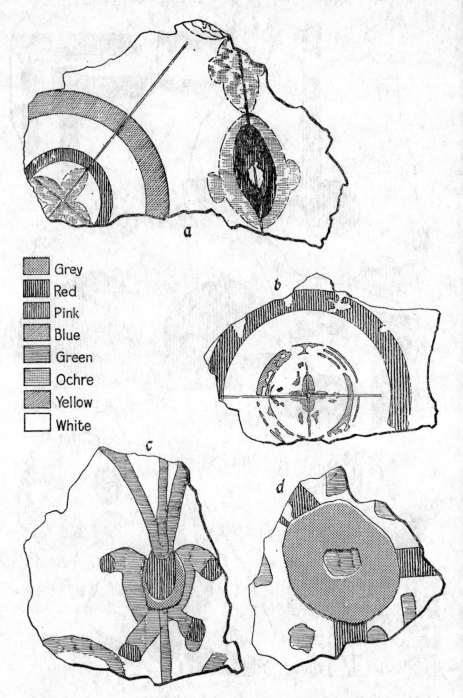

Fig. 4.4. Curvilinear designs; (a, b) Hadstock, Essex (Cambridge University Museum of Archaeology and Ethnology); (c, d) Ham Hill, Somerset (by courtesy of Castle Museum, Taunton). *John Christiansen.*

regular intervals with beads shaded in blue.[1] Kintbury (Berks.) produced such bobbles in profusion varying from $\frac{1}{4}$ to $\frac{1}{2}$ inch in diameter. Part of one border consisted of an ochre yellow line $\frac{1}{2}$ inch wide edged with fine red lines, with gay red and black beads painted over the yellow (Fig. 4.3e). Another border has them in red and black on white, and these also form part of a more elaborate pattern with a motif in red and yellow, all on a white ground (Fig. 4.3f, g).[2]

Various types of curvilinear design occur and some of them could equally well have decorated either panels or dado. One of the more elaborate and colourful examples survives from the Hadstock villa and in this case the centre of a panel seems the most likely position (Fig. 4.4a). It consists of a yellow quatrefoil in a red circle enclosed in a wider blue one. This was surrounded by an outer zone made up of red and white ovals outlined in yellow. Another fragment shows a green quatrefoil enclosed by yellow and red circles and here the mark of the Roman compass at the point where two guide-lines intersect can be clearly seen (Fig. 4.4b). From the same site come a blue roundel outlined in black, and also pink, red and black concentric circles. All these designs are painted on a white ground.[3]

Kintbury is another site which has produced concentric circles, boldly painted in red and black on white, as well as various patterns in yellow and red in which curves appear. Pieces preserved in Taunton Museum from the Ham Hill excavations of 1907 are typical of the designs frequently encountered, which can only be vaguely and unsatisfactorily described as curvilinear or geometric (Fig. 4.4c, d). Red, green and grey are the colours used, on a white ground.[4] Also typical are the deep purple curves and loops of a large fragment found at Darenth, spattered with lighter purple and black spots (Fig. 4.5a). They seem to decorate a white stripe, above which came a grey ground with a black line. Below appear yellow and black lines and more purple, all three applied over a yellow ground. Possibly this should be considered as more marbling, but the same type of design was found in shades of red at Lullingstone, dating from the 4th century and

[1] *North Warnborough* (1931a), 227. My thanks are due to Mr M. Parsons for showing me drawings of this material.

[2] I am much indebted to Mr D. B. Connah for enabling me to study the Kintbury material.

[3] Liversidge (1951), 13, 14, pl. 1

[4] My thanks are due to the Curator and the Taunton Museum for permission to use the Ham Hill material for Fig. 4.4c, d. A brief reference to the paintings occurs in *Ham Hill* (1913), 133

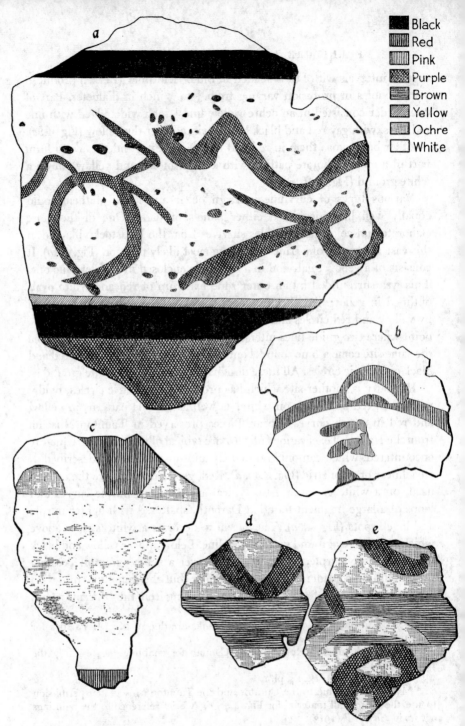

Black
Red
Pink
Purple
Brown
Yellow
Ochre
White

Fig. 4.5. Curvilinear designs; (a) Darenth, Kent (by courtesy of the Eastgate House Museum, Rochester; (b–e) Landwade, Exning, Suffolk (Cambridge University Museum of Archaeology and Ethnology). *John Christiansen*.

with no signs of stippling. Another variation of it comes from the 2nd-century house excavated at Landwade in 1959. In purplish-brown on a ground of two shades of yellow, the pattern sometimes runs over on to lines of pale and dark brown about $\frac{1}{2}$ inch wide (Fig. 4.5*d*, *e*). Earlier excavations on the same site also produced a design of yellow and white or grey semicircles painted on a red ground. Possibly these formed a border to a white band edged with red or purple and with faint traces of a black pattern (Fig. 4.5*c*). With it were found fragments with purple lines wandering over a white ground which also occurred among the 1959 material, together with one piece with a shaded pink and red curve with white highlights and a red or purple design (Fig. 4.5*b*). All this plaster probably dates from the 3rd century or later. The 4th-century bath-house at Old Durham, the most northerly villa so far found in Britain, also produced walls painted with green curvilinear designs.[1]

In many cases these curving lines are also decorated with leaves and flowers. A striking design, showing a white geometric flower at the centre of a scarlet roundel enclosed in black and white circles from which spring black and green, and green and yellow leaf sprays, was found at the Yorkshire villa of Harpham in 1950 (Fig. 4.6*a*). Mr Mellor, the excavator, considered this might occupy the centre of a panel decorated with more leaves, some of them growing out of the border which was further embellished with semicircular motifs and beads of colour on grounds of white and ochre yellow (Fig. 4.6*e*). Leaf sprays spring in even greater profusion from other concentric circles 10 inches in diameter (Fig. 4.6*b*, *c*), and in one case a more elaborate flower is surrounded by circles striped in a sort of 'tartan' design. From this depend small medallions containing birds and, in one case, a human figure (Fig. 4.6*d*).[2] These are so far unique in Roman Britain, but individual details such as the geometric flowers are not uncommon. A four-petalled variety in yellow and red occurred at Darenth, and part of an eight-petalled example in the same colours at Landwade. Rockbourne has delightful smaller flowers with six petals in greenish-blue on a purple ground or white on black, as well as a green leaf of Harpham type. A suburban villa at Greetwell, just outside Lincoln, has produced the larger blossoms illustrated (Pl. 4.8). No. 1 has green and blue petals and a red and yellow centre, and no. 4 red petals with a centre of green

---

[1] *Old Durham* (1944), 10

[2] I am much indebted to Mr Eric Mellor for his generous permission to make use of this unpublished material from his Harpham excavations.

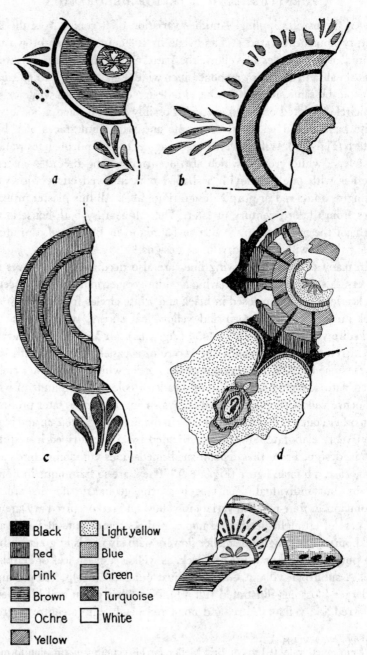

Black

Red

Pink

Brown

Ochre

Yellow

Light yellow

Blue

Green

Turquoise

White

Fig. 4.6. Designs from Harpham, Yorks. (by courtesy of E. Mellor). *John Christiansen*.

and blue. The single petal, no. 6, is yellow with red markings. Green leaf sprays (?) spring from the red, blue and black circles of no. 2, and no. 7 is a gay medley of yellow, red, green, black and blue.[1] Twelve-petalled flowers probably of Greetwell type are also recorded from Castle Dykes in brown on white or vice versa.[2]

Other motifs of a less formal type also occasionally appear. One found at North Warnborough (Fig. 4.7a) may be some form of water plant[3] and something like it in red and black occurred at Kintbury. A more naturalistic design of lilies (?) in pale-green and white on a red ground is preserved in a sketch from Darenth (Fig. 4.7b) and a parallel to this seems to have been found at Magor Farm, Camborne.[4] A similar design has survived from the Roman town at Caistor-by-Norwich and is now in the Norwich Castle Museum. Lullingstone has also produced beautiful lilies. Roses, lovingly painted in several shades of red and green, survive from the Ickleton villa; the piece illustrated is shaped to fit some architectural feature (Colour Pl. 1).[5] Roses depicted in outline decorate the dado below the Lullingstone Christian paintings, and designs with red buds are recorded from Clanville[6] and Appleshaw (Hants.),[7] Frindsbury (Kent)[8] and Fifehead Neville (Dorset).[9]

Some of these leaves and flowers must have formed part of wreaths and garlands of the type found decorating panels at Verulamium.[10] A sketch survives from Darenth of a scrap of a swag of this kind, with green leaves with white highlights and shadows of brown, painted on a red ground (Fig. 4.7c). A background of the same colour was used for a piece from Lockleys which may come from the lower room of the tower of late 2nd-century date. It is moulded into a slight curve (Fig. 4.7d). The decoration consists of very delicate greyish-green leaves on a dark brown band.[11]

---

[1] I am indebted to the Curator and the City Museum, Lincoln, for pl. 4.8, a photograph of a drawing by W. Ramsden.

[2] *Castle Dykes* (1875), 138

[3] My thanks are due to Mr M. Parsons for permission to publish fig. 4.7a

[4] *Magor Farm* (1932), 71

[5] Liversidge (1951), 14

[6] *Clanville* (1898), 6

[7] VCH, Hants, i (1900), 297

[8] *Frindsbury* (1889), 191, pl. II, opp. 190

[9] Drawing in the Brown Portfolio, Society of Antiquaries of London.

[10] Frere (1957), pl. IIIa

[11] My thanks are due to Mr J. B. Ward-Perkins and to the Curator and the Letchworth Museum for permission to publish this fragment.

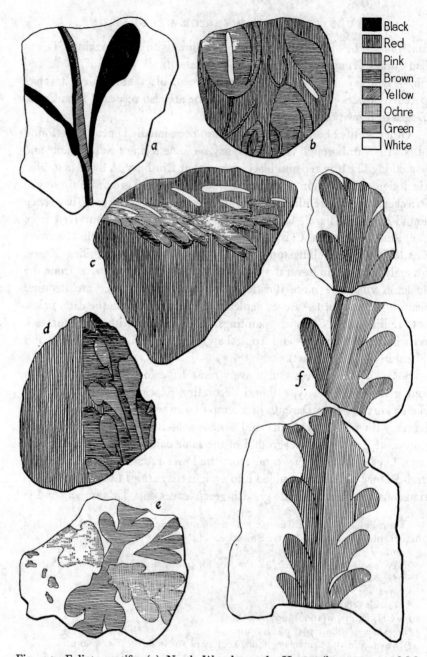

■	Black
	Red
	Pink
	Brown
	Yellow
	Ochre
	Green
□	White

Fig. 4.7. Foliate motifs: (a) North Warnborough, Hants. (by courtesy of M. Parsons); (b, c) Darenth, Kent (by courtesy of the Eastgate House Museum, Rochester); (d) Lockleys, Herts. (by courtesy of Letchworth Museum); (e) Witcombe, Glos. (by courtesy of Mrs E. Clifford); (f) Brading, Isle of Wight (by courtesy of the late Major D. Oglander). *John Christiansen.*

Another fragment, from Witcombe, may show strands from two garlands crossing each other, in green and in yellow respectively, or the two may outline rectangles containing flowers or birds (Fig. 4.7*e*).[1]

This type of leaf recalls a more formal type of 'fern' pattern which was also frequently used vertically on the strips between panels. Brading provides a good example of it in pink, shaded on one side with red (Fig. 4.7*f*). This method of showing a shadow on the underside of garlands or on one side of a vertical foliate line of this type is customary, and a close parallel to the Brading example exists among the unpublished material from Verulamium. Whittlebury (Northants.)[2] and Landwade are other sites at which it was present. The fleur-de-lis was also sometimes used in this way. A scrap of one in black survives from Lockleys and pieces of it in red on a

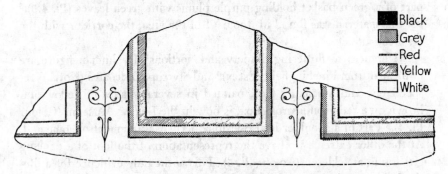

Black
Grey
Red
Yellow
White

Fig. 4.8. Witcombe, Glos. (by courtesy of the Society of Antiquaries of London, after a sketch in the Red Portfolio). *John Christiansen.*

yellow ground can be seen from Ickleton, although there it may possibly have formed part of a trellis (Colour Pl. 2). It was also found at Lullingstone. A graceful motif, possibly the base of an ornamental candelabrum appears on a decorated wall from Witcombe (Fig. 4.8).[3] Apparently a stretch 32 feet wide survived *in situ*, painted white with the panels outlined in black, yellow, and red, and with black candelabra. Darenth also produced a design of this type in white on red.

Not many representations of living creatures have so far been recovered

[1] I am much indebted to Mrs E. Clifford for information about Witcombe and for leave to publish this fragment.

[2] *Whittlebury* (1852), 109, pl. XI

[3] My thanks are due to the President and Fellows of the Society of Antiquaries of London for permission to publish Fig. 4.8 based on a drawing in the Red Portfolio.

from villa walls, but there are enough to arouse hopes of future discoveries. A fish, possibly a roach, seems to have been seen in the baths at High Wycombe in 1862,[1] perhaps part of some decoration recalling the mosaic floors from Lufton. A possible representation of a bird's head is among the material from Compton Abdale (Glos.), a bird on a branch is recorded from Acton Scott (Shropshire),[2] and birds, stars and other fanciful objects are said to have been found at Ickleton.[3] A fine blue bird with red beak and wings can be seen at Brading (Colour Pl. 3).[4] It is placed under a yellow garland with a few green leaves fluttering near by. Further fragments probably depict the tails of this and other birds and another piece also shows two green figs, all painted on a white ground. In the British Museum is a painting on a yellow background, also from Brading, and showing part of a green basket holding purple plums with green leaves (Pl. 4.5).[5] All this material was found in Room VI of the villa, the corridor with the Orpheus mosaic.

References to fluttering drapery and portions of a human figure are published from Finchingfield (Essex)[6] and Styrrup, Oldcoates (Notts.)[7] respectively, and a striking face, painted in several shades of yellow and brown on a red ground from Box, is now in the Devizes Museum (Colour Pl. 4).[8] Part of a shoulder is also visible, perhaps a fragment of some god. At the other extreme we have the representation of the foot of a dancing girl found at Ickleton (Colour Pl. 5). This is the only evidence for a life-sized figure painting so far found in Britain and it is a pity the 1848 excavations failed to find more of it. Another most peculiar fragment in the same collection may depict part of an animal skin used as a drapery, perhaps in some scene of Maenads and Satyrs. The foot is 8 inches in length, suggesting a figure about 5 feet tall and, like the rose mentioned above, is most delicately painted in flesh tints while the pale-green drapery has a brownish border.

Other figures, but not life-size, are known from Otford (Kent). One

---

[1] *High Wycombe* (1878), 3

[2] VCH, Shropshire, i (1908), 260

[3] Liversidge (1951), 14

[4] I am much indebted to Major D. Oglander for facilities to study the Brading paintings and for permission to publish fig. 4.7*f* and Colour Pl. 3

[5] For Pl. 5 I am indebted to the Trustees of the B.M.

[6] *Finchingfield* (1937), 200

[7] *Oldcoates* (1871), 67

[8] For permission to publish Colour Pl. 4 I am indebted to the Curator, Devizes Museum, and to the Wiltshire Archaeological and Natural History Society.

4. 1   South-west angle of the 'painted room', Iwerne, Dorset.
Copy of a photograph of 1897 taken by H. St George Gray, now,
in Dorset County Museum. R.C.H.M. (England), crown copyright

4. 2   Bignor, Sussex, Room 33. After Lysons (1817), Pl. XXIV

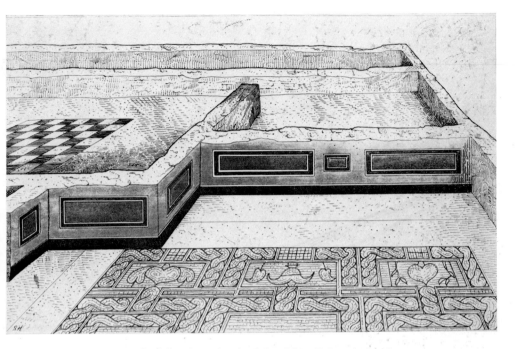

4. 3　Carisbrooke, Isle of Wight. After C. Roach Smith (1868), 126

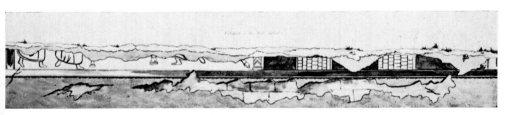

4. 4　Wall-painting, Comb End, Glos. After Lysons (1813), Plate I

4. 5 Wall-painting, Brading.
Isle of Wight

4. 6 Wall-painting, Otford, Kent

4. 7 Wall-painting, Otford, Kent. Photos British Museum,
by courtesy of the Trustees

Scale 6 Inch to one Foot

4. 8 Motifs from wall-painting at Greetwell, Lincs. Photo
Record and Central Photographs Ltd, by courtesy of Lincoln
Municipal Museum

4. 9 Wall-painting, Farningham, Kent. Photo Lieut.-Col. G. W. Meates

4. 10 *Graffito* on plaster, Hucclecote, Glos. Photo by kind permission of Mrs E. Clifford

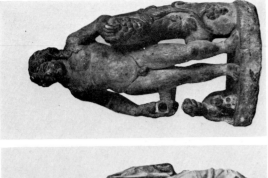

4. 12　*left* Statue of Luna, Woodchester, Glos.

4. 13　*right* Statue of Bacchus, Spoonley Wood, Glos.

Photos British Museum, by courtesy of the Trustees

4. 11　Relief, Wellow, Som.

4. 14 Statue of Venus, Froxfield, Wilts. Photo British Museum, by courtesy of the Trustees

4. 15 Detail of marble bust, Lullingstone, Kent. Photo Warburg Institute (Otto Fein)

4. 16 Pipeclay statuette of Mother-Goddess, London. Photo London Museum, by courtesy of the Trustees

4. 17   Wall-painting, Trier, Germany. Photo Landesmuseum, Trier

4. 18 Tombstone of Julia Velva, York, Yorkshire Museum.
Photo R.C.H.M. (England), crown copyright

4. 19   Tombstone of Aelia Aeliana, York, Yorkshire Museum.
Photo R.C.H.M. (England), crown copyright

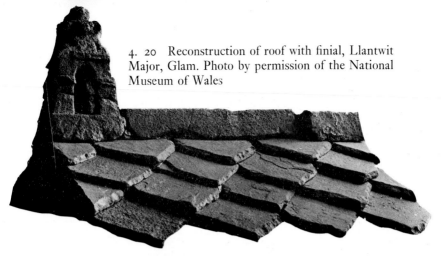

4. 20 Reconstruction of roof with finial, Llantwit Major, Glam. Photo by permission of the National Museum of Wales

4. 21 Shale table-foot. Upper Langridge Farm, Bath, Som. Photo by kind permission of J. Gardner, Esq.

4. 22 Bronze foot, Stanton Low, Bucks. Photo by permission of the National Museum of Wales

4. 23 *far right* Bronze foot, Caerwent, Mon. Photo by permission of the National Museum of Wales

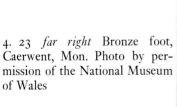

4. 25 Shale table-leg, Frampton, Dorset. Dorset County Museum. Photo J. M. C. Toynbee

4. 24 Shale table-leg, Dorchester. Dorset County Museum. Photo J. M. C. Toynbee

4. 26 Shale table-leg, Preston, Dorset. Dorset County Museum. Photo J. M. C. Toynbee

4. 27   Shale table-leg, Rothley, Leics.
Photo Leicester City Museum

4. 29   Top of shale table-leg, Foscott, Bucks. Cambridge
University Museum of Archaeology and Ethnology. Photo L. P.
Morley

4. 28   Shale table-leg, Norden, Dorset. Photo Dorset County
Museum

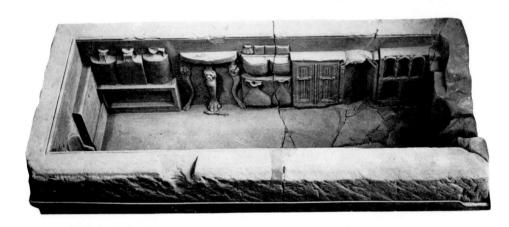

4. 30   Sarcophagus, Simpelveld, Netherlands. Photo Rijksmuseum van Oudheden te Leiden

showed two men and a second piece, measuring approximately 11 by 10 inches and now in the British Museum, depicts part of the arm and body of a man flourishing a spear (Pl. 4.6), painted in flesh tones on a black ground. With it are three fragments showing lettering, BINA MANV L (Pl. 4.7). These words are believed to be part of a quotation from the *Aeneid* (I: 313): *bina manu lato crispans hastilia ferro*.[1] The painted figure probably represents Achates and the walls of the room may have been decorated with Virgilian scenes of the same type as those which appear on the floor of the *frigidarium* at Low Ham (see p. 90). And, of course, Lullingstone only a few miles from Otford also has an allusion to the *Aeneid* in the elegiac couplet which accompanies the mosaic of Europa and the Bull (see p. 91). Fragments of lettering which may have explained other paintings of this type were also found at Greetwell and Woodchester.[2]

In 1779 a stretch of wall-painting 135 feet in length was found *in situ* at Comb End (Glos.) and fortunately recorded by Lysons (Pl. 4.4).[3] It shows part of a large figure-scene with the lower portions of two individuals, perhaps a man and a woman, advancing through the pillars of a portico to meet two more figures who come running in from the right. Beyond them dark brown panels and a design of black and white rectangles, possibly intended to indicate masonry, interrupt the sequence. Another scene may have followed farther to the right. The figures are shown in black outline shaded in red on a white background and the pillars are also sketched in black. Below comes a red band edged with white and black lines, and an orange dado. A later redecoration still covers part of the band and dado with more rectangles outlined in black on white. Possibly here we have more incidents from Virgil or some other event from Roman literature or mythology.[4] Unpublished material from recent excavations includes traces of female figures from the villa at Brantingham (Yorks.).[5] These may be water-nymphs echoing the design of the mosaic in the same room (*cf.* above, ch. III, p. 105). Across the Humber a large site at Winterton (Lincs.) produced wall-paintings from several buildings. In the baths (F) there seems to have been a scene including Cupid and a larger figure

[1] *Otford* (1927), 153; Hinks (1933), 56, no. 84. For Pls. 6 and 7 I am indebted to the Trustees of the B.M.
[2] *Woodchester* (1797), pl. xxxi
[3] Lysons (1815), ii, pl. i
[4] Toynbee (1964), 220
[5] *J.R.S.*, liii (1963), 131

on one wall, while fragments depicting fish and water-plants came from elsewhere in the same room.[1]

A few other scraps of architectural painting survive. Hemsworth (Dorset) produced a column with a capital which may come from a landscape with a colonnade or temple.[2] A small piece from Hadstock probably represents the gable end of a house, and a larger one from Ickleton (Colour Pl. 6) clearly shows a building outlined in black on a brown ground with a red-tiled roof. One would like to imagine this to be a picture of the Ickleton villa itself, but it is more likely to have formed part of one of the country scenes popular at Pompeii, Herculaneum and elsewhere. A well-preserved provincial parallel was found at Trier and shows a handsome villa with a colonnade connecting buildings two storeys high, while in the foreground farm-labourers are at work (Pl. 4.17). In Britain we also have a *graffito* sketch of a building incised on a piece of plaster found at Hucclecote (Glos.). This suggests a timbered construction on stone wall-footings (Pl. 4.10).[3]

It has already been noted that the majority of villas produce evidence for wall-painting, but perhaps the detailed discussion of designs and motifs largely based upon scattered fragments from a number of sites has rather obscured the general picture of the extent of such decoration in an individual house. Let us consider a few villas singly or in groups, especially those where future discoveries seem possible. The published accounts of the excavations of 1818 and 1938–9 at Witcombe suggest that most of the rooms were decorated and mention that, when first discovered, Room 1 had plaster *in situ* up to 6 feet high, painted in panels of various colours. These soon perished on exposure to the weather and in 1938 only pink plaster remained on the walls. A drawing in the Red Portfolio of the Society of Antiquaries of London, however, shows pale blue panels with a framework of red stripes and fine pink lines and white panels framed in red, above a pink dado. In 1938, Room 2, the corridor with the staircase, was found with the pink, yellow and green decoration described on p. 129. Lysons also saw there panels formed by light blue and orange stripes on a white ground, 'having elegant ornaments of ivy leaves etc. between them'.[4] The panelled design with candelabra (Fig. 4.8) may come from Room 5,

[1] *J.R.S.*, liv (1964), 159; Liversidge (1968), pl. 17a
[2] *Hemsworth* (1909), 8
[3] *Hucclecote* (1933), pl. xiv, fig. 22, also 328, 344, 348
[4] *Witcombe* (1821), 179

which had a geometric mosaic floor with a fluted chalice. Room 4, a passage, was decorated in pinkish purple, white and pale yellow with a red stripe and much the same colour scheme was used for Room 3 next door, the latrine. Cream, red, yellow and white plaster was also found in Room 41a and the unpublished 1961 excavations noted more plaster lying about the courtyard. Fragments showing fish were recovered from the cold bath, Room 7a, in 1962.[1] Excavation at Witcombe is continuing for several seasons and fresh discoveries there are very probable. Cirencester, of course, has produced good wall-painting and may well have been the artistic centre for the Cotswold villas, most of which have produced evidence of decoration, but little of it recorded. Lysons tells us that the exterior of Woodchester was plastered in red and such exterior plastering seems to have existed at many houses, red and white being popular colours. Some interior wall-painting is also mentioned at Woodchester in Rooms 10, 25, 26 and 27,[2] and one cannot help feeling that at this rich site some exciting discoveries must surely have been overlooked.

Continuing farther west, we find more decorated villas in Wales. Notable among them is Llantwit Major, where several walls showed two layers of wall-painting still *in situ*. The earlier decoration consisted of pink marbling below a multicoloured panel framework, the topmost stripe of yellow embodying an undulating red line. The later replastering had covered this with pale blue paint flecked with dark blue and crimson. A similar sequence of plasterings with the same designs was also found in three other rooms.[3] Some red and black stippling from Llantwit Major seems to have been echoed at the Ely villa,[4] Newton Nottage appears to have produced a trellis of blue and dark ochre[5] and now wall-painting has been found at Llys Brychan Farm between Llangadog and Llandeilo in Carmarthenshire.[6]

Sites in three other counties may perhaps be mentioned here, although every group produces something of interest. The surprising finds at Harpham have already been described. The 'tartan' pattern found there (Fig. 4.6d) with its pendants of birds and possible human figures is one of the most sophisticated designs found in Roman Britain, suggesting that

[1] Information from Mr E. Greenfield.

[2] *Woodchester* (1797), 7, 9

[3] *Llantwit* (1953), 102, 104–5, 110, 112, 119, 133

[4] *Ely* (1895), 126, 128; (1920), 31

[5] *Newton Nottage* (1853), 97

[6] *Llys Brychan* (1962), 5, fig. 2

some north country wall-painters may have been more skilful than local mosaicists, although this does not apply to the artists who worked at Brantingham. Much unpublished plaster of great interest has been found in the settlement at Malton, where some of it can be seen in the Museum. Possibly this was one centre for the painters and, remembering the perspective painting found there, Aldborough may well have been another.[1] Material is also known from the villas at Rudston,[2] Langton,[3] North Newbald,[4] Collingham[5] and Gargrave.[6] Castle Dykes, in addition to the flowers already mentioned (p. 141), also had marbling, trellis and foliate designs. One wall showed evidence of three periods of decoration.

Passing over much of the midlands, where recent excavations at Leicester and Southwell[7] have produced new exciting material which is now being studied, the large Oxfordshire villa of North Leigh should be mentioned. This is another site first excavated in the 19th century, when a large heated room with a mosaic floor and frescoes not only on the walls but also from the ceiling were discovered. The account tells us it was probably vaulted and finished with a coating of very thin plaster formed into compartments by red, yellow and green fillets on a cream ground, decorated with the foliage of the olive. One piece showed the groin of an arch with a fillet on each side of it. The walls had a narrow dark brown skirting 6 inches high, and then a white stripe and more brown and above this Etruscan yellow. More yellow, with a red skirting, was found in Room 3 next door. Room 32 had green plaster and Room 35, a heated room in the baths, red and black stripes.[8] The description of the ceiling is the most notable feature here and recent discoveries at Verulamium suggest it is probably an accurate one. The 19th-century account of Headington, another Oxfordshire site, tells us that there, too, plaster moulding was found as from a cornice, ornamented with a beaded cavetto.[9]

The last group of villas to be mentioned are all in Kent. Along the Darent valley between Sevenoaks and Dartford dwellings of varying size occur at surprisingly regular intervals, ranging from small houses at

[1] Liversidge (1958), 374, fig. 1
[2] *Rudston* (1934), 370
[3] *Langton* (1932), 20
[4] *North Newbald* (1941), 237
[5] YMH (1891), 94
[6] *Kirk Sink* (1912), 360
[7] Toynbee (1964), 219
[8] Skelton (1823), Wootton Hundred 10
[9] *Headington* (1851), 66

Otford and Farningham to the large country seat at Darenth. As many of the important wall-paintings from these sites have already been described, it now only remains to consider another site in this area, Lullingstone. In view of the new account of the villa due to appear in the near future it is not proposed to discuss it in great detail, but its importance is so great in any study of wall-painting that some aspects of the work there must be considered.[1]

At present the name Lullingstone in this connection usually calls to mind the 4th-century Christian paintings and it is not always remembered that this villa also produced material from several earlier periods. The exterior of the late-2nd-century house, for instance, was painted cream and stippled in red, blue and yellow. A little plaster found *in situ* at the foot of the staircase in the baths showed a cream dado with a few red spots, and then pink stippled with red as a background for a red panel drawn in perspective and outlined by fine white and dark blue lines above a yellow band. Redecoration took place in the 3rd century but of this only some red-spotted pink plaster survives. Other 2nd-century fragments from the bath block include a pink and blue fish, possibly a trout, swimming in pale blue water. In the 4th century the corridors were painted brown with groups of fine orange lines and the south corridor wall, on the side adjacent to the room with the mosaics, had white panels enlivened with purple curvilinear motifs between deep red and purple pillars.

At the north end of the villa a room had been cut at a low level in the late 2nd century and it was reached down a staircase with walls with a painted latticework. The room itself was rendered in white with a dado of rectangles and lozenges, and panels outlined by fine lines of red, orange and green in a wider orange border. Between the panels are orange-coloured trees with leaf fronds and bunches of scarlet fruit. These have been tentatively identified as date-palms and in 1956 similar decoration was found in the neighbouring corridor and in Room 17. The appearance of these trees enabled the excavator to realise that he was indeed working in a late-2nd-century context. In 1957 a walled-up niche nearly 3 feet high in the south wall of the basement room was cleared out and a charming painting unexpectedly revealed.[2] It shows three girls, probably water-

---

[1] My thanks are due to Lt.-Col. G. W. Meates and the late Mr C. D. P. Nicholson for facilities to see and discuss the Lullingstone material throughout the excavations. This account is based on *Lullingstone* (1951) and (1955)

[2] *J.R.S.*, xlviii (1958), 149; Toynbee (1964), 220, pl. LIII

nymphs, one standing and the others seated on either side of her. All seem to have had aureoles of green leaves although the heads of the two seated figures are much damaged. One girl, half draped in a dark blue cloak, is sitting with her right hand resting on an overturned flagon out of which flows blue water. Little but blue and dark red drapery survives of her companion. The standing figure is clad in yellow; she wears a yellow and red diadem and a necklace of blue beads, and carries a green frond. Jets of blue water gush from her nipples. Her face is painted with great delicacy and the whole composition is one of great beauty. The painting was damaged when a shelf or something similar was inserted in the niche, and at a later date the basement room was repainted in cream with a few scarlet stripes and then blocked off.

In the mid-4th century the room above the basement room was probably turned into some form of domestic chapel or house church. At the end of the 4th or early in the 5th century the house was destroyed by fire and this upper room crashed into the basement. Much painted plaster from its walls was recovered and patiently pieced together, showing that the west wall had been occupied by six human figures nearly 3 feet tall standing between the columns of a portico. One is a young man with dark eyes and red hair, richly dressed in garments edged with pearls and standing in front of a curtain. Three at least of the other figures are similarly clad and stand in the attitude of an *Orans* or early Christian at prayer. The presence of the curtain indicates that the young man is dead and the others may be praying for his soul. One figure may possibly depict a child. Elsewhere in the room was a painting of the Chi-Rho monogram in red on a white ground, enclosed in a gaily coloured wreath secured by ribbon. Scarlet berries fall from it and are eyed hungrily by two birds standing on the fluttering ends of the ribbon, one on each side. Fragments of two more Chi-Rho monograms were also found, one from the east wall and the other from the ante-room. Both are surrounded by a wreath and the one from the ante-room also had part of an *omega* in the field to the right.[1]

Lullingstone is one of the few villas with wall-painting securely dated to different periods. Up till recent years chronological data are normally entirely lacking from reports of plaster finds. The discoveries at Fishbourne, the Flavian material from Manor Farm, Farningham, and a fragment with green marbling in the first Roman House at Lockleys

[1] Toynbee (1963), nos. 175, 176

near Welwyn, Herts.[1] show that walls were already being decorated in the second half of the 1st century A.D. and the Lockleys foliate design (Fig. 4.7*d*) may be of mid-2nd-century date. Plaster of two or three periods was found at High Wycombe in 1954; the earliest came from a stratified deposit of mid-2nd-century date in the baths.[2] Landwade and Llantwit Major also showed at least two periods of decoration, the earliest dating to the 2nd century. Other sites include Lufton and Low Ham, where the wall-paintings may belong to the 3rd or 4th centuries, while the 'Painted Room' at Iwerne probably dates to some time after 300. The suburban villa at Great Casterton[3] produced a dado *in situ* in the annexe reconstruction of A.D. 370–80, and the material from Brantingham and Winterton is also of 4th-century date. In dating wall-painting there is the added complication that we have no way of knowing how often villa rooms were redecorated. Presumably redecoration would be necessary more often than the rebuilding of the house, but its frequency must have depended very much upon such factors as financial status, standards of housekeeping, and domestic events such as the arrival of a new bride or the activities of a member of the household inspired by ideas seen in towns such as Verulamium, or even farther afield in Trier or Rome. All these might lead to the summoning of the decorators and their pattern-books.

How far can we assess the achievements of the Romano-British villa wall-painters? For the present it is possible to say very little. We need more material and more stratified deposits and there seems little doubt that they will be forthcoming. Any such assessment also needs detailed discussion of the discoveries from such Romano-British towns as Leicester, Cirencester, Malton, and above all, Verulamium, where house after house produced wall-painting in varying quantities. Most of this material is not yet published. Consequently only a few comments and suggestions of a general nature are offered here.

Stippled decoration seems to have been popular in Britain at all periods and this taste is shared with Italy and other provinces. Random examples of 'fried egg' marbling, for instance, can be mentioned from the House of Menander at Pompeii,[4] the Hunting Baths at Lepcis Magna,[5] the Swiss

[1] *Lockleys* (1938), 347, 348 n. 1
[2] *High Wycombe* (1959), 254
[3] *Great Casterton* (1954), 29, pl. x
[4] Beyen (1958), colour pl. 1, opp. 352
[5] Ward-Perkins and Toynbee (1949), pl. xld

villa at Seeb,[1] or the Dutch villa at Vlengendaal, near Bochholz, South Limburg. The foliate line or fern design from Brading also appears in Holland at Arentsburg,[2] and in Switzerland at the villas of Gränichen, Le Buy, and Herzogenbuchsee, with the same effect of light and shadow.[3] Blossoms resembling those from Greetwell have been found in Holland at Plasmolen, Kloosterberg;[4] and at Stein, where the designs also recall those from Harpham.[5] Such flowers occur at Virunum in Austria[6] and also at Augst in Switzerland;[7] in fact, a casual inspection of the pages of Dr Drack's book reveals many motifs similar to those found in Britain.

A good illustration of the division of the wall into dado and panels is provided by the discoveries at the Roman temple of Elst, near Arnhem. Here Period II produced evidence for a wall with a dado with brown and yellow rectangles and a black oblong decorated with a white beaded line above a stippled pink band. Brown panels outlined in green and white were painted on a black ground, separated from each other by candelabra in pink, green and white. This wall may have been painted soon after A.D. 70 and it was preceded by earlier decoration which also includes marbling, dating from shortly after A.D. 50.[8] Recent research on material found in Cologne suggests that this type of panelled decoration began to die out in the 3rd century. The architectural details, such as pillars and candelabra, were omitted and the panels were probably placed side by side with no intervening details until in some cases the wall-decoration consisted largely of vertical stripes.[9] Possibly the wall from Bignor mentioned on p. 130 illustrates a British example of this tendency. Alternatively, the walls were covered with an all-over pattern more reminiscent of wallpaper; this has been found at Virunum, wall-painting from Silchester may also have been inspired by it,[10] and a very fragmentary foliate design from 2nd-century levels at Landwade might just possibly be an early form of it. How the figure paintings from Otford, Comb End or Ickleton fit in with

[1] Drack (1950), fig. 108
[2] I am much indebted to Dr J. Kern and the Rijksmuseum van Oudheden, Leiden, for facilities to study the wall-paintings from Vlengendaal and Arentsburg.
[3] Drack (1950), figs. 33, 67, 69
[4] *Kloosterberg* (1934), fig. 8
[5] *Stein* (1928), colour figs. 22, 23
[6] Praschniker and Kenner (1947), fig. 155
[7] Drack (1950), fig. 18
[8] Bogaers (1955), colour pl. xx–xxiv
[9] Doppelfeld (1956), fig. 18
[10] Boon (1957), fig. 29

such artistic development is not very clear. Discoveries such as the Low Ham mosaic or the splendid portraits of the empresses from 4th-century Trier[1] suggest they may be of 3rd- or 4th-century date, but similar discoveries in a better chronological context are needed to confirm this and it is necessary to remember that Comb End, at least, was covered by a later redecoration. It appears probable, therefore, that Roman Britain shared the same fashions in decoration as the neighbouring provinces, but it is not impossible that some concessions to purely Romano-British taste may yet be discovered. It is also possible we may one day be in a position to identify local schools of wall-painters working from centres such as Cirencester or Winchester.

A little evidence survives for other forms of wall decoration. A bath in the Wingham villa produced traces of a wall mosaic still *in situ*, worked in small grey and white tesserae.[2] Elsewhere walls or floors of *opus sectile* seem probable. Square, oblong, triangular or kite-shaped pieces of coloured stone from the Wealden series, Sussex marble and white limestone from north Italy were found at Angmering, some worn by use.[3] Similar-shaped fragments of English or foreign marble are recorded from Woodchester,[4] Folkestone,[5] Fingringhoe (Essex)[6] and Ely (Glam.),[7] and other probable examples come from Ashtead[8] and Abbotts Ann (Hants).[9] *Opus sectile* and wall-mosaic are features found in luxurious houses at Pompeii and Ostia, and fresh evidence for the existence of the former in Roman Britain has been found recently during the excavation of the buildings at Fishbourne, near Chichester.[10]

In addition to mosaic floors and wall-paintings British villas must also have possessed statues, carvings in relief, and various types of architectural decoration. Regrettably little evidence for these embellishments has survived, but at Woodchester, a site which one would expect to be rich in such features, Lysons notes a few examples. In Room 25 two fragments of small pedestals were found, one with the feet of a statue and an animal's

[1] Kempf (1959), 10, 18
[2] *Wingham* (1882), 135 and pl. opp.
[3] *Angmering* (1938), 15–17, 43
[4] *Woodchester* (1797), 9
[5] *Folkestone* (1925), 109
[6] Information from Colchester Museum
[7] *Ely* (1925), 45
[8] *Angmering* (1938), 17, n. 5
[9] VCH, Hants, i (1900), 300
[10] *Fishbourne* (1963), 7

foot still forming part of it. With these pieces was a marble statuette about 20 inches high, representing the goddess Luna standing, with a bull lying at her feet (Pl. 4.12). Lysons suggests that one of her hands (now lost) originally held a torch, part of the flame of which survives by her right shoulder, but the figure is too damaged for this to be certain.[1] In Room 26 next door lay part of the drapery of a bust described as being of very heavy calcareous spar, accompanied by several small columns of local stone decorated with mouldings. On the west side of the great court more columns occurred and also a marble fragment depicting a group of Cupid and Psyche. The statue of Luna is now in the British Museum and with it are a small marble group of Bacchus accompanied by a panther, found in a grave at Spoonley Wood (Glos.) (Pl. 4.13), a statue probably representing Venus from Froxfield (Wilts.) (Pl. 4.14)[2] and an oolite panel 14 inches high from one of the villas at Wellow (Pl. 4.11). This shows three figures carved in relief, two of them very well-draped females each holding an object which may be a staff or branch and wearing a necklace of large square ornaments or a torc. The end figure on the left appears to be resting her hand on something, rather than grasping another object. This might be the end of a couch with a cushioned seat indicated by the horizontal lines visible near the figure's skirt. The third figure, on the right, is a man, nude apart from a cloak and carrying a purse in one hand and a staff in the other. The heads of all three are missing, but it seems probable that they represent Mercury and two mother goddesses.

Other finds, not in the British Museum, include a head of Ceres unfortunately stolen from Bignor, but recorded by Lysons,[3] and fragments of statues from Wadfield[4] and Hucclecote in Gloucestershire[5] and Tracy Park and Lansdown, both near Bath.[6] Relief sculpture is also known from Box and includes a fragment of a hand holding a trident, framed in an ornamental border.[7] Another piece shows a headless male figure standing in a niche, apparently a hunter or a hunter god, returning from the chase, as he has a hare hanging from his right shoulder and a bird from his left. North Wraxall produced a carving showing Diana killing

---

[1] *Woodchester* (1797), 10, 11
[2] Toynbee (1964), 82
[3] Lysons (1817), iii, pl. xxxii
[4] Dent (1877), pl. opp. 15
[5] *Hucclecote* (1933), 336
[6] *Lansdown* (1909), 34
[7] *Box* (1927), 335

a stag[1] and two votive reliefs from Customs Scrubs, Bisley, show, respectively, a figure holding a cornucopia, and a warrior.[2] The latter is identified by its inscription as the god Romulus, dedicated by Gulioepius. Several crudely carved altars were also found at Chedworth.[3]

The outstanding examples of the sculptor's art, however, discovered in a British villa are the two well-known busts from Lullingstone. Of Greek, probably Pentelic, marble, they are both over life-size. Bust I depicts a man aged forty-five or fifty with thick curly hair growing low over the brow and a short beard (Pl. 4.15). His head is turned slightly to the left and he has a benign and rather dreamy expression. He wears a tunic under a cloak with a fringed border, fastened on the right shoulder with a large brooch, and is believed to date from A.D. 125–35. Bust II is larger but less well preserved. At some time within the Roman period its shoulders were shaved off, probably so that it could be fitted into a niche or recess. When found, the head and the body were in two pieces. A man of rather severe aspect is depicted, a little older than Bust I and with thinner and straighter hair and a square-cut beard. He is clad in tunic and toga and may have been carved A.D. 155–65 or even later. A strong family likeness exists between the two faces; possibly they were uncle and nephew, or even father and son if the dating is stretched to its limits. Both may be the work of east Mediterranean sculptors and they form a notable addition to our small collection of works of art from villas.[4]

Apart from figure sculptures, however, there are a few more examples of carving in relief, among them part of a frieze of green sandstone built into the walls at Longstock (Hants),[5] and more green sandstone showing part of a spiral ornament noted at Putley (Herefords.).[6] Pieces of a sandstone slab of late 1st-century date decorated with a design of scrolls and cornucopias were discovered among the debris in the gutter surrounding the dwelling-house at Ashtead (Fig. 4.9).[7] Witcombe and Chedworth have both produced fragments from the railings of a veranda or balcony decorated with an open-work S motif.

---

[1] *North Wraxall* (1862), pl. LXV, 15

[2] Lysons (1815), pl. XXVIII, nos. 5, 6; R.I.B. 132

[3] Toynbee (1964), 176, 179, 181

[4] *Lullingstone* (1950), Appendix V by J. M. C. Toynbee; 35–43, pl. II–IV; Toynbee (1964), 60

[5] *J.R.S.*, xii (1922), 271

[6] *Putley* (1925), lxxvi

[7] *Ashtead* (1930), 135, fig. 11. I am indebted to Mr A. W. G. Lowther for permission to use his drawing for fig. 4.9, and for information about this slab

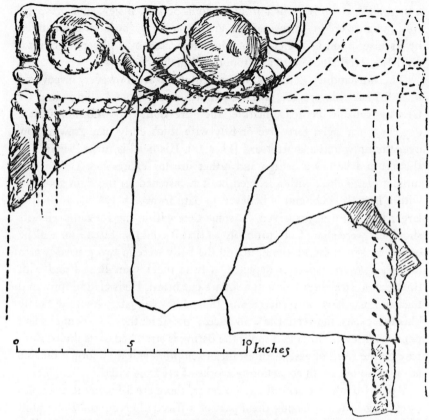

Fig. 4.9. Carved sandstone slab, Ashtead, Surrey (by courtesy of A. W. G. Lowther and the Surrey Archaeological Society).

Dwarf pillars from exterior corridors or verandas are of frequent occurrence. Examples are illustrated in the reports on Acton Scott[1] and Wincanton,[2] and fragments of six may be seen at Chedworth. They usually measure about 9 inches in diameter and are lathe-turned, with moulded capitals and bases. Dwarf capitals and bases of various types were found at Spoonley Wood,[3] made of the local oolite, and fragments from columns of various sizes turned up at North Wraxall.[4] Larger pillars were used to support the archway of Room 1 at North Leigh[5] and a fine column from a site

[1] *Acton Scott* (1846), opp. 340
[2] *W.A.M.*, xvi (1871), pl. opp. 14 (excursion notes)
[3] *Spoonley Wood* (1890), 656, pl. xix
[4] *North Wraxall* (1862), 65, pl. iv
[5] Skelton (1823), Wootton Hundred, 10

at Bathford had a carved composite capital (Fig. 4.10).[1] In the 4th century Ditchley seems to have had an elaborate entrance with tall columns supporting an ornamental cornice.[2] Stone roofs were crowned by the crest and ridge stones found at sites including Keynsham,[3] and carved finials are known from North Wraxall,[4] Wellow,[5] Chew Stoke,[6] Atworth[7] and Llantwit Major (Pl. 4.20). They all bear a fairly close resemblance to one

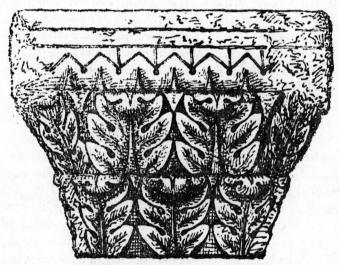

Fig. 4.10. Column capital, Warleigh, Bathford, Somerset (from Scarth (1864), (Pl. li).

another and may have come, perhaps, from workshops at such centres as Bath and Caerwent, where similar specimens occur. A decorative earthenware finial from a tiled roof was also found at Ashtead.[8]

Apart from pottery, an inventory of the furnishings so far found inside British villas would not occupy much space, even if it included agricultural implements and other metalwork concerned with the day-to-day life of the farm. Cato, however, has given us a list of the requirements of an

[1] Scarth (1864), 119, pl. LI
[2] *Ditchley* (1936), 42, 43
[3] *Keynsham* (1926), 131
[4] *North Wraxall* (1862), 65, pl. IV
[5] VCH, Som., i (1906), 313
[6] *ibid.*, 309
[7] *Atworth* (1942), 67
[8] *Ashtead* (1930), 133, fig. 2, opp. 6

Italian *villa rustica*, designed for a bailiff and his wife and the farm slaves in the 2nd century B.C. This includes bronze cauldrons and plates, a kneading-table, a wash-basin and pitchers, a tray, a lampstand, a store closet, a chest for clothing, tables, long benches, low stools, four chairs and two large chairs, one bed, presumably for the bailiff and his wife, several beds with woven thongs, mattresses, pillows and bedspreads, coverlets and towels.[1] Metal objects such as the cauldrons have been found, of course, in Britain, but most of the other essential furnishings on this list are made of wood or textiles which do not often survive the years in this country. We have a few fragments of furniture, but otherwise the gaps in our knowledge have to be filled by material from the towns, funerary reliefs and other sculptures, and evidence from other parts of the Empire.

Let us consider first the most important item, the bed. Cato says 'beds with woven thongs', meaning probably a wooden frame filled in with a latticework of cords or strips of leather and standing on four legs. Good examples of this are shown in the paintings of the Healing of the Paralytic in the Catacomb of St Calixtus in Rome and in the Tomb of Vestorius Priscus outside the Porta Vesuvio at Pompeii;[2] the latter example has bedroom slippers placed ready beside it. Other beds at Pompeii fit into alcoves or corners of bedrooms and are larger, with strips of wood placed at right-angles to each other strengthening or replacing the latticework of their frames. With high straight backs and ends, they either have legs decorated with mouldings or else are completely boxed in by a panel along the front reaching to ground-level. At Herculaneum a bed made of rare wood with inlaid decoration was found in a house occupied by a gem-cutter.[3] The skeleton of a youth lay on it and near by stood a one-legged marble table, a four-legged stool and a small loom or embroidery frame. Thick mattresses were used on these beds.

High-backed couches of the same type as the beds were also in use, and the deceased are shown reclining on them in the funeral banquet scenes which appear on many tombstones. Good clear British examples can be seen at York and Chester. In some cases the head- and footboards partially retain the curves of the head- and footrests of the earlier backless type of couch. The tombstone of Aelia Aeliana at York shows a typical

[1] Cato, *Agr.*, x, xi
[2] Spinazzola (1953), i, fig. 514
[3] Maiuri (1958), fig. 420

high-backed couch with this feature (Pl. 4.19).[1] The legs are usually decorated with mouldings, but some of the Chester examples have shorter fatter legs, sometimes standing on blocks.[2] A moulded leg made of Kimmeridge shale and turned on the lathe was found during the Silchester excavations and is now in the Reading Museum.[3] It is believed to be part of a couch. Little evidence survives for any other types of decoration, but the front of some of the couches is sometimes carved in the shape of a dolphin, its head resting on the end of the seat and the body and tail curving up the head- or footboard. Aelia Aeliana's couch may have had this feature, which also appears very clearly on one of the Chester tombstones.[4] In Italy, at least, the earlier backless couches were elaborately embellished with bronze or silver plating and their head- and footrests might be ornamented with small bronze busts or inlaid with various designs or bone plaques. British craftsmen may also have used veneers of fine woods or bronze plating in couch-making, with inlays or incised decoration for details such as seat-bars.

Another type of couch in use at this time was more in the nature of a bench with a very upright back and either a solid seat or one panelled down to the ground along the front and sides. Mother goddesses seem to prefer this type of furniture.[5] Simple wooden benches without backs, but sometimes with curved legs, and work-tables of the type Cato probably had in mind must have existed in all villas. They appear not infrequently on the walls of houses at Herculaneum and Pompeii and the famous paintings of Cupids plying various trades illustrate them clearly (Fig. 4.11).

The only type of chair pictorially represented in Britain is a substantial piece of furniture presumably made of wood. It has a rounded back to about shoulder height, made in one piece with the sides and it often stands on a rectangular or semicircular base. The well-known tombstone in the Tullie House Museum, Carlisle, shows a woman seated in such a chair, and another appears in profile on a small relief showing men coming to worship a seated deity, probably a mother goddess. This was found at Daglingworth and is now in the Corinium Museum, Cirencester. A lighter and probably more comfortable version of this chair was made of wickerwork, as is clearly shown on some of the imported Gaulish pipeclay

[1] Liversidge (1955), fig. 9 (*R.I.B.*, 682)
[2] *ibid.*, figs. 6, 7 (*R.I.B.*, 558, 568)
[3] *ibid.*, 8, fig. 33; Boon (1957), 162
[4] Liversidge (1955), fig. 14
[5] *e.g. ibid.*, fig. 21 from Ancaster.

figurines of mother goddesses. One good example is in the London Museum (Pl. 4.16). The plaited design round the front of another such chair is clearly visible on the tombstone of Julia Velva at York (Pl. 4.18) and a statue of a goddess seated in one was found at Birdoswald. The best picture of a chair of this type appears on the well-known relief of a toilet scene at Trier, where the decorative effect of varying the weave of the

Fig. 4.11. Cupids playing at shoemakers. Wall-painting from Herculaneum (from Richter (1926), fig. 343).

wickerwork is easily discerned. A full-scale stone model of a more upright variety was found in a tomb at Weiden, near Cologne, and this, being unoccupied, shows us that these chairs had a good thick seat cushion.[1]

Other types of chair in use in the Roman Empire at this period include the high-backed throne, usually occupied by deities or other people of importance, the cathedra, a lighter chair with slightly curved back and legs, and a straight-backed chair, sometimes with a solid or panelled seat which might have legs decorated with mouldings.[2] Basketwork tuffets and four-legged stools are also represented on Gaulish reliefs and a piece of iron which might belong to the leg of a stool of this type was found in the villa of Mansfield Woodhouse.[3]

Along the shores of the Mediterranean the convenience of the folding stool was appreciated long before the Roman period and it often appears on Imperial coins, reliefs or wall-paintings. Two types were known, one with curved legs, the other with straight. Actual examples of the latter

[1] For all these chairs, see *ibid.*, figs. 3 (*R.I.B.*, 688), 15 (*R.I.B.*, 129), 25–29, 32
[2] *ibid.*, 26
[3] *ibid.*, 28, fig. 37

have been found in Britain in Roman barrow burials at Holborough and Bartlow (Fig. 4.12).[1] They have straight legs joined just above the feet by stretcher-bars and by seat-bars which came behind the sitter and under his thighs, as with a deck chair, instead of on either side as is the case with a modern folding stool. The front seat of the two British examples is split

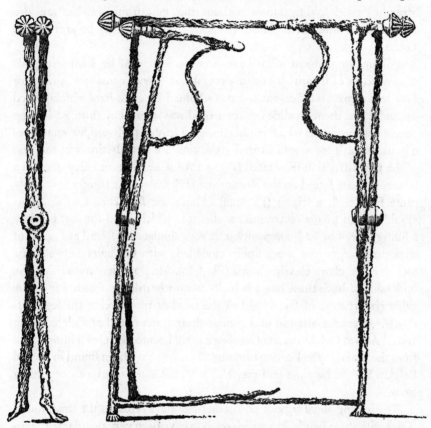

Fig. 4.12. Folding stool, Bartlow, Cambs. (by courtesy of the Society of Antiquaries of London). *John Christiansen.*

into two small sections supported by an S-shaped bracket attached to the legs. Probably this arrangement gave added flexibility when the leather seat was piled with cushions. Both stools were made of iron with bronze decorations. The Bartlow specimen had bronze or bronze-capped rivets holding the legs together, bronze caps adorned with a geometric design

[1] *ibid.*, 29; Jessup (1954), 22

161

encased the ends of the seat-bars and it stood on small bronze feet. A small Roman house existed not far from the barrows, so we may be justified in claiming it as an item of villa furniture. A similar stool was found in the Belgian villa of Fouron-le-Comte, and another one is exhibited in the Museum at Stara Zagora in Bulgaria, showing that the type was widespread. Straight-legged folding stools without the split front seat-bar are also known and a fine silver-plated specimen from Ostia may be seen in the Louvre.[1]

Folding stools must often have been accompanied by folding tripods of bronze, or of iron with bronze decorations. These consisted of three or four legs, ornamented in various ways, joined by cross-bars which moved up and down them on slides as the tripod was opened or shut. At the top came busts or tenons which could support a tray or table-top, or sometimes a hook on each leg would fit under the rim of a large basin as in the case of the reconstruction illustrated (Fig. 4.13).[2] A small bronze claw-foot on a hexagonal base found on the Roman site at Stanton Low (Bucks.) probably came from such a tripod (Pl. 4.22). Above the foot comes an acanthus moulding and then a rectangular socket into which fitted the leg, fixed by a filling of lead or lead-composition. A very similar foot found at Caerwent is slightly larger and more finely modelled, with the hairs between the toes and the claws clearly shown (Pl. 4.23). Mr Boon has noted that the underside of both these bases is badly worn towards the front, due to the sideways pressure of the weight of the bowl or tray forcing the legs outwards.[3] A cruder attempt at a similar design was found at Colchester in 1951.[4] Also at Colchester may be seen a small bronze model of a human foot from the burial in the Lexden tumulus. Such feet have been found in several Belgian Roman barrows and may also have belonged to tripods or folding stools.[5]

The folding metal tripods may sometimes have replaced the small round tables with three bandy legs which seem to have been very popular through-

[1] Liversidge (1955), 32

[2] My thanks are due to Dr D. K. Hill and the Walters Art Gallery for permission to use this illustration; see D. K. Hill, 'Roman Panther Tripods', *American Journal of Archaeology*, lv (1951), 344, pl. xxxviii

[3] I am very much indebted to Mr G. Boon and the National Museum of Wales for information and photographs of the Stanton Low foot. A brief report of the site, excavated by Mrs M. U. Jones for the Ministry of Public Building and Works, appears in *J.R.S.*, xlix (1959), 119

[4] Hull (1958), 30, fig. 9

[5] Liversidge (1955), 34

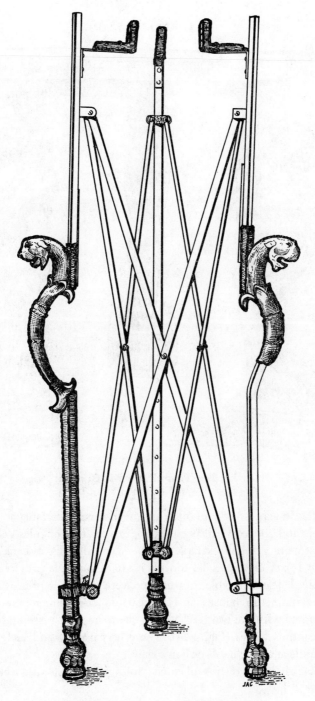

Fig. 4.13. Reconstruction of a Roman bronze tripod, Baltimore (by courtesy of Dr
D. K. Hill and the Walters Art Gallery, Baltimore).

Fig. 4.14. Marble table from Pompeii (from P. Gusman: *Pompeii: the City, its Life and Art* (1900)).

out the Roman world and often appear in funeral banquet scenes. A very simple and undecorated specimen appears in front of Julia Velva (Pl. 4.18) and a more graceful example can be seen on Aelia Aeliana's tombstone (Pl. 4.19). A close parallel to this, made of wood, is preserved at Herculaneum.[1] Beautiful tables of this type were also made of marble, and some still standing in houses at Herculaneum and Pompeii have their legs decorated with the heads of lions or panthers which rise up out of collars of acanthus leaves (Fig. 4.14). These legs usually end in feet carved to resemble antelope hoofs or lion's claws.

In Britain fragments of such tables have been discovered made of

[1] *ibid.*, fig. 16

Kimmeridge shale, a substance rather like slaty coal which could be turned on the lathe and polished. A possible Roman villa site at Upper Langridge Farm, near Bath, produced a claw-foot and the lower part of a leg (Pl. 4.21)[1] and similar isolated feet have been found at Dorchester, Caerleon and Silchester. The only complete table-leg so far found comes from a 2nd-century town house in Colliton Park, Dorchester, and this again has the claw-foot (Pl. 4.24). Like the Italian marble tables, the upper parts of these Kimmeridge shale fragments were usually decorated with animal heads. The most naturalistic is the piece found in the Rothley villa (Leics.), a lion with a bristling mane (Pl. 4.29). The same type of head, but less realistic and without the mane, appears on the Colliton Park leg (Pl. 4.24) and on a fragment from the near-by villa of Frampton (Pl. 4.25). These are strange beasts; their eyes stare out into space and from their open mouths protrude long outstretched tongues which rest on the curve of the leg. At first sight one is tempted to identify them as some peculiarly British beast worked by a Celtic artist, were it not for the fact that very similar creatures appear carved on a marble table support in the Museo Nazionale in Naples (Fig. 4.15). These even have manes which could well have inspired the artist at Rothley, and so it appears that we must regard the classical lion-headed, winged and claw-footed griffin as the prototype for the decoration of our tables of Kimmeridge shale. The head on the Colliton Park leg rises out of a collar of fluted ornament and this is probably the equivalent of the acanthus foliage of Pompeii and Herculaneum (Fig. 4.14), which it would be impossible to copy in shale and difficult, indeed, to copy in wood. This is demonstrated by a wooden table found in the Casa dell'Atrio Corintio at Herculaneum which has animal heads with outstretched tongues closely akin to the Dorset beasts and below each of them a band of incised fluting.[2]

A small piece from the top of a table-leg comes from the villa at Foscott (Bucks.) with a spiral carved in relief as its only ornamental feature (Pl. 4.29). It is possible that this is all the decoration there was, as legs with such spirals appear in funeral banquet scenes from Cologne and Narbonne and also on actual bronze specimens found at Pompeii. However, the discovery in 1938 of the upper part of another shale leg at Norden, Corfe Castle, Dorset, offers an alternative solution to the Foscott mystery as the new discovery was decorated with a head with fine curling horns (Pl. 4.28). Obviously on occasion the lion-headed griffin with rams' horns, of the type

[1] Liversidge (1952), 233
[2] Liversidge (1955), 40

Fig. 4.15. Marble table support, Pompeii. *H. J. Mellon.*

seen on the table support in the House of Cornelius Rufus at Pompeii, was
included in the British craftsman's repertoire.[1]

There remains one further addition to our menagerie. Running up from
the claw, on the inner edge of the Colliton Park leg, is a detail which
probably represents the slender leg of another animal, ending in a double
hoof just below the fluting (Pl. 4.24). The idea which inspired this is
illustrated by the last item on our list of shale fragments from villas, the

[1] *ibid.*, 44, fig. e

fine piece from Preston, Dorset (Pl. 4.26).[1] Here we have the usual animal head near the top of the leg, although the tongue has been broken away. Below it we find no fluted ornament, but in its place the head of another animal, climbing up the leg which it grips between its forepaws. For some years this was a unique find, but in 1958 another piece was found in Dorchester, broken off just above the outstretched tongue of the upper animal, but showing most of the creature climbing up the leg towards it. This is a much poorer representation, however, with feeble foreshortened paws, and little of the head survives apart from the long ears.[2]

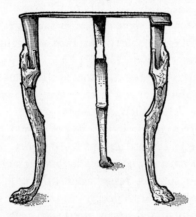

Fig. 4.16. Bronze table, Pompeii (Museo Nazionale, Naples). *John Christiansen.*

The identity of this secondary animal remains in doubt and, indeed, different animals may be depicted. The slender leg of Pl. 4.24 and of a further fragment found in Dorchester which also shows this feature,[3] may belong to a deer or antelope, while the long-eared animals of Preston and the 1958 Dorchester discovery might be hares resembling those familiar to us from hunt scenes on Castor ware beakers. If these identifications are correct, then these animals could be the griffin's prey. The Preston animal, however, seems rather too virile and full of attack for a hare about to be consumed by a griffin, and it is possible that here again we can learn from Italian parallels. In the Naples Museum is a bronze table from Pompeii, and up each of its legs climbs a dog of greyhound type with pointed nose and long outstretched legs, emerging from a band of acanthus foliage (Fig.

[1] *ibid.*, 38, 46
[2] Liversidge (1960), 72
[3] Liversidge (1955), 46, fig. 50

4.16). A wooden table in a house at Herculaneum has the same decoration, a leg from another was found in Egypt,[1] and fragments of this design are known from elsewhere.[2] Dogs of rather similar type also appear in the Castor ware hunting scenes. The Italian tables lack the griffin heads, but even so it seems not impossible that in Britain a conflation of ideas occurred and some tables showed one of the hunting dogs for which the province was renowned, bravely leaping to the attack.

A notch behind the griffin head (Pl. 4.24) shows that the shale tables had stretcher-bars. Pieces of the circular tops have been found at Silchester, Caerwent and Gloucester, and two fragments from the Brading villa may also belong to table-tops. In some cases they may have been supported by one leg rather than three, as tables of this type, decorated with lions' heads, appear on reliefs from Arlon or Trier.[3]

From literary references we know that the Romans used sideboards to display their most valued household treasures.[4] Fragments from a series of rectangular stone slabs which may have been used for this purpose in Britain have been recovered from the sites of several villas. One found at Wincanton (Somerset) measured about 3 feet 6 inches by 2 feet 4 inches and had three of its sides cut away underneath, forming a chamfered edge. The fourth side, which presumably rested against the wall, was left plain. The front edge was ornamented with deeply cut triangular indentations with a scallop shell in the centre, and square stops with geometric flowers at each end.[5] Another fragment, decorated with a similar flower and a more angular series of rosettes in the same chip-carving technique, was found at Bawdrip in 1956,[6] and other pieces from Whitsbury and Kingsworthy are in Salisbury and Winchester Museums respectively. The most impressive specimen so far found was excavated in 1960 by Mr A. T. Morley Hewitt at Rockbourne (Hants.).[7] It measures 2 feet 9 inches by 2 feet and is decorated with a central scallop shell. A row of triangles runs just under the edge and below it come geometric flowers and other motifs. A leg may have fitted under the squared corner which survives at one end of the slab, as

---

[1] Aldred (1956), 235, fig. 208

[2] Liversidge (1955), 46

[3] *ibid.*, 52

[4] Richter (1926), 142

[5] *W.A.M.*, xvi (1871), pl. opp. 14 (excursion notes)

[6] *J.R.S.*, xlvii (1957), 222, pl. vii, 4

[7] To whom I am much indebted for this information. *J.R.S.*, lii (1962), 185, pl. xxii (2), fig. 29

4. 1 Ickleton. Cambs. Cambridge University Museum of Archaeology and Ethnology. Photo L. P. Morley

4. 2 Ickleton, Cambs. Cambridge University Museum of Archaeology and Ethnology. Photo L. P. Morley

4. 3 Brading, Isle of Wight. Photo W. J. Nigh. By courtesy of the late Major D. Oglander.

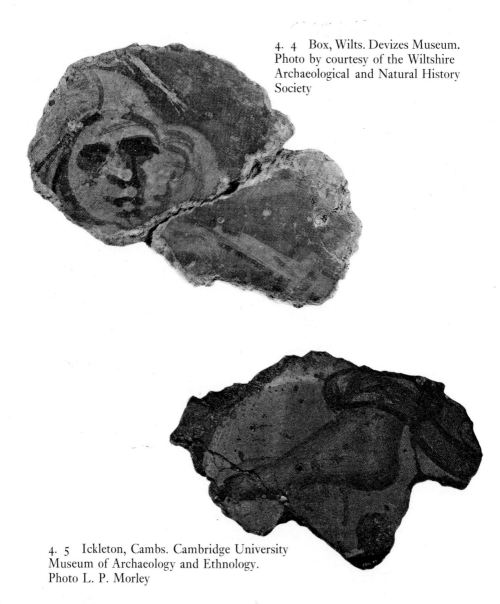

4. 4   Box, Wilts. Devizes Museum. Photo by courtesy of the Wiltshire Archaeological and Natural History Society

4. 5   Ickleton, Cambs. Cambridge University Museum of Archaeology and Ethnology. Photo L. P. Morley

4. 6   Ickleton, Cambs. Cambridge University Museum of Archaeology and Ethnology. Photo L. P. Morley

another slab found at Tockington (Glos.) is recorded as standing on four supports.[1] Two pieces of stone also found at Rockbourne might have belonged to pillar-shaped legs and one has a moulding on three sides, the fourth side being left rough. Another piece of stone had a chamfered groove and it is believed that this was built into the wall and into it fitted the back of the slab, the front resting on two legs. Another unique feature about the Rockbourne discovery is the fact that the top of the slab is decorated with an incised circle, while semicircles appear in the centre of the sides and at the corners. This decoration rather recalls the ornament on the oblong panels of Kimmeridge shale, sometimes described as trays or wall-veneers, which are found coming mostly from the Dorset area. They might have decorated the tops of tables or sideboards of this type.

Items of Roman furniture for which we have so far no definite evidence in Britain include sets of shelves and cupboards. Fig. 4.11 shows a shelf fixed to the wall with brackets (and a little artistic licence) and occasionally traces of such fixtures are suspected in villas. The painting of the nymphs at Lullingstone, for instance, had been damaged in Roman times by the insertion of some item of furniture before the niche was finally blocked up. Fig. 4.11 also shows a cupboard, and wooden cupboards with panelled doors are preserved at Herculaneum. A good representation of a cupboard from a neighbouring Roman province also appears among the reliefs on the inside of the Simpelveld sarcophagus, now in Leyden Museum (Pl. 4.30). These depict a Gallo-Roman lady, the mistress of a 2nd-century villa, lying on her couch or bed among her cherished household possessions. Her round-backed chair, three-legged table decorated with feline heads and claw-feet, and sets of shelves with toilet articles, are also depicted, as well as several buildings from the villa, giving us a clear idea of a Roman home. Among the furnishings not portrayed are the footstools which frequently accompany the chairs and high couches, and the strong boxes and chests. These do occasionally appear, however, on Romano-British tombstones.[2] Bronze lock-plates and other fittings from chests are also uncovered fairly frequently. Fragments of burnt wood at Brading were associated with sixteen bronze studs, a key, two drop handles with acorn-shaped ends and four iron clamps, all possibly the remains of a casket.[3] Evidence for another iron-bound box was found at Brislington.

[1] *The Builder*, liii (1887), 554
[2] Liversidge (1955), 61
[2] *Brading* (1881), 21

Cato's list of household necessities includes mattresses, pillows, bedspreads, coverlets and towels. Mattresses are clearly visible on the couches represented on reliefs (*e.g.* Pls. 4. 18, 19) and Julia Velva is provided with a particularly well-upholstered specimen. Such mattresses often had elaborately decorated covers, and traces of bands of woven ornament are faintly visible on Victor's tombstone in the Museum at South Shields. Couches which form the covers of sarcophagi in Rome and Athens depict such stripes very clearly and traces of a design also decorate the rest of the textile.[1] Mattresses of varying thickness and pillows of several different shapes can be found on the Chester tombstones, and at South Shields, Victor's elbow rests on an elaborate bolster ornamented with fringe or a frill.[2] Mattresses and cushions must have been very necessary for the springless seats and chairs, and the cushion on the seat of the Cologne basket chair has already been noted (p. 160). Reliefs found in or near Cologne also show fringed or frilled cushions.[3] Traces of vegetable matter adhering to the framework of the Holborough folding stool may be evidence for a seat-cushion stuffed with straw or chaff and trimmed with bronze ribbon.[4] Such vegetable material, or feathers, wool or flax, was the customary stuffing for mattresses and cushions. Fragments of both wool and linen textiles have been identified in Britain, but they mostly come from graves. Actual specimens of colourful coverlets or curtains, also used as grave wrappings, occasionally turn up in the Near East, and curtains, fringed coverings and fringed tablecloths appear on tombstones.[5]

From this survey it becomes apparent that, like wall-painting, Romano-British furnishings were chiefly developed from ideas current in Italy and in the other provinces. We know from such discoveries as the Lexden tumulus that, even before the Roman invasion of A.D. 43, Belgic chieftains occasionally possessed luxurious bronze tripods or folding stools, and possibly most of the collapsible furniture of this type continued to be imported from Italy or Gaul. Prototypes of the wooden couches could easily have been copied in this country and the Chester tombstones suggest that local fashions soon developed. Craftsmen who learnt their trade in centres in Italy, Greece or Syria may have settled in Britain and manu-

[1] Charbonneaux and Peters (1955), pl. 93, 94
[2] Liversidge (1955), 53
[3] Espérandieu (1922), viii, nos. 6418, 6467
[4] Jessup (1954), 23
[5] Liversidge (1955), 54–56

factured more elaborate furniture with bone, bronze or fine wood veneers. Wickerwork was a pre-Roman craft, found, for example, at Glastonbury, so the production of basket chairs would present no difficulties. The most interesting developments occur with the tables. As we have seen, their decoration seems largely inspired by lions, griffins and dogs found in Italy, but, so far as I know, no other province has yet combined animal heads with a secondary animal climbing up a table-leg, and only in Britain does one seem to find such tables made of Kimmeridge shale. It would appear, therefore, that the ideas which poured across the Channel for over 400 years were not merely imitated; they were also assimilated and sometimes developed. Possibly this traffic was not entirely one-way and British designs in soft furnishing, for instance, may well have found their way to the Continent. We may also wonder whether our strange Dorset beasts had any descendants among the art of post-Roman Britain.

We know that Roman sculptured reliefs were often coloured, but so far no helpful traces of paint have been found on any British funeral banquet scenes and our wall-decorations have provided no pictures of a furnished room. The wooden furniture, however, must have been polished or painted, and the markets of London and other large towns would supply a variety of textiles, imported or homespun. So perhaps we are justified in turning again to Italy for a few ideas for colour schemes. The famous mosaic from Pompeii depicting three actors in a scene from a play, for example, includes a brown and yellow table and a stool covered with brown, yellow and white check drapery. On this lies a cushion with purple, red and yellow stripes.[1] Paintings also in the Naples Museum show Apollo seated on a chair or stool with white moulded legs picked out in red (no. 9543), and a woman with a cream-coloured chair (no. 9022). The matron presiding over the ceremonies depicted on the walls of the Villa dei Misteri also sits on a cream chair, with green and purple cushion and draperies.[2] Another lady sits on a yellow bed, its legs picked out in red and with a gaily painted purple design along its front. On the bed are diaphanous white pillows and coverlets.[3] And finally, there is the picture of the courtship of Venus and Mars from the house of Marcus Lucretius Fronto, the gold and white bed hung with white drapery and spread with a purple mattress and coverlets striped with red and gold. Beside it sits Venus on a blue and yellow cushion

[1] B. Maiuri (1957), 117
[2] A. Maiuri (1953), 52
[3] *ibid.*, 106

in a chair draped in blue and red with long gold tassels, her feet on a brown and red footstool.[1]

This is the type of colouring we have to imagine in Romano-British houses. The tints used for the wall-paintings are sometimes described as either garish or dull and depressing, but it has to be remembered that the final effect must have depended upon the lighting, either daylight, entering through windows which might be thickly glazed or merely shuttered, or artificial light provided by numbers of small oil lamps, torches or candles. Pompeii has shown us that decorators carefully considered this problem and also such factors as the height and size of rooms. In Britain surely, gay textiles, furniture with coloured veneers and inlays, wall-decorations, often painted on grounds of red, white or yellow, and polychrome mosaics must have turned the interiors of our wealthy villas into a gorgeous spectacle and brightened up many a less luxurious dwelling.

[1] *ibid.*, 78

CHAPTER FIVE

Social and Economic Aspects

A. L. F. RIVET

The Problem

THE PRECEDING CHAPTERS have dealt with various physical aspects of Romano-British villas, drawing mainly on the archaeological evidence. As the reader will have realised, this evidence, though of varying precision, is remarkably plentiful, and if we were dealing with a prehistoric period we should count ourselves fortunate indeed. Quite what sort of society a prehistorian would derive from it is a matter not, perhaps, beyond all conjecture but fortunately irrelevant here. For in making their deductions from the archaeological evidence the authors have been able to confirm their findings by reference both to the chronological skeleton provided for Britain by the ancient historians and to the solid body of literary and epigraphic evidence relating to the rest of the Roman Empire.

It remains true, however, that the period of Roman Britain is not, in the epistemological sense, a fully historical period, for no local literature concerning it has survived. This makes difficulties enough when we are dealing with urban affairs, but in their case there are some mitigating factors. Towns do at least achieve occasional mention both in itineraries and in the chronicles of the Empire as a whole, and beyond this they often

173

yield some monumental inscriptions, so that the story of their origin and development, as derived from archaeology, can be checked at several points. Villas, on the other hand, together with the whole field of rural affairs, were beneath the notice of imperial historians, while such few inscriptions as are found in them are likely to provide personal rather than historical information. In fact, the word 'villa' occurs only once in contemporary writing in connection with Britain—in the Antonine Itinerary, where *Villa Faustini* is listed as a staging-point between Colchester and Caister St Edmunds.[1] We lack not merely a Varro or a Columella to tell us how British villas were organised, but even an Ausonius or a Sidonius to illustrate the life of their owners. Above all—and this is not peculiar to Britain—we lack any statistical information whatever.

The effect of this can be seen most clearly if we consider what would be expected of an economic survey of a class of establishments comparable with villas today, or in any other well-documented period of history. First of all, there would be a clear determination of the subject, with the villa defined in terms of size—either by acreage, or by number of persons employed, or by some similar factual criterion—and account would be taken of the form of ownership and land tenure; freehold, leasehold and so on. Questions of labour relations would be raised—is the labour force free, servile, or a mixture of the two, and what wage rates apply? The efficiency of villas as productive units would be assessed, again statistically, in terms of yield per acre and yield per man. Consideration would be given to the relationship of villas to the country's economy as a whole and much attention would be paid to markets and their fluctuation, to the profitability of different crops at different times and to the incidence of taxation. Most of this information would be neatly tabulated in statistical appendices and on the basis of them we should be in a position to set about tracing the history of the rise, and possibly the fall, of our villas in the economic and in the social sense too.

Such a survey would no doubt include much else, but this is enough to suggest not only how little we do know but how little we can know about the economy of Romano-British villas. We cannot begin to compile our statistical appendices, first because the direct written evidence does not exist and secondly because archaeology cannot give us the sort of informa-

---

[1] *Itin. Anton.*, 474, 5. For the buildings at Scole (which do not correspond with orthodox ideas of a Roman villa), see R. R. Clarke, *Norfolk Archaeology*, xxx (1949–52), 151

tion we require. The most obvious reason for this is the sporadic nature of the archaeological material. Out of some 600 known structures in Britain which are loosely referred to as villas there are, to be generous, a score which have been examined in what could be called a scientific manner, and none has been completely excavated. Without this, such scraps of evidence as are forthcoming are bound to be equivocal and can be misleading, especially from the economic point of view. The ideal villa produced everything the household needed, and the discovery of a ploughshare or a pair of cropping-shears does not justify us in assuming that corn on the one hand or wool on the other was the main, let alone the exclusive, concern of the owner. And even when we have achieved the long-overdue feat of the total excavation of a villa we shall not thereby discover the size of the estate related to it. In this matter, which should be central to our inquiry, some slight progress has been made by the methods of historical geography, with some assurance in Gaul,[1] more tentatively in Britain,[2] but nothing has yet emerged on which any general conclusions can be based.

In these circumstances it is evident that very few firm statements regarding the economic aspects of our villas can be made. We must recognise that we have to deal not with fully authenticated facts but at best with probabilities, and in establishing such probabilities two approaches are open to us. Either we can try to construct a probable economy from the scattered scraps of archaeological evidence and then relate it to what we know of the history and economics of the Roman Empire in general and of Britain in particular, or we can begin with the history and the economics and see at what points the archaeology comes out to meet us. Of these two approaches the former, which one might call the prehistorian's approach, has more often been taken in Britain and it has some virtues to commend it; in particular, nothing is more hostile to sound archaeological practice than to set out with the aim of proving a preconceived idea. Nevertheless, in the case of villas there is a special reason why the second course is to be preferred—the fact that we do not really know what, in a British context, the word 'villa' means.

This problem is of comparatively recent growth. While villa excavation

[1] Earlier work summarised by Grenier (1934), 885–941. The most notable recent example is the identification by M. G. Fouet of the medieval *petit pays* of the Nébouzan as the domain of the villa at Montmaurin: *Montmaurin* (1949)

[2] Especially H. P. R. Finberg: *Withington* (1955)

was confined to the uncovering of stone walls and mosaics and hypocausts, and while the native Britons were still thought of as naked blue-painted savages, no such difficulty arose; the elaborate buildings were clearly villas and they were equally clearly Roman, not British. More recently, however, increases in our knowledge have undermined the foundations on which this simple proposition was based. Haverfield, relying on what is known of Roman policy elsewhere, demonstrated that 'Roman' and 'British' were not mutually exclusive terms and that the villa-owners were more likely to be of native than of Italian stock, while archaeological research revealed an agricultural society which in its origins owed nothing at all to Roman influence. For a time it seemed possible that a valid distinction could still be made between the 'village economy' of the native Britons on the one hand and the specifically Roman 'villa economy', centred on the single farm, on the other, and most of Collingwood's writing on the subject was based on such an hypothesis; but further work has shown that this, too, is oversimplified and that the single farm was, though not universal, at least normal in Celtic society. So we are reduced to Collingwood's classic definition:

> 'Villa', in Latin, means farm. It is an economic term; it refers to the fact that the place so designated is an agricultural establishment. . . .
> Any house of the Roman period may be called a villa, provided that it was the dwelling of people, somewhat Romanised in manners, who farmed a plot of land; as opposed to a town house on the one hand and a cottage on the other.[1]

This seems to suggest that the mere rebuilding of a Celtic farm *more Romanorum*, with baked tiles and mortar to replace the wattle and thatch, converted it into something different, something that qualifies for the definition 'villa'; but that this something turns out still to be no more than a farm.[2]

Now it can, of course, be argued that when we are dealing with a society whose official language was Latin it is appropriate that we should use Latin terms, but the argument is only valid where a term has no satisfactory English synonym. Such terms do occur: *civitas* is one and *colonia* is another, and the use of the English word 'colony' for the latter is instructively misleading. But does the word 'villa' really fall into this category? Super-

[1] Collingwood (1930), 113; *cf.* his more expanded discussions in Collingwood and Myres (1937), 209–10, in Frank (1937), 73–76, and in *C.A.H.*, xii (1939), 284–5
[2] As might, indeed, be suggested by *C.A.H.*, xii, 284

ficially the evidence is contradictory. On the one hand we have the definition given in the *Digest*,[1] which seems to bear out Collingwood's; on the
other we have the fact that neither Caesar nor Tacitus, nor any other
classical writer, ever uses the word, even by analogy, to describe a native
Celtic farm. Further reflection, however, reveals that the contradiction is
more apparent than real. The lawyers of the *Digest* were legislating for a
specifically Roman society, and it was from this society that Caesar and
Tacitus were looking out upon the Celtic world. Our difficulty is resolved
if we amend Collingwood's definition to read: 'Villa, in Latin, means farm,
but a farm which is integrated into the social and economic organisation of
the Roman world.'

Something like this may, indeed, be read into his phrase 'somewhat
Romanised in manners', but the point is that the Romanisation that is
significant inheres not so much in the farm itself as in its relations with the
outside world. As Mr Bowen has shown (ch. I), the Romans did introduce
some improvements in agricultural practice, but they were of a marginal
character and by themselves they might only have resulted in the development of the Celtic economy at a higher level. In fact, this was not the result,
because the Romanisation of the farms of Britain did not take place in
isolation, but was a secondary and accidental effect of the deliberate replacement of the old diffuse Celtic economy by a centralised system, based
on the towns, which approximated to the mediterranean model. The transi-
tion was a long process—in some parts of the province it was never
achieved at all—and whether or not a farm can properly be called a villa
must depend not only on the character of the building itself but also on
its relationship to towns and roads. This is cold comfort for the excavator
who wants to know what to call his site, but we should by now be inured
to the limitations of archaeological inference.[2] That the villas and the
towns did indeed form connected parts of the same economic system is

---

[1] *Digest.*, L, 16, 211: 'Fundi appellatione omne aedificium et omnis ager
continetur; sed in usu urbana aedificia aedes, rustica villae dicuntur; locus vero
sine aedificio in urbe area, rure autem ager appellatur: idemque ager cum
aedificio fundus dicitur.' (In the country buildings are called *villae*, and land
without buildings *ager*; and *ager* with a building is called *fundus*.) Contrast Varro,
R.R., III, ii, 6: 'Nam quod extra urbem est aedificium, nihilo magis ideo est villa,
quam eorum aedificia, qui habitant extra portam Flumentanam aut in Aemilianis.'

[2] For a recent attempt to define a villa in purely archaeological terms, see
Manning (1962). This fails because it overlooks the fact that in the late Iron Age
round houses are a British peculiarity. This is not an exclusively British problem,
and a fuller realisation of its implications is shown by J. Harmand, 'Sur le valeur

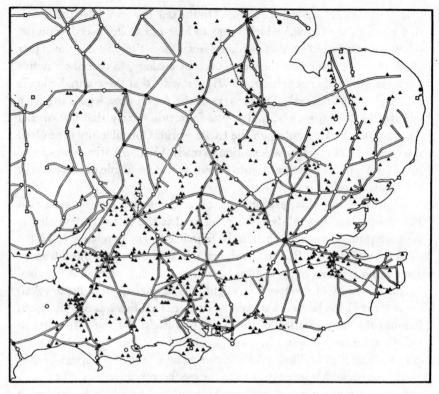

Fig. 5.1. Distribution of villas in relation to towns and roads.

amply demonstrated by their geographical distribution (Fig. 5.1); and this interdependence explains not only the consistent grouping of villas round towns but equally their absence where no towns exist, even in so favoured a part of the country as south Devon.

Definition of the Villa in Roman Terms

The question of what the word 'villa' means in its proper context of Roman civilisation can be answered fairly fully by reference to the Roman

archéologique du mot "Villa" ' (*Revue Archéologique*, xxxviii (1951), 155–8), concluding: 'Tout bien considéré, la vraie solution ne consisterait-elle pas à user *seulement* de la terminologie qui nous est naturelle: établissement, exploitation, ferme, habitation, résidence . . . ?' (M. Harmand practises what he preaches—*cf.* *Les Origines des Recherches Françaises sur l'Habitat Rural Gallo-Romain* (1961))

writers on agriculture—Cato, Varro, Columella, Pliny the Elder and Palladius, but especially Varro and Columella. How far their actual precepts are relevant to British farming in the Roman period does not immediately concern us; their own writings indicate that they had a healthy respect for the working farmer's empirical knowledge of his local conditions and that they would have been the last to suggest that British farms should automatically conform to Italian practice. What we are concerned with are the broader assumptions on which their dissertations rest. Varro does confirm Collingwood when he says that a farmhouse is no less a villa because it lacks all the decoration and amenities of a town house,[1] but the reasons he supposes for such examples of austerity have little to do with the wealth or social standing of the owners. To Varro, a villa is a self-contained unit and the key figure in it is not really the owner (*dominus*) but the bailiff (*vilicus*), and a similar attitude is adopted by Columella, who devotes sections of his treatise not only to the *vilicus* but also to his wife, the *vilica*;[2] whether or not the *dominus* chooses to relax there is a side issue. Of course, the advice offered by Varro and Columella is addressed to the *dominus*, because he directs policy; and in both cases they were writing propaganda, with the aim of restoring Italy—their appeal is to the Roman national stereotype of the solid Cato-like farmer. But it is perfectly clear that the villa as they envisaged it could and did function without the presence of the *dominus*, who in a sense stood outside it and did not necessarily live in it; they were merely concerned that he should visit it fairly often.[3] Varro, with his love of playing on words, does indeed set the scene for his dialogues at a villa, but it is the *Villa Publica*, as it might be the Mansion House, in the great city of Rome itself, and his dramatis personae, though all expert in their several fields, are first and foremost citizens.

Further, to these writers a villa is a rural enterprise which can be not

---

[1] Varro, *R.R.*, III, ii, 9: 'Num minus villa tua erit ad angulum Velini, quam neque pictor neque tector vidit umquam, quam in Rosia quae est polita opere tectorio eleganter, quam dominus habes communem cum asino? Cum significasset nutu nihilo minus esse villam eam quae esset simplex rustica, quam eam quae esset utrumque, et ea et urbana, . . . '

[2] Columella, *R.R.*, XII; *cf.* Cato, *Agr.*, cxliii

[3] Columella, *R.R.*, I, i, 18. Varro *R.R.*, II, *praef.* 1, contrasts contemporary habits with those of the ancients, who spent seven days out of the eight in the country; encouragement to villa-owners to visit the country had evidently been necessary for some time—*cf.* Cato, *Agr.*, iv: 'Villam urbanam pro copia aedificato. In bono praedio si bene aedificaveris, bene posiveris, ruri si recte habitaveris, libentius et saepius venies.'

merely bequeathed or inherited but also bought and sold; the fact that his wife has just bought one (for we have female owners too) is made the occasion for Varro's first book. Varro is at pains to make it clear that to invest in the countryside is not only the good Roman's duty (again the appeal is to Cato) but also to his interest,[1] and this carries two important implications. First, anyone could buy a villa who had the necessary money, and it made no difference how he had acquired it. Trimalchio, the outrageous freedman in the *Satyricon*, is the classic example of this. One could invest in land without being a working farmer. Varro and Columella thought that the owner should make a serious effort to know something about farming, but they did not suggest that he should give up town life altogether.[2] For the good citizen villa-owning is one activity among many, not a whole way of life; so that the correct form of the question, 'What was the status of villa-owners?' becomes rather, 'Who owned the villas?' Secondly, if a man had enough money, he could buy several villas, as we know many Romans did. Such multiple owners included the Emperors, and in parenthesis we may note that many imperial estates would probably be indistinguishable, at least in archaeological terms, from those of other multiple owners. Nor was the situation static: in time, properties tended to be consolidated, producing in Italy the *latifundia*, against which the poets and moralists inveigh, echoing the words of Isaiah the prophet, 'Woe unto them that join house to house, that lay field to field, till there be no place, that they may be placed alone in the midst of the earth.'

It is true that even in Italy not all the land was accounted for by estates of this character. On the one hand there were independent peasants and small farmers, a class which, though it declined in numbers, never entirely disappeared. On the other hand, a good deal of land was worked by people who lived in towns. It is important that we should remember this, because this was the concept that lay behind the *coloniae* which Rome planted in the provinces and which, in Britain as elsewhere, represented the first impact of Roman ideas on the countryside. Because we have only three *coloniae* of the traditional kind (for York is different), we tend to overlook this aspect of the matter, but it strikes one forcefully in the lower Rhône valley, for example, where the *coloniae* positively jostle one another

[1] Varro, *R.R.*, I, ii, 8: 'Nemo enim sanus debet velle impensam ac sumptum facere in cultura, si videt non posse refici.'

[2] This was Mago's idea. Columella (*R.R.*, I, i, 18–19) considers it an ideal, but quite impracticable; Pliny (*N.H.*, XVIII, vii, 35) denounces it as contrary to the public interest.

and where, significantly, known villas are very few. We should not expect our *coloniae*, either, to sprout villas in their earlier stages, but in a barbarian land like Britain, with no native form of town life, the same pattern must have applied even more widely. The metropoleis which Rome provided for the tribal *civitates* to be the seats of local government were not *coloniae*, in the legal sense, in that they were not communities of Roman citizens, but they were deliberate Roman foundations none the less and designed to a similar model. The land around them too would certainly have been worked by their inhabitants and this may account for the fact that most of the larger groups of villas are centred not on the original tribal capitals but on the secondary towns, which were both smaller than the capitals and later to develop.[1]

Viewing it in the light of this traditional mediterranean form of land use, we can the better recognise the idea of the villa, as expressed in Varro and Columella, for what it really is—a means by which the townsman can exploit the countryside. The typical villa-owner is a citizen who has invested in land. In time, of course, either of two variations might develop: the owner might so thoroughly convert a villa to his urban ideas of style and comfort that the farmyard was segregated from it, or even given up altogether, thus producing rural palaces of the type of Hadrian's Villa or Piazza Armerina; or, at the other extreme, he might become so preoccupied with his rural interests that he abandoned town life completely, both in fact and in ideas, thus producing a villa which would be indistinguishable from the farm of a wealthy peasant. The fact that in the latter case the degenerate may resemble the primitive must not blind us to the difference between the two, the essential difference between the native Celtic farm and the Roman, or Roman-inspired, villa. It is true that Roman and Celtic society shared in a common Bronze Age heritage, but it is irrelevant in this context, for they had in the meantime been subjected to totally different influences and Roman development was so far advanced that, as we have already noted, the classical authors could not see even the likeness of a villa in the Celtic world. Apart from the neutral, functional, terms, *fundus* and *aedificium*, the words used to describe Celtic farms are those which in Italy refer to the dwellings of the backward peasantry—*casa* and *tugurium*; even in Gaul, which had a century's start over Britain in Romanisation, the first use of the word 'villa' does not occur until A.D. 21.[2] But *casa* and

---

[1] For comparative sizes of the groups, see Corder (1955), fig. 1
[2] Tacitus, *Ann.*, iii, 46: 'Sacrovir primo Augustodunum, dein metu deditionis in

tugurium are not appropriate names for the houses which yielded the decoration dealt with by Miss Liversidge and Dr Smith. Assuredly villas did
develop in Roman Britain and, bearing in mind the guiding principles we
have derived from Varro and Columella, we may consider how and when
this can have happened under the three headings of possession, productivity
and profitability.

Conditions in pre-Roman Britain

First, then, possession. The typical Roman villa could be not only bequeathed and inherited but also bought and sold on the open market;
would this have been possible in pre-Roman Britain? In view of the equivocal nature of the evidence, which consists of much later survivals on the
one hand and chance references in the ancient authors on the other, we
must not expect an unequivocal answer. The survivals occur in predominantly pastoral societies, which have been modified by many influences,
both secular and religious, and the very fact that they have preserved
archaic features suggests that they are atypical;[1] and since none of the
ancient authors was a trained anthropologist we can never be quite sure
that they understood what they were looking at.[2] This is a difficulty that
recurs throughout history: one society inevitably interprets the customs of
another in terms of its own usage. In the 19th century vast areas of Africa
fell into European hands by the enforcement of treaties which were not
understood and which, had they been understood, would have been invalid
under tribal law. Just so in early Celtic society it seems that the ownership
of land was vested in the tribe[3] and while there was a clear stratification
into classes, and the nobles effectively controlled the land, it was not fully

[1] 'Predominantly pastoral' does not, of course, mean exclusively pastoral, *cf.*
G. Jones (1961), 222; nor were the prehistoric Celts of south-eastern Britain
exclusively agricultural. But L. Alcock is right (Alcock and G. Jones (1962), 51)
to remind us of the inevitability of change.

[2] Probably the best was Posidonius. On him, and on Caesar's debt to him, see
Tierney (1960)

[3] *cf.* Powell (1958), 75–83; C. E. Stevens, in Thomas (1966), 108–28

villam propinquam cum fidissimis pergit. Illic sua manu, reliqui mutuis ictibus
occidere; incensa super villa omnis cremavit.' For a detailed discussion of the
terms, see d'Arbois de Jubainville, *Recherches sur l'origine de la propriété foncière et des
noms de lieux habités en France* (1890), 90–98

theirs to dispose of. The commoner was bound to the noble in a relationship which the Romans interpreted as that of the client to his patron, which is not quite the same as the relationship between tenant and landlord. Celtic society was organised for war, not for commerce, and both the duty which the client owed to his patron and the benefits he received from him had warlike rather than financial implications. Of course, a client can be converted into a tenant, and where land is involved it may be that such a change is inevitable. To take another example from the 19th century, at the time of the Sutherland clearances the first reaction of the inhabitants of Strathnaver was sheer incredulity that the Countess, their hereditary chieftain, should have authorised their eviction.[1] Though already formally tenants, they still thought as clients, and what to the landlord was an economically progressive and perhaps even benevolent action represented to them the end of their way of life. A similar degradation of clients had taken place in Gaul, and for a similar reason—the influence of a stronger and more developed economy to the south.[2] Caesar, drawing on Posidonius, illustrates it in two ways: by his statement that the common people were treated almost as slaves,[3] and by his reference to the existence of private property in land—a matter in which he contrasts the Gauls with the more primitive Germans.[4] These developments were largely due to increased contact with the mediterranean world, which stimulated trade and led to a measure of urbanisation.

But the fact that this had already happened in Gaul does not necessarily mean that it had happened in Britain too. Caesar says that the Britons generally resembled the Gauls, but that their ways were more primitive,[5]

[1] Gen. Stewart of Garth, quoted in A. Mackenzie, *History of the Highland Clearances* (2nd edn, 1946), 46–47

[2] For a review of the evidence and of opposing arguments based on it, see Grenier, in Frank (1937), 406–10

[3] *B.G.*, vi, 13: 'Nam plebes paene servorum habetur loco, quae nihil audet per se, nullo adhibetur consilio. Plerique, cum aut aere alieno aut magnitudine tributorum aut iniuria potentiorum premuntur, sese in servitutem dicant nobilibus, quibus in hos eadem omnia sunt iura quae dominis in servos.'

[4] *B.G.*, vi, 21–22: 'Germani multum ab hac [*sc.* Gallorum] consuetudine differunt. . . . Neque quisquam agri modum certum aut finis habet proprios; sed magistratus ac principes in annos singulos gentibus cognationibusque hominum, qui una coierunt, quantum et quo loco visum est agri attribuunt atque anno post alio transire cogunt.' Whether or not this system of runrig applied to the Germans generally (the point has been disputed), Caesar's statement specifically excludes it from Gaul.

[5] *B.G.*, v, 12–13; *cf.* Strabo, IV, v, 2 (C 200)

and the truth of his statement is fully borne out by the archaeological evidence. Further, he makes a distinction between conditions in the backward hinterland and those in Kent, the part of the country most affected by Continental influences, and in this, too, he is supported by archaeology.[1] There was certainly a notable difference between the Belgic south-east (which by the time of the Claudian conquest comprehended much more than Kent) and the areas to the west and north. In the Belgic lands, though some hill-forts continue in occupation, we can discern the beginnings of a more civilised pattern of settlement. Centralised power is recognisable in the great low-lying *oppida*, such as Camulodunum, while the appearance of Continental imports at a number of sites (Fig. 5.2*d*),[2] and of slave-chains at Park Street,[3] indicates that men of substance could occupy open farms. Outside these areas, by contrast, the older way of life persisted and the characteristic element remains the local (not tribal) hill-fort with an aura of open farms and hamlets dependent on it. While much still remains to be learned of the precise nature of the relationship between the hill-forts and the farms,[4] they surely suit the older, cliently, system better than the harsher, more materialistic, society described by Caesar in Gaul.

In summary, then, it is probable that from the point of view of possession the necessary conditions for the emergence of Roman villas had already developed in parts of the south-east, but hardly in other areas, before the conquest. The conquest itself might have stimulated the process in two ways, economically and legally. Its economic effects will be discussed below; its legal effects were probably slower to take effect. Certainly all land had to be brought within the system of taxation at an early date, but beyond this it was not the practice of the Romans to impose their law wholesale on the conquered, still less on those who, like several of the British tribes, were initially treated as *socii*, or allies; and Mr Stevens has even detected a survival of primitive land tenure as late as the 4th century.[5] Nevertheless one would expect most of the anomalies to have been cleared up by A.D. 212, when Caracalla's *Constitutio Antoniniana* made Roman citizens of all

[1] *B.G.*, v, 14: 'Ex eis omnibus longe sunt humanissimi qui Cantium incolunt, quae regio est maritima omnis, neque multum a Gallica differunt consuetudine.'

[2] Including fourteen farm sites; see *OSSBIA* (1962), Index, pp. 50–53, for their identity.

[3] *Park Street* (1945), 35 and 66. On slave-chains in Iron Age Britain in general, see R. F. Jessup, *Arch. J.*, lxxxix (1932), 108–10

[4] For a recent discussion, see G. Jones (1961), 221–32, and Alcock and G. Jones (1962), 51–55

[5] Stevens (1947), commenting on *Cod. Theod.*, XI, vii, 2

free provincials. This was not merely a legal fiction; according to Dio, one of its aims was economic, to increase the yield from the *vicesima hereditatum*, the 5 per cent estate duty to which none but Roman citizens were liable,[1] and this could only have been realised if at least the majority of provincial land was by then heritable in the full Roman sense.

Turning from the social to the economic, we must next consider productivity. The typical Roman villa is a productive unit able to support quite handsomely a master and his family, who are not actually expected to labour; and in a country like Britain, which could grow few vines and no olives, this meant not merely producing enough food for the household but also a surplus for sale, so that the other necessities of a civilised life could be purchased. Was this possible in the Britain which the Romans conquered? One is tempted to assume so, because the nobility, to judge by the fragments of imported amphorae and by their metalwork and other equipment, had already achieved some degree of splendour. But we must not forget that barbaric splendour may still fall short of the basic standards of civilised comfort—as Samuel Johnson found in Ulva, when, undressing before an elegant bed of Indian cotton, spread with fine sheets, he felt his feet in the mire.[2] The archaeological evidence suggests that even the nobleman in pre-Roman Britain was in like case with Mr Macquarry, and this holds good not only in the farms but in a great centre like Camulodunum, too.[3] We must, therefore, look a little more carefully at the evidence for native British productivity. The technical aspects of this, the actual methods of farming employed, have been dealt with by Mr Bowen (ch. I); here we shall be concerned with generalities.

In the earlier part of the Iron Age the economy of Britain, apart from a limited trade in metalwork, was essentially a subsistence economy, but as time went on this had been modified. First, there was the rise of non-productive classes in the community, especially the *equites* or nobility, evidently affecting the whole country. Secondly, from the late 2nd century onwards, we see the introduction and spread of coinage, a clear indication

[1] Dio, LXXVIII, ix, 5: Οὗ ἕνεκα καὶ ῾Ρωμαίους πάντας τοὺς ἐν τῇ ἀρχῇ αὐτοῦ, λόγῳ μὲν τιμῶν, ἔργῳ δὲ ὅπως πλείω αὐτῷ καὶ ἐκ τοῦ τοιούτου προσίῃ διὰ τὸ τοὺς ξένους τὰ πολλὰ αὐτῶν μὴ συντελεῖν, ἀπέδειξεν. Stevens' qualifications (Thomas (1966), 109) should not apply to the villa-owning class.

[2] *Journey to the Western Islands of Scotland* (1775). Though recorded by Johnson under Ostig in Skye, the incident occurred at the house of M'Quarrie, 'intelligent, polite and much a man of the world', in Ulva (Boswell, *Journal of a Tour to the Hebrides*, 16 October).

[3] cf. Hawkes and Hull (1947), 46–48

of a system of tribute and trade, followed in the years between Caesar and Claudius by a great expansion of commerce with the Continent, especially with Gaul. These commercial developments are again associated primarily with the Belgic kingdoms of the south-east, but they affected some of the tribes on the periphery, too. Coins were used not only by the Catuvellauni and the Atrebates, but by the Coritani, the Dobunni, the Durotriges and the Iceni, each coinage having a distribution which defines a distinct state as a social and economic unit, probably ruled by a Belgic dynasty.[1] Similarly Continental imports are found not only at Camulodunum and Calleva but likewise at the Dobunnic capital at Bagendon.[2] Working from such distributions as these, we can define fairly closely the area of Britain which at the time of the Roman conquest was economically viable, in the sense that it could support not only the working population but an administrative superstructure, too, and could engage in a significant amount of trade (Fig. 5.2). Not surprisingly, it corresponds fairly closely with Fox's 'Lowland Zone', but it is notable that, with very minor additions, it is likewise the area in which we shall find our Roman villas; and it is also the area which was enclosed in the original Roman province, as defined by Aulus Plautius and Ostorius Scapula.[3]

While archaeology can tell us a good deal about imports into Britain, it can tell us virtually nothing about exports from it. For these we have to turn to the literary evidence, specifically to the statements made by Strabo. Strabo says that Britain imported ivory bracelets and necklaces, amber, glassware and pottery, and exported corn, cattle, gold, silver, iron, hides and hunting dogs.[4] Having already considered the imports, we may merely remark that, judging by the number of amphora fragments found, wine and oil should certainly be added to Strabo's list, though the very fact that he omits them should warn us against overestimating their importance. Of the exports, those that most concern us are corn and cattle, and here we find an anomaly. Strabo says that Britain exported corn, but he does not tell us who bought it, and we may well wonder. Grain is easily transported by sea and for long distances—whether from Alexandria to Ostia in the ancient world or from Australia to England in more modern times—this

[1] D. F. Allen, in *OSSBIA* (1962), Introduction, 19–22; *Arch.*, xv (1944), 1–43; and in Frere (1960), 97–128

[2] *OSSBIA* (1962) and Index.

[3] Tacitus, *Ann.*, xii, 31; Collingwood and Myres (1937), 91; Dudley and Webster (1965), fig. 24; G. Webster, *Arch. J.*, cxv (1958), 59ff.

[4] Strabo, IV, v, 2: C 199 (exports); IV, v, 3: C 200 (imports).

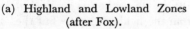

(a) Highland and Lowland Zones (after Fox).

(b) Approximate tribal areas, showing known coin mints.

(c) Distribution of Celtic coins.

(d) Distribution of Continental imports, excluding coins, from 100 B.C. to the Roman conquest.

Fig. 5.2. Pre-Roman economic development.

is the ideal method, because it avoids the difficulties of unloading and re-loading. But this hardly applies to the passage between Britain and the Continent and it is thus not a 'natural' export. Strabo indicates that the trade was with Gaul,[1] but he also says that north of the olive and fig country of Narbonensis all Gaul produced grain in large quantities, and that in his day the population were made to concentrate on agriculture, presumably to feed the Roman army.[2] Germany is an unlikely destination, for bread was not in demand there and in any case the country is described by Tacitus as '*satis ferax*', fertile in seed crops.[3] The explanation may be that this was not a regular traffic at all but a special measure, and that here we have one form of that notorious aid given by Britain to the Gauls in their struggles against Caesar[4]—and a very necessary form, since, Roman forag-ing apart, we know that the Gauls did on occasion practise a 'scorched earth' policy.

Such other literary evidence as we have is also equivocal. Caesar was able to feed a considerable army off the land, but we cannot estimate the hardship that this entailed for the Britons in the succeeding year. Most of the Britons themselves were summoned from the fields to fight,[5] but the force of 4,000 charioteers which Cassivellaunus retained in 54 B.C. suggests a standing army,[6] and it seems likely that his successors could do rather better than this. Our authorities indicate that intertribal warfare was endemic among the Britons,[7] and bearing in mind the productive capacity that its cessation would release, and the evidence for trade, we may conclude that even if it was not yet realised the productive capacity

[1] Four routes were in normal use: from the mouths of the Rhine, the Seine, the Loire, and the Garonne (Strabo IV, v, 2 (C 1999))

[2] Strabo, IV, i, 2 (C 178): ἡ δ' ἄλλη πᾶσα σῖτον φέρει πολὺν καὶ κέγχρον καὶ βάλανον καὶ βοσκήματα παντοῖα, ἀργὸν δ'αὐτῆς οὐδέν, πλὴν εἴ τι ἕλεσι κεκώλυται καὶ δρυμοῖς . . . νῦν δ'ἀναγκάζονται γεωργεῖν, καταθέμενοι τα ὅπλα.

[3] Caesar, *B.G.*, vi, 22, 1; Tacitus, *Germ.*, v, 1

[4] Caesar, *B.G.*, iv, 20, 1. The ear of corn on Catuvellaunian coins cannot be taken (as by M. Grant, *Roman History from Coins* (1958), 88) to suggest large-scale corn production. It is an abstract emblem derived from the wreath of Apollo and parallel to the vine-leaf on the coins of the Atrebates—hardly a local product; see D. F. Allen, *Arch.*, xc (1944), 25n.

[5] Caesar, *B.G.*, iv, 27, 7; v, 19, 1

[6] Caesar, *B.G.*, v, 19, 1

[7] Tacitus, *Agr.*, xii, 1–2. This is a change from the statement (possibly derived from Pytheas) in Diodorus Siculus, V, xxi, 6, that the Britons πρὸς ἀλλήλους κατὰ τὸ πλεῖστον εἰρηνικῶς διακεῖσθαι, but it is well supported by Caesar's experience and the whole history of Roman relations with Britain between the invasions of Caesar and Claudius (*cf.* C. E. Stevens, in Grimes (1951))

of Britain was already sufficient to support a profitable agriculture.

The question of its realisation brings us to our third heading, that of profitability. We may begin by looking once more at Strabo's list of exports. The metals—gold, silver (to which we may add lead) and iron—were what brought the Romans to Britain and they were not slow to seize hold of them. The Mendip mines were working within six years of the landing,[1] but they were working under imperial control, and so brought no profit to the Britons. The export of hunting dogs continued, and there are several references to them in the literature, but they can hardly have formed a main prop of the British economy. As for slaves, there can be no doubt that the wars of conquest produced a flood of them—again to the profit of the Romans, not the Britons—but thereafter the suppression of tribal warfare would have reduced it to a mere trickle: the chief drain on the population of Roman Britain was not into the slave market but, perhaps equally forcibly, into the auxiliary units of the Roman army. There remain the foodstuffs and animal products: corn, cattle and hides.

Now, agriculturally southern Britain is exceptionally productive, and one's first thought is that grain production should have been automatically profitable, especially in an economy like that of the Roman world, where bread was, in a very real sense, the staff of life. There are, however, two complicating factors that must be borne in mind. First, civilised Roman life required other things besides bread, and these had to be purchased; and since many of them, especially wine and oil, had to be imported, their price would be inflated by transport costs and probably also by import duties.[2] Secondly, bread was, in fact, so important in the Roman world that special measures were taken to ensure the supply of it to the consumers who mattered most—the citizens of Rome itself and the army. It was these special measures that came to be comprehended in the term 'annona'.

The Economic Effects of Roman Military Demands

The first responsibility of a general is to feed his troops, both during the campaign and after it. It is true that at least until the time of Severus the

[1] *C.I.L.*, vii, 1201

[2] *Portoria* were normal within the Empire as well as at its boundaries, though several provinces, as the three Gauls, were grouped together for this purpose. The often-cited passage of Strabo (IV, v, 3: C 200–1) does not envisage the abolition of duties if Britain were conquered, but only their reduction (ἀνάγκη γὰρ μειοῦσθαι τὰ τέλη φόρων ἐπιβαλλομένων).

Roman legionary, as a citizen soldier, paid for his own keep, or had a proportion of his pay stopped for it, but the supplies had obviously to be obtained centrally and they normally came from the conquered territory; the Imperial Government was not accustomed to paying its own occupation costs. The necessary items might be obtained by purchase, with money raised as tribute, or by direct taxation in kind. The liquid part of the soldiers' rations in Britain, the wine, had in any case to be bought from overseas, but a well-known passage in Tacitus suggests that the grain was, for a time at least, raised by direct levy. He says that Agricola

eased the levy of corn and tribute (*frumenti et tributorum exactionem*) by distributing the burden fairly, and cancelled those charges, contrived by profiteers, which were more bitterly resented than the tax itself. The provincials had actually been compelled to wait at the doors of closed granaries, buy back their own corn and pay farcical prices. Delivery was ordered to destinations off the map or at a great distance, and states that had permanent quarters of troops close by them had to send to remote and inaccessible spots, until a service that should have been easy for all ended by benefiting a few scoundrels only.[1]

Note that Agricola, in his benevolence, did not cancel the levies; he was merely implementing the advice which Tiberius had given to one of his provincial governors, that it is the duty of a good shepherd to shear the sheep, not to skin them.[2]

Britain was unfortunate in that for a considerable time the shears had to cut close, for two reasons. First, the military effort, and the number of troops to be supplied, was unduly large, and second, the area available to supply them was unduly small. We may appreciate these points if we look briefly at the military establishment in Britain from an economic point of view. The assimilation of a new province to the Roman Empire had three stages: first, the actual war of conquest; second, the planting of military garrisons in the conquered territory to control, subdue and civilise; and third, the withdrawal of the troops, except for frontier guards, and the

---

[1] Tacitus, *Agr.*, xix, 4–5 (trans. H. Mattingly *Tacitus on Britain and Germany*, pp. 70–71). Taxes in kind as well as money seem also to be implied in Dio, LXII, iii, 3: οὐ πρὸς τῷ τἆλλα πάντα καὶ νέμειν καὶ γεωργεῖν ἐκείνοις, καὶ τῶν σωμάτων αὐτῶν δασμὸν ἐτήσιον φέρομεν; but this may be anachronism. A token payment for the levy was indeed made, but it was much below the market price, which in turn was evidently lower than the price demanded at the granary doors.

[2] Suetonius, *Tiberius*, xxxii, 2: 'Boni pastoris esse tondere pecus, non deglubere.'

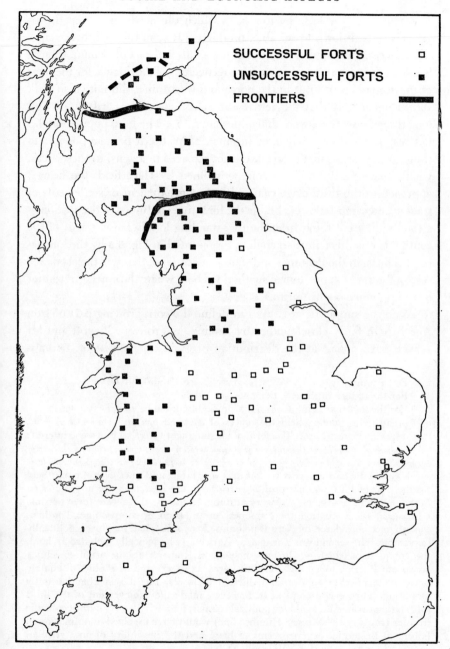

Fig. 5.3. The military occupation of Britain.

replacement of the forts by towns, in which the newly enlightened provincials settled down to sensible, productive Roman life. All three stages
were successfully carried through in the south and east of Britain, though
it is only in recent years that we have recovered solid evidence for the forts
of the second stage.[1] But in the north and west things did not go so well.
It was not merely that the actual war of conquest was hard fought and
long drawn out; there were difficulties later, too. The local population did
not respond and even when, as in much of Wales, it became possible to
thin out the garrisons, the forts were not replaced by towns. In these areas,
which comprise the military zone as defined by Haverfield, the nearest
approach to the third stage came with the development of settlements of
traders and camp-followers beside the forts that continued in occupation—
a totally different thing from the free-standing locally based towns of the
south.[2] It was this failure to civilise, represented in Fig. 5.3 by the 'unsuc-
cessful forts' in the Pennines and southern Scotland, that was the economic
reason for the most un-Roman swithering about where the northern frontier
of the province ought to run.[3]

As to the supplying area, we can define the corn-growing part of Iron
Age Britain fairly closely either by looking, as Professor Piggott and Mr
Bowen have done,[4] at the distribution of grain-storage pits or, perhaps

[1] For a summary, see G. Webster, *Arch. J.*, cxv (1960), 49–98

[2] For the nature of these settlements, see Salway (1965)

[3] For the fact that Britain was not a profitable province we have the testimony
of Appian, who, having held the offices of *advocatus fisci* and *procurator Augusti*,
might be expected to know. The form of his statement (*praef.* 5) is of some interest:
καὶ τὸν βόρειον ὠκεανὸν ἐς τὴν Βρεττανίδα νῆσον περάσαντες, ἠπείρου μεγάλης μείζονα, τὸ κράτιστον
αὐτῆς [οἱ ῾Ρωμαῖοι] ἔχουσιν ὑπὲρ ἥμισυ, οὐδὲν τῆς ἄλλης δεόμενοι· οὐ γὰρ εὔφορος αὐτοῖς ἐστιν
οὐδ᾽ ἣν ἔχουσιν. Britain was very remote and very large, and since even the part held
(in the time of Pius) was not profitable to them, the Romans were not interested
in the rest. This is a typical Treasury attitude. In theory, there were three possible
solutions: total evacuation, total conquest, or an economic compromise. The first,
though once considered by Nero (Suetonius, *Nero*, xviii), had long been politically
impossible. The second was pursued by Agricola (who logically included Ireland,
the conquest of which would have helped, 'si Romana ubique arma et velut e
conspectu libertas tolleretur' (Tacitus, *Agr.*, xxiv, 3)) and it should ultimately
have made possible an overall reduction of forces, but it was abandoned by
Domitian. The very attempt at it, however, made the achievement of the third
solution more difficult, again for political reasons, for a withdrawal to the economic
frontier (roughly the Mersey–Humber line) would have involved an admission of
failure in Brigantia. Severus seems to have had the possibility of an Agricolan
solution in mind (Dio, LXXVII, xiii, 1)

[4] Richmond (1958), 10, Map 2

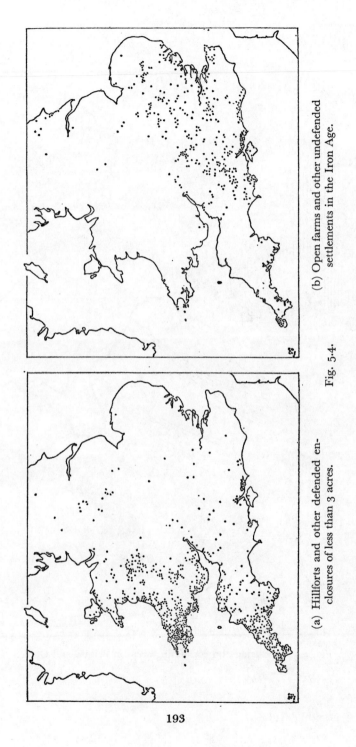

(a) Hillforts and other defended enclosures of less than 3 acres.

(b) Open farms and other undefended settlements in the Iron Age.

Fig. 5.4.

193

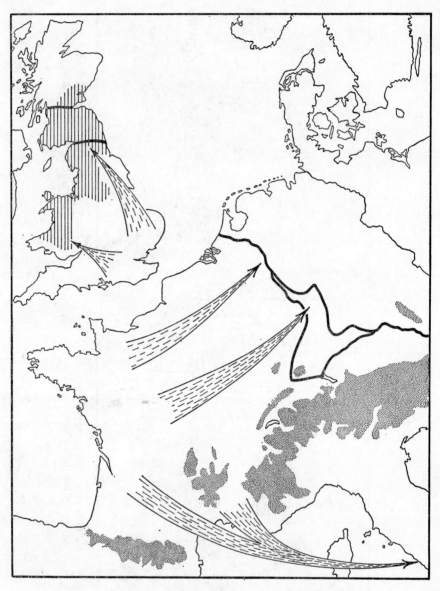

Fig. 5.5. Producing and consuming areas in Britain and Gaul.

more comprehensively, by contrasting the so-called open farms of the agri-
culturalists with the enclosed homesteads of the pastoralists (Fig. 5.4). The
pastoralists would not, of course, have got off scot-free. Like the Frisians,
whose case is mentioned by Tacitus,[1] they probably had to pay their levy
in hides, but that did not reduce the burden on the agricultural areas.

Just how unfortunate Britain was may be seen by comparing her lot with
that of the other provinces of western Europe, Gaul and Spain. Spain,
though it contained a number of wild and mountainous districts, had no
hostile frontiers to be defended and so no permanent military zone; abut-
ting on another province on one side and bounded on the others by the sea,
it was in a position that Britain could only have achieved if the aspirations
of Veranius and the policy of Agricola had come to fulfilment and the whole
island had been subdued.[2] Gaul had, indeed, a frontier army to supply,
but she was a notoriously rich country, more developed than Britain at the
time of the Roman conquest, and even allowing for the fact that parts of
Provence and Aquitania contributed to the *annona* of Rome itself,[3] the
ratio of the productive area to the area to be supplied was much more
favourable than in the case of Britain; moreover, from an early date the
productive area extended right up to the frontier zone (Fig. 5.5). Gaul could
have been placed in a position similar to that of Britain, at least tempo-
rarily, if the intention had been fulfilled of carrying the frontier forward
to the Elbe, but the events of A.D. 9 destroyed the possibility of that.
It is a truism that but for the *clades Variana* we should today have a
different Germany from what we have; but we might also have a different
France.

Turning from comparisons to an absolute assessment of the burden, we
are once again hampered by the lack of statistical evidence. We know that
the initial Roman force in Britain included four legions—II Augusta, IX
Hispana, XIV Gemina and XX Valeria. These were reduced to three when
XIV Gemina was withdrawn in A.D. 66, but restored to four, first by the
temporary return of XIV, and then by the arrival of II Adiutrix in 71. With
its recall in 86, the number sank again to three, at which it remained for
the rest of the period. Thus, for much of the 1st century, Britain was
required to feed four legions of some 6,000 men each—approximately
24,000 men—and since the legionary's ration of wheat was approximately

[1] Tacitus, *Ann.*, iv, 72
[2] See p. 192 note 3 above; for Veranius, Tacitus, *Ann.*, xiv, 29
[3] Grenier, in Frank (1937), 578–9, with references.

11 bushels a year,[1] this gives a figure of 265,000 bushels. Besides the legions, however, there was a force of auxiliaries, and while we do not know its precise strength there is reason to believe that it was similar to that of the legions. Since the men in the auxiliary units were drawn from barbarian tribes, they probably consumed less bread than the legionaries, who in this period were still predominantly Italians, but many of them were mounted and would require winter feed for their horses. Moreover, there is a third force to be considered, the staff of the *legatus* and, more numerous, that of the *procurator*. Thus we should probably be justified in doubling the legionary figure and assuming a total requirement of the order of 530,000 bushels a year. Taking the average yield as about 10 bushels an acre,[2] this represents the total produce of 53,000 acres.

For a marauding army it was merely necessary to strip so many acres of their crop, and Caesar no doubt did just this in his campaigns. But Plautius was not conducting a punitive expedition; he was establishing a new province, and he had to think of the future. Seed grain had to be provided for the next harvest, labourers kept alive to grow it, and the land had sometimes to be rested. For seed corn, most modern writers on the subject suggest that about one-third of the yield would be required—that is, about 3⅓ bushels per acre;[3] by contrast, Varro recommends that wheat should be sowed at 5 *modii* to the *iugerum* (that is, 1·9 bushels to the acre) and mentions yields varying from tenfold to a hundredfold.[4] The discrepancy is not so great as might appear, because Varro is discussing

---

[1] Polybius, vi, 39, 13: σιτομετροῦνται δ'οἱ μὲν πεζοὶ πυρῶν 'Αττικοῦ μεδίμνου δύο μέρη μάλιστά πως . . . εἰς τὸν μῆνα, . . . 'The ration of corn for a foot-soldier is about two-thirds of an Attic *medimnus* a month.' Two-thirds of a *medimnus* is 0.96 bushels, which is very close to four Roman *modii* (0.952 bushels). This presumably means the issue of a *modius* of corn each *nundinum* (or market-day), thus preserving the rhythm of civil life for the citizen soldiers. There is no reason to suppose that this legionary scale had been altered, but Polybius' scale for Italian *socii* cannot, of course, be transferred automatically to the barbarian *auxilia* of the Empire.

[2] Bowen (1961), 13; Piggott, in Richmond (1958), 23; G. Bersu, *P.P.S.*, vi (1940), 104, estimates 11 bushels of wheat or barley per acre or 14 bushels of oats. All these figures merely represent a third of the modern yield off the chalk, and a considerable margin of error is possible. For a recent discussion of the ancient literary evidence (relating to the Mediterranean area), see K. D. White, 'Wheat-farming in Roman times', *Ant.*, xxxvii (1963), 207–12

[3] *e.g.* Bersu, Piggott, *loc. cit.*, the latter citing W. H. Beveridge, *Economic History* No. 2 (1927), 155–67, for medieval analogies.

[4] Varro, *R.R.*, I, xliv, 1–2; for comment, see C. E. Stevens, *Cambridge Economic History of Europe*, i (1966), 104

autumn sowing in Italy, while the modern estimates are for spring sowing on the chalk. By no means all the British crop came from the chalk, however, and we may compromise by allowing an average of 2 bushels per acre, giving a fivefold yield. For the labourers, Columella estimates that 200 *iugera* (124·6 acres) of treeless land, again in Italy, can be worked by two yoke of oxen, two ploughmen and six common labourers.[1] This can only be applied approximately to Britain, but if we allow each of these men a (barbarian) ration of, say 4 bushels a year and add something for animal feed, we need to subtract something over a quarter of a bushel per acre. So between them these two items of seed corn and labourer's rations mean that about a quarter of the total yield had to be set aside for maintenance. Thus, the production of our 530,000 bushels would actually have required some 70,666 acres or, allowing for fallow every third year, 106,000 acres. This, which includes no provision for headlands, pasture, waste land, woods, roads or buildings, and allows for no profit at all to the owner, is considerably more than the total acreage (97,273) of the modern county of Rutland and must have represented a noticeable proportion of the total arable land available at the time of the conquest. For further comparison, Professor Piggott estimates the surviving areas of field systems of Iron Age or Romano-British type in the Berkshire Downs and Dorset as 8,000 acres and 30,000 acres respectively;[2] that is to say, between them they would provide about one-third of our total requirement.

In fact, it is probable that something more than 530,000 bushels was demanded, for it was not a direct transaction. Soon after the conquest of a province a census was taken, which included not only the numbering of the people but also details of the character and extent of cultivated land and of other property, and this, subject to periodic review, served as the basis for all taxation. The rate of the corn levy could thus be fixed to yield a specified return, but some overestimation was necessary to cover contingencies. A shortfall would be insured against, and the reference to native purchasing in the passage of Tacitus quoted above (p. 190) clearly indicates that a surplus was sometimes obtained. The responsibility for producing the quantity demanded was laid on the tribal authorities, which were themselves made up of the landowning class, and they had to distribute the burden in their own areas as best they could. Simultaneously they

---

[1] Columella, *R.R.*, II, xii, 7. Like Polybius' auxiliary rations, the scale for farm workers given by Cato (*Agr.*, lvi) cannot be transferred to barbarian Britain.

[2] In Richmond (1958), 23

had to supply labour, which was thus diverted from the fields, for the construction of roads and other public works.

It is in any case clear that in the first period of the Roman occupation the productive capacity of British agriculture was under strain, though the intensity of the strain would have varied according to the degree of military activity, the excellence or otherwise of the harvests, and the efficiency of governors like Agricola in checking abuses—or the actions of procurators like Decianus Catus in encouraging them. On the other hand, this pressure must have had some good results. One was the bringing into cultivation of land which had previously lain unused. The most far-reaching manifestation of this is the occupation of the Fenland which, though it seems to have reached its peak under Hadrian, began in the 1st century.[1] A different kind of result must have been a tightening of discipline. It is probably not unfair to attribute to the British peasantry of this period an outlook similar to that of some highlanders in more recent times, whose watchwords are 'Tomorrow is also a day' and 'When God made time He made plenty of it'; not because this attitude is specifically Celtic—it is not—but because it is the universal human reaction to a near-subsistence situation, in which it is not too difficult to live but impossible to live well.[2] It is an approach to life whose attractiveness to the observer varies in inverse proportion to the urgency of his business, and it can hardly have been unaffected by the conditions that we have envisaged.

The Emergence and Development of Villas in Britain

Thus in the 1st century, and perhaps even for a part of the 2nd, British agriculture, though compelled to develop, cannot have been very profitable; and this applies whether one regards it from the point of view of the established British farmer or from that of the tycoon, whether British or foreign, who was looking for an investment. It is also borne out by what we know from archaeology of the farmsteads of this period. The plans of some of these have been discussed by the late Sir Ian Richmond (ch. II) and it is only necessary here to refer briefly to the two best-known examples of the earlier type: those at Park Street and Lockleys. We may note, first,

[1] P. Salway, paper read to Royal Geographical Society, 21 Jan. 1963: results summarised in Thomas (1966), 27

[2] It was certainly widespread in parts of East Africa, for example, twenty-five years ago.

that apart from their rectangular shape and their mortared stone footings, the 1st-century houses do not compare so very favourably with the much earlier Iron Age hut at Little Woodbury.[1] Secondly, the plans are simple and suggest family working rather than the master-servant relationship which is typical of the true villa. It is only in the later versions, with the corridor added, that some sort of segregation appears possible, and these belong to the 2nd century. This general line of development, with variations in detail and in timing, is followed in most parts of southern Britain— for example, at Saunderton in Buckinghamshire, Ditchley in Oxfordshire, Catsgore in Somerset and (though here the variations are greater) Lullingstone in Kent; in the north, as at Langton in the East Riding, a very similar development is seen, but it comes at a much later date. The use of the corridor plan, with the segregation it implies, is clearly significant, but whether it indicates the segregation of a resident *dominus*, of a superior tenant or tacksman, or merely that of the *vilicus* from the underservants,[2] it is difficult to decide; this is a question to which we shall return later. In the meantime it is obvious that money was being spent on the buildings. The farmhouse was growing in size, and in a small way in comfort, and British agriculture must have been showing some signs of prosperity. Why, in a 2nd-century context, should this have been so?

The answer to this question is twofold, and probably threefold—probably a reduction in official demands, certainly an increase in production and the development of new markets. There is no direct evidence that the corn levy was relaxed in Britain, but it is very likely because the system was normally used only when an actual war was in progress. Its cancellation would have been in accordance with the trends of the times, for provincial oppression was no part of the policy of the better Emperors.[3] This may even have been one of the things which, as the *Historia Augusta* claims, Hadrian 'corrected' in Britain,[4] and it would be a natural corollary to his consolidation of the frontier and to the public works which were now undertaken in the Fens.[5] If the change was made, the result would have

[1] For a comparison on the same scale, see Rivet (1964), fig. 7

[2] A principle insisted on by Varro (*R.R.*, I, xiii, 2) and Columella (*R.R.*, XI, i, 13) in the interests of discipline.

[3] Pliny, *Paneg.*, xxix; Dio, LXIX, 8–9; *cf.* R. P. Longden, *C.A.H.*, xi (1936), 213 (Trajan), and W. Weber, *ibid.*, 316 (Hadrian).

[4] *S.H.A.*, Hadrian, xi, 2; but this is not a source on which anything substantial can be built.

[5] P. Salway, *loc. cit.*

been that, instead of having to hand over the grain itself and pay for its transport, the Britons would have been liable for somewhat higher taxes in money than previously and would have sold the grain to the authorities at the market price. This would vary, but the arrangement would be preferable to the other system and it would leave more scope for manœuvre.

The increased production and the new markets are more certain. We have already dealt with one reason for an increase in production, the sheer pressure of official demands. But there was another pressure too, in the salesmanship of merchants from other parts of the Empire. As we have seen, there is both literary and archaeological evidence that some of them had a foothold in the country even before the conquest, but following the invasion there must have been a great rush of them—Gauls and Greeks and Italians, Jews and Armenians, a whole pentecost of traders, all crying their wares. Their first prey was the military, to whom they could sell a variety of goods, from wine more interesting than the ration issue to souvenirs like the Rudge Cup, and they early established themselves in the lee of the forts. But they did not neglect the civilian population, and a British settlement like Verulamium grew into a Roman city. More than that, London, which did not exist at all before the conquest, was by the time of the Boudiccan revolt already a commercial centre, thronged, says Tacitus, with traders.[1] The Britons were under pressure to buy, and buy they did, even though it led some of them into debt.[2] A little later, first under Agricola and again under Hadrian, official encouragement was given to the adoption of Roman ways, and so the numerous towns of Roman Britain came into full existence. It was these towns that provided the new markets for British agricultural produce. Here was no forced levy, but free exchange—at the least, a market controlled by the tribal notables themselves—and as the urban population grew, so did the profitability of British agriculture. Thus it was that a situation was reached in which capitalist farming became a reasonable proposition, and this accounts for what we may call the first wave of Romano-British villas, which flourished especially in the second half of the 2nd century.

But this is not the end of the story. The golden age of the British villas was still to come, and before it came there was a recession. At almost every

[1] Tacitus, *Ann.*, xiv, 33

[2] Dio, LXII, ii, 1, on Seneca's alleged loans to the Britons, amounting to 40 m. sesterces; Syme (*Tacitus* (1958), 763, 551) discounts this as a manifestation of Dio's hostility to Seneca, but the story is circumstantial and other demands for repayment are mentioned.

villa which has been carefully excavated—though there are few indeed of these—there seems to have been a period of decay in the 3rd century. This is true at Park Street, Lockleys, Saunderton, Lullingstone, Ditchley, Catsgore, and others too, and it appears to have been very widespread. From the economic point of view it is not difficult to find possible reasons for it. First, there was the disastrous episode of Albinus, who took troops away to fight for the crown, and the devastation that followed: the physical devastation was confined to the north, but its economic effects must have been felt all over the province. Then there were the Severan wars of re-conquest, when the Emperors invaded Scotland and re-established Hadrian's Wall. Britain had for a time to support an increased military establishment, and the probability is that she had to do it by the direct method. Hitherto the legionary had paid for his keep, and especially in parts of the Empire where the supplies could not be obtained locally he had felt the chill wind of inflation—even though his pay had been more than doubled since the time of Augustus. It has been credibly suggested that the institution of the *annona militaris* and the issue of free rations, which by the end of the 3rd century had certainly come to represent the most important element in a soldier's pay, dates back to the period of the Severi.[1]

So, in this respect, the economy of Britain was back where it had been at the beginning of the Roman period, and it is not surprising that the first half of the 3rd century should see a recession in British agriculture. Quite what form the recession took, we cannot be sure. Some excavators write confidently of the actual abandonment of a villa. This is not completely impossible, because if the building in question were a master's house it could be allowed to collapse without the tenantry, who lived elsewhere, ceasing production; in such cases we might suppose that the masters continued to control the estates, but gave up the expense of a country residence and concentrated on their town houses—in the towns which, for reasons that we do not yet fully understand, were being walled in this same period. But the very nature of the crisis forbids us to accept the idea of the abandonment of the land itself, at any rate on any large scale, for the crops had still to be produced. What the archaeological record reveals is a general lack of maintenance and rebuilding.

Later in the 3rd century, however, and continuing on into the 4th, the

[1] Van Berchem (1937), 166–81; A. H. Jones (1964) 30–31; on soldier's pay in the 1st and 2nd centuries, see Brunt (1950)

archaeological evidence points equally clearly to a renaissance—or rather, to remarkable new developments, because we find not only the rebuilding of most of the old villas but also, almost for the first time in Britain, the appearance of really large and luxurious establishments, some of them, like Keynsham in Somerset, on entirely new sites. It is to this time that belong the extensive houses, with elaborate heated rooms and elegant mosaics, which are usually considered typical of the 'villa system' in Britain.

Now this is remarkable, because in the western Empire as a whole this period was a time of troubles. Emperor fought and deposed Emperor with disastrous frequency, and on at least two occasions, in 253 and 275, Gaul suffered full-scale invasion by the barbarians. Britain was not entirely immune: there were the beginnings of Saxon piracy, which Carausius was appointed to combat, and there were also the raids that followed the denuding of the northern frontier by Allectus. But Britain was fortunate in that, this one episode apart, the civil wars were not fought over her territory and she thus suffered less, both directly by destruction and indirectly by taxation and levies, than did Gaul. And in one respect she actually benefited by the discomfiture of the neighbouring provinces, for economically the period is marked by a growing trend towards self-sufficiency.

We can see this best in the case of durable goods, which survive as archaeological evidence, and the clearest example of all is provided by pottery. In the first two centuries of the Roman occupation samian pottery from Gaul had been imported into Britain on a truly colossal scale, so that the sites not of towns and villas only but even of hovels like those in Cranborne Chase are littered with it. In the 3rd century this traffic stops. It was not merely that the Continental potteries were put out of action by the barbarian invasions, which was indeed the case, but the British potteries had already begun to take over, and now they had, at least for a time, a clear field. The effects of such a change would have been complex. Instead of the purchase price of the pottery going out of the country, it stayed here. The profits helped to swell the class of the wealthy, as is illustrated by the group of rich villas round the potteries at Castor,[1] while the workmen employed in the various factories up and down the country had to be fed, providing yet another market for the produce of British farms. Other industries were developing too, such as the manufacture of pewter at places like Camerton,[2] and, perhaps most important of all, the

[1] Artis (1828)
[2] Wedlake (1958)

weaving industry. British woollen goods had an international reputation and at least two lines, the *birrus Britannicus* and the *tapete Britannicum*, were sufficiently well established by the end of the 3rd century to be given specific mention in Diocletian's price-fixing edict.[1] And as success bred success, we have the rise of service industries, such as the firms of mosaic-ists, no longer confined to the towns, discussed by Dr Smith (ch. III). Britain could never, of course, be completely self-sufficient. Imports continued to arrive, notably glassware, and while the Emperor Probus included Britain among the provinces to which he restored the right to grow vines,[2] one shrinks from believing that the native vintage supplanted the imported. But there is every sign that the British economy was buoyant, and all this would have made farming more attractive.

Reasons such as these may help us to understand how it was possible that in the late 3rd and the 4th centuries we should have this remarkable efflorescence of British villas, but they do not fully explain it. For instead of a slow and steady recovery, such as we might expect, we appear to be faced by a completely new phenomenon. The problems it poses are social as well as economic, and since the appearance of these large villas is the last significant development before the decline sets in, this is an appropriate point at which to look back and consider the social implications of the changes we have been discussing.

Social Implications

The stratification of Celtic society is well attested both by literary references and by analogy, but how it is reflected in the settlement pattern of Iron Age Britain is not so clear. Mr Glanville Jones has stated a case for something similar to the medieval Welsh *maenor*, with bond hamlets (nucleated settlements of about nine houses) dependent on a hill-fort (representing the *llys*),[3] and this would appear to be appropriate in the hill-fort area. How far the tenantry were at this time bond or nominally free, and whether the dependent settlements were normally nucleated, are questions that need not detain us. What does need to be stressed is that by the time

---

[1] *Edict*, XIX; on the *birrus Britannicus*, see J. P. Wild, *Ant.*, xxxvii (1963), 193–202; on the *tapete Britannicum*, I. A. Richmond, *J.R.S.*, xlv (1955), 114

[2] *S.H.A.*, Probus, xviii, 8

[3] G. Jones (1961)

of the Roman conquest much of south-eastern Britain, under Belgic influence, appears already to have passed out of the hill-fort phase and to have developed a more sophisticated pattern. This is not to say that there were no occupied hill-forts here, but that private enterprise forts were discouraged by the central power. Instead, we have open farms like Park Street, evidently occupied by men of substance, and it is in these that we must seek the south-eastern equivalents of the fortified lords of the west and north. It might be inferred that they too had farms or hamlets dependent on them, but the known pattern is altogether too thin for certainty; to cite only the most obvious example of its inadequacy, very few of the *creberrima aedificia* remarked on by Caesar in Kent have yet been located.[1]

These two types of site—the smaller hill-forts and the richer open farms—should represent the rural seats of the noble *equites*, the men whom the Romans converted into *decuriones*. Even in pre-Roman conditions we do not need to conceive of them as in permanent residence, for some of their time would have been spent away at the wars and some in attendance on the kings at their tribal *oppida*.[2] Nevertheless, so far as the farms are concerned, their layout suggests that, when at home, they were very much in the bosom of their family. There is evidence that some of them owned a few slaves, and on Mr Jones's hypothesis the cultivation of at least some of their land would have been carried out for them by their tenantry, but there is no indication that the domestic staff, indoor or outdoor, were segregated from the master. In Roman terms they were probably nearer to Cincinnatus than to Cato.

The initial effect of Roman rule on these people, while leaving their tenurial position unchanged, would probably be to require them to spend longer away from their farms than previously. Membership of the tribal *ordo* was no sinecure and they were compelled to concentrate on founding and developing their tribal centres. The *templa fora domos* which Agricola encouraged them to build were to embellish the towns, and while the earliest *domus* were, on present evidence, no palaces, they had at least to

[1] Caesar, *B.G.*, v, 12, 3; compare *OSSBIA* (1962), with comment on p. 12 of the Introduction.

[2] It is, of course, impossible in many cases to distinguish between 'local' and 'tribal' hill-forts, but the great variation in size, complexity and density of occupation indicates that a division must be made somewhere, and the figure of 15 acres enclosed (as on *OSSBIA*) seems to offer a reasonably satisfactory measure (provided that it is recognised as a guess and an approximation).

conform to urban standards.[1] A side effect of this was that when farmhouses were rebuilt in the 1st century they too were constructed on the new rectangular plan, but they still remained units suitable for family working.

With the second phase of rebuilding, however, which is manifest in the first half of the 2nd century, we see the introduction of the new type of corridor house. This is not only more elaborate than the old type but, as we have noted, provides for the first time some evidence of segregation, and it is surely at this point that we can begin with some confidence to speak of true villas. As we have seen, there are good economic reasons why this development should take place just at this time, but the reasons are such that we must be cautious in the social interpretation we put upon it. It may be that a number of noble families had now reached the stage at which they could afford both a town and a country house, but there are several possible variations. For example, some landowners may have settled sons or other relations either in the ancestral manor itself or in one of its dependencies, and the creation of a class of tenants-in-chief, analogous to the tacksmen of Scotland, is not impossible. More important, an owner could now sell his whole estate or a part of it and the purchaser might be anyone, Briton or foreigner, who had the money to buy. Both in this way and by the transfer of property in payment of debts (for it would now have been acceptable), many farms may have passed into few hands and the living standards they reflect would be those of the bailiff, not of the master. On the other hand, while the buildings we are considering can hardly have been the homes of mere peasants (they are distinct from the humbler dwellings discussed by Mr Bowen), not all the purchasers need have been very rich or very powerful and the large estate was probably far from universal.

The effect of such developments on the pattern of settlement would have been complex, shifting the centre of gravity of some estates, fragmenting others, and in some cases creating entirely new units. A number of villas—undoubtedly many more than is at present recognised—succeeded Iron Age homesteads, and here the new house is regularly built on precisely the same site as the old. If this could be attributed to a desire to preserve the ancestral hearth it might suggest continuity of ownership, but an equally cogent reason could be the rigidity of the farm's layout

[1] Tacitus, *Agr.*, xxi, 1. For the disappointing standard of buildings in early Verulamium, see S. S. Frere, 'Verulamium–Then and Now', *Bulletin of the Institute of Archaeology (London)*, iv (1964), 69

when once it had been established. In these cases no less than in those of new foundations, such as Ditchley appears to be, the suitability of the land for profitable cultivation in terms of soil and aspect would obviously be of supreme importance; this rules out most of the hill-forts[1] and it is significant that with negligible exceptions the old-established sites are those of Belgic or Belgic-influenced farms. But soil was not the only consideration. To be profitable—that is, to be viable as Roman villas— these establishments had also to have access to their markets and so had to be related to towns and roads—a point which is constantly stressed by the ancient authors.[2] It is this fact, rather than a difference between light and heavy soils, which distinguishes the Roman from the pre-Roman settlement pattern, and this applies to the first wave of villas no less than to the second; it is most unlikely that any land which was already under cultivation was allowed to revert to waste, but the focal points are different.

To accept these 2nd-century houses as Roman villas within our defini-tion of the term implies the acceptance of their owners as people already integrated into the Roman way of life, but it does not imply that we believe them to have been either large or luxurious, and indeed all the evidence points to the contrary. Their standard of comfort, though certainly above that of peasant dwellings, was still below that of the 2nd-century towns, even of Britain, and they do not begin to compare with the larger contemporary villas of Gaul, such as Anthée or Chiragan or Montmaurin. It is not simply the vast areas covered by the buildings of these establishments (30, 41 and 44 acres respectively), for that could be explained by different systems of working; even for Italy, Columella recommends that cornland should be leased out to tenants[3] and this

[1] Exceptions are Ham Hill in Somerset, where the house may have been associated with quarrying; and perhaps Borough Hill, near Daventry, Northants.

[2] *cf.* Cato. *Agr.*, i, 3: 'Oppidum validum prope siet aut mare aut amnis, qua naves ambulant, aut via bona celebrisque'; Varro, *R.R.*, I, xvi, 1: '[Among the matters which] vehementer pertinent ad culturam [are] . . . si quo neque fructus nostros exportare expediat neque inde quae opus sunt adportare; tertium, si viae aut fluvii, qua portetur, aut non sunt aut idonei non sunt; . . .'; *ibid.*, 6: 'Eundem fundum fructuosiorem faciunt vecturae, si viae sunt, qua plaustra agi facile possint, aut flumina propinqua, qua navigari possit, . . . '; Columella, *R.R.*, I, iii, 3: 'Multum conferre agris iter commodum', quoting Cato and expand-ing him.

[3] Columella, *R.R.*, I, vii, 6: 'In longinquis tamen fundis, in quos non est facilis excursus patris familiae, cum omne genus agri tolerabilius sit sub liberis colonis quam sub vilicis servis habere, tum praecipue frumentarium, quem et minime, sicut vineas aut arbustum, colonus evertere potest et maxime vexant servi, . . . '

)iscuss the function of villas in Roman Britain

ik Street I
- 2↑ rooms in a row, a passage through
  in the centre
- extension in later
- a half-underground stable

3↑
- The latin word — agriculture
  established.

: much Types of villas
  farmhouse to more leisure site?

hedwe↑ Roman Villa
- Religeous function?
  → shrine in the courtyard

method, rather than the concentration of estate workers in a compound, is to be expected in Britain. But at each of these three Continental examples the main house, the *villa urbana* itself, had already reached its full extent and it was much larger and more luxurious than anything, with the exception of Fishbourne and possibly Eccles, that we can show in Britain.

This difference is important when we come to consider the 3rd-century recession and the revival that followed it. A popular explanation used to be that about this time the official duties (*munera*) demanded of the local aristocracy, the *curiales*, began to be so oppressive that they sought refuge on their country estates, thus avoiding their responsibilities and the expenses that they involved.[1] This argument is difficult to accept for a number of reasons. First, it is evident that the plight of the *curiales* throughout the Empire in the 3rd and 4th centuries has been somewhat exaggerated; while there is ample evidence that they complained both about taxes and about their duties and while much legislation was certainly devoted to keeping them at their posts, there is, as Professor Jones points out, little to suggest that they had to draw on their capital, and most of them remained relatively wealthy.[2] Second, to be effective such a manœuvre required more resources than one would expect the *curiales* of Britain to command; as always, large-scale tax evasion was for the really rich. Third, whatever the truth in Gaul, it is unlikely to apply in Britain also. A 3rd-century Gaulish decurion might view with equanimity a withdrawal to his country estate, for the mansion was already there to receive him; for his British counterpart it still needed construction, and that would have required both an act of faith and an outlay of money, of which he was, in the nature of the case, desperately short. Further, many Gaulish cities suffered heavily in the barbarian raids of the 3rd century and this produced a strange situation. The noble cities celebrated by Ausonius indeed went on—Trier, Toulouse, Narbonne and his own Bordeaux—and so did some others, like Autun, but many were reduced to mere strong-points, with none of the amenities of city life. It is difficult to imagine what attractions 4th-century Paris or Bavai or Périgueux could hold for the decurions of the Parisii or the Nervii or the Petrucorii—or even Tours for the Turones, despite the fact that it became the capital of

[1] *cf.* Collingwood, in Collingwood and Myres (1937), 203–7, and *C.A.H.*, xii (1939), 285, adapting Rostovtzeff (1957), chaps. ix–xi

[2] A. H. Jones (1964), 737–57

Lugdunensis Tertia. By contrast, the cities of Britain, which in the 2nd century had been poor by comparison, kept their full size in the later period.[1]

A general 'flight to the villas' therefore seems highly improbable, but our very reasons for rejecting it make it still more difficult to understand how, in the conditions of the 4th century, a British decurion could both perform his civic duties and maintain a luxurious country seat; and this raises the question whether all these late villas were, in fact, in such hands. There were, of course, other landowners. Both the State and the Church held property in all provinces, and so also did members of the senatorial class,[2] but in all these cases the estates would have been worked by bailiffs or tenants, and luxurious mansions are unlikely to have resulted; while at the other end of the scale the peasant proprietor, so far as he survived, could not have afforded such ostentation. What we are seeking is men who were rich by provincial rather than by imperial standards and who are likely to have resided in Britain.

This last qualification narrows the field of search, for, hunting apart, Britain held little to attract people from the Mediterranean area. On the other hand, in the second half of the 3rd century the island may well have appeared as a haven of safety to Gaulish landowners, especially those living near the frontier, and it is not impossible that some of them migrated from one country to the other. Such a conclusion has been hinted at by Dr Smith (p. 114) in dealing with the mosaics, and it can be supported by a number of other considerations. Connections between the peoples, and especially the tribal notables, of Belgic Gaul and Britain reach back before the conquest, and their persistence into Roman times is to be expected. On the commercial side it is suggested, for example, by the probably Rhenish origins of the Castor potteries, which were established in the 2nd century,[3] and socially by the presence in Britain of several Gaulish citizens and by the appearance here of dedications to Rhineland

[1] P. Corder, *Arch. J.*, cxii (1955), 20–42; S. S. Frere, in Wacher (1966), chap. viii; A. L. F. Rivet, *ibid.*, 106–8; the addition of bastions in the 4th century, which involved filling the old town ditches and digging new ones, would surely have invited contraction, if it had been practicable, on grounds of economy.

[2] For the state, *Not. Dig.*, xii, 15, *Rationalis rei privatae per Britannias*; for a senatorial holding, *Vita Sanctae Melaniae Junioris*, Latin version 10, Greek version 11 (*Analecta Bollandiana*, viii (1889), 27; xxii (1903), 14; both versions mention Britain); for a general review of land-ownership in the later Empire, A. H. Jones (1964), chap. xx

[3] Hartley (1960), 21

deities (the most suggestive being that to the Treveran Mars Lenus at Chedworth), while Dr Applebaum has drawn attention to the remarkable similarity of plan between the villa at Houdeng-Goegnis in Belgium and the final phase of Ditchley.[1] All such evidence must be circumstantial, but it may be that the instinct of the older antiquaries did not mislead them when they saw our richer villas as owned by foreigners; only the foreigners were not generals who had come over with the conqueror, but captains of another, less heroic, kind.

In considering the implications of this possibility, we must not forget that only a proportion of the new villas, rather less than a hundred, would have been involved. The remaining 500-odd, which seem rather to be trying to copy them, do probably represent some continuity of ownership and a renaissance of the old order. Nevertheless, such a movement from the Continent could mean that in some places, instead of one ruling class, the descendants of the old British aristocracy with such additions to it as chance had brought, we now have two—the one primarily town based and carrying the burden of routine administration, the other primarily villa based and avoiding civic responsibility. This could help to explain why in 4th-century Britain the towns are so much more tenacious of life than in Gaul; it may also help to explain one of the peculiarities of the distribution of villas in Britain.

The Distribution of Villas in Britain

Taking the distribution of villas as a whole, they present very much the picture we should expect. When we plot all the 604 possible examples (Fig. 5.6)[2] we find them to be fairly evenly distributed over that part of Britain which we defined as economically viable at the time of the conquest. Grouping the *civitates* according to the criteria we applied then (and including villas near *coloniae* with their nearest native *civitas*), we get the following figures:

[1] S. Applebaum, in Thomas (1966), 104, also adducing the evidence of *R.I.B.*, 110, 140 and 149 for Gauls, and 126 and 309 for Gaulish deities in civil areas; the dedication to the Treveran Mars Lenus from Chedworth (*R.I.B.*, 126) is especially significant in this context. For the plan of Houdeng-Goegnis, see de Maeyer (1937), p. 83, afb. 19a

[2] Fig. 5.6 includes 'Villas', 'Probable Villas' and 'Other Substantial Buildings' as defined on p. 10 of the Introduction to *OSRB* (1956); new discoveries up to and including *J.R.S.*, liv (1964) have been added.

Civitates of the 'primary Belgic area'

Catuvellauni	95
Trinovantes	20
Atrebates	39
Regnenses (*ex* Atrebates)	42
Cantiaci	47
Belgae (eastern part, *ex* Atrebates)	50
Total	293

Civitates of the other coin-using tribes

Belgae (western part, *ex* Dobunni)	54
Durotriges	59
Dobunni	65
Coritani	49
Iceni	35
Total	262

Civitates of tribes who did not use coins

Parisi	13
Brigantes	12
Cornovii	9
Silures	10
Demetae	4
Dumnonii	1
Ordovices	0
Deceangli	0
Total	49

These figures can, of course, be only a rough guide, especially as the tribal boundaries adopted are largely arbitrary,[1] but bearing in mind the size of the territory attributed to each tribe, we can see that the degree of Romanisation of the countryside was generally uniform throughout the civilised part of the province, but petered out rapidly at its fringes.

For the earlier period we cannot be more precise than this, because the

[1] The boundaries are those adopted in Rivet (1964), where they are explained in chap. vi

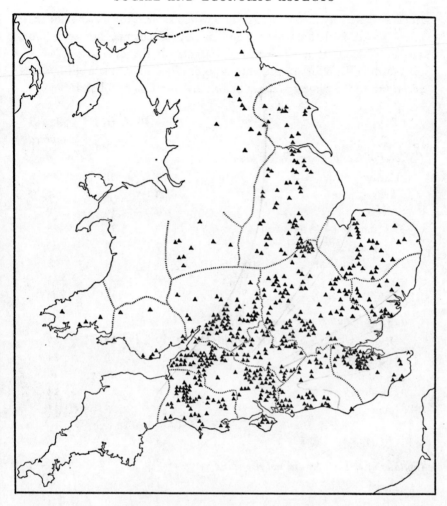

Fig. 5.6. Total distribution of villas in Britain.

evidence is altogether too slight. For the 4th century, however, it is possible at least to attempt a classification and to divide our villas into three categories, according to their size and luxury (Fig. 5.7). In Class A we may put those which might rank with the Continental examples—remembering that what we are comparing is the *villa urbana*, for the extent of the workers' quarters is irrelevant; though all our villas evidently have an element of the *villa rustica*, it still comprises no more than the home farm.

In Class B we may include those villas which aspired to similar standards, often having both bath-houses and mosaic pavements, but were on a smaller scale. And finally we may relegate all the others to Class C, disregarding them for our present purpose. When we tabulate our findings according to the same system as before, the result is as follows:

	Class A[1]	Class B	Classes A and B combined
Civitates of the 'primary Belgic area'			
Catuvellauni	10	35	45
Trinovantes	3	4	7
Atrebates	4	16	20
Regnenses (*ex* Atrebates)	5	23	28
Cantiaci	7	18	25
Belgae (eastern part, *ex* Atrebates)	4	24	28
Totals	33	120	153
Civitates of the other coin-using tribes			
Belgae (western part, *ex* Atrebates)	10	23	33
Durotriges	12	19	31
Dobunni	19	21	40
Coritani	9	15	24
Iceni	3	8	11
Totals	53	86	139
Civitates of tribes who did not use coins			
Parisi	4	3	7
Brigantes	2	2	4
Cornovii	0	5	5
Silures	2	3	5
Demetae	0	0	0
Dumnonii	0	0	0
Ordovices	0	0	0
Deceangli	0	0	0
Totals	8	13	21

[1] For the identity of the villas classed as A, see pp. 265–279

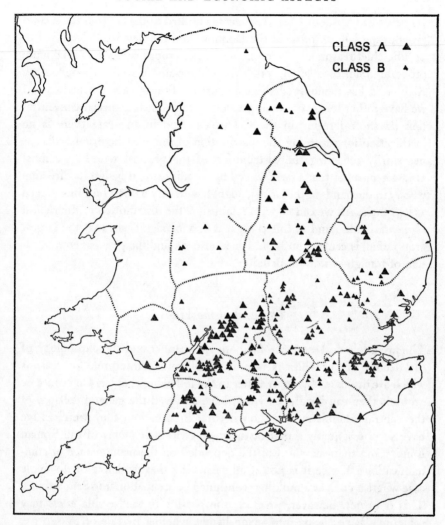

Fig. 5.7. Distribution of 3rd–4th century villas of classes A and B (*see text for definition*).

All the same uncertainties and qualifications apply to this table as to the other, and there is here the additional difficulty that much of the classification is inevitably subjective. Nevertheless, if the general picture can be accepted, it does seem to indicate an interesting trend and one for which we should seek an explanation. Whereas the 'primary Belgic area' leads in the overall total, and maintains its lead in the case of Class B, the very richest villas, our Class A, are concentrated in the lands of the second group, especially in those of the Dobunni and the western Belgae.

The chief reason may be economic; other crops may have proved more profitable than cereals, and one thinks especially of wool—though, since Richmond has demolished the evidence for fulling vats at Chedworth,[1] we have rather less cause than previously to suppose a special concentration on sheep-farming in the Cotswolds. And in any case there is no justification for regarding the distribution of the most luxurious villas as necessarily reflecting the distribution of the greatest wealth; we must always remember that a farm owned by a millionaire, if he left its direction wholly in the hands of the *vilicus*, might have a very modest building indeed as its centre. All we can hope to establish is the distribution of the richest *residential* villas, and in this context it may be significant that the largest group of all is centred on Bath, where also we find the greatest concentration of foreign visitors to Britain.

The End of the Villas

The archaeological evidence for both the manner and the chronology of the decline of our villas is peculiarly difficult to interpret, for reasons which are discussed by Dr Webster in the following chapter. On economic grounds they can hardly, as villas, have survived the general collapse of the central administration; though rural in situation, they were, as we have seen, essentially a part of the town-centred economy of the Roman Empire and their standard of life depended on the maintenance of communications. Hence it is not at all surprising that we know of no single case where a villa, as a building, continued in occupation into Saxon times. This does not, however, preclude the possibility that a villa *estate* may sometimes have passed into Saxon hands, whether by sale or by seizure, as a working unit and, as Dr Webster points out, examples of this are still to be looked for. Moreover, as in the 3rd century, so also in the 5th, it is most unlikely that the cultivated area of the country as a whole was ever abandoned, and the collapse of the centre of an estate does not necessarily imply that all of its land reverted to bush. The tenants, or *coloni*, have still to be reckoned with. Much has been written of the degradation of the *coloni* in the later Empire, from the reforms of Diocletian onwards, and it

[1] Chedworth (1960)

is clear that by the 5th century many of them were reduced to mere serfs, tied to their holdings and completely subject to their lords.[1] But the fact that they were tied does not mean that most of them wished to leave the land, and if they could shake off the burden of rents and taxes—as the *coloni* of Brittany succeeded for a time in doing—they would be most tenacious of their holdings. For them the collapse of the central administration spelled release, not deprivation, and it is the relations of the Saxons with them, not with the villa-owners, that pose the great social and economic question of the Dark Ages. In fact, survival is to be sought not in the villas of the rich, but rather in the humbler settlements—farms or hamlets or villages—described by Mr Bowen.

Summary

As we anticipated at the outset, this chapter has been highly speculative, dealing with possibilities and probabilities rather than with facts. We have established no dates and proved no theories. Nevertheless some purpose may have been served if attention has been concentrated on some of the historical realities of which any viable interpretation of the evidence must take account. These may be summarised as follows:

First, the Roman occupation involved a fundamental change in the economy of Britain, from that of a diffuse and loosely knit collection of tribes to that of coherent town-centred states. The Roman villa was but one manifestation of this economy and it cannot profitably be considered in isolation from it. More than this, the Roman villa, as distinct from the Celtic farm, depended on the town for its very existence, both socially and economically.

Second, in view of this special relationship, the social and economic information we can obtain from a villa, as a building, is strictly limited, since it represents only a part of the owner's life. In particular, the appointments of the *villa urbana* do not necessarily reflect fully the wealth and social standing of the owner, who often had other interests elsewhere.

Third, the Roman economy itself was of such a character that official demands, especially for cereals, played a large part in it. But precisely because these demands were official, the form they took varied from time to time according to political and military considerations, so that they

[1] See A. H. Jones (1964), 795–803

did not automatically spell prosperity for the British farmer; rather, the whip and the carrot seem to have alternated.

Fourth, and finally, in the Roman villa we are considering a specific and peculiar method of exploiting the land, not the extent of agriculture itself; other forms of exploitation continued, as Mr Bowen has shown (ch. I). It may well be that, besides taking over farms that already existed, the villa owners formed some new ones from virgin bush, and the same may be true of the Saxons who came later, but such additions were marginal rather than central. In both cases—in that of the profit-seeking Romano-Celtic capitalists on the one hand and in that of the invading Saxons on the other—the initial incentive must have been land that was already under cultivation. It follows that in both cases continuity of occupation is to be expected—but with a difference. Since the villa-owners seem largely to be derived from the native stock, probably being the descendants of the Celtic farmers themselves, one would expect the change of method to be reflected in a rebuilding of the old farmhouse on the same site; and this is, in fact, what we find. The Saxons, on the other hand, were aliens, with no such links with the past, and a ruined villa would be an embarrassment to them. But it was desire for good land that brought them here and it must have been on land that was already in good order that they settled.

CHAPTER SIX

The Future of Villa Studies

GRAHAM WEBSTER

The Evidence Available

IT IS THE PURPOSE of this final chapter to consider in what direction future studies of the villa may lie. Students should by now be aware that the whole subject bristles with problems; on its historical, economic, sociological and architectural bearings our present knowledge is lamentably defective, and this is due entirely to the lack of evidence. Although the sites of 500–600 villas are known or suspected, the amount of information supplied by their investigators is, for the most part, extremely meagre. Normally the evidence falls into one of the following categories:

1. A scatter of pottery and building debris turned up by the plough is noted. In some cases an aerial photograph may show fragments of structures and enclosures. The information merely denotes the presence of some kind of building, possibly a villa, and the pottery may, when studied, indicate the period of occupation.

2. An excavation may have taken place many years ago and a plan of a building, or part of it, may even have been published. From this it may be possible to identify the building as part of a house or some other structure.

It is unlikely that pottery and coins will be more than barely noted,[1] but if these remains can be traced to a museum they can be studied there. This summarises the kind of information available for most of the British villas discovered more than thirty years ago: a fragment of a plan, usually the house, possibly with some dating evidence. In the 18th and 19th centuries attention was often given to the pavements, and lavish illustrations were occasionally published. At least they show something of the internal decoration and may even be dated on stylistic grounds. Most of these excavations, however, were superficial and only revealed the upper and latest structures, and so tell us nothing of the origins and early history of the buildings. The concept of growth involving the reconstruction of buildings rarely seems to have been envisaged by these early excavators.

3. A partial excavation may have been carried out and published more recently. This may have been done in a competent manner and may reveal something of the history of the site and answer a few of our questions. But all too often work of this kind, excellent as it may be, is concerned with only a fragment of the total establishment.

4. A reliable full-scale excavation may have been recently carried out and fully published. This may show the plan of the whole establishment during its various stages of construction, not only of the house but of the outbuildings which are so important in making an assessment of the economic implications. If fifty or sixty such excavations had been completed in a competent manner, it might now be possible to draw some useful conclusions and seek reliable answers to our basic questions. Unfortunately there are reports of only seven or eight such excavations, and they are of varying quality and some by no means complete. It is on these and on the scattered and scanty information from the rest that any assessment has, for the time being, to be based.

Our knowledge depends on sources which are too diverse and fragmentary. The villas can supply some of the answers to the many problems only if they can be investigated on a large enough scale. Merely to uncover a few rooms or even the complete dwelling-house will not materially add to what is already known. A carefully planned programme is needed, aimed at nothing short of the complete excavation of a number of establishments, carefully selected as typical of a region or, if within a region,

[1] As in the case of Keynsham (*Keynsham* (1926), 132), 'The pottery was disappointing, consisting chiefly of the usual culinary types . . . ' The coins, however, are carefully listed.

typical by reason of size, physical environment or other determinable factors. It might be another thirty or forty years before this work is completed and the results are available, and it may therefore be pertinent at this stage to examine the kind of archaeological evidence which will help towards a closer understanding of some of the main problems. Two aspects selected here for discussion are (1) types of agriculture and (2) chronology.

(1) Apart from the pioneer work of Dr Applebaum[1] little attention has been given to the problems of the kinds and the extent of agricultural practice in Roman Britain. The only possible approaches towards such problems must be a more intensive study of field systems, implements, plant remains and livestock. The pattern of Celtic fields has at present little relationship to villas, mainly because the latter are found on the best arable land which has been under constant cultivation over the centuries. Yet there must be some villas where traces of field systems can still be detected and surveyed either on the ground or by aerial reconnaissance. The finds of ironmongery from villas have rarely been published extensively.[2] Large-scale excavations should produce sufficient quantities of material which, when related to the chronology of the site, could be used to demonstrate changes in practice. Similarly, detailed studies of animal bones are lacking in spite of pioneer work by McKenny Hughes[3] and Pitt-Rivers. Much could be done on a study of breeds, age and physical condition of the animals and methods of butchery, but this leads to more intensive studies than most specialists are at present able or willing to attempt.[4] Similarly, seeds and plant remains, especially from wells and other damp places, deserve serious study.

(2) The main data of chronology are coins and pottery, and one must first inquire as to their precise significance and just how much or how little information can be gleaned from their discovery. The mint date of a coin can often be established within very narrow limits, and this has led in the past to undue archaeological reliance being placed on it. In the first place, to be of any real use the coin ought to be found, not in a surface scatter, but in a structure or stratified layer. Even then it only tells us

[1] Applebaum (1958)

[2] A notable exception is that by H. F. Cleere from Brading (Cleere (1958)); but this survey has no chronological basis.

[3] *Arch.*, lv (1896–7), 125–58

[4] An exception must be made here of the Passmore Edwards Museum (*Ant.*, xxxix (1965), 204–11)

that the structure or layer in which it was found could not have been placed in position before the coin was minted. What is not known is precisely how long after the coin had been minted it came into this position. The coin may have been lost centuries earlier and have been moved several times during either reconstruction or pit-digging for rubbish disposal before it came to its final resting-place. Before being lost it may have been in circulation for many years, and this is often reflected in the amount of wear. One has also to take into account the complicated history of coinage in Roman Britain. Some issues stayed in circulation much longer than others, and this is especially true of the late 3rd century radiates, the numerous imitations of which clearly imply shortage of coins. It seems possible that these coins may have remained in use until the large-scale Constantinian issues of c. 330. The most difficult and perplexing problem is that of dating 5th-century occupation. The almost complete closure of the western mints in 396[1] and the withdrawal of officials and army units mean that very few coins minted after 410 came across the Channel, since after this date no pay-chests were dispatched to Britain. The movement of coins in the course of trade was restricted by imperial edict. The fact that the coin series of a villa ends about A.D. 400 does not mean that life came to an end at that time, but merely that the inhabitants used no coins minted after this date because very few were reaching Britain. Indeed, the archaeological implications from structural sequences are, in some cases, that life continued for a considerable time thereafter.

Pottery may eventually be found to be more valuable than coins. It was purchased, used, broken and discarded at a fairly regular rate and has none of the vagaries in minting, circulation and hoarding to which coins are subject. It is unfortunate that the study of 3rd- and 4th-century pottery is still in its infancy, and it is not yet possible to date types to narrow limits. The wares are in such quantity and variation of form and fabric that their classification and close study is no mean task. Much of it, too, had a very localised manufacture and distribution, and one cannot always be sure of giving similar dates to similar pieces from different parts of the country. More work is needed on the centres of production, and in time it may be possible to use pottery for dating purposes with the pre-

[1] Some of these mints opened again later; most of the coins found in Britain were minted at Trier, Lyons and Arles, which finally ceased activity in 450, 423, and 415 respectively; Carson (1960); J.P.C. Kent, 'Coin Evidence for the Abandonment of a Frontier Province', *Carnuntina*, 1956, pp. 85–90

cision and certainty which is at present achieved with the decorated samian of the 1st and 2nd centuries. Nor must the prospects of scientific aids be overlooked. The Carbon 14 method has been gradually refined and it may yet be possible to give an absolute date for organic material of the 5th and 6th centuries with reasonable certainty. Other techniques, as yet unknown, may eventually provide some answers.

Problems of Survival

Of all the many perplexing questions facing the student of the Roman countryside, those which are the most difficult and at the same time of the greatest interest and importance are those of survival. This applies equally to both ends of the period. With the advent of the Romans the lives of Britons must have changed very little and this is especially true of the countryside. The complex cultural pattern of Iron Age and Late Bronze Age peoples remained, with all the regional differences in ways of life that this implies. The real problem is that of assessing the effect of Romanisation on these different communities. The produce of pre-Roman Britain would have been unlikely to have exceeded the needs of the social unit to which they belonged and the demands of the overlords and priests. In those parts of Britain which became a Roman province this situation was immediately changed, firstly by the sudden demands of the army and secondly by the establishment of communications and markets. The economic revolution implied by the latter in the production and marketing of surpluses for capital gain must have had a profound effect on the countryside. This is, however, closely related to ownership, and on this important matter there is little evidence. Large-scale confiscations of estates by the Roman Government would have taken place where hostility was maintained or revolts occurred at a later date. Some of this land may have been kept as an imperial estate, some sold, some given away. All this means change, but perhaps only by degrees did the British landowners begin to appreciate the full significance of their being precipitated into a capitalist society.

It is not proposed to develop this particular topic, which has been discussed by Mr Rivet in the previous chapter, but to concentrate on the other end of the period. Here there are the very difficult considerations of the continuity of life in the villas and the native homesteads into the

221

5th and 6th centuries and the effect on the country population of the Saxon settlements.

The problems associated with the date of abandonment of the villas raise many important issues. With the gradual decline of Romanised life in Britain, the following seem to be the main possibilities for the fate of these country establishments towards the end of the 4th century:

1. The whole or greater part of the buildings were destroyed by external agents and were never rebuilt or reoccupied.

2. The buildings were abandoned by all their occupants, who never returned, and they gradually fell into ruins.

3. The Romanised occupants left and the buildings or part of them were taken over by others accustomed to a lower standard of life.

4. The same family continued in occupation, but slowly became less and less Romanised in their way of life.

5. The buildings and/or lands were taken over by immigrants.

The historical accounts of the period provide a number of agents of violent destruction. These have, in fact, been used by earlier historians to portray the sudden and violent end of Roman Britain in a torrent of destruction in A.D. 367; but there had been occasions before this date. Towards the end of the 3rd century the south and east coasts were troubled by Frankish and Saxon raiders, a menace countered by the establishment of the coastal defences known as the forts of the Saxon Shore. The accounts of the reign of Carausius show that some of the raiders were successful in obtaining loot, and a source of this would have been the unprotected villas near the coasts and larger rivers. If the owners could be surprised, there might be useful pickings, but activities of this kind would leave little archaeological trace, for the raiders' main interest was gold and silver plate and they would not necessarily have set buildings alight. This would indeed have given a signal of their presence, and a warning to neighbouring villa occupants and to any troops in the area. Small bands of raiders would presumably have operated with swift but quiet cunning. Only when larger bodies roamed the country at will would there have been an element of wanton destruction for its own sake.

The stiffening of the coastal defences and the concentration of units of the fleet off the south and east of England must have reduced the dangers of any serious trouble during the early part of the 4th century. This appears to be the hey-day of the villa in Britain and the period in which the large houses with their splendid pavements were constructed.

The emergency which brought Constans to Britain in the winter of 342-3 appears to be associated not with the raiders but with mass movements of people from Ireland and Scotland, who had established themselves in frontier areas. The Emperor deemed it prudent to accept their presence, and presumably the treaties he made with them gave recognition of the tribes as part of the defensive scheme; they could, in other words, retain the lands they had seized providing they protected them against any potential settlers of the future. The first serious trouble which may have affected the prosperity of the countryside was in 360, when Julian sent a field army to Britain to deal with Picts and Scots who had broken the treaties made with Constans and who were creating trouble in the frontier areas, but even this may have been confined to northern territories and the Welsh Marches. Soon, however, a new threat developed with a concerted attack by Picts, Scots and Saxons in 367, known as the barbarian conspiracy.[1]

The total collapse of the defences and defeat of the army in the field opened the whole province to the raiders. Bands must have swarmed all over the countryside, picking up all the portable valuables they could find. The only safety lay in the towns, with their substantial walls and bastions equipped with spring guns.[2] Here, for the very first time in Britain since 196, there was an opportunity for the total destruction of the villas. Nor did relief come immediately, as it was some time before Theodosius could bring a field army to Britain and deal with the situation. Many historians in the past have accepted this date as the end of Roman Britain, and considered that such civilised life as survived this holocaust faded rapidly away in the succeeding decades. That Britain remained worth saving is clear from the work of Theodosius. Not only did he restore the northern frontier, but he also extended the coastal defences into Yorkshire. Invaders continued to infest the shores of Britain, but not in the same combined strength. Stilicho is said to have freed Britain from the fear of the invader by 399, but soon after this the Imperial Government was withdrawing army units from Britain. From the early years of the 5th

[1] The late Sir Ian Richmond reminded us (*Roman Britain* (1963), 62) that the very fact of this remarkable and unusual alliance clearly demonstrated the effectiveness of the Roman defences. Even so, the army might have dealt with the barbarians, but for the treachery of the northern frontier scouts, won over by bribes.

[2] Provided, of course, that the town defences had been strengthened by this date. Prof. Frere has argued that the bastions were the work of Theodosius (*Britannia* (1967) 256)

century any defences against potential invaders and raiders had to be organised by the Britons themselves. Such help as Rome could afford must have been scanty and sporadic.

Raiders from across the sea were not the only threat to the villas. Early in the 5th century there was probably a revolt started by the peasants, similar to that in Gaul where they were known as 'Bacaudae'.[1] It appears to have been a reaction against the rich and powerful. There was little hope of personal advancement in a society which during the 4th century had become almost a caste system. Every man was born into a level in which he remained. For the slaves and serfs, the raiders represented a chance of escape and joining in the general pillage. Britain may have been the source of this menace, which spread to northern Gaul, where it became a serious problem. The Bacaudae of Armorica, having established an independent state, maintained themselves for ten years. It has been argued that such was the nature of the threat to the rich land of central and southern Gaul that it was as a protection that the Visigoths were brought from Spain and settled on officially appropriated land.[2] This evidence suggests that the Bacaudae represent something more than a mere peasants' revolt. It was probably a movement of Britons and Gauls against the authority of Rome. Their main enemies were the rich absentee landowners, the tax-collectors and bureaucrats. It is even possible that military aid was not forthcoming from Rome because Britain rejected it, and it would have been in keeping with the spirit of the times if Honorius had sent barbarian mercenaries to Britain to crush the Romanised Britons. This is precisely the kind of situation which was developing in Gaul. It is unfortunate that we know so little of these interesting events and it is unlikely that archaeology will be able to add to the story.

Having briefly reviewed the agents and possible times of destruction, it is necessary to examine the archaeological evidence for confirmation. Destruction by fire normally leaves a substantial amount of evidence in the form of a thick ash layer, burnt objects and stones. Many of the earlier antiquaries assumed there must have been a destruction by the barbarians and any evidence of burning was sufficient for them to conclude that the whole house had been enveloped. Ash is often found in quantity from

[1] E. A. Thompson, 'Zosimus on the end of Roman Britain', *Ant.*, xxx (1956), 163–7

[2] E. A. Thompson, 'The Settlement of the Barbarians in Southern Gaul', *J.R.S.*, xlvi (1956), 65–75

hearths and hypocaust stoke-holes, and when a site is investigated critically the idea of total destruction by hostile invaders melts away. It has been rare in the last few decades for an excavator to claim this for his villa. A notable exception is Norton Disney, Lincs.,[1] where the excavator concludes that 'it is difficult to avoid the conclusion that the end of the occupation was a violent one and that it took place in the troublesome times which the country endured in the mid-fourth century'. The evidence which, it is claimed, supports this view is in the form of a skeleton on a threshold. The report reads: 'The adjoining rooms and all the levels of this period bear traces of a fierce fire. It is perhaps permissible to suggest that these people were trying to escape from the burning building and that as the man on the wall passed over the threshold of the door, the lintel collapsed on top of him, crushing the body into the distorted condition in which it was found. The photograph published of the skeleton 'on the wall' (pl. XLIII, no. 1) does not support the theory, as it does not show the smooth threshold stone below the skeleton. It is, in any case, almost impossible structurally for a wall to collapse in this manner, as lengths with openings would normally fall outwards or inwards as the building collapsed. Secondary burials are very common on villa sites, and it would be simpler to conclude that this is yet another example and reject the rather fanciful suggestion put forward. It is, however, a good example of the archaeological evidence being interpreted in the light of presumed historical knowledge, instead of being assessed on its own merits.

Another example of destruction was found at Great Casterton, Rutland.[2] This was, however, confined to a single building, a small barn in the southern range of the establishment. The burning was distinguished by a thick layer of black charcoal particularly rich in pottery, small objects and coins, which included an issue of Valens minted A.D. 375. The destruction, therefore, must have taken place subsequent to this date—at least a decade after the barbarian conspiracy. If this had been the only area investigated, one might have been tempted to consider a violent end to the establishment, but when the excavation was extended to other parts of the building no further evidence of fire was discovered. It was most probably a local conflagration, without any historical significance, and it so happens that the particular building involved was never replaced.

[1] *Norton Disney* (1937)
[2] *Great Casterton* (1951), 18

Similar evidence is recorded from Whittington Court, Glos., where remains of burnt rafters were found under a fall of slates on both floors (i.e. of two rooms of the villa), and where also a spread of charred wheat and much debris was lying directly on the pavement.[1] Elsewhere the excavator considered that the building gradually collapsed 'for want of occupants and maintenance'. Nor does destruction by fire always bring the occupation to an end. An example of this is Lockleys, Herts, where a disaster of this nature occurred early in the 4th century. The suggestion is advanced that 'the site probably lay desolate for a short while and was used as a quarry for building materials. Little, if anything, can have been standing when it was reoccupied and a fresh building erected across the site of the southern end of the earlier house in complete disregard of the former plan'.[2] The practice of having cooking-hearths and corn-drying kilns inside barns and sheds where straw and hay were stored must have been the cause of many local fires. The greater part of the structure of such buildings would have been timber. Although one finds stone foundations, the height of the masonry itself would have varied with the availability of suitable stone. In the Cotswolds, even today, there are farm buildings with stone walls as much as 10–15 feet high surmounted by half-timbered constructions. Where stone was not so plentiful the walls would have been merely low sills. Even in stone country there was much inflammable material in villas, especially among the outbuildings. Fires would be common, and would be due to the careless farm hand and not the barbarian raider. There are, in fact, very few clear examples of violent destruction. One is provided by the large and wealthy villa at North Wraxall, partially excavated in 1859,[3] where human remains were found in the well, together with architectural fragments, but there are also coins of Gratian and a late 4th century belt-buckle to show that this incident was probably later than 367.[4] Another comes from Brislington, Som., where again human remains were found in a well.[5]

A careful survey of the published reports of recent years, when excavators have been observing their work with diligence, fails to provide a single example of the total destruction of a villa which can be placed with

[1] *Whittington Court* (1953), 34
[2] *Lockleys* (1938), 350
[3] *N. Wraxall* (1862): the finds include marble veneer and 2nd century samian (*Cat. of Antiquities in the Museum of Devizes*, 1911, Nos. 417–51)
[4] Hawkes and Dunning (1965), 25
[5] *Brislington* (1906)

certainty to the year 367. Perhaps the nearest approach is that of Park Street, Herts.[1] Here destruction was limited to the cellar, which contained the charred remains of wheat and barley, but the coins cease with issues of 361. Of a total of sixty-nine coins, there is not a single one of later date and the reasonable deduction is drawn that life in the villa ceased at this time. On the other hand, when the small group of coarse pottery found in the cellar floor is examined (fig. 20), it will be seen to contain close parallels with the Verulamium theatre types dated by coins to post-379[2] and also to examples from the Great Casterton destruction deposit post-375. It could perhaps be argued that twenty years is too short a time in which to expect to see changes in this type of pottery. Until much more is known about this complex subject it would be wise to suspend judgement. The Park Street villa was excavated with great care and its chronological problems weighed with considerable thought and discernment. This unfortunately cannot be said of many of the earlier reports, where one looks in vain for even the mention of coins and pottery. When the former do receive notice it is rare that the number found is given, or any details. A typical comment is : 'A number of small coins was found, including some of the House of Constantine'.

A survey has been attempted of two classes of sites where some 4th-century occupation is evident: those, on the one hand, whose coin series does not extend beyond the reign of Magnentius, which ended in 353, and those, on the other, whose coin series extends beyond that date; dividing the latter class into certainties and probabilities. This has been based on the Ordnance Survey classification of villas and bath-houses, supplemented by reference to the annual reports in the *Journal of Roman Studies* up to and including 1964.

Of the total of 334 buildings classified in this manner, for no less than 199, almost two-thirds, there is no satisfactory evidence of a date; of those which offer some dating evidence, sixty-five appear to have come to an end *c.* 360; thirty-two certainly went on after 367, and thirty-eight probably did so. Statistically this evidence may be considered to have little value, and even where coins have been found and recorded in sufficient detail, one is left in considerable doubt as to the implications. Coins listed merely as of the family or house of Constantine cover a wide range down to the last issue of Constantius II (A.D. 361). Often only one or two

[1] *Park Street* (1945)
[2] *Arch.*, lxxxiv (1935), 257, fig. 11

coins have been identified, and one is left in complete ignorance of the remainder. There is also the problem, by no means an easy one, of giving a precise identification of these small 4th-century coins. Often one is left in some doubt as to the accuracy of the observations of earlier antiquaries. Some villas have produced very few coins, others a hundred or more. This may not always reflect the care of the excavators, but may have a close association with the status of the villa. Where only four or five coins are found they are far too few in number to offer a terminal date that can be accepted with confidence. Then one has to consider the implication of a considerable number of issues to *c*. 350 and only one or two coins of later date. This may indicate a sudden change in the type of occupancy, perhaps the wealthy landowning family leaving and being superseded by poor tenants or serfs. There is other archaeological evidence to support this state of affairs, which must be considered below. For the moment, attention is merely drawn to the possibility of life continuing on these sites beyond the period suggested by the coins.[1]

Only a careful study of the coarse pottery will ever fill this gap. There are cases where logic compels one to go beyond the circumstantial evidence that the coins appear to provide. A typical example of the kind of problem raised by coin evidence can be quoted from Wraxall, Som.,[2] where there were twenty-five coins ending with a worn FEL TEMP REPARATIO type (*c*. 350), but a 'much worn' Constantinopolis type (335–7) was found below the stone flagging of the courtyard. This could have been the result of a repair, but it was found in the mortar, which seems to have been homogeneous, and a repair would have presumably been discernible. The conclusion to be drawn is that, after adding at least twenty years for the degree of wear, one may arrive at the date of construction and one must assume thereafter a period of some occupancy. The pottery is unfortunately not drawn, but merely described, and one piece noted as 'should be later than A.D. 330'. The implication of this evidence is that the villa came to an end *c*. 360–70, but, as the report indicates, there may have been a 'decline in intensity' much earlier than this.

The results of the attempted survey, inadequate as they may seem, are shown on the two maps (Fig. 6.1 and Fig. 6.2). The villas where life seems to end before *c*. 360 are for the most part spread evenly over the

---

[1] This problem is considered in more detail in the writer's first interim report, *Barnsley Park* (1967)

[2] *Wraxall* (1961)

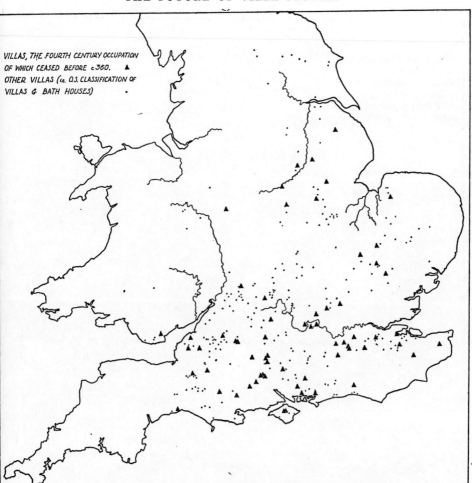

VILLAS, THE FOURTH CENTURY OCCUPATION
OF WHICH CEASED BEFORE c.360.   ▲

OTHER VILLAS (i.e. O.S. CLASSIFICATION OF
VILLAS & BATH HOUSES)   •

Fig. 6.1. Villas where occupation ceased before A.D. 360.

general distribution of villas, with several possible exceptions. There are
three areas where there appears to be an undue proportion: first, Hampshire, Dorset and Wiltshire; secondly, Somerset; and thirdly, Surrey and
west Kent. The first of these is especially striking and implies circumstances,
social, economic or related to invaders, which brought the villas to an end
in the middle or towards the end of the 4th century. The evidence from
Somerset is not so clear, but it is noticeable that it is the villas grouped
round the towns of Ilchester and the great temple of Bath which survived

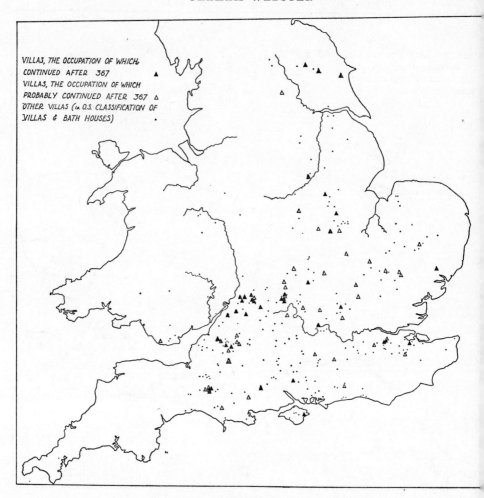

VILLAS, THE OCCUPATION OF WHICH
CONTINUED AFTER 367 ▲
VILLAS, THE OCCUPATION OF WHICH
PROBABLY CONTINUED AFTER 367 △
OTHER VILLAS (ie O.S. CLASSIFICATION OF
VILLAS & BATH HOUSES) •

Fig. 6.2. Villas occupied after A.D. 367.

the period of 367; some of those near the exposed coastline have not
survived. At present there is no evidence of any coastal defences along
the Bristol Channel, except the fort at Cardiff on the Welsh coast. It seems
unlikely that such precautions would have been neglected, but until forts
have been found and studied we must remain in a state of ignorance. The
third area, to the south of London, may require explanation in social or
economic terms, unless invaders were permitted to approach so close to
the most important city in Britain.

The distribution of villas surviving the troubles of 367 raises some interesting points. The most solid block appears in the Cotswolds. This area contains the most important concentration of rich villas, the finest, at Woodchester, being comparable with the splendid palaces of southern Gaul; and the great wealth represented by these magnificent buildings would be an obvious focus for attack, but also for protection. Here must have gathered some of the greatest landowners and men of importance in Roman Britain. Such men could ensure adequate security both from without and from within, and it is perhaps not so surprising that few members of the group show signs of abandonment or destruction in the 4th century. Another group which tends to stand out conspicuously is that in Yorkshire. It might have been thought that in an area so exposed to invaders from the north and the sea, survival would be unlikely. Perhaps it was the protection given by the forts, and by Malton in particular, that created a zone of security. But these villas are not so exposed and isolated as Llantwit Major on the coast of South Wales, which also survived, but in reduced circumstances. This change in the conditions inside the villa is disclosed by archaeological evidence, and as this may have an important bearing on the fate of the villas in general, it is necessary to study it in more detail.

One aspect of this change, mentioned above, is the reduction of coinage. Whereas there may be ten or more issues of the house of Constantine, there may be one or two of Valens, Valentinian and their successors. This can be no reflection on the amount of coinage issued, since where the use of coinage continues unchecked, as in the towns, there is little diminution at this later period. The implication is that there was a change of occupancy of these villas, a change to people who had to manage with a tenth or less of the money used by the previous occupants. A reduction in the standard of living can be seen in the abandonment of the bath-house, one of the appurtenances most closely associated with civilised life as conceived by the Romans. This occurs at Llantwit Major, where it was the opinion of the excavator that the block had been deliberately demolished for its materials and the area sealed off from the rest of the house with a blocking of the only door which originally gave access. Before this happened there had been an attempt to reduce the size of the cold and hot plunges of the baths, presumably in the interests of economy. The furnace area provided further evidence, for inserted into the layer of demolition was an iron smelting hearth. This clearly indicates not only continuing life, but life of a self-sufficient kind. The house itself must have been demolished or allowed to fall into complete decay, since there were burials inserted into the walls and pavements of two of the rooms. The careful orientation of the bodies suggested formal Christian interments of people still resident in another part of the establishment. One part, known as the basilican house, in the south-east corner, was considered to have been the servants' quarters when the complete house was occupied. Part of it may have had this function, but the presence of corn-drying kilns at the east end suggests that it was a barn. This rare example of an extensive excavation revealing the whole of the plan of the establishment thus offers useful evidence of a change of occupancy, which the excavator suggested took place early in the 4th century. The evidence for this date is not very secure, and it may have been later. The case is considered more fully below (p. 238). Here it is interesting to note that almost all the coarse pottery published belongs to the 4th century and although the coin series ends with Constantius II, this may merely date the end of the more civilised occupation.

At Lullingstone, Kent, another villa which has been subject to a careful and critical investigation, the bath-house was found to have been dismantled and a thick layer of yellow clay spread over the site.[1] A similar situation was found at Atworth, Wilts.,[2] but the bath-house, having fallen into disuse, was partly converted into a corn-drying kiln and two other kilns were discovered in rooms of the house. At Barnsley Park, near Cirencester, too, a small bath-house appears to have been dismantled and the site converted into a stackyard.[3] The baths would be the most substantial structure in the villa. In order to retain the heat and obviate fire risk, the building would have to be of stone throughout, even to the barrel-vaulted or domed roofs, although lighter materials like tufa were also used. Such a building would not decay and fall into ruins like the rest of the establishment, but stand, a target for those looking for building material.

There are other kinds of evidence indicating a lowering of standards of civilised life. Very often excavators have noted hearths built on tessellated pavements and have identified them as occupation by 'squatters'. The implication here is that the house in its abandoned and ruinous

---

[1] *Lullingstone* (1955), 159

[2] *Atworth* (1942), 49

[3] Investigations still in progress as a training excavation; interim report in *T.B.G.A.S. LXXXVI* (1967), 74–87

condition attracted vagrants. Taking the evidence as a whole, it would seem more likely that these 'squatters' hearths' are the cooking-places of the regular inhabitants content to exist in a more barbarous way than their luxury-loving predecessors, because they knew no other way of life. Their cooking-hearths in the palmy days of the villa are to be found in the barns and outbuildings where they had previously lived out their days of serfdom. As soon as these less substantial buildings began to fall down, they moved into better quarters. There are examples like Keynsham, Som.,[1] where the hearth has been carefully laid with flat tiles and the excavators noticed there was $1\frac{1}{2}$–$2\frac{1}{2}$ inches of black earth between the hearth and the tessellated pavement. The old floor had been covered over, possibly with dirt and straw, and lost to view before the hearth was laid down. The hearth in Room VII at Whittington Court, Glos.,[2] had been carefully built, and the heavy burning of the stone surround demonstrates its long use, nor is it likely that such a hearth would have been constructed in the open.

The absence of restraint in the more barbarous days is also shown in the burial habits. No doubt in better times each villa had its little cemetery or mausoleum at a discreet distance from the buildings, following the tradition in urban centres. This practice comes to an end in the new *ménage*, and soon the occupants are interring their relatives nearer at hand, in the ruins of the old house. There are many examples of burials on villa sites apart from those at Llantwit Major and Norton Disney mentioned above. These are not to be confused with new-born infants, whose bodies were normally put in the roof and often leave a scatter of tiny bones on the floors, but are properly arranged adult burials, though rarely with any grave goods. That some of these may belong to Christians need occasion little surprise, as these beliefs had become widespread among the Celtic people by the end of the 4th century. Indeed, one wonders how many of the larger villas had possessed private chapels like Lullingstone. The apparent continuity of worship on villa sites in the presence of the parish church, as at Woodchester and Frocester, Glos.,[3] is indicative of a similar arrangement. Christianity may thus have spread from urban centres into the large estates through the great landowners and continued into the twilight period. Corn-drying ovens, already

[1] *Keynsham* (1926), 124
[2] *Whittington Court* (1953), 43
[3] *Frocester* (1959), 23; *T.B.G.A.S. LXXXII* (1963), 148

mentioned, are another sign of continuing rural life. An example at Great Casterton, Rutland,[1] was found built into one of the main walls of the house. It has not the distinctive T-shape and may, of course, be many centuries later.

This brings us to the most crucial question: if there is continuity after the end of the 4th century, how long does it last? The chief evidence for precise dating, that of coinage, ceases to be of any help, not, as Dr J. P. C. Kent has indicated, that the mint had ceased production, but because the Roman Government was no longer paying its soldiers and officials. The western mints had closed down, but that at Rome was still in full production in the early 5th century. It is possible that there are more of these later coins found in Britain than has been realised, but they were clearly never plentiful.[2] It is noticeable also that very few of these late issues are found on villa sites, but occur for the most part in the towns where trade undoubtedly continued. The same is true of late coin hoards: of the seventy-two listed by B. H. St J. O'Neil[3] only four could be associated with villas, and even in these the connection is doubtful. Apart from the obvious raider's loot, most of the hoards have been found near roads. By the beginning of the 5th century the rural communities had become self-sufficient and in little need of a coinage, since they could obtain all they needed for their existence by a system of barter with one another and the people of the towns. Their most important need was for iron for replacing their tools, and this occurs so widely in Britain that there would be little difficulty in mining and smelting the ores. It would appear that even if some early 5th-century coins are found and identified on the villa sites, we shall still be unable to date occupation during the rest of the century. This is a problem already faced by Professor Frere at Verulamium,[4] where a sequence of structural changes forces the dating well into the middle of the 5th century. The same kind of situation is found on the villas, and Great Casterton, Rutland,[5] may be cited as an example. Here the barn which had been in use during the first half of the 4th century was converted into a small dwelling-house, not before c. 350. After this several major reconstructions took place, including the laying of a mosaic pavement

[1] *Great Casterton* (1954), 33

[2] J.P.C. Kent, *Archaeological News Letter*, v (1954), 115–19; *Carnuntina*, 1956, 86; *Limes-Studien, Vorträge des 3 Internationalen Limes-Kongress in Rheinfelden* (1957), 61–68

[3] *Arch., J.* xc (1933), 398–405

[4] Frere (1961), 77

[5] *Great Casterton* (1951), (1954), (1961)

which needed repair and eventual replacing in part with stone flagging. These alterations show an increase in prosperity, but it is difficult to compress the structural phases into fifty years, and one may reasonably assume that the history of this establishment extended into the 5th century. It is possible that a closer study of coarse pottery types will eventually help in this direction. An attempt has been made in associating a type of pottery, known as Romano-Saxon, with this difficult period and thus bridging the gap between the coarse Roman wares and pagan Saxon types.[1] Some of this pottery, in particular the stamped ware, is now known to be late Roman with a centre of manufacture in the Nene Valley,[2] but other wares common in East Anglia may be due to the introduction of Saxon and Frisian mercenaries to protect the east coast.

It is now widely recognised that some kind of Celtic life survived in Britain, especially in areas of the south and west, throughout the 5th and probably into the greater part of the 6th century.[3] It would not, therefore, be at all unreasonable to suppose that rural life continued, for example, in the Cotswolds, based on the villas, for at least two centuries after 400. Most of the buildings would by now be in ruins, but traces of this long occupation must somewhere survive and may one day be recognised. This is one of the most difficult of the archaeological lacunae which at present embarrass the student of Romano-British and early medieval archaeology.[4] It would appear that the people were without any form of pottery, metal tools or ornaments which can be recognised. Yet there were many datable objects coming to Britain from Ireland, the Continent and the Mediterranean. Their distribution seems at present to be almost entirely a coastal one, and the rural communities appear to be completely cut off and isolated. This may be an entirely false picture, for the Cotswolds had much to offer in trade exchanges in their wool, corn and possibly even wine. Satisfactory evidence is lacking even in the towns like Caerwent and Cirencester, where one would expect some continuity even at a modest level.

The first break towards a re-assessment of the situation has been made by Mrs Sonia Chadwick Hawkes.[5] Her study of buckles and belt-fittings

---

[1] J. N. L. Myres, 'Romano-Saxon Pottery', in Harden (1956), 16–39
[2] Hartley (1960), 20
[3] Evidence summarised by Myres (1961)
[4] The study by H. P. R. Finberg, *Roman and Saxon Withington: a Study in Continuity* (1955) is ingenious, but lacks real proof.
[5] Mrs S. C. Hawkes and G. C. Dunning, 'Soldiers and Settlers in Britain, fourth

which may have belonged to Germanic warriors of the 5th century has revealed the surprising fact that examples of such equipment have been found in at least fourteen Romano-British towns and nine villas.[1] The conclusion which has been drawn from this evidence is that bands of Teutonic warriors were employed by the tribes of Britons as protection against the new invaders, a logical continuation of official Roman policy. But the tribes would not be able to support such forces by payment in coin or bullion alone, and the only way to secure their services on a permanent footing would have been by substantial land-grants such as were allotted to the Visigoths in Gaul.[2] This may explain the presence of Germanic equipment on these nine villas with such a widespread geographical distribution. The difficulty about accepting such an interesting suggestion is that if this practice had been widespread in Britain its effect would have been to continue the occupation of the villas into even later times, especially in the west, where the pressure created by the incoming colonists cannot have been very great. But evidence of such continuity is very rare, occurring, so far as present evidence suggests, only at Whittington Court, Glos. On the other hand, such scant attention was paid to pottery by the 18th- and 19th-century excavators that it is possible that similar examples escaped notice.

Such, then, is the present state of our ignorance, and further speculation is useless. Rather, ways must be considered of closing this serious gap between the declining villas on the one hand and the rising Saxon economy on the other. The attack can be mounted from both ends, and while the continued careful and complete excavation of villas may perhaps produce some evidence in due course, better rewards are probably to be sought from the Saxon end. It is, of course, true that our knowledge of early Saxon settlement in Britain is extremely scanty; many cemeteries are known, but rarely has any trace of living sites of these early centuries

[1] Clipsham, Rutland; Spoonley Wood and Chedworth, Glos.; Popham and Hotbury (= West Dean), Hants; North Wraxall and Holbury, Wilts.; Lullingstone, Kent; and Icklingham, Suffolk.

[2] Landowners were obliged to surrender two-thirds of their arable and one-half of their pasture lands to the barbarian settlers: E. A. Thompson, *J.R.S.*, xlvi (1956), p. 66, who refers for full discussion to F. Lot, 'Du régime de l'hospitalité', *Revue belge de philologie et d'histoire*, vii (1928), 975–1011

to fifth century: with a catalogue of animal-ornamented buckles and related belt-fittings', *Medieval Archaeology*, v (1965), 1–70; a slightly expanded version appeared in *Bericht der Römisch-Germanischen Kommission*, 1964, 155–231

been found.[1] Perhaps the best place to start is the deserted medieval village, working its history back to the original settlement. In any case there must clearly be fuller co-operation between the excavators of the two periods. When a villa is being excavated attention must also be paid to the nearest and earliest Saxon occupation site in the district. The barriers which tend to be subconsciously erected between archaeologists of different periods must be broken down if any real progress is to be made on this extremely difficult series of problems.

A Reappraisal of Three Excavation Reports of Villas

When excavators begin to assess their evidence and draw conclusions they are inhibited by the limits of their own knowledge and, if they are aware of them, of ideas under current discussion. It is inevitable, therefore, that interpretation of archaeological evidence should be shaped by these factors. As knowledge grows and our perception of the past deepens, so we gradually edge nearer the truth. One cannot, therefore, be critical of excavators of a past generation merely on the grounds that their conclusions were different from what they would be in the context of our knowledge today. On the other hand, if we are to derive full advantage from our increasing knowledge we must be prepared constantly to re-appraise the work of the past without any disparagement to those who were or may be still concerned. As we noted at the beginning of this chapter, most villa excavations have been very scrappily recorded; in such cases one may perhaps be able to re-date the pottery (if indeed it has been preserved), but short of physical re-excavation there is little that can be done significantly to increase our knowledge. It is otherwise, however, with the small minority of excavations that were carried out and reported in a thorough and complete manner, and these deserve special attention for two reasons. Firstly, it is on these few reports that most of our pre-conceptions about villas in Britain rest, and they are constantly used for references and analogies; thus, a correct understanding of them has an importance that extends far beyond the particular sites that are their subject. But secondly, it is precisely because these excavations were so well conducted and so fully reported that such an operation can be reward-

[1] *Ordnance Survey Map of Britain in the Dark Ages*, 2nd edn, 1966, and Introduction; Vera I. Evison, *The Fifth Century Invasions south of the Thames*, 1965, Map 1

ing. Thus, the reports reassessed here, to demonstrate a method which others may apply more widely, are selected not for their possible shortcomings but rather, *honoris causa*, for their general excellence.[1]

1. THE ROMAN VILLA AT LLANTWIT MAJOR IN GLAMORGAN

by V. E. Nash-Williams

Published in *Arch. Camb.* cii (1953), 89–163. (Plan, p. 58, above)

This investigation was carried out in two seasons, 1938 and 1939; the war intervened and a third season completed the work in 1948. The result was a plan of buildings spread over an area approximately 250 feet square. Earlier excavations of 1887–8, when the villa was first discovered, had removed evidence from one area of the buildings. There were some earthworks apparently associated with the buildings, but the excavator's sections show that, while the visible ditch and bank are post-Roman, they concealed an earlier ditch system which was contemporary with the Roman buildings. Unfortunately, these interesting features, which showed evidence of at least two systems and recutting, were not fully explored and no conclusions could be drawn as to their history or function.

The buildings of the villa range round two courtyards in an irregular manner which in itself strongly suggests periods of alteration and rebuilding. The excavator, however, concluded that the whole of the villa was constructed in its final form at the same time, about the middle of the 2nd century A.D. There were traces of earlier occupation, but these are dismissed as 'slight incidental occupation of the site anterior to the founding of the villa [which] probably represented no more than the preparatory activities of the villa-builders'. The only way this statement can be checked is by an examination of the sections taken through the buildings. Fortunately these were carefully drawn and reproduced. Section MN across Building C shows a foot thickness of pre-building occupation with a possible hearth. Section OP across the same building shows that the north wall foundations actually rest on the earliest cobbling of the yard which

---

[1] One cannot do better than quote Prof. C. F. C. Hawkes's well-known reassessment of Pitt-Rivers: 'He recorded it so well, and preserved his finds so carefully, that this process can really amount to re-excavation of his sites. One can pay no greater tribute to his genius' (*Arch J.*, civ (1948), 36).

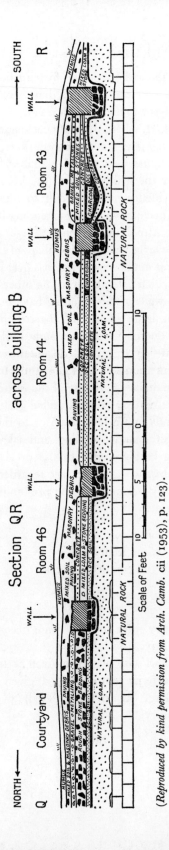

Fig. 6.3. Section QR, Llantwit

(*Reproduced by kind permission from Arch. Camb. cii (1953), p. 123*).

ceases at this point, but the earlier spread of occupation clearly continues under the building itself. One conclusion is that there must have been an earlier building, probably of timber. Similar evidence can be seen in the North Range in Section GH, where the early occupation extends as far as the north wall of this range and stops abruptly there, as if this wall had also replaced an earlier division, possibly in timber. There is a thinner occupation spread under the main range of the house. Building B, the basilican barn, offers evidence more difficult to interpret; Section QR (Fig. 6.3) shows an early occupation spread extending beyond the building to the north, but in the centre there is a concrete layer at foundation-level. In Room 43 this concrete layer has actually collapsed into what must have been a large pit, which was not observed, and has over it a mass of charcoal more than a foot thick which extends on to the other side of the wall. It seems therefore that the walls of this building have been inserted into an earlier structure and the large amount of charcoal may even suggest a destruction by fire. The concrete floors of the stone building, all at the same level, are clearly seen, but they are separated from the earlier concrete floor by this charcoal and occupation soil. It is most unfortunate that when we have been given such a tantalising glimpse of the earlier timber structures the pottery and coins are not treated in stratified groups. There is only a broad division of the finds into a level anterior to the stone building, a level contemporary with the stone building, and a level posterior to the occupation of the stone building. But this is precisely how it can be expected to be arranged by the excavator, who regarded the building as all of one period. The pottery belonging to the pre-building period is small in quantity, but consists of:

Samian   No.   32   Antonine; form 37.

43   Antonine, from 37.

45   Late-2nd century, form 31.

Coarse wares

No.   17   A grey ware jar with comb decoration given as 2nd century.

131   A bowl with plain rim given as 2nd century.

152   A large jar (not illustrated) given as 2nd century.

153   A large jar (not illustrated) given as 2nd or 3rd century.

154 A black-burnished pie dish 'with short, grooved rim',
dated 'late 2nd to 4th century'. Although this is not
illustrated, a Leicester parallel is quoted which could
not be earlier than the end of the 3rd century. Mr
J. P. Gillam gives a reasonably close parallel from
Lancaster with a date bracket A.D. 260–320 (type
227, *Arch. Ael.*,[4] xxxv (1957), fig. 24).

The small quantity of pottery recovered from these early levels may
indicate that they were not extensively explored,[1] and this would have been
reasonable had the excavator assumed that they were merely builders'
levels. Apart from No. 154, all the pieces are of the 2nd century. This
particular sherd was found on the east side of Building C outside Room
51, but the Section OP clearly indicates that it must have belonged to a
pre-stone building phase. The evidence of the coins is not very helpful, but
it should be noted that nos. 21 and 23, both Constantinian, are given as
pre-stone or stone period. There is, however, one coin, no. 31, which is
considered as pre-stone period; this was found in the first occupation
period of the yard associated with the *praefurnium* of the baths, and as it is
Constantinian, in worn condition, it must mean that the yard was not in
use until the mid-4th century.

Admittedly the evidence is limited to one pottery sherd and one coin,
but the careful record of the sections and comments in the text render
it conclusive. It is doubtful if there were any stone buildings before the
4th century, and the whole of the west range, which is clearly of one build,
is probably mid-4th century. In considering the general arrangement of
the buildings a speculation may be permitted. The nucleus of the early
timber buildings seems to be the outer yard and the main ranges, consisting
of the house, may be a 4th-century extension. In this case there may be the
demolished remains of the first timber house below the central area of the
courtyard between Building B and the workshops, which are on the same
alignment. In support of this suggestion it is clear that the western end of
the workshops has been demolished and the reduced building fitted on to
the new range. Unfortunately the relevant stratigraphy is not shown, as
Section JI is not extended into the older building. There is no evidence

---

[1] It is significant that of Building B the excavator writes: 'Owing to limitations
of time and labour it was unfortunately not possible to make a detailed clearance
of the whole building' (p. 121)

that the yards were extensively stripped, the excavator being content to test the statification at selected points.

The coin list of thirty-two items is sufficient to indicate the main period of activity; the earliest is one of Gallienus (A.D. 252–68) and there are seventeen coins of the late 3rd century. The rest are all of the house of Constantine, with nothing later than A.D. 341–6 (reign of Constantius II). One would not expect any coins of the early 3rd century, but the lack of 2nd-century specimens tends to suggest that occupation could not have started until the end of that period, and this is supported by the samian ware, of which forty-eight pieces are listed with the general comment: 'There is nothing earlier than A.D. 150 and the Lezoux ware may, in fact, be much nearer the end of the second century than this.' Of the 180 sherds of coarse ware listed, only sixty-nine are illustrated and of these thirty-three are definitely of the 4th century.

It would seem from this that occupation started towards the end of the 2nd century in a modest way with mainly timber buildings. The conversion to stone may be associated with the expansion and the new west wing, and such indications as there are tend towards an early 4th-century date for this. Wealth represented by the coins is limited to the first half of this century. The excavator, however, interpreted his evidence as showing that the villa reached 'the zenith of its prosperity somewhere in the third century, after which a decline set in'. This decline is deduced from a remodelling of the baths involving a reduction of the main furnace and some of the rooms. The alterations involved the fitting of seats to the hot bath and apparently also to the cold bath, while the main furnace flue was relined, having the effect of forming a narrower opening. These, then, could be interpreted as added amenities and increase of efficiency rather than the inauguration of a period of economy. It is clear, however, that the baths had a considerable life before they became disused and the site of the *praefurnium* was adapted for iron smelting. It seems that the whole house itself became unoccupied, but that Building B continued in use; presumably, as the excavator surmised, it was the servants who remained there and who eventually began to bury their dead on the site previously occupied by the house. This small cemetery, with its hint of Christianity in the alignment of the bodies, could only have been started when the main house had disappeared totally from view, since at least four of the burials are placed across walls, which is difficult to understand had these remained above ground.

This must drastically affect the chronology, since time must be allowed for the building to fall into decay and eventually be demolished. On the basis of the coin evidence it is suggested that the hey-day of the villa must have been the first half of the 4th century. The coin-using people, that is those who lived in the house, departed some time after *c.* A.D. 350, but the farm continued in use, with the servants and workers occupying the basilican house as they had previously done. They could hardly have started their cemetery before the end of the 4th century or even later, and just how long this continued it is impossible to say. The two sets of interpretation can be summarised as follows:

Excavator's interpretation	*Suggested reinterpretation*
c. A.D. 150, the whole villa built.	*c.* A.D. 180, occupation started with modest timber buildings.
Third century, zenith of prosperity.	*c.* A.D. 300, large-scale rebuilding in stone, including the extension to the west with a new house.
c. A.D. 300, a decline with a period of austerity.	
Fourth century, occupation continuing in Building B only until the end of the century.	*c.* A.D. 350, family occupying the house leave, but servants and workers continue in Building B.
	c. A.D. 400+, cemetery in use.
	? Occupation finally ceases.

2. THE ROMAN VILLA AT LOCKLEYS, WELWYN

by J. B. Ward-Perkins

Published in *Ant. J.*, xxviii (1938), 339–76. (Plan, p. 54, above)

This villa was discovered in 1930 and excavated in 1937. The area investigated was limited to the house itself, a small corridor type; walls extended beyond the house at each end, but ploughing had removed all traces of these extensions. The excavation was conducted with great thoroughness and the full and prompt publication made it a model of its kind, much influenced by Sir Mortimer Wheeler's brilliant work at Verulamium immediately prior to this. It stands as one of the earliest studies of a villa using the new techniques of stratification and pottery study, and looking back from a distance of almost thirty years one does not seriously question the quality of the work so much as the basic interpretation of the chronology. This report has been cited on many occasions as evidence of continuity from Late Iron Age into Roman times. That a Belgic family should continue to occupy the same site and be subject to Roman influences soon after the conquest is an important conclusion. As the excavator himself writes, 'It is clear that the Roman invasion had no catastrophic consequences for this Belgic farmer. He went on living just as he had done before. A certain number of new objects came his way, but considering the situation of his farm they were surprisingly few. It is tempting to recall in this connection the description which Tacitus gives[1] of the administrative conditions which led up to the revolt of Boudicca. In any case we have at Welwyn an interesting commentary upon the character and intensity of Romanisation in the early years after the conquest.'

The evidence for this consists of what are described as two Belgic houses. But the first of these was merely a shallow depression with two small sockets which may have been in association. Although this is classified as a house, it appears on the plan as a hut and is described in the text as a lean-to tent; it can only represent occupation of a most ephemeral kind, but the pottery from the floor and a pit is Belgic. Of the second Belgic house no structural elements were found. The evidence for its presence lies entirely in fragments of daub, pottery and charcoal sealed by the first Roman building. All that this need imply, however, is that there was some occupation of the building. The pottery is described as overwhelmingly Belgic, with a scarcity of imported wares, but the small amount of samian is definitely Claudian, together with three brooches, and, to clinch the matter, Roman brick was also found. This occupation must therefore have extended into the post-conquest period, and the coarse pottery is little different from most of the wares still made and in use in the first four decades of the occupation. A building may have existed somewhere near the site, but the evidence is not sufficient to support a pre-Roman phase, except that of the modest tent-like structure.

The first Roman house is dated to the period A.D. 60–70 on the evidence of the pottery in the builders' rubbish, which included a samian sherd of early Flavian date. But this could all have been rubbish survival from the early Roman phase. It is striking that the coin series includes an example of Claudius and then two of Hadrian, one worn smooth, and the next

[1] *Agr.*, xv; *Ann.*, xiv, 31–32

Emperor is Victorinus (A.D. 265–8). Even more telling is the pottery, for not a single piece is illustrated of the 1st and 2nd centuries apart from the early group and a fragment of samian with a stamp of TINTIRVS, who also appears on a Walters form 80 from London of late Antonine date.[1] This, with two other fragments of samian, is the sole evidence for continuity of occupation through the 2nd century; the typical kitchen wares of *mortaria* and cooking-pots are completely absent. It is difficult to avoid the conclusion that there was no occupation on this part of the site during this period. Thus, the house has been dated by residual material which may be 200 years earlier than the actual date of construction.

The pottery and coins which are abundant are wholly 4th-century and the building plans have a coherence which suggests uniformity, except in the final phase. One fact emerges very clearly—the destruction of the building in the early 4th century by fire.[2] Sealed in the debris was a considerable amount of pottery (figs. 9, 10, 11 and 12), datable to the middle of the 4th century; unfortunately no coins were found in these deposits. In a final phase a new building was erected at the south end of the site, cutting across the earlier one and implying a complete break with the previous plan. The date of this new phase is given by three coins (*c.* A.D. 330–40) from a pit built into a corner. Two later coins of Gratian and Valens suggest that this occupation continued down to the last quarter of the 4th century. A summary of the excavator's interpretation and a suggested revision can be compared as follows:

Excavator's interpretation	*Suggested reinterpretation*
c. A.D. 0–25, first Belgic house.	Casual Belgic occupation.
c. A.D. 25–60, second Belgic house.	*c.* A.D. 50–120, a timber phase on or near the site of the later buildings.[3]
c. A.D. 60–150, first Roman house.	
c. A.D. 150–300(?), second Roman house destroyed by fire.	*c.* A.D. 300, house (Excavator's Phases 1 and 2) destroyed *c.* 340.
c. A.D. 340–75, third Roman house.	*c.* A.D. 340–75, final phase.

[1] Oswald and Pryce, *An Introduction to the Study of Terra Sigillata* (1920), 200

[2] There are two statements on the date of the fire: according to p. 347, it was late in the 3rd century; according to p. 349, it was early in the 4th. But the pottery in the destruction layer could not be earlier than *c.* A.D. 340

[3] To this may belong the line of flint foundations for timber posts in the veranda, which are slightly out of alignment with the later building.

It would, however, be most unwise to be too firm about this reassessment, since the excavation may have been a small part of what originally was a large site. Nevertheless the evidence fails to support the suggestion of continuity from Belgic into Roman times.

3. A ROMAN VILLA AT LANGTON, NEAR MALTON, E. YORKSHIRE

by Philip Corder and John L. Kirk

Published as Roman Malton and District Report No. 4, 1932.

This report is a landmark in the study of villas, since it was a serious attempt to investigate the whole of a large and difficult site (about 250 feet by 650 feet). Although the remains were in poor condition, careful attention was given to all the buildings and structures and their functions fully discussed. Some of the conclusions can now be reconsidered in the light of more recent work.

The earliest features on the site were ditches forming a square enclosure identified as a small military fort of Flavian date. The work of Mr George Jobey in Northumbria[1] on the native sites of the Roman period has shown that a more probable explanation is that this enclosure is that of a native farmstead. The pottery (fig. 7) is an interesting collection of native wares with Romanised types. The local imitation of a black-burnished dish (no. 12) and the type of rusticated ware (no. 1) would seem to place this pottery somewhat later than the Flavian period, probably into the middle of the 2nd century, where it would fit with the coins of Trajan, the brooch (fig. 18, no. 1) and fragments of samian (fig. 23), which extend this phase of the occupation to the end of the 2nd century. The earliest pottery associated with the villa itself is the group from the filling of the stoke-hole of the bath building (fig. 12). This was recognised as belonging to the 3rd century, and one would be inclined in the light of present knowledge to assign it to the period c. 200–30. Presumably the flue went out of use at this time. The hypocaust system is clearly an insertion into an earlier building so it became possible to visualise a continuity of rural life from c. 150, but whether any of the stone buildings are as early as this it is impossible to say. One is, however, struck by the way the two rectangular buildings are carefully set inside the ditched enclosure, although, in fact,

[1] *Arch. Ael.*, xxxviii (1960), 1–38; xxxix (1961), 371–3; xli (1963), 19–35, 211–13

the footings have been built into the filling of one of the ditches (Section F. 2, p. 28). These buildings are therefore later, but the builders seemed to be aware of the presence of the enclosure and they may have replaced timber buildings contemporary with it. The coins and pottery demonstrate an intensity of occupation in the 4th century and continuing until the very end, including the latest issues normally found in Britain. This led the excavators to suggest that life may have extended into the 5th century, a very shrewd observation to have made as early as 1932.

The stone buildings underwent a long sequence of change lasting over 200 years, and land clearance and ploughing had caused much damage. In spite of the devoted labours of the excavators, the story remains far from complete. The 'bath building' was first equipped for animals, as is indicated by the gulley along the main axis. The added 'hypocaust' and tanks do not make a satisfactory bath-house, and now that other examples are available they would be better interpreted as a corn-drying oven[1] and wool-washing tanks. One of the most interesting and important aspects of this investigation is the study of the farm buildings and ancillary structures. Seven or eight of the buildings are merely rectangular in plan and offer little evidence of function. The presence of corn-driers in two of them, and of two others in the open (K1 and K2), indicates the importance of grain production. The circular building was identified, with some reservations, as a manual mill for grinding corn, but the evidence of the small socket with signs of wear is opposed to this, and it could be better interpreted as a pigeon-house with a revolving wooden post bearing projecting arms which functioned as a ladder to give access to the wall recesses. Such structures are common in later times and may even still survive. The large platform (P), 30 feet by 35 feet, was thought to have been a threshing-floor, but it seems too large and of unnecessarily solid construction for this, and the suggestion is now made that it was a rick-stand.[2]

The method used in excavating the villa was that of cutting trenches at 8-foot intervals, but most of the buildings were stripped. If this had been

[1] For a corn-drier supported by columns and built into a barn, see *Great Casterton* (1961), fig. 23. Another, but with channels, occurs in an aisled building, also with a series of tanks, at Huntsham, Herefords.: *Trans. of the Woolhope Naturalists Field Club*, 37 (1962), p. 182 and fig. 3

[2] Several of these have been found on the villa at Barnsley Park, near Cirencester (interim report forthcoming), and it is possible that stone fillings in the demolished villa at Star, Somerset, is a similar example (*Star* (1964))

done for the whole area, in accordance with modern practice, more smaller structures might have been revealed. There remains also the problem of the area enclosed by the east ditch, where occupation was noted but not explored (pl. 35). Perhaps the most important factor, which it was not possible in 1930 to develop, is the relationship between this site and the villa known to exist only 400 yards to the west. The two sites in such close proximity can hardly not be associated in some way. The chronological sequences can be summarised as follows:

Excavators' interpretation	*Suggested reinterpretation*
c. A.D. 80–120 small fort.	A.D. 150 small rural settlement begun with gradual additions of buildings and re-adaptations. Occupation continuing in strength to the end of the 4th century and possibly later.
c. A.D. 200–300 modest farm buildings.	
c. A.D. 320–400+, period of greatest prosperity.	

Summary

It must be conceded that the evidence for forming an assessment of most of the problems relating to villas in Roman Britain is at present woefully inadequate. In important respects relating to social and economic questions it scarcely exists. Very little can be gained by further small-scale trenching or exposure of a few rooms of large establishments. More large-scale exhaustive work is required both in the field and in excavation. The following may be considered as guide-lines:

1. Careful regional surveys in which ground features are surveyed and aerial reconnaissance pursued with a view to producing plans of field systems, enclosures and farmsteads and their relationship to villas. This should also include a subsoil survey to enable agricultural potentialities to be considered.

2. Excavation reports can be re-studied to see if there is a need for the revision of the chronology originally laid down. Such reassessment may inevitably raise other problems, as seen above.

3. A body like the Iron Age and Roman Research Committee of the Council for British Archaeology might consider the initiation of a long-term programme of villa excavation. This would start with the careful

selection of a few villas of differentiated type and background and their total excavation under skilled direction over a number of years, with the opportunity of comprehensive reports.

4. The problem of continuity, both from the Late Iron Age and into the medieval period, should be carefully considered in consultation with those interested in these periods. Sites should be sought where there may be possibilities of such continuity and even a joint excavation might eventually be considered.

Ancient Authorities
Cited

Appian	*Roman History*, ed. with parallel translation, H. White, Loeb Library, 1912
Athenaeus	*The Deipnosophists*, ed. with parallel translation, C. B. Gulick, Loeb Library, 1927–41
Caesar, *B.G.*	*De Bello Gallico*, ed. R. du Pontet, O.U.P., 1900; trans. S. A. Handford (*Caesar: The Conquest of Gaul*), Penguin Classics, 1951
Cato, *Agr.*	*De Agri Cultura*, ed. with parallel translation, W. D. Hooper and H. B. Ash, Loeb Library, 1935 (in one volume with Varro)
Cicero, *ad Fam.*	*Epistulae ad Familiares*, ed. L. C. Purser, O.U.P., 1901
Cod. Theod.	Theodor Mommsen, *Theodosiani libri xvi cum constitutionibus sirmondianis*, Berlin, 1905; *The Theodosian Code and Novels and the Sirmondian Constitutions*, trans. C. Pharr, Princeton, 1952
Columella, *R.R.*	*Res Rustica*, ed. with parallel translation, H. B. Ash, E. S. Forster, and E. H. Heffner, Loeb Library, 1941–55
de Laudibus Constantini	Migne, *Patrologia Graeca*, XX, col. 1409
Digest.	*Justiniani Digestorum seu Pandectarum fasciculi viii*, Berlin, 1870
Dio	Cassius Dio Cocceianus, *Roman History*, ed. with parallel translation, E. Cary, Loeb Library, 1914–27
Diodorus Siculus	*History*, ed. with parallel translation, C. H. Oldfather, Loeb Library, 1933–54
Edict	Diocletian's *Edict on Prices*; text in T. Frank: *An Economic Survey of Ancient Rome*, Volume V, Johns Hopkins, 1940,

251

	with subsequent additions from *l'Année Epigraphique*, 1947, 148f., and *J.R.S.*, XLV (1955), 106ff.
Itin. Anton.	*Itinerarium Provinciarum Antonini Augusti*, in *Itineraria Romana*, vol. I, ed. O. Cuntz, Teubner, 1929
Not. Dig.	*Notitia Dignitatum Omnium tam Civilium quam Militarium, in Partibus Orientis, in Partibus Occidentis*, ed. O. Seeck, 1876
Ovid, *Metam.*	*Metamorphoses*, ed. with parallel translation, F. J. Miller, Loeb Library, 1916
Pliny, *N.H.*	Pliny the Elder, *Naturalis Historia*, ed. with parallel translation, H. Rackham, Loeb Library, 1938–56
Pliny, *Paneg.*	Pliny the Younger, *Panegyricus Dictus Traiano Imperatori*, in *XII Panegyrici Latini*, ed. R. A. B. Mynors, O.U.P., 1964
Polybius	*Histories*, ed. with parallel translation, W. R. Paton, Loeb Library, 1922–7
S.H.A.	*Scriptores Historiae Augustae*, ed. with parallel translation, D. Magie, Loeb Library, 1921–32
Strabo	*Geography*, ed. with parallel translation, H. L. Jones, Loeb Library, 1917–32
Suetonius	*De Vita Caesarum*, ed. with parallel translation, J. C. Rolfe, Loeb Library, 1914
Tacitus, *Agr.* } Tacitus, *Germ.* }	*Agricola* and *Germania*, in *Opera Minora*, ed. H. Furneaux and J. G. C. Anderson, O.U.P., 1938; trans. H. Mattingly (*Tacitus on Britain and Germany*), Penguin Classics, 1948
Tacitus, *Ann.*	*Annales ab Excessu Divi Augusti*, ed. C. D. Fisher, O.U.P., 1906; trans. M. Grant, Penguin Classics, 1956
Varro, *R.R.*	*Res Rusticae*, ed. with parallel translation, W. D. Hooper and H. B. Ash, Loeb Library, 1934 (in one volume with Cato)
Virgil	*Opera*, ed. A. Hirtzel, O.U.P., 1900; *Aeneid*, trans. W. F. Jackson Knight, Penguin Classics, 1956

(For texts and translations of passages from Athenaeus, Diodorus Siculus, Strabo and Caesar, see also J. J. Tierney: 'The Celtic Ethnography of Posidonius' (*Procs. of the Royal Irish Academy*, Vol. LX, Sect. C, No. 5, 1960)

Modern Authorities Cited

Aberg (1957) A. Aberg, 'The Early Plough in Europe', *Gwerin*, I (1956–7), 171–81

Alcock and G. Jones (1962) L. Alcock and G. R. Jones, 'Settlement Patterns in Celtic Britain', *Ant.*, XXXVI (1962), 51–55

Aldred (1956) Cyril Aldred, 'Furniture: To the End of the Roman Empire', in C. Singer *et al.* (ed.): *A History of Technology*, II, Oxford, 1956

Allen (1958) D. F. Allen, 'Belgic Coins as Illustrations of Life in the late pre-Roman Iron Age of Britain', *P.P.S.*, XXIV (1958), 43–63

Applebaum (1954a) S. Applebaum, 'The Agriculture of the British Early Iron Age as exemplified at Figheldean Down, Wiltshire', *P.P.S.*, XX (1954), 103–14

— (1954b) S. Applebaum, 'A Note on three Romano-British Place-names', *J.B.A.A.*, XVII (1954), 77–79

— (1958) S. Applebaum, 'Agriculture in Roman Britain', *Ag. H.R.*, VI (1958), 66–86

Artis (1828) E. T. Artis: *The Durobrivae of Antoninus*, privately, 1828

Ashbee (1963) P. Ashbee, 'The Wilsford Shaft', *Ant.*, XXXVII (1963), 116–20

Becatti (1961) G. Becatti: *Scavi di Ostia*: IV, *Mosaici e Pavimenti Marmorei*, Rome, 1961

Beesley (1848) A. Beesley: *The History of Banbury*, London, 1848

Bersu (1940) G. Bersu, 'Excavations at Little Woodbury, Wiltshire', *P.P.S.*, VI (1940), 30–111

— (1946) G. Bersu, 'Celtic Homesteads in the Isle of Man', *Journal of the Manx Museum*, V (1945–6), 177–92

Beyen (1958)   H. G. Beyen, 'Das stilistische und chronologische
                  Verhaltnis der letzten drei pompejanischen Stile',
                  Antiquity and Survival, 1958, 349–72

Blanchet (1928)   J. A. Blanchet: *La Mosaïque*, Paris, 1928

Blanchet and   A. Blanchet and G. Lafaye: *Inventaire des mosaïques de la*
  Lafaye   *Gaule*, Paris, 1909
  (1909)

Bogaers (1955)   J. E. A. Th. Bogaers: *De Gallo-Romeinse Tempels te Elst in*
                  de Over-Betuwe, The Hague, 1955

Boon (1957)   G. C. Boon: *Roman Silchester*, London, 1957

Borda (1958)   M. Borda: *La Pittura Romana*, Milan, 1958

Bowen (1961)   H. C. Bowen: *Ancient Fields*, London, 1961

Bowen and   H. C. Bowen and P. J. Fowler, 'The Archaeology of
  Fowler   Fyfield and Overton Downs, Wilts.', *W.A.M.*, LVIII
  (1962)   (1962), 98–115

Boyd, Doney,   J. M. Boyd, J. M. Doney, R. G. Gunn, and P. A. Jewell,
  Gunn and   'The Soay sheep of the Island of Hirta, St Kilda', *Procs.*
  Jewell (1964)   *of the Zoological Society of London*, No. 142 (Jan. 1964),
                  129–63

Bradford (1942)   J. S. P. Bradford, 'An Early Iron Age Settlement at
                  Standlake, Oxon.', *Ant. J.*, XXII (1942), 202–14

Brailsford   J. W. Brailsford, 'Excavations at Little Woodbury',
  (1949)   *P.P.S.*, XV (1949), 156–68

— (1955)   J. W. Brailsford: *The Mildenhall Treasure: a Handbook*,
                  B.M., London, 2nd edn, 1955

Brewster (1963)   T. C. M. Brewster: *The Excavation of Staple Howe*,
                  Scarborough, 1963

Briscoe (1958)   Lady (Grace) Briscoe, 'Combined Early Iron Age and
                  Romano-British Site at Wangford, West Suffolk',
                  P.C.A.S., LI (1958), 19–29

Brunt (1950)   P. A. Brunt, 'Pay and Superannuation in the Roman
                  Army', *Papers of the British School at Rome*, XVII (N.S. V),
                  1950, 50–71

Bulleid and   A. Bulleid and H. St G. Gray: *The Glastonbury Lake*
  Gray (1911)   *Village*, vol. 1, Glastonbury, 1911

Burstow and   G. P. Burstow and G. A. Holleyman, 'Late Bronze Age
  Holleyman   Settlement on Itford Hill, Sussex', *P.P.S.*, XXIII
  (1957)   (1957), 167–212

Cabrol and   F. Cabrol and H. Leclercq: *Dictionnaire d'archéologie*
  Leclercq   *chrétienne et de liturgie*, Paris, 1903–53

Calkin (1962)   J. B. Calkin, 'The Bournemouth Area in the Middle and

Late Bronze Age, with the "Deverel-Rimbury" Problem reconsidered', *Arch. J.*, CXIX (1962), 1–65

Carson (1960) R. A. G. Carson, P. V. Hill, and J. P. C. Kent: *Late Roman Bronze Coinage, A.D. 324–498*: Part II, by R. A. G. Carson and J. P. C. Kent, London, 1960

Charbonneaux R. Viollet: *Greece in Photographs*, text by J. Charbonneaux
and Peters and E. Peters, London, 1954
(1954)

Childe (1950) V. Gordon Childe: *Prehistoric Migrations in Europe*, Oslo and London, 1950

Clark, G. J. G. D. Clark, 'Excavations on the Cambridgeshire Car
(1949) Dyke', *Ant. J.*, XXIX (1949), 145–63

Clark, G. and J. G. D. Clark and C. I. Fell, 'The Early Iron Age Site
Fell (1953) at Micklemoor Hill, West Harling, Norfolk, and its Pottery', *P.P.S.*, XIX (1953), 1–40

Clark, M. K. M. Kitson Clark, *A Gazetteer of Roman Remains in East*
(1935) *Yorkshire*, Leeds, 1935

Clarke, R. R. R. Clarke, 'The Iron Age Treasure from Snettisham,
(1954) Norfolk', *P.P.S.*, XX (1954), 27–86

Clay (1924) R. C. C. Clay, 'Excavations on Fifield Bavant Down', *W.A.M.*, XLII (1924), 457–96

Cleere (1958) H. F. Cleere, 'Roman Domestic Ironwork, as illustrated by the Brading, Isle of Wight, Villa', *Bulletin of the Institute of Archaeology* (London), I (1958), 55–74

Clifford (1961) E. M. Clifford: *Bagendon: a Belgic Oppidum*, Cambridge, 1961

Collingwood R. G. Collingwood: *The Archaeology of Roman Britain*,
(1930) London, 1930

— (1932) R. G. Collingwood: *Roman Britain*, rev. edn, Oxford, 1932

Collingwood R. G. Collingwood and J. N. L. Myres: *Roman Britain and*
and Myres *the English Settlements*, 2nd edn, Oxford, 1937
(1937)

Corder (1955) P. Corder (ed.): *Romano-British Villas: some current Problems* (CBA Research Report No. 1 = *Archaeological News Letter*, VI, No. 2), London, 1955

Cotton (1961) M. A. Cotton, 'Robin Hood's Arbour: and Rectilinear Enclosures in Berkshire', *Berks. A.J.*, LIX (1961), 1–35

Cra'ster (1961) M. D. Cra'ster, 'The Aldwick Iron Age Settlement, Barley, Hertfordshire', *P.C.A.S.*, LIV (1961), 22–46

Crawford O. G. S. Crawford: *Archaeology in the Field*, London, 1953
(1953)

Crawford and   O. G. S. Crawford and A. Keiller: *Wessex from the Air*,
  Keiller   Oxford, 1928
  (1928)
Cumont (1914)   F. V. M. Cumont: *Comment la Belgique fut romanisée*,
                Brussels, 1914
Cunnington   Mr and Mrs B. H. Cunnington, 'Casterley Camp',
  (1913)   *W.A.M.*, XXXVIII (1913), 53–105
— (1923)   M. E. Cunnington: *The Early Iron Age Inhabited Site at All
                Cannings Cross Farm, Wiltshire*, Devizes, 1923
Curwen (1933)   E. C. Curwen, 'Excavations on Thundersbarrow Hill,
                Sussex', *Ant. J.*, XIII (1923), 109–51
— (1939)   E. C. Curwen, 'The Iron Age in Sussex', *Sx A.C.*, LXXX
                (1939), 214–16
d'Arbois de   M. H. d'Arbois de Jubainville: *Recherches sur l'origine de
  Jubainville   la propriété foncière et des noms de lieux habités en France*,
  (1890)   Paris, 1890
Davey (1961)   N. Davey: *A History of Building Materials*, London,
                1961
de Maeyer   R. de Maeyer: *De Romeinsche Villa's in België*, Antwerp,
  (1937)   1937
Dent (1877)   Emma Dent: *Annals of Winchcombe and Sudely*, London,
                1877
Doppelfeld   O. Doppelfeld, 'Von Postumus zu Konstantin', *Wallraf-
  (1956)   Richartz-Jahrbuch*, XVIII (1956), 1–26
Drack (1950)   W. Drack: *Die römische Wandmalerei der Schweiz*, Basel,
                1950
Dudley and   D. R. Dudley and G. Webster: *The Roman Conquest of
  Webster   Britain*, London, 1965
  (1965)
Dyer (1961)   J. F. Dyer, 'Dray's Ditches, Bedfordshire, and Early Iron
                Age Territorial Boundaries in the Eastern Chilterns', *Ant.
                J.*, XLI (1961), 32–43
Espérandieu   E. Espérandieu: *Recueil général des bas-reliefs, statues et bustes
                de la Gaule Romaine*, Paris, 1907–47
Field (1966)   N. H. Field, 'A Romano-British Settlement at Studland,
                Dorset', *P.D.N.H.A.F.C.*, LXXXVII (1966), 142–99
Forbes (1955)   R. J. Forbes: *Studies in Ancient Technology*, Leiden, 1955–8
Forde (1948)   C. Daryll Forde: *Habitat, Economy and Society*, London, 6th
                edn, 1948
Forde-Johnston J. F. Forde-Johnston, 'Excavations on Knowle Hill, 1957',
  (1957)   *P.D.N.H.A.F.C.*, LXXIX (1957), 106–7

Fowler   W. Fowler: *Engravings of the Principal Mosaic Pavements*,
 (1796–1818) Winterton, 1796–1818
Fowler (1964)   P. J. Fowler, 'Cross-dykes on the Ebble-Nadder Ridge',
                 W.A.M., LIX (1964), 46–57
Fowler, Musty,   P. J. Fowler, J. W. G. Musty, and C. C. Taylor, 'Some
  and Taylor   Earthwork Enclosures in Wiltshire', *W.A.M.*, LX (1965),
  (1965)   52–74
Fox (1943)   Sir Cyril Fox: *The Personality of Britain*, 4th edn, Cardiff,
                 1943
— (1946)   Sir Cyril Fox: *A Find of the Early Iron Age from Llyn Cerrig
                 Bach, Anglesey*, Cardiff, 1946
Frank (1937)   T. Frank (ed.): *An Economic Survey of Ancient Rome*, Vol.
                 III (Britain, Spain, Sicily, Gaul), Baltimore, 1937
Fream (1955)   *Fream's Elements of Agriculture*, 13th edn (ed. D. H. Robin-
                 son), London, 1955
Frere (1957)   S. S. Frere, 'Excavations at Verulamium, 1956', *Ant. J.*,
                 XXXVII (1957), 1–15
— (1960)   S. S. Frere (ed.): *Problems of the Iron Age in Southern Britain*,
                 London, 1960
— (1961)   S. S. Frere, 'Excavations at Verulamium, 1960', *Ant. J.*,
                 XLI (1961), 72–85
Glob (1951)   P. V. Glob: *Ard og Plov i Nordens Oldtid*, Aarhus,
                 1951
Goodchild   R. G. Goodchild, 'T-shaped Corn-drying Ovens in
  (1943)   Roman Britain', *Ant. J.*, XXIII (1943), 148–53
Green (1959)   H. J. M. Green, 'A Romano-British Farm at St Ives',
                 P.C.A.S., LII (1959), 23–29
Grenier (1934)   A. Grenier: *Manuel d'archéologie gallo-romaine*, Vol. II (ii)
                 (*l'archéologie du sol: occupation du sol*), Paris, 1934
Gresham (1939)   C. A. Gresham, 'Spettisbury Rings, Dorset', *Arch. J.*,
                 XCVI (1939), 114–31
Grimes (1951)   W. F. Grimes (ed.): *Aspects of Archaeology in Britain and
                 Beyond*, London, 1951
Hallam (1964)   S. J. Hallam, 'Villages in Roman Britain: some evidence',
                 Ant. J., XLIV (1964), 19–32
Harden (1956)   D. B. Harden (ed.): *Dark Age Britain*, London, 1956
Harding and   D. W. Harding and I. M. Blake, 'An Early Iron Age
  Blake (1963)   Settlement in Dorset' [Pimperne], *Ant.*, XXXVIII
                 (1963), 63–64
Harmand   J. Harmand, 'Sur le valeur archéologique du mot
  (1951)   "villa" ', *Revue Archéologique*, XXXVIII (1951), 155–8

Hartley (1960)   B. R. Hartley: *Notes on the Roman Pottery Industry in the Nene Valley*, Peterborough, 1960

Haverfield   F. Haverfield: *The Romanization of Roman Britain*, 4th edn
(1923)   (ed. G. Macdonald), Oxford, 1923

Haverfield and   F. Haverfield, *The Roman Occupation of Britain*, revised by
Macdonald   George Macdonald, Oxford, 1924
(1924)

Hawkes (1940)   C. F. C. Hawkes, 'The Excavations at Quarley Hill, 1938', *P.P.H.F.C.*, XIV (1940), 136–90

— (1948)   C. F. C. Hawkes, 'Britons, Romans and Saxons round Salisbury and in Cranborne Chase', *Arch. J.*, CIV (1948), 27–81

Hawkes and   S. C. Hawkes and G. C. Dunning, 'Soldiers and Settlers
Dunning   in Britain, fourth to fifth Century', *Medieval Archaeology*,
(1965)   V (1965), 1–70

Hawkes and   C. F. C. Hawkes and M. R. Hull: *Camulodunum* (Soc. of
Hull (1947)   Antiquaries Research Report XIV), Oxford, 1947

Helbaek (1952)   H. Helbaek, 'Early Crops in Southern England', *P.P.S.*, XVIII (1952), 194–233

— (1964)   H. Helbaek, 'The Isca Grain: a Roman Plant Introduction in Britain', *New Phytologist*, LXIII (June 1964), 158–64

Higgs and   E. S. Higgs and J. P. White, 'Autumn Killing', *Ant.*,
White (1963)   XXXVII (1963), 282–9

Hinks (1933)   R. P. Hinks: *Catalogue of the Greek, Etruscan and Roman Paintings and Mosaics in the British Museum*, London, 1933

Hoare (1810)   R. Colt Hoare: *The History of Ancient Wiltshire*, Part I, London, 1810

— (1819)   R. Colt Hoare: *The History of Ancient Wiltshire*, Part II, London, 1819 (= 1821)

Holmes (1885)   T. V. Holmes, 'Portland Beehives', *Procs. of the Geological Association*, VIII (1885), 404–10

Horsley (1732)   J. Horsley: *Britannia Romana*, London, 1732

Hull (1958)   M. R. Hull: *Roman Colchester* (Soc. of Antiquaries Research Report XX), Oxford, 1958

Jackson (1953)   K. H. Jackson: *Language and History in Early Britain*, Edinburgh, 1953

— (1964)   K. H. Jackson: *The Oldest Irish Tradition: a Window on the Iron Age*, Cambridge, 1964

Jessup (1954)   R. F. Jessup, 'Excavation of a Roman Barrow at Holborough, Snodland', *Arch. Cant.*, LXVIII (1954), 1–61

Jewell (1962) P. A. Jewell, 'Changes in Size and Type of Cattle from Prehistoric to Mediaeval Times in Britain', *Zeitschrift für Tierzüchtung und Züchtungsbiologie*, Band 77, Heft 2 (1962), 159–67

A. H. Jones (1964) A. H. M. Jones: *The Later Roman Empire 284–602*, Oxford, 1964

— (1966) A. H. M. Jones: *The Decline of the Ancient World*, London, 1966

G. Jones (1960) G. R. Jones, 'The Pattern of Settlement on the Welsh Border', *Ag. H.R.*, VIII (1960), 66–81

— (1961) G. R. Jones, 'Settlement Patterns in Anglo-Saxon England', *Ant.*, XXXV (1961), 221–32

Kempf (1959) Th. K. Kempf: *Legende, Überlieferung, Forschung*, Trier, 1959

Kendrick (1938) T. D. Kendrick: *Anglo-Saxon Art to A.D. 900*, London, 1938

Levi (1947) D. Levi: *Antioch Mosaic Pavements*, Princeton, 1947

Lewis (1960) G. D. Lewis, 'Some Recent Discoveries in West Sussex', *Sx A.C.*, XCVIII (1960), 12–28

Liddell (1934) and (1937) D. M. Liddell, 'Excavations at Meon Hill', *P.P.H.F.C.*, XII (1932–4), 127–62; second season, *P.P.H.F.C.*, XIII (1935–7), 7–54

Liversidge (1951) J. Liversidge, 'Painted Wall-Plaster from Roman Villas in the Cambridge Region', *P.C.A.S.*, XLIV (1951), 13–17

— (1952) J. Liversidge, 'A Shale Foot of a Roman Table from Upper Langridge Farm', *P.S.A.N.H.S.*, XCVI (1952), 233

— (1955) J. Liversidge: *Furniture in Roman Britain*, London, 1955

— (1958) J. Liversidge: 'Wall Painting in Roman Britain: a Survey of the Evidence', *Antiquity and Survival*, II (1958), 373–86

— (1960) J. Liversidge, 'A New Roman Shale Table-leg from Dorset', *Ant. J.*, XL (1960), 72–73

Lowndes (1963) R. A. C. Lowndes, ' "Celtic" Fields, Farmsteads and Burial Mounds in the Lune Valley', *T.C.W.A.A.S.*, LXIII (1963), 77–94

Lysons (1813–17) S. Lysons: *Reliquiae Britannico-Romanae*, I (1813), II (1817), III (1817), London

Maiuri (1953) A. Maiuri: *Roman Painting*, Geneva, 1953

— (1957) B. Maiuri: *Museo Nazionale di Napoli*, Novara, 1957

— (1958) A. Maiuri: *Ercolano: I Nuovi Scavi 1927–1958*, I, Rome, 1958

Manning (1962) W. H. Manning, 'The Villa in Roman Britain', *Ant.*, XXXVI (1962), 56–58

— (1964a)   W. H. Manning, 'A Mill Pivot from Silchester', *Ant. J.*, XLIV (1964), 38–40

— (1964b)   W. H. Manning, 'The Plough in Roman Britain', *J.R.S.*, LIV (1964), 54–65

Mau (1899)   A. Mau: *Pompeii, its Life and Art* (trans. F. W. Kelsey), New York, 1899

Megaw,   J. V. S. Megaw, A. C. Thomas, and B. Wailes, 'The Thomas, and Bronze Age Settlement at Gwythian, Cornwall', *Procs. of* Wailes (1961) *the West Cornwall Field Club*, II (1961)

Mertens (1958)   J. Mertens, 'Römische Skulpturen von Buzenol, Provinz Luxemburg', *Germania*, XXXVI (1958), 386–92

Morgan (1886)   Thomas Morgan: *Romano-British Mosaic Pavements*, London, 1886

Myres (1961)   J. N. L. Myres, 'Archaeology and History: Britons and Saxons in the post-Roman Centuries', CBA Annual Report No. 11, 1961, 35–45

Neville (1856)   R. C. Neville, 'Description of a Remarkable Deposit of Roman Antiquities of Iron found at Great Chesterford, Essex, in 1854', *Arch. J.*, XIII (1856), 1–13

Nightingale   M. D. Nightingale, 'A Roman Land Settlement near (1952)   Rochester', *Arch. Cant.*, LXV (1952), 150–9

Northcote and J. Spencer Northcote and W. R. Brownlow: *Roma Sot-* Brownlow   *terranea*, London, 1879 (1879)

OSRB (1956)   *Map of Roman Britain*, 3rd edn, Ordnance Survey, 1956

OSSBIA   *Map of Southern Britain in the Iron Age*, Ordnance Survey, (1962)   1962

Parlasca (1959)   K. Parlasca: *Die römischen Mosaiken in Deutschland*, Berlin, 1959

Payne (1947)   F. G. Payne, 'The Plough in Early Britain', *Arch. J.*, CIV (1947), 82–111

— (1957)   F. G. Payne, 'The British Plough: Some Stages in its Development', *Ag. H.R.*, V (1957), 74–84

Pernice (1938)   E. Pernice: *Die hellenistische Kunst in Pompeii*: VI, *Pavimente und figürliche Mosaiken*, Berlin, 1938

Piggott, C. M. C. M. Piggott, 'Five Late Bronze Age Enclosures in (1942)   North Wiltshire', *P.P.S.*, VIII (1942), 48–61

Piggott, S.   S. Piggott: *Ancient Europe*, Edinburgh, 1965 (1965)

Plesters (1963)   J. Plesters, 'Examination of Painted Wall Plaster', *W.A.M.*, LVIII (1963), 337–41

Pobé (1961)   M. Pobé: *The Art of Roman Gaul*, London, 1961

Powell (1958)   T. G. E. Powell: *The Celts*, London, 1958

Praschniker and C. Praschniker and H. Kenner: *Der Bäderbezirk von Viru-*
   Kenner   *num*, Vienna, 1947
   (1947)

Rahtz (1962)   P. A. Rahtz, 'Excavations at Shearplace Hill, Sydling St
               Nicholas, Dorset', *P.P.S.*, XXVIII (1962), 289–328

RCHM (1928)   RCHM (England): *Inventory of the Historical Monuments
               in London*: III, *Roman London*, London, 1928

— (1959)   RCHM (England): *Inventory of the Historical Monuments in
               the City of Cambridge*, London, 1959

— (1960)   RCHM (England): *A Matter of Time: an Archaeological
               Survey*, London, 1960

— (1962)   RCHM (England): *Inventory of the Historical Monuments in
               the City of York*: I, *Eburacum, Roman York*, London, 1962

— (1963)   RCHM (England): *Monuments Threatened or Destroyed, a
               Select List*, London, 1963

Richardson   K. M. Richardson, 'The Excavation of Iron Age Villages
   (1951)   on Boscombe Down West', *W.A.M.*, LIV (1951), 123
               –68

Richmond   I. A. Richmond: *Roman Britain* ('Britain in Pictures'
   (1947)   Series), London, 1947

— (1950)   I. A. Richmond: *Archaeology and the After-life in Pagan and
               Christian Imagery*, Durham and London, 1950

— (1958)   I. A. Richmond (ed.): *Roman and Native in North Britain*,
               Edinburgh, 1958

— (1963)   I. A. Richmond: *Roman Britain*, 2nd edn, Harmonds-
               worth, 1963

Richter (1926)   G. M. A. Richter: *Ancient Furniture*, Oxford, 1926

Riehm (1961)   K. Riehm, 'Prehistoric Salt Boiling', *Ant.*, XXXV (1961),
               181–91

Rivet (1964)   A. L. F. Rivet: *Town and Country in Roman Britain*, 2nd edn,
               London, 1964

Rostovtzeff   M. I. Rostovtzeff: *The Social and Economic History of the
   (1957)   Roman Empire*, 2nd edn, revised by P. M. Fraser, Oxford,
               1957

Salway (1965)   P. Salway: *The Frontier People of Roman Britain*, Cambridge,
               1965

Savory (1959)   H. N. Savory, 'The Excavations at Dinorben Hillfort,
               Abergele, 1956–59', *Trans. of the Denbigh Historical Society*,
               VIII (1959), 18–39

Scarth (1864)   H. M. Scarth: *Aquae Solis*, Bath, 1864

Skelton (1823)   J. Skelton: *Engraved Illustrations of the Principal Antiquities of Oxfordshire*, Oxford, 1823

Smith, C. R. (1848–80)   C. Roach Smith: *Collectanea Antiqua*, I (1848), II (1852), III (1854), IV (1857), V (1861), VI (1868), VII (1880), London

Smith, D. J. (1965)   D. J. Smith, 'Three Fourth-Century Schools of Mosaic in Roman Britain', in Stern (ed.): *La Mosaïque Gréco-Romaine*, Paris, 1965, 95–116

Smith, H. (1852)   Henry Ecroyd Smith: *Reliquiae Isurianae*, London, 1852

Smith, J. T. (1963)   J. T. Smith, 'Romano-British Aisled Houses', *Arch. J.*, CXX (1963), 1–30

Spinazzola (1953)   V. Spinazzola: *Pompei alla Luce degli Scavi Nuovi di Via dell' Abbondanza* (Anni 1910–23), Rome, 1953

Stamp (1955)   L. Dudley Stamp: *Man and the Land*, London, 1955

Steensberg (1943)   A. Steensberg: *Ancient Harvesting Implements*, Copenhagen, 1943

Stern (1953)   H. Stern: *Le Calendrier de 354*, Paris, 1953

— (1957–63)   H. Stern: *Recueil général des mosaïques de la Gaule*, I: fasc. 1 (1957), fasc. 2 (1960), fasc. 3 (1963), Paris

— (1965)   H. Stern (ed.): *La Mosaïque Gréco-Romaine*, Paris, 1965

Stevens (1947)   C. E. Stevens, 'A Possible Conflict of Laws in Roman Britain', *J.R.S.*, XXXVII (1947), 132–4

Stuart and Birkbeck (1936)   J. D. M. Stuart and J. M. Birkbeck, 'A Celtic Village on Twyford Down, Winchester, excavated 1933–34', *P.P.H.F.C.*, XIII (1936), 188–207

Swoboda (1919)   K. M. Swoboda: *Römische und romanische Paläste*, Vienna, 1919

Sumner (1914)   H. Sumner: *Excavations on Rockbourne Down, Hampshire*, London, 1914

Syme (1958)   R. Syme: *Tacitus*, Oxford, 1958

Taylor (1966)   C. C. Taylor, 'Strip Lynchets', *Ant.*, XL (1966), 277–84

Thomas (1966)   A. C. Thomas (ed.): *Rural Settlement in Roman Britain* (CBA Research Report No. 7), London, 1966

Thorpe (1964)   H. Thorpe, 'Rural Settlement', chap. 19 in J. W. Watson and J. B. Sissons (ed.): *The British Isles: a Systematic Geography*, London, 1964

Tierney (1960)   J. J. Tierney, 'The Celtic Ethnography of Posidonius', *Procs. of the Royal Irish Academy*, LX, Sect. C, No. 5 (1960), 189–275

Toynbee (1953) J. M. C. Toynbee, 'Christianity in Roman Britain', *J.B.A.A.* (3rd ser.), XVI (1953), 1–24

— (1963) J. M. C. Toynbee: *Art in Roman Britain*, 2nd edn, London, 1963

— (1964) J. M. C. Toynbee: *Art in Britain under the Romans*, Oxford, 1964

Unger (1965) H. Unger: *Practical Mosaics*, London, 1965

van Bath (1963) B. H. S. van Bath: *The Agrarian History of Western Europe A.D. 500–1850*, London, 1963

van Berchem (1937) D. van Berchem, 'L'annone militaire dans l'empire Romain au IIIe siècle', *Mémoires de la Société Nationale des Antiquaires de France*, XXX (8th ser. X) (1937), 117–202

Veale (1957) E. M. Veale, 'The Rabbit in England', *Ag. H.R.*, V (1957), 85–90

Volbach and Hirmer (1961) W. F. Volbach and M. Hirmer: *Early Christian Art*, London, 1961

von Gonzenbach (1961) V. von Gonzenbach: *Die römischen Mosaiken der Schweiz*, Basel, 1961

Wacher (1966) J. S. Wacher (ed.): *The Civitas Capitals of Roman Britain*, Leicester, 1966

Ward (1911) John Ward: *Romano-British Buildings and Earthworks*, London, 1911

Ward-Perkins and Toynbee (1949) J. B. Ward-Perkins and J. M. C. Toynbee, 'The Hunting Baths at Lepcis Magna', *Arch.*, XCIII (1949), 165–95

Watkin (1886) W. T. Watkin: *Roman Cheshire*, Liverpool, 1886

Webster (1955) G. Webster, 'A Note on the Use of Coal in Roman Britain', *Ant. J.*, XXXV (1955), 199–216

Webster and Hobley (1965) G. Webster and B. Hobley, 'Aerial Reconnaissance over the Warwickshire Avon', *Arch. J.*, CXXI (1965), 1–22

Wedlake (1958) W. J. Wedlake: *Excavations at Camerton, Somerset*, Camerton, 1958

Wheeler (1932) R. E. M. and T. V. Wheeler: *Report on the Excavation of the Prehistoric, Roman and Post-Roman Site in Lydney Park, Gloucestershire* (Soc. of Antiquaries Research Report IX), Oxford, 1932

— (1936) R. E. M. and T. V. Wheeler: *Verulamium, a Belgic and two Roman Cities* (Soc. of Antiquaries Research Report XI), Oxford, 1936

— (1943) R. E. M. Wheeler: *Maiden Castle, Dorset* (Soc. of Antiquaries Research Report XII), Oxford, 1943

— (1956) [Note on Cypriote Storage-pits sent to Sir Mortimer Wheeler by Mr Vlassios Krestos,] *Ant.*, XXX (1956), 223

Wolseley, Smith, and Hawley (1927) G. R. Wolseley, R. A. Smith, and W. Hawley, 'Prehistoric and Roman Settlement on Park Brow', *Arch.*, LXXXVI (1927), 1–40

Wood and Whittington (1959) P. D. Wood and G. Whittington, 'The Investigation in 1957 of Strip Lynchets North of the Vale of Pewsey', *W.A.M.*, LVII (1959), 163–72

YMH (1891) *A Handbook to the Antiquities in the Grounds and Museum of the Yorkshire Philosophical Society*, York, 1891

Bibliography of Individual Villas and Similar Buildings

I BRITAIN (WITH NATIONAL GRID REFERENCES)

*Abbotts Ann, Hants	1900	VCH, Hants, I, 300
(SU 3141)		
Acton Scott, Salop	1846	Arch., XXI, 339–45
(SO 4589)	1908	VCH, Shropshire, I, 259
*Alresford, Essex	1885	Trans. Essex Archaeological Society, III, 136–9
(TM 0619)	1963	VCH, Essex, III, 37
Angmering, Sussex	1938	Sx A.C., LXXIX, 3–44
(TQ 0504)	1939	Sx A.C., LXXX, 89
	1943	Sx A.C., LXXXIII, xxi
	1945	Sx A.C., LXXXIV, 83
	1947	Sx A.C., LXXXVI, 1–21
*Apethorpe, Northants.	1859	Associated Architectural Societies Reports, V, 97–107
(TL 0294)		
	1868	C. R. Smith (1868), 280
	1902	VCH, Northants., I, 191–2
Ashtead, Surrey	1929	Sy A.C., XXXVII, 144–63
(TQ 1760)	1930	Sy A.C., XXXVIII, 1–17, 132–48
*Atworth, Wilts.	1942	W.A.M., XLIX, 46–95
(ST 8566)	1957	VCH, Wilts., I (i), 30
*Barnsley Park, Glos.	1951	J.R.S., XLI, 135
(SP 0706)	1963	J.R.S., LIII, 143, 164
	1964	J.R.S., LIV, 171
	1965	J.R.S., LV, 216
	1966	J.R.S., LVI, 212
	1967	T.B.G.A.S., LXXXVI, 74–87

*Barton Farm, Ciren- cester, Glos. (SP 0102)	1850	J. Buckman and C. H. Newmarch: *Remains of Roman Art in . . . Corinium*, 32, pl. VIII
	1910	*T.B.G.A.S.*, XXXIII, 67–77
	1952	*T.B.G.A.S.*, LXX, 51–53
*Bedwyn Brail, Wilts. (SU 2862)	1930	*W.A.M.*, XLV, 174
	1938	*W.A.M.*, XLVIII, 318–20
	1957	VCH, Wilts., I (i), 75
*Bignor, Sussex (SU 9814)	1817a	Lysons (1817)
	1817b	*Arch.*, XVIII, 203–21
	1821	*Arch.*, XIX, 176–7
	1934	S. E. Winbolt and G. Herbert: *The Roman Villa at Bignor*
	1935	VCH, Sussex, III, 22
	1963	*J.R.S.*, LIII, 155–6

Bisley see Bournes Green

*Borough Farm, Pul- borough, Sussex (TQ 0620)	1910	*P.S.A.L.²*, XXIII, 121–9
	1935	VCH, Sussex, III, 25
Borough Hill, Daven- try, Northants. (SP 5863)	1848	C. R. Smith (1848), 113
	1853	*Arch.*, XXXV, 383–95
	1854	C. R. Smith (1854), 208
	1902	VCH, Northants., I, 195
*Bournes Green, Bisley, Glos. (SO 9104)	1846a	*J.B.A.A.*, I, 44–45
	1846b	*Arch. J.*, II, 42–45
	1847	*J.B.A.A.*, II, 324–7
*Box, Wilts. (ST 8268)	1904	*W.A.M.*, XXXIII, 236–69
	1927	*W.A.M.*, XLIII, 335
	1957	VCH, Wilts., I (i), 44
*Brading, Isle of Wight (SZ 6086)	1881	J. E. P. and F. G. H. Price: *Description of the Remains of Roman Buildings at Morton near Brading, Isle of Wight*
	1900	VCH, Hants, I, 313–16
	1958	*Bulletin of the Institute of Archaeology* (London), I, 55–74

Bradley Spring see Littleton

*Bramdean, Hants (SU 6228)	1823	*Gents. Mag.*, 1823, i, 631–2
	1824	*Gents. Mag.*, 1824, ii, 100–1
	1839	J. Duthy: *Sketches of Hampshire*, 33
	1900	VCH, Hants, I, 307–8

*Brantingham (Cockle 1951   *Y.A.J.*, XXXVII, 514–20
Pits), Yorks., E.R. 1963   *J.R.S.*, LIII, 131
(SE 9328)   Report by I. M. Stead forthcoming

Brislington, Bristol   1901   W. R. Barker: *Account of Remains of a Roman
(ST 6170)   Villa discovered at Brislington, Bristol, December
                  1899*
          1906   VCH, Somerset, I, 304

Bromham (West   1819   Hoare (1819), *Roman Aera*, 123
Park), Wilts.   1957   VCH, Wilts., I (i), 51
(ST 9765)

Calne Without (Wans 1796   *Gents. Mag.*, 1796, i, 472–3
House), Wilts.   1957   VCH, Wilts., I (i), 51 (s.v. *Bromham*)
(ST 9667)

*Castle Dykes, North 1875   *Arch. J.*, XXXII, 135–54
Stainley, Yorks.,
W.R. (SE 2975)

Castlefield, Andover, 1867   *J.B.A.A.*, XXIII, 268–81
Hants   1868   *J.B.A.A.*, XXIV, 402–4
(SU 3946)   1900   VCH, Hants, I, 302

*Castor Village,   1828   Artis (1828)
Northants.   1902   VCH, Northants., I, 171–2
(TL 1298)

*Castor (Mill Hill)   1828   Artis (1828)
Northants.   1900   VCH, Northants., I, 172–4
(TL 1297)

Catsgore, Som.   1951   *P.S.A.N.H.S.*, XCVI, 41–77
(ST 5026)

*Chedworth, Glos.   1868   *J.B.A.A.*, XXIV, 129–35
(SP 0513)   1887   *Arch. J.*, XLIV, 322–36
          1905   *Arch.*, LIX, 210–14
          1960   *T.B.G.A.S.*, LXXVIII, 5–23, 162–5
          1965   *J.R.S.*, LV, 215–16
          1966   *J.R.S.*, LVI, 212

Cherhill, Wilts.   1914   *W.A.M.*, XXXVIII, 222
(SU 0370)   1939   *W.A.M.*, XLVIII, 390
          1957   VCH, Wilts., I (i), 55

Clanville, Hants   1898   *Arch.*, LVI, 1–20
(SU 3148)   1900   VCH, Hants, I, 296

Cockle Pits see *Brantingham*

*Colerne, Wilts.	1856	Arch. J., XIII, 328–31
(ST 8171)	1932	W.A.M., XLV, 184
	1957	VCH, Wilts., I (i), 59
*Collingham (Dalton Parlours), Yorks., W.R. (SE 4044)	1854	Procs. Yorkshire Philosophical Society 1849–1854, 270–81
	1949	Y.A.J., XXXVII, 237–9
Combe Down, Som.	1864	Scarth (1864), 117
(ST 7662)	1906	VCH, Som., I, 309
*Comb End (Stockwood), Glos. (SO 9811)	1789	Arch., IX, 319–22
	1817	Arch., XVIII, 112–13
Cox Green, Maidenhead, Berks. (SU 8779)	1958	J.R.S., XLVIII, 99
	1960	J.R.S., L, 232–3
	1962	Berks. A.J., LX, 62–91
*Cromhall, Glos. (ST 6889)	1910	P.S.A.L.², XXIII, 20–23

Dalton Parlours see Collingham

*Darenth, Kent	1897	Arch. Cant., XXII, 49–84
(TQ 5670)	1932	VCH, Kent, III, 111–13

Daventry see Borough Hill

*Dell Farm, Latimer, Bucks. (SU 9998)	1870	Records of Bucks., III, 181–5
	1908	VCH, Bucks., II, 8–9
	1967	Records of Bucks., XVIII, 138
Denton, Lincs. (SK 8730)	1950	J.R.S., XL, 100
	1960	J.R.S., L, 221
	1964	Lincs. Architectural and Archaeological Society Reports and Papers, X, 75–104
Ditchley, Oxon.	1936	Oxoniensia, I, 24–69
(SP 3920)	1939	VCH, Oxon., I, 311
Downton, Wilts. (SP 1821)	1963	W.A.M., LVIII, 303–41
*Eastbourne, Sussex	1849	Sx A.C., II, 257–9
(TV 6198)	1935	VCH, Sussex, III, 24
East Coker, Som.	1852	C. R. Smith (1852), 51–52
(ST 5413)	1906	VCH, Som., I, 329
	1954	C. A. R. Radford and H. S. L. Dewar: The Roman Mosaics from Low Ham and East Coker, 5–6

East Dean see Holbury

East Grimstead, Wilts. 1924 Heywood Sumner: *Excavations at East Grim-*
 (SU 2327) *stead*
 1957 VCH, Wilts., I (i), 75
*Ebrington (The 1959 *J.R.S.*, XLIX, 127
 Grove), Glos. 1961 *J.R.S.*, LI, 186
 (SP 1840)
*Eccles, Kent 1963a *Arch. Cant.*, LXXVIII, 125–41
 (TQ 7260) 1963b *J.R.S.*, LIII, 158
 1964a *Arch. Cant.*, LXXIX, 121–35
 1964b *J.R.S.*, LIV, 177
 1965a *Arch. Cant.*, LXXX, 69–91
 1965b *J.R.S.*, LV, 220, 224, 226
 1966 *J.R.S.*, LVI, 217, 224
*Eling, Yattendon, 1871 *Trans. Newbury Field Club*, I, 183–4
 Berks. 1880 *J.B.A.A.*, XXXVI, 27–29
 (SU 5375) 1906 VCH, Berks., I, 210
Ely, Cardiff, 1895 *Trans. Cardiff Naturalists Society*, XXVI, 125–8
 Glamorgan 1920 *Trans. Cardiff Naturalists Society*, L, 24–44
 (ST 1476) 1921 *J.R.S.*, XI, 67
 1925 *Trans. Cardiff Naturalists Society*, LV, 19–45
Engleton, Staffs. 1938a *Historical Collections, Staffs.*, 1938, 267–93
 (SJ 8910) 1938b *J.R.S.*, XXVIII, 183–4
Ewhurst (Rapsley 1963 *J.R.S.*, LIII, 151
 Farm), Surrey 1965 *J.R.S.*, LV, 218–19
 (TQ 0841) 1966 *J.R.S.*, LVI, 214–16
Exning (Landwade), 1907 *P.C.A.S.*, XI, 210
 Suffolk (TL 6167) 1960 *J.R.S.*, L, 228
*Fifehead Neville, 1881 *P.S.A.L.*², VIII, 543–5
 Dorset (ST 7711) 1883 *P.S.A.L.*², IX, 66–70
 1903 *P.D.N.H.A.F.C.*, XXIV, lxxiv–lxxxvi, 172–7
 1928 *P.D.N.H.A.F.C.*, L, 92–95
Finchingfield, Essex 1937 *Trans. Essex Archaeological Society*, XXI,
 (TL 6633) 219–29
 1963 VCH, Essex, III, 129–30
Fishbourne, Sussex 1962 *Ant. J.*, XLII, 15–23
 (SU 8303) 1963 *Ant. J.*, XLIII, 1–14
 1964 *Ant. J.*, XLIV, 1–8
 1965a *Ant. J.*, XLV, 1–11
 1965b *Ant.*, XXXIX, 177–83
 1966 *Ant. J.*, XLVI, 26–38
 1967 *Ant. J.*, XLVII, 51–59

*Folkestone, Kent   1925   S. E. Winbolt: *Roman Folkestone*
  (TR 2437)   1932   VCH, Kent, III, 114

Foscott (Foxcote),   1838   *Gents. Mag.*, 1838, i, 302
  Bucks. (SP 7235) 1841   *Gents. Mag.*, 1841, i, 81
                  1843   *Gents. Mag.*, 1843, i, 303
                  1908   VCH, Bucks., II, 7

*Frampton, Dorset   1813   Lysons (1813), iii, 1–6
  (SY 6195)   1952   RCHM, Dorset, I, 150

Frilford, Berks.   1897   *Arch. J.*, LIV, 340–54
  (SU 4297)   1906   VCH, Berks., I, 207

Frindsbury, Kent   1889   *Arch. Cant.*, XVIII, 189–92
  (TQ 7469)   1932   VCH, Kent, III, 115

*Frocester Court, Glos. 1959   *T.B.G.A.S.*, LXXVII, 23–30
  (SO 7802)   1960   *J.R.S.*, L, 230
                  1962   *J.R.S.*, LII, 182
                  1963   *J.R.S.*, LIII, 143
                  1964   *J.R.S.*, LIV, 171, 183
                  1965   *J.R.S.*, LV, 216
                  1966   *J.R.S.*, LVI, 212

Froxfield see *Rudge Farm*

Fullerton (Wherwell), 1905   *Athenaeum*, 25 Feb. 1905, 250
  Hants (SU 3740) 1922   *J.R.S.*, XII, 250
                  1964   *J.R.S.*, LIV, 174
                  1965   *J.R.S.*, LV, 217

Gadebridge, Hemel   1965   *J.R.S.*, LV, 211
  Hempstead, Herts. 1966   *J.R.S.*, LVI, 208–9
  (TL 0507)

*Gayton Thorpe,   1928   *Norfolk Archaeology*, XXIII, 166–209
  Norfolk (TF 7318)

*Great Casterton,   1951   P. Corder (ed.): *The Roman Town and Villa at*
  Rutland   *Great Casterton: First Interim Report*
  (TF 0009)   1954   ditto: *Second Interim Report*
                  1961   ditto: *Third Interim Report*

Great Staughton,   1959   *J.R.S.*, XLIX, 118
  Hunts. (TL 1363) 1960   *J.R.S.*, L, 224–5
                          Report by E. Greenfield forthcoming

*Great Tew, Oxon.   1939   VCH, Oxon., I, 310–11
  (SP 4027)

*Great Weldon,   1885   *Publications of the Surtees Society*, LXXX,
   Northants.   40–42, 58, 61–62
   (SP 9290)   1902   VCH, Northants., I, 193
                1953   *Trans. Ancient Monuments Soc.*, N.S.I, 74–76
                1954   *J.R.S.*, XLIV, 93
                1955   *J.R.S.*, XLV, 135
                1956   *J.R.S.*, XLVI, 131
                     Report by D. J. Smith forthcoming

*Great Wymondley   1886   *Trans. Herts. Natural History Society*, IV, 43–
   (*Purwell Mill*),   46
   Herts. (TL 2029)   1914   VCH, Herts., IV, 170–1

*Greetwell, Lincs.   1891a   *Associated Architectural Societies Reports*, XXI,
   (SK 9971)   48–52
               1891b   *Arch. J.*, XLVIII, 187
                1892   *Arch. J.*, XLIX, 259–62

*Grimston, Norfolk   1907   *Norfolk Archaeology*, XVI, 219–27
   (TF 7121)

Gullet, The see *Whittlebury*

Hales see *Tyrley*

Hambleden, Bucks.   1921   *Arch.*, LXXI, 141–98
   (SU 7885)

Ham Hill, Som.   1913   *J.R.S.*, III, 127–33
   (ST 4816)

*Hampstead Norris   1863   *J.B.A.A.*, XIX, 60–63
   (*Well House*),   1906   VCH, Berks., I, 209
   Hants (SU 5272)

*Harpham, Yorks.,   1907   *Trans. East Riding Antiquarian Society*, XIII
   E.R. (TA 0863)   (ii), 141–52
                1935   Clark, M. K. (1935), 87
                1941   *J.R.S.*, XXXI, 126
                1955   *Y.A.J.*, XXXVIII, 117–18
                1965   *Y.A.J.*, XXXIX, 55

Harpole, Northants.   1850   *J.B.A.A.*, V, 375–6
   (SP 6859)   1851   *J.B.A.A.*, VI, 126–7
                1902   VCH, Northants., I, 197

*Hartlip, Kent   1852   C. R. Smith (1852), 1–24
   (TQ 8263)   1932   VCH, Kent, III, 117

*Headington (Wick   1851   *J.B.A.A.*, VI, 52–67
   Farm), Oxon.*   1939   VCH, Oxon., I, 320–2
   (SP 5409)

*Hemsworth, Dorset 1909 *P.D.N.H.A.F.C.*, XXX, 1–12
 (ST 9605)

High Wycombe, 1878 J. Parker: *The Early History and Antiquities of*
 Bucks. (SU 8792)   *Wycombe*
   1906 VCH, Bucks., II, 17–19
   1959 *Records of Bucks.*, XVI, 227–57

*Hinton St Mary, 1964a *P.D.N.H.A.F.C.*, LXXXV, 116–21
 Dorset (ST 7816) 1964b *J.R.S.*, LIV, 7–14
   1965 *P.D.N.H.A.F.C.*, LXXXVI, 150–4
   1967 *B.M. Quarterly*, XXXII, 15–35

Holbury, East Dean, 1872 *W.A.M.*, XIII, 33–41, 276–9
 Hants (SU 2827) 1900 VCH, Hants, I, 312

*Holcombe, Uplyme, 1854 *Arch. J.*, XI, 49–51
 Devon (SY 3192) 1877 *Arch.*, XLV, 462–5

*Horkstow, Lincs. 1813 Lysons (1813), i, 1–4
 (SE 9819) 1872 E. Trollope: *Sleaford and the Wapentakes of*
    Flaxwell and Aswardhurn, 61–62

Hotbury see *West Dean*

*Hovingham, Yorks., 1885 *Publications of the Surtees Society*, LXXX, 354–6
 N.R. (SE 6675) 1935 Clark, M. K. (1935), 88–92

Hucclecote, Glos. 1933 *T.B.G.A.S.*, LV, 323–76
 (SO 8717) 1961 *T.B.G.A.S.*, LXXIX, 159–73
   1962 *T.B.G.A.S.*, LXXX, 42–49

*Ickleton, Cambs. 1849a *J.B.A.A.*, IV, 356–68
 (TL 4943) 1849b *Arch. J.*, VI, 14–26

*Ipswich (Castle Hill), 1933 *Procs. Suffolk Institute of Archaeology*, XXI,
 Suffolk (TM 1446)   240–62

Itchen Abbas, Hants 1878 *J.B.A.A.*, XXXIV, 233–4, 258, 504
 (SU 5234) 1879 *J.B.A.A.*, XXXV, 109–10, 208–9
   1900 VCH, Hants, I, 307

Iwerne, Dorset 1947 *Arch. J.*, CIV, 48–62
 (ST 8513)

*Keynsham, Som. 1926 *Arch.*, LXXV, 109–38
 (ST 6469)

*Kings Weston, 1950 *T.B.G.A.S.*, LXIX, 5–58
 Bristol (ST 5377)

Kirk Sink, Gargrave, 1878 T. D. Whitaker: *History of Craven*, 3rd edn,
 Yorks., W.R.   229
 (SD 9353) 1912 *Bradford Antiquary* (N.S.), III, 353–68
    New excavations in progress

Landwade see *Exning*

Langton, Yorks., E.R. (SE 8167)	1932	P. Corder and J. L. Kirk: *A Roman Villa at Langton, near Malton, E. Yorkshire*
Lansdown, Bath, Som. (ST 7368)	1906	VCH, Som., I, 301–2
	1908	*Procs. Bath Branch, Som. Arch. Soc., 1905–1908,* 152–74, 204–18
	1909	*P.S.A.L.*², XXII, 34–35
	1913	*Procs. Bath Branch, Som. Arch. Soc., 1909–1913,* 126–8
Lenthay Green, Sherborne, Dorset (ST 6215)	1846	*J.B.A.A.*, I, 57
	1865	*Arch. J.*, XXII, 360–1
	1952	RCHM, Dorset, I, 199
*Litlington, Cambs. (TL 3142)	1829	*Gents. Mag.*, 1829, i, 546
	1836	*Arch.*, XXVI, 376
	1915	*P.C.A.S.*, XIX, 4
*Littlecote Park, Ramsbury, Wilts. (SU 2970)	1813	Lysons (1819), iv, pl. IX and X
	1819	Hoare (1819), *Roman Aera,* 117–21
	1957	VCH, Wilts., I (i), 98
Little Milton, Oxon. (SP 6200)	1950	*J.R.S.*, XL, 102
	1953	*J.R.S.*, XLIII, 94
*Littleton (Bradley Spring), Som. (ST 4931)	1827	*Gents. Mag.*, 1827, ii, 113–14
	1831	R. Colt Hoare: *The Pitney Pavement,* No. 11
	1906	VCH, Som., I, 323–4
*Llanfrynach, Brecon (SO 0625)	1785	*Arch.*, VII, 205–10
	1949	*B.B.C.S.*, XIII, 106–7
*Llantwit Major, Glamorgan (SS 9569)	1888	*Arch. Camb.*⁵, V, 413–17
	1953	*Arch. Camb.*, CII, 89–163
Llys Brychan, Llangadog, Carmarthen (SN 7025)	1962	*Carmarthen Antiquary,* IV, 2–8
Lockleys, Welwyn, Herts. (TL 2316)	1938	*Ant. J.*, XVIII, 339–76
*Low Ham, Som. (ST 4328)	1946a	*P.S.A.N.H.S.*, XCII, 25–28
	1946b	*J.R.S.*, XXXVI, 142
	1947	*J.R.S.*, XXXVII, 173
	1949	*J.R.S.*, XXXIX, 109
	1954a	*J.R.S.*, XLIV, 99–100
	1954b	C. A. R. Radford and H. S. L. Dewar: *The Roman Mosaics from Low Ham and East Coker*

Lufton, Som.	1952	*P.S.A.N.H.S.*, XCVII, 91–112
(ST 5117)	1962	*J.R.S.*, LII, 182–4
	1963	*J.R.S.*, LIII, 146
*Lullingstone, Kent	1950	*Arch. Cant.*, LXIII, 1–49
(TQ 5365)	1952	*Arch. Cant.*, LXV, 26–78
	1954	*Arch. Cant.*, LXVI, 15–36
	1955	G. W. Meates: *Lullingstone Roman Villa*
	1956	*Arch. Cant.*, LXX, 249–50
	1958	*Arch. Cant.*, LXXII, xlviii–l
Magor Farm, Illogan,	1932	*Ant. J.*, XII, 71–72
Cornwall	1933	*J.B.A.A.*, XXXIX, 117–75
(SW 6342)		
*Maidstone (Loose	1876	*Arch. Cant.*, X, 163–72
Road), Kent	1932	VCH, Kent, III, 99–100
(TQ 7654)		
Mansfield Woodhouse,	1787	*Arch.*, VIII, 363–76
Notts. (SK 5264)	1910	VCH, Notts., II, 28
	1939	*J.R.S.*, XXIX, 206
	1953	*Trans. Thoroton Society*, LIII, 1–14
Medbourne, Leics.	1801	*Gents. Mag.*, 1801, i, 1182–3
(SP 7992)	1907	VCH, Leics., I, 214
	1911	*Arch. J.*, LXVIII, 218–20
*Mersea Island, Essex	1898	*Trans. Essex Archaeological Society* (N.S.), VI,
(TM 0012)		173–4
	1963	VCH, Essex, III, 158–9
Mill Hill see *Castor*		
Nether Heyford,	1806	Gough's Camden, II, 277
Northants.	1886	Morgan (1886), 115
(SP 6658)	1902	VCH, Northants., I, 196
Newton Nottage,	1853	*Arch. Camb.*², IV, 90–98
Glamorgan		
(SS 8077)		
Newton St Loe, Som.	1838	W. Ll. Nichols: *Description of the Roman Villa discovered at Newton St Loe*
(ST 7165)	1906	VCH, Som., I, 302
	1936	*J.R.S.*, XXVI, 43–46
North Leigh, Oxon.	1826	H. Hakewill: *An Account of the Roman Villa discovered at Northleigh*
(SP 3915)	1939	VCH, Oxon., I, 316–18
	1944	*J.R.S.*, XXXIV, 81

North Newbald,   1941   *Procs. Leeds Philosophical Society,* V, 231–8
Yorks., E.R.
(SE 8936)

North Stainley see *Castle Dykes*

North Warnborough   1931a   *P.P.H.F.C.,* X, 225–36
(Lodge Farm),   1931b   *J.R.S.,* XXI, 242
Hants (SU 7352)

*North Wraxall   1860   *Gents. Mag.,* 1860, ii, 157–9
(Truckle Hill),   1862   *W.A.M.,* VII, 59–74
Wilts. (ST 8376)   1957   VCH, Wilts., I (i), 92

Norton Disney, Lincs.   1937   *Ant. J.,* XVII, 138–78
(SK 8560)

Oldcoates, Styrrup,   1871   *Arch. J.,* XXVIII, 66–67
Notts. (SK 5988)   1886   *Arch. J.,* XLIII, 32–34
              1910   VCH, Notts., II, 34–35

Old Durham, Co.   1944   *Arch. Ael.*[4], XXII, 1–21
Durham   1951   *Arch. Ael.*[4], XXIX, 203–12
(NZ 2841)   1953   *Arch. Ael.*[4], XXXI, 116–26

*Olga Road, Dorches-   1900   *P.D.N.H.A.F.C.,* XXI, 162–3
ter, Dorset   1901   *P.D.N.H.A.F.C.,* XXII, xxviii–xxix
(SY 6890)

Otford, Kent   1927   *Arch. Cant.,* XXXIX, 153–8
(TQ 5359)   1932   VCH, Kent, III, 122

Park Street, Herts.   1945   *Arch. J.,* CII, 21–110
(TL 1403)   1961   *Arch. J.,* CXVIII, 100–35

Pit Meads, Sutton   1787   *Gents. Mag.,* 1787, i, 221–2
Veny, Wilts.   1819   Hoare (1819), *Roman Aera,* 111–17
(ST 9043)   1932   *W.A.M.,* XLV, 204
              1957   VCH, Wilts., I (i), 110

*Pitney, Som.   1831   R. Colt Hoare: *The Pitney Pavement*
(ST 4530)   1863   *P.S.A.N.H.S.,* XI, 23–24
              1906   VCH, Som., I, 326–8

Preston, Weymouth,   1872   *J.B.A.A.,* XXVIII, 94–96
Dorset (SY 7082)   1889   *P.D.N.H.A.F.C.,* X, xxviii–xxix
              1900   *P.D.N.H.A.F.C.,* XXI, 205–9
              1933   *P.D.N.H.A.F.C.,* LIV, 21–34

Putley, Herefords.   1908   VCH, Herefords., I, 193
(SO 6437)   1925   *Trans. Woolhope Naturalists Field Club,* 1925,
                      lxxvi

Ramsbury see *Littlecote Park*

Rapsley see *Ewhurst*

*Rockbourne, Hants	1943	*J.R.S.*, XXXIII, 75
(SU 1217)	1945	*J.R.S.*, XXXV, 88
	1960	A. T. Morley Hewitt: *Roman Villa, West Park, Rockbourne, near Fordingbridge, Hants: Interim Report*
	1962	ditto: *Second Interim Report*
	1963	*J.R.S.*, LIII, 150, 164
	1965	*J.R.S.*, LV, 217, 228
	1966	*J.R.S.*, LVI, 214, 219–20, 225
Rodmarton, Glos.	1817	*Arch.*, XVIII, 113–16
(ST 9498)		
*Rothley, Leics.	1904	*Trans. Leicester Archaeological Society*, IX, 157–8
(SK 5612)	1907	VCH, Leics., I, 217
Roxby, Lincs.	1806	Gough's Camden, II, 376
(SE 9216)	1869	*Publications of the Surtees Society*, LIV, 212
	1876	*P.S.A.L.*², VI, 114–15
Rudge Farm, Frox-	1819	Hoare (1819), *Roman Aera*, 121
field, Wilts.	1934	*W.A.M.*, XLVI, 108–9
(SU 2769)	1950	*W.A.M.*, LIII, 332
	1957	VCH, Wilts., I (i), 71–72
*Rudston, Yorks., E.R.	1934	*Y.A.J.*, XXXI, 366–76
(TA 0866)	1936	*Y.A.J.*, XXXII, 214–20
	1938	*Y.A.J.*, XXXIII, 81–86, 222–4, 320–38
	1963a	I. A. Richmond: *The Roman Pavements from Rudston*
	1963b	*J.R.S.*, LIII, 130–1
		Report by I. M. Stead forthcoming
Sapcote, Leics.	1792	J. Throsby: *Select Views in Leicestershire*, II, 231
(SP 4993)	1811	J. Nichols: *History and Antiquities of the County of Leicester*, IV, 898
	1907	VCH, Leics., I, 217
	1935	*Trans. Leicester Archaeological Society*, XVIII, 157–94
Saunderton Mill,	1940	*Records of Bucks.*, XIII, 398–426
Bucks. (SP 7902)		
*Scampton, Lincs.	1808	C. Illingworth: *Topographical Account of the Parish of Scampton*, 6, 9
(SK 9578)		

*Southwell, Notts.	1910	VCH, Notts., II, 34
(SK 7053)	1960	J.R.S., L, 223
	1966	Trans. Thoroton Society lxx, 13–54
*Southwick, Sussex	1932	Sx A.C., LXXIII, 13–32
(TQ 2405)	1935	VCH, Sussex, III, 25, 70
	1966	J.R.S., LVI, 214
*Spoonley Wood, Glos.	1882	J.B.A.A., XXXVIII, 215
(SP 0425)	1890	Arch., LII, 651–68
*Stanton Chair, Suffolk	1936	Procs. Suffolk Institute of Archaeology, XXII,
(TL 9574)		339–41
Star, Shipham, Som.	1906	VCH, Som., I, 308
(ST 4358)	1964	P.S.A.N.H.S., CVIII, 45–93
*Stonesfield, Oxon.	1806	Gough's Camden, II, 15
(SP 4017)	1939	VCH, Oxon., I, 315–16
	1941	Oxoniensia, VI, 1–8
Stroud, Petersfield,	1908	Arch. J., LXV, 57–60
Hants (SU 7223)	1909	Arch., J., LXVI, 33–52
Sturton-by-Scawby,	1872	E. Trollope: Sleaford and the Wapentakes of
Lincs. (SE 9604)		Flaxwell and Aswardhurn, 57–58
	1931	H. E. Dudley: History of Scunthorpe, 33

Styrrup see Oldcoates

Sutton Veny see Pit Meads

Thruxton, Hants	1851	RAI, Salisbury volume, 241–5
(SU 2946)	1900	VCH, Hants, I, 299
* Titsey, Surrey	1869	Sy A.C., IV, 214–37
(TQ 4054)	1905	Arch., LIX, 214–18
	1912	VCH, Surrey, IV, 367–9
* Tockington Park,	1888	T.B.G.A.S., XII, 159–69
Glos. (ST 6285)	1889	T.B.G.A.S., XIII, 196–204
* Totternhoe, Beds.	1957	J.R.S., XLVII, 214–15
(SP 9920)	1963	C. L. Matthews: Ancient Dunstable, 61–64
Tyrley (Hales),	1929	Trans. North Staffs. Field Club, LXIII, 98–110
Staffs. (SJ 7233)	1967	J.R.S., LVII, 185
* Wadfield, Sudeley,	1877	Dent (1877)
Glos. (SP 0226)	1895	J.B.A.A. (N.S.), I, 242–50
* Walton Heath, Surrey	1849	Sy A.C., II, 1–13
(TQ 2353)	1912	VCH, Surrey, IV, 369
	1950	Sy A.C., LI, 65–81

Wans House see *Calne Without*

Well, Yorks., N.R.	1951	R. Gilyard-Beer: *The Romano-British Baths at*
(SE 2681)		*Well*

Well House see *Hampstead Norris*

*Wellow, Som.	1787	*Gents. Mag.*, 1787, ii, 961
(ST 7258)	1807	*Gents. Mag.*, 1807, ii, 969
	1906	VCH, Som., I, 312
West Coker, Som.	1862	*J.B.A.A.*, XVIII, 392–5
(ST 5213)	1863	*J.B.A.A.*, XIX, 322
	1906	VCH, Som., I, 312
	1931	*P.S.A.N.H.S.*, LXXVII, 112–14
*West Dean (Hotbury),	1885	*W.A.M.*, XXII, 243–50
West Tytherley,	1900	VCH, Hants, I, 311
Hants (SU 2527)	1957	VCH, Wilts., I (i), 119

West Park see *Bromham*

Whatley, Som.	1838	*Gents. Mag.*, 1838, i, 435
(ST 7447)	1839	*Gents. Mag.*, 1839, ii, 77
	1906	VCH, Som., I, 317

Wherwell see *Fullerton*

Whittington Court,	1953	*T.B.G.A.S.*, LXXI, 13–87
Glos. (SP 0120)		
*Whittlebury (The	1851	*J.B.A.A.*, VI, 73–76
Gullet), Northants.	1852	*J.B.A.A.*, VII, 107–14
(SP 7344)	1902	VCH, Northants., I, 199
*Wigginton, Oxon.	1848	A. Beesley: *History of Banbury*, 41–43
(SP 3933)	1939	VCH, Oxon., I, 309
	1966	*J.R.S.*, LVI, 208
Wingham, Kent	1882	*Arch. Cant.*, XIV, 134–9
(TR 2457)	1883	*Arch. Cant.*, XV, 351
	1932	VCH, Kent, III, 125
	1943	*Ant.*, XVII, 210–12
	1944	*Ant.*, XVIII, 52–55
*Winterton, Lincs.	1966	*Ant. J.*, XLVI, 72–84
(SE 9318)		
*Witcombe, Glos.	1821	*Arch.*, XIX, 178–83
(SO 8914)	1954	*T.B.G.A.S.*, LXXIII, 5–69
	1961	*J.R.S.*, LI, 186
	1963	*J.R.S.*, LIII, 141
	1966	*J.R.S.*, LVI, 212

*Withington, Glos.   1817   Arch., XVIII, 118–21
  (SP 0314)   1955   H. P. R. Finberg: Roman and Saxon Withing-
                             ton: a Study in Continuity

*Woodchester, Glos.   1797   S. Lysons: An Account of Roman Antiquities dis-
  (SO 8303)   covered at Woodchester in the County of Gloucester
                 1813   Lysons (1813), Pt i
                 1927   T.B.G.A.S., XLVIII, 75–96
                 1956   T.B.G.A.S., LXXIV, 172–5

*Woolaston, Glos.   1938   Arch. Camb., XCIII, 93–125
  (ST 5998)

*Woolstone, Berks.   1886   Morgan (1886), 119
  (SU 2987)   1906   VCH, Berks., I, 222
                 1939   Berks. A.J., XLIII, 138

*Wraxall, Birdcombe,   1961   P.S.A.N.H.S., CV, 37–51
  Som. (ST 4771)

*Wynford Eagle,   1864   J.B.A.A., XX, 273
  Dorset (SY 5795)   1952   RCHM, Dorset, 269

*Yatton (Wemberham),   1886   P.S.A.N.H.S., XXXI, 1–9, 64–73
  Som. (ST 4065)   1887   J.B.A.A., XLIII, 353–62
                 1906   VCH, Som., I, 306

*Yeovil, Som.   1928   P.S.A.N.H.S., LXXIV, 122–43
  (ST 5415)

*Note: Villas marked with an asterisk are classified as 'A' in the table on page 212 (4th century).

II GAUL AND GERMANY

Anthée, Belgium   1879   Annales de la Société Archéologique de Namur,
                             XIV, 165ff.
                 1881   ibid., XV, 1ff.
                 1934   Grenier (1934), 843–50
                 1937   de Maeyer (1937), 77–83

Basse Wavre (Hosté),   1914   Cumont (1914), 41
  Belgium   1934   Grenier (1934), 820–3
                 1937   de Maeyer (1937), 73

Chiragan (Martres-   1900   L. Joulin: Les établissements gallo-romains de
  Tolosane), Haute-   Martres-Tolosane (Mémoires de l'Académie
  Garonne, France   des Inscriptions et Belles Lettres, 1ère série,
                             XI)
                 1934   Grenier (1934), 832–7, 850–8, 888–97

Kastell Larga, Haut-Rhin, France	1907	*Westdeutsche Zeitschrift für Geschichte und Kunst*, XXVI, 273–80
	1931	A. Grenier: *Manuel d'Archéologie Gallo-Romaine*, I, 452–4
Kloosterberg, Netherlands	1934	*Oudheidkundige Mededeelingen*, XV, 4–13
Maulévrier, Seine-Maritime, France	1934	Grenier (1934), 800, 802, 805
Mayen, Germany	1928	*Bonner Jahrbücher*, CXXXIII, 51–152
	1934	Grenier (1934), 784–95
Mienne, Eure-et-Loir, France	1934	Grenier (1934), 839, 842–3
Montmaurin, Haute-Garonne, France	1949	*Gallia*, VII, 23–54
Müngersdorf, Köln, Germany	1933	F. Fremersdorf: *Der römische Gutshof Köln-Müngersdorf*
	1934	Grenier (1934), 814–19
Nennig, Germany	1908	*Trierer Jahresbericht*, I, 83ff.
	1934	Grenier (1934), 862–5
St Ulrich, Moselle, France	1919	Swoboda (1919), 26
	1934	Grenier (1934), 830–2
Stein, Netherlands	1928	*Oudheidkundige Mededeelingen*, IX, 4–9

Index of Places

(bib.) = Bibliographical reference
(ill.) = Illustration in the text
Pl. = Plate
* An asterisk indicates a villa

*Abbotts Ann, Hants, 153, 265 (bib.)
*Acton Scott, Salop., 144, 156, 265 (bib.)
Aldborough (Isurium Brigantum), W.R. Yorks., 148
Alexandria, Egypt, 186
All Cannings Cross, Wilts., 9, 13 (ill.), 16
*Alresford, Essex, 265 (bib.)
*Angmering, Sussex, 75–76, 124 (bib.), 153, 265 (bib.)
*Anthée, Belgium, 206, 279 (bib.)
Antinoé, Egypt, 91
Antioch, Syria, 93
*Apethorpe, Northants., 107, 122 (bib.), 265 (bib.)
*Appleshaw, Hants, 141
*Arentsburg, Netherlands, 152
Arlon (Orolaunum), Belgium, 168
*Ashtead, Surrey, 153, 155, 156 (ill.), 157, 265 (bib.)
Athens, Greece, 170
*Atworth, Wilts., 157, 232, 265 (bib.)

Augst (Augusta Raurica), Switzerland, 152
Autun (Augustodunum Aeduorum), France, 207
Avon Valley (War.), 25

Bagendon, Glos., 186
*Barnsley Park, Glos., 40, 232, 265 (bib.)
Bartlow, Essex, 161 (ill.)
*Barton Farm, Cirencester, Glos., 97–101, 120 (bib.), 266 (bib.), Pl. 3.12
Bath (Aquae Sulis), Som., 157, 229–30
Bathford, Som., 157 (ill.)
Bavai (Bagacum Nerviorum), France, 207
Bawdrip, Som., 168
*Bedwyn Brail, Wilts., 266 (bib.)
Besançon (Vesontio), France, 75
Bigbury, Kent, 18
*Bignor, Sussex, 24, 53, 57, 58 (plan), 62, 83, 85, 94, 124 (bib.), 130, 131 (ill.), 134, 152, 154, 266 (bib.), Colour Pl. 3.1, Pl. 4.2

281

Bilbury, Wilts., 30

Birdoswald (Camboglanna), Cumb., 160

*Bisley, Glos., 155, 266 (bib.)

Blagden Copse, Hurstbourne Tarrant, Hants, 5 (plan), 23

Blandford, Dorset, 22

Bordeaux (Burdigala), France, 207

*Borough Farm, Pulborough, Sussex, 266 (bib.)

*Borough Hill, Daventry, Northants., 266 (bib.)

Boscombe Down, Hants, 5 (area), 11, 25

*Box, Wilts., 130, 144, 154, 266 (bib.), Colour Pl. 4.4

*Brading, I.O.W., 38, 39 (ill.), 43 (plan), 44, 54 (plan), 56, 58 (plan), 60, 66 (plan), 68, 83–85, 91, 93, 121 (bib.), 142 (ill.), 143, 144, 152, 168, 169, 266 (bib.), Pl. 3.8, 4.5, Colour Pl. 4.3

*Bramdean, Hants, 23, 83, 121 (bib.), 266 (bib.), Pl. 3.4

*Brantingham, E.R. Yorks., 80, 85, 105–7, 125 (bib.), 145, 148, 151, 267 (bib.), Pl. 3.19

*Brislington, Bristol, 123 (bib.), 169, 226, 267 (bib.)

Brittany (Armorica), 215, 224

*Bromham, Wilts., 86, 124 (bib.), 267 (bib.)

Brough-on-Humber (Petuaria), E.R. Yorks., 97, 102, 105, 106

Caburn, The, Sussex, 13, 25

Caerleon (Isca), Mon., 165

Caerwent (Venta Silurum), Mon., 157, 162, 168, 235, Pl. 4.23

Caistor St Edmund (Venta Icenorum), Norfolk, 141, 174

*Calne Without, Wilts., 124 (bib.), 267 (bib.)

Camerton, Som., 202

Cardiff, Glam., 230

*Carisbrooke, I.O.W., 130, 133, 134, Pl. 4.3

Carlisle (Luguvalium), Cumb., 159

Casterley, Wilts., 24

*Castle Dykes, North Stainley, W.R. Yorks., 141, 148, 267 (bib.)

*Castlefield, Andover, Hants, 67, 267 (bib.)

*Castor, Northants., (see also Mill Hill), 107, 202, 267 (bib.)

*Catsgore, Som., 37, 38, 199, 201, 267 (bib.)

*Chedworth, Glos., 50, 60, 62, 63 (plan), 64, 68, 69, 84, 85, 97, 100, 101, 113, 120 (bib.), 134, 155, 156, 267 (bib.)

*Cherhill, Wilts., 116, 124 (bib.), 267 (bib.)

Chester (Deva), 158, 159, 170

Chettle, Dorset, 47

*Chew Stoke, Som., 157

Chiltern Hills, 26

*Chiragan (Martres Tolosane), France, 206, 279 (bib.)

Chisenbury Warren, Wilts., 6 (plan), 24, 33

Cirencester (Corinium Dobunnorum), Glos., 97–99, 112, 116, 147, 151, 153, 235

*Clanville, Hants, 58 (plan), 60, 66 (plan), 67, 69, 141, 267 (bib.)

Colchester (Camulodunum), Essex, 162, 185, 186

*Colerne, Wilts., 86, 94, 124 (bib.), 268 (bib.)

*Collingham (Dalton Parlours), W.R. Yorks., 148, 268 (bib.)

Colliton Park, *see* Dorchester

Colsterworth, Lincs., 10

*Combe Down, Som., 268 (bib.)

*Comb End, Glos., 120 (bib.), 145, 152, 153, 268 (bib.), Pl. 4.4

*Compton Abdale, Glos., 131 (ill.), 134, 144

Cotswold Hills, 26, 226, 231

Cottenham, Cambs., 31

*Cox Green, Maidenhead, Berks., 56, 268 (bib.)

Cranborne Chase, Wilts., 25, 31, 32, 202

Crosby Garrett, Westmorland, 28

*Cromhall, Glos., 268 (bib.)

Crowland, Lincs., 30

Cuckoo Bridge, Spalding, Lincs., 30, 46 (ill.), Pl. 1.3

Cyprus, 16

Daglingworth, Glos., 159

*Darenth, Kent, 132 (ill.), 133, 137, 138 (ill.), 141, 142 (ill.), 143, 149, 268 (bib.)

Dartmoor, 28

Denmark, 20

*Denton, Lincs., 68, 79, 81, 107, 109, 119, 122 (bib.), 268 (bib.), Pl. 3.26

Dinorben, Denbighs., 4

*Ditchley, Oxon., 50, 54 (plan), 55, 60, 69, 157, 199, 201, 206, 209, 268 (bib.), Pl. 2.1

Dorchester (Durnovaria), Dorset, 35, 97, 111, 112, 165–167, Pl. 4.24 (*see also* Olga Road)

*Downton, Wilts., 81, 124 (bib.), 268 (bib.)

Draughton, Northants., 10

*Eastbourne, Sussex, 268 (bib.)

*East Coker, Som., 83, 86, 91, 92 (ill.), 123 (bib.), 268 (bib.)

Ebsbury, Wilts., 34

*East Grimstead, Wilts., 269 (bib.)

*Ebrington, Glos., 269 (bib.)

*Eccles, Kent, 75, 121 (bib.), 207, 269 (bib.), Pl. 3.1

*Eling, Yattendon, Berks., 269 (bib.)

Elst, Netherlands, 152

*Ely, Cardiff, Glam., 55, 147, 153, 269 (bib.)

*Engleton, Staffs., 54 (plan), 55, 57, 269 (bib.)

Ewe Close, Westmorland, 28

*Ewhurst (Rapsley), Surrey, 269 (bib.)

*Exning (Landwade), Suffolk, 65, 133, 138, 139 (ill.), 143, 151, 152, 269 (bib.)

Farley Mount, Ashley, Hants, 5 (plan), 8, 23

*Farningham (Manor Farm), Kent, 134, 149, 150, Pl. 4.9

Fenland, The, 29, 31–33, 37, 44, 199

*Fifehead Neville, Dorset, 84, 86, 87, 110, 111, 119 (bib.), 141, 269 (bib.), Pl. 3.30

*Finchingfield, Essex, 144, 269 (bib.)

Fingringhoe, Essex, 153

*Fishbourne, Sussex, 45, 59, 64, 72, 74–78, 124 (bib.), 150, 153, 207, 269 (bib.), Pl. 3.2

*Folkestone, Kent, 39 (ill.), 57 (plan), 58 (plan), 59, 60, 64, 153, 270 (bib.)

Fosbury, Wilts., Pl. 1.1

*Foscott, Bucks., 165, 270 (bib.), Pl. 4.29

*Fouron-le-Comte, Belgium, 162

*Frampton, Dorset, 82–86, 88, 94, 101, 109–12, 119 (bib.), 165, 270 (bib.), Pl. 3.27, 3.28, 4.25

*Frilford, Berks., 54 (plan), 55, 270 (bib.)

*Frindsbury, Kent, 141, 270 (bib.)

*Frocester Court, Glos., 55, 81, 120 (bib.), 233, 270 (bib.)

Froxfield, Wilts., (see also Rudge), 154, Pl. 4.14

*Fullerton (Wherwell), Hants, 85, 121 (bib.), 270 (bib.)

Fyfield Down, Wilts., 42

*Gadebridge, Hemel Hempstead, Herts., 270 (bib.)

Gargrave, see Kirk Sink

Gaul, 2–4, 40, 44, 52, 53, 113, 114, 183, 184, 188, 194 (map), 195, 202, 207–9

*Gayton Thorpe, Norfolk, 69, 270 (bib.)

Germany, 16, 53, 55, 56, 68, 114, 188, 195

Glastonbury, Som., 11, 18, 20, 171

Gloucester (Glevum), 168

Goldberg, Switzerland, 8

*Gränichen, Switzerland, 152

Grassington, W.R. Yorks., 28

*Great Casterton, Rutland, 66 (plan), 68, 79, 81, 107, 108, 123 (bib.), 151, 225, 227, 234, 235, 270 (bib.)

Great Chesterford, Essex, 38, 39 (ill.), 40, 56

*Great Staughton, Hunts., 54 (plan), 55, 81, 107, 108, 121 (bib.), 134, 135 (ill.), 270 (bib.), Pl. 3.25

*Great Tew, Oxon., 270 (bib.)

*Great Weldon, Northants., 79, 80, 107, 108, 122 (bib.), 132 (ill.), 133, 271 (bib.), Pl. 3.21

Great Witcombe, see Witcombe

Great Woodbury, Wilts., 25

*Great Wymondley (Purwell Mill), Herts., 271 (bib.)

*Greetwell, Lincs., 139, 145, 152, 271 (bib.), Pl. 4.8

*Grimston, Norfolk, 271 (bib.)

Grovely Ridge, Wilts., 30

Gussage All Saints, Dorset, 5 (plan), 8

*Hadstock, Essex, 136 (ill.), 137, 146

Hales, see Tyrley

*Hambleden, Bucks., 45, 50, 53, 56, 57 (plan), 58 (plan), 60, 271 (bib.)

*Ham Hill, Som., 136 (ill.), 137, 271 (bib.)

*Hampstead Norris (Well House), Hants, 271 (bib.)

*Harpham, E.R. Yorks., 80, 125 (bib.), 139, 140 (ill.), 147, 152, 271 (bib.)

*Harpole, Northants., 107, 122 (bib.), 271 (bib.)

*Hartlip, Kent, 271 (bib.)

*Headington, Oxon., 148, 271 (bib.)

Heath Row, Middlesex, 11

*Hemsworth, Dorset, 83, 84, 86, 111, 119 (bib.), 146, 272 (bib.)

Herculaneum, Italy, 146, 158, 159, 160 (ill.), 164, 165, 168, 169

*Herzogenbuchsee, Switzerland, 152

*High Wycombe, Bucks., 56, 68, 78, 119 (bib.), 144, 151, 272 (bib.)

*Hinton St Mary, Dorset, 81, 83, 84, 86–88, 109–113, 117, 118, 119 (bib.), 272 (bib.), Pl. 3.29

Hockwold, Norfolk, 37

Hod Hill, Dorset, 6, 12, 30, 31, 35

Hog Cliff Hill, Maiden Newton, Dorset, 5 (plan), 11, 23

Holborough, Kent, 161, 170

*Holbury, East Dean, Hants, 66 (plan), 67, 272 (bib.)

*Holcombe, Uplyme, Devon, 70, 272 (bib.)

*Horkstow, Lincs., 84–86, 89 (ill.), 90, 102–7, 122 (bib.), 272 (bib.)
*Hosté, Basse Wavre, Belgium, 59, 279 (bib.)
Hotbury, see West Dean
*Houdeng-Goegnis, Belgium, 209
Housesteads (Vercovicium), Northumb., 42
*Hovingham, N.R. Yorks., 272 (bib.)
*Hucclecote, Glos., 79, 81, 120 (bib.), 146, 154, 272 (bib.), Pl. 4.10

*Ickleton, Cambs., 66 (plan), 68, 141, 144, 146, 152, 272, (bib.), Colour Pl. 4.1, 4.2, 4.5, 4.6
Ilchester (Lindinis), Som., 229
Illogan, see Magor Farm
*Ipswich (Castle Hill), Suffolk, 272 (bib.)
Ireland, 2, 4
Isle of Man, 9
*Itchen Abbas, Hants, 85, 121 (bib.), 272 (bib.)
Itford Hill, Sussex, 16
*Iwerne, Dorset, 6 (plan), 33, 37, 38, 53, 66 (plan), 69, 70, 130, 151, 272 (bib.), Pl. 4.1

*Kastell Larga, France, 65, 280 (bib.)
*Keynsham, Som., 58 (plan), 61, 70, 83, 84, 123 (bib.), 157, 202, 233, 272 (bib.)
*Kings Weston, Bristol, 54 (plan), 55, 56, 80, 120 (bib.), 272 (bib.)
Kingsworthy, Hants, 168
*Kintbury, Berks., 135 (ill.), 137, 141
*Királyudvar (Königshof), Hungary, 65
*Kirk Sink, Gargrave, W.R. Yorks., 44, 148, 272 (bib.)

*Kloosterberg, Netherlands, 152, 280 (bib.)
Knook Down, Wilts., 33, 34
Knocking Hoe, Herts., 26
Knowle Hill, Purbeck, Dorset, 23
Köln (Colonia Agrippinensis), Germany, 152, 165, 170
Kreuznach, Germany, 65

Landwade, see Exning
*Langridge, Som., 165, Pl. 4.21
*Langton, E.R. Yorks., 69, 148, 199, 246–8, 273 (bib.)
*Lansdown, Som., 154, 273 (bib.)
*Latimer, Bucks., 268 (bib.)
*Le Buy, Switzerland, 152
Leicester (Ratae Coritanorum), 148, 151
*Lenthay Green, Sherborne, Dorset, 83, 119, 120 (bib.), 273 (bib.), Pl. 3.31
Lepcis Magna, Africa, 151
Lexden, Essex, 162, 170
Lincolnshire, 20
*Litlington, Cambs., 273 (bib.)
*Littlecote Park, Ramsbury, Wilts., 84, 85, 102, 125 (bib.), 273 (bib.), Pl. 3.16
*Little Milton, Oxon., 50, 53, 54 (plan), 273 (bib.)
*Littleton, Som., 94, 123 (bib.), 273 (bib.)
Little Woodbury, Wilts., 5 (plan), 6ff., 11ff., 16, 20, 21, 25, 31, 32, 199
*Llanfrynach, Brecon, 86, 119 (bib.), 273 (bib.)
*Llantwit Major, Glam., 58 (plan), 60, 68, 120 (bib.), 133, 147, 151, 157, 231–3, 238–43, 239 (section), 273 (bib.), Pl. 4.20

*Llys Brychan, Llangadog, Carm., 147, 273 (bib.)

*Lockleys, Welwyn, Herts., 50, 53, 54 (plan), 141, 142 (ill.), 143, 150, 151, 198, 201, 226, 243–6, 273 (bib.)

London (Londinium), 160, 200, 230, Pl. 4.16

Longbridge Deverill Cow Down, Wilts., 9

*Longstock, Hants, 155

*Low Ham, Som., 69, 80, 83, 85, 90, 91, 102, 117, 123 (bib.), 145, 151, 153, 273 (bib.), Pl. 3.5

*Lufton, Som., 69, 81, 86, 111, 123 (bib.), 133, 134, 144, 151, 274 (bib.)

*Lullingstone, Kent, 69, 70 (plan), 81, 83, 85, 90, 94, 117, 118, 121 (bib.), 127–9, 137, 141, 143, 145, 149, 150, 155, 169, 199, 201, 232, 233, 274 (bib.), Pl. 3.7, 4.15

Lydney Park, Glos., 4, 79, 80, 109

*Magor Farm, Illogan, Cornwall, 141, 274 (bib.)

Maiden Castle, Dorset, 4, 17

*Maidstone (Loose Road), Kent, 274 (bib.)

Malton (Derventio), E.R. Yorks., 148, 151, 231

Mancombe Down, Warminster, Wilts., 5 (plan), 11

*Mansfield Woodhouse, Notts., 54 (plan), 55, 58 (plan), 60, 66 (plan), 67–69, 107, 108, 122 (bib.), 160, 274 (bib.), Pl. 3.23

Martin Down, Hants, 22

*Maulévrier, France, 65, 280 (bib.)

*Mayen, Germany, 53, 56, 65, 280 (bib.)

*Medbourne, Leics., 107, 108, 122 (bib.), 274 (bib.)

Mendip Hills, 189

Meriden Down, Winterbourne Houghton, Dorset, 35, 36 (plan)

Meon Hill, Hants, 8

*Mersea Island, Essex, 274 (bib.)

*Mill Hill, Castor, Northants., 107, 122 (bib.), 267 (bib.), 274 (bib.), Pl. 3.24

Milston Down, Wilts., 22

*Montmaurin, France, 206, 280 (bib.)

*Müngersdorf, Köln, Germany, 53, 280 (bib.)

Narbonne (Narbo Martius), France, 165, 207

*Nennig, Germany, 59, 280 (bib.)

*Nether Heyford, Northants., 107, 108, 122 (bib.), 274 (bib.)

*Newton Nottage, Glam., 274 (bib.)

New Timber Hill, Lewes, Sussex, 42

*Newton St Loe, Som., 84, 97–99, 100, 101, 123 (bib.), 274 (bib.), Pl. 3.10

Norden, Corfe Castle, Dorset, 166, Pl. 4.28

*North Leigh, Oxon., 58 (plan), 60, 61 (plan), 62, 64, 68, 97, 100, 123 (bib.), 148, 156, 274 (bib.)

*North Newbald, E.R. Yorks., 148, 275 (bib.)

*North Warnborough, Hants, 67, 134, 135, 141, 142 (ill.), 275 (bib.)

*North Wraxall, Wilts., 154–7, 226, 275 (bib.)

*Norton Disney, Lincs., 225, 233, 275 (bib.)

*Oldcoates (Styrrup), Notts., 84, 122 (bib.), 144, 275 (bib.)

*Old Durham, Co. Durham, 69, 139, 275 (bib.)

*Olga Road, Dorchester, Dorset, 275 (bib.)

Ostia, Italy, 101, 153, 162, 186

*Otford, Kent, 91, 144, 145, 149, 152, 275 (bib.), Pl. 4.6, 4.7

Paris (Lutetia Parisiorum), France, 207

Park Brow, Sussex, 6 (plan), 33

*Park Street, Herts., 24, 50, 53, 54 (plan), 55, 56, 184, 198, 201, 204, 227, 275 (bib.)

Périgueux (Vesunna Petrucoriorum), France, 207

*Piazza Armerina, Sicily, 181

Pimperne Down, Dorset, 9, 47

*Pit Meads, Wilts., 84, 88, 97–99, 125 (bib.), 275 (bib.)

*Pitney, Som., 83, 85, 102, 124 (bib.), 275 (bib.), Pl. 3.3

Pompeii, Italy, 53, 64, 146, 151, 153, 158, 159, 164–7 (ill.), 168, 171

Portland, Dorset, 17

Prae Wood, St Albans, Herts., 24

*Preston, Dorset, 167, 275 (bib.), Pl. 4.26

Purbeck, Isle of, Dorset, 20, 47

*Putley, Herefords., 155, 275 (bib.)

Quarley Hill, Hants, 22

Rapsley, see Ewhurst

Rhineland, The, 52, 208

Rhône Valley, 180

Robin Hood's Arbour, Berks., 24

*Rockbourne, Hants, 47, 134, 135 (ill.), 139, 168, 169, 276 (bib.)

Rockbourne Down, Hants, 42, 44

*Rodmarton, Glos., 120 (bib.), 276 (bib.)

Rome, Italy, 151, 158, 170

Rotherley, Wilts., 31, 32

*Rothley, Leics., 165, 276 (bib.), Pl. 4.27

*Roxby, Lincs., 108, 122 (bib.), 276 (bib.)

*Rudge Farm, Froxfield, Wilts., 85, 200, 276 (bib.)

*Rudston, E.R. Yorks., 81, 83–86, 95, 107, 118, 119, 125 (bib.), 148, 276 (bib.), Pl. 3.20

St Albans (Verulamium), Herts., 79, 128, 141, 143, 148, 151, 200, 234, 243

*St Ulrich, France, 280 (bib.)

Salisbury Plain, 33

*Sapcote, Leics., 134, 135 (ill.), 276 (bib.)

*Saunderton Mill, Bucks., 199, 201, 276 (bib.)

*Scampton, Lincs., 107, 108, 122 (bib.), 276 (bib.), Pl. 3.22

*Scole (Villa Faustini), Norfolk, 174

*Seeb, Switzerland, 152

Sétif, Algeria, 102

Severn Valley, 25

Shearplace Hill, Dorset, 21, 34

Silchester (Calleva Atrebatum), Hants., 38, 152, 159, 165, 168, 186

Simpelveld, Netherlands, 169, Pl. 4.30

*Šmarje-Grobelce, Hungary, 65

Snettisham, Norfolk, 10

Soldier's Ring, Damerham, Hants, 23

South Shields (Arbeia), Co. Durham, 170

*Southwell, Notts., 123 (bib.), 148, 277 (bib.)

*Southwick, Sussex, 61, 64, 277 (bib.)

Spettisbury, Dorset, 8

*Spoonley Wood, Glos., 56, 57 (plan),

Spoonley Wood, Glos.—contd.
64, 66 (plan), 67, 69, 85, 120 (bib.),
154, 156, 276 (bib.), Pl. 4.13
*Stanton Chair, Suffolk, 277 (bib.)
*Stanton Low, Bucks., 162, Pl. 4.22
Staple Howe, N.R. Yorks., 28
*Star, Shipham, Som., 277 (bib.)
Stara Zagora, Bulgaria, 162
*Stein, Netherlands, 152, 280 (bib.)
Stonehenge, Wilts., 34
*Stonesfield, Oxon., 82–84, 97, 100,
123 (bib.), 277 (bib.), Pl. 3.15
*Stroud, Petersfield, Hants, 58 (plan),
60, 66 (plan), 67, 69, 277 (bib.)
*Sturton-by-Scawby, Lincs., 122
(bib.), 277 (bib.)
Styrrup, *see* Oldcoates

Tallington, Lincs., 13
Tarrant Hinton, Dorset, 47
Thames Valley, 25
*Thruxton, Hants, 82, 85, 94, 121
(bib.), 277 (bib.), Pl. 3.9
Thundersbarrow Hill, Sussex, 25, 34,
42
*Titsey, Surrey, 277 (bib.)
*Tockington Park, Glos., 97, 100, 113,
120 (bib.), 169, 277 (bib.)
*Totternhoe, Beds., 277 (bib.)
Toulouse (Tolosa), France, 207
Tours (Caesarodunum Turonum),
France, 207, 208
Tracy Park, nr Bath, Som., 154
Trier (Augusta Treverorum), Germ-
any, 116, 146, 151, 153, 160, 168,
207, Pl. 3.32, 4.17
Twyford Down, Hants, 18
*Tyrley (Hales), Staffs., 277 (bib.)

Verulamium, *see* St Albans
Virunum, nr Klagenfurt, Austria, 152
*Vlengendaal, Netherlands, 152

*Wadfield, Sudeley, Glos., 154, 277
(bib.)
Wadi Qelt, Palestine, 59
*Walton Heath, Surrey, 78, 124 (bib.),
277 (bib.)
Wangford, Suffolk, 26
War Ditches, Cherry Hinton, Cambs.,
13, 26
Water Newton (Durobrivae), Hunts.,
97, 108
Weiden, Germany, 160
*Well, N.R. Yorks., 78, 125 (bib.), 278
(bib.)
Welland Valley, 13, 16, 24, 25
*Wellow, Som., 84, 154, 157, 278 (bib.),
Pl. 4.11
West Blatchington, Sussex, 31
*West Dean (Hotbury), Hants, 68, 278
(bib.)
West Harling, Norfolk, 8, 9
West Hill, Plush, Piddletrenthide,
Dorset, 35
Westminstone Down, Frampton,
Dorset, 35
*Whatley, Som., 85, 86, 111, 124
(bib.), 278 (bib.)
Whitsbury, Wilts., 168
*Whittington Court, Glos., 80, 120
(bib.), 226, 233, 278 (bib.)
*Whittlebury, Northants., 143, 278
(bib.)
*Wigginton, Oxon., 97, 100, 113, 123
(bib.), 278 (bib.)
*Wincanton, Som., 156, 168
Winchester (Venta Belgarum), Hants,
153
*Wingham, Kent, 153, 278 (bib.)
*Winterton, Lincs., 9, 78, 81, 82, 84,
102–7, 122 (bib.), 145, 146, 151,
278 (bib.), Pl. 3.17, 3.18
*Witcombe, Glos., 42, 86, 120 (bib.),

142 (ill.), 143 (ill.), 146, 147, 155, 278 (bib.)

*Withington, Glos., 83, 84, 86, 90, 97–101, 112, 113, 116, 121 (bib.), 279 (bib.), Pl. 3.11

*Woodchester, Glos., 58 (plan), 61, 62, 64, 68, 72, 83–86, 94, 95, 97–101, 103, 105, 116, 121 (bib.), 145, 147, 153, 154, 231, 233, 279, (bib.) Pl. 3.13, 3.14, 3.32, 4.12, Colour Pl. 3.2

Woodcuts, Dorset, 31

Woodhouse Hill, Studland, Dorset, 25, 33, 38

*Woolaston, Glos., 279 (bib.)

*Woolstone, Berks., 279 (bib.)

Worthing, Sussex, 44

*Wraxall, Birdcombe, Som., 228, 279 (bib.)

*Wynford Eagle, Dorset, 111, 112, 120 (bib.), 279 (bib.)

*Yatton (Wemberham), Som., 279 (bib.)

*Yeovil, Som., 279 (bib.)

York (Eburacum), 158–160, 180, Pl. 4.18, 4.19

Yorkshire Wolds, 28

General Index

(ill.) = Illustration in the text
Pl. = Plate

Abraxas, in mosaic, 84, 91
Achates, in wall-painting, 145
Aedificium, meaning of, 177, 181
Aelia Aeliana, tombstone of, 158–9, 164, Pl. 4.19
Aeneas and Dido, in mosaic, 83, 90, Pl. 3.5, 3.6
Agricola, Cn. Iulius, 190, 195, 198, 200, 204
Agriculture, 1–48, 51, 204, 215–16, 219
Air photography, 25, 30, 47, 50, 60; Pl. 1.1, 1.3, 2.1
Aisled houses, 64–68, 66 (plans)
Albinus, D. Clodius, 201
Allectus, 202
Amber, imported, 186
Ambrosia, in mosaic, 92
Amphitheatre, scenes from, in mosaic, 85, 86, Pl. 3.20
Andromeda, in mosaic, 93, 94
Animal forms of table legs, 167–8
Animal husbandry, 15, 20–21, 44–45, 47, 51, 195
Annona, 189–98, 191 (map), 194 (map), 201
Antonine Itinerary, 174

Apollo and Marsyas, in mosaic, 83, 119, Pl. 3.31
Applebaum, S., 24, 45, 209, 219
Architectural subjects in wall-painting, 146
Army recruiting, 189
Army, supplies for, 188, 189–198, 191 (map), 194 (map)
Artis, E. T., 108
Astronomy, personification of, in mosaic, 84, Pl. 3.8
Athenaeus, 2, 12, 20
Atrebates (in Britain), 186, 187 (map) villas of, 210, 211 (map), 212, 213 (map)
Augustus (Emperor), 201
Ausonius, D. Magnus, 174, 207
Axes, 24, 38, 39 (ill.)

Bacaudae, 224
Bacchus (Dionysus), in mosaic, 82, 87, 91, 92 (ill.), 93–94, 109, 110, Pl. 3.9, 3.15
  statue of, 154, Pl. 4.13
Bailiff (*vilicus*), 158, 179, 199, 205
'Banjo'-shaped enclosures, 23

291

Barley, 19
Barns (see also Granaries), 65
Barrows, Roman, finds in, 161–62
Basilican houses, see Aisled houses
Bath-houses, 51, 59, 62, 68–69, 86
Beans, 19
Beds and couches, 158–9, Pl. 4.30
Bedspreads, 170
Beer, 19
Belgae, villas of, 210, 211 (map), 212, 213 (map)
Bellerophon and Chimaera, in mosaic, 83, 110–11, 118, Pl. 3.27, 3.29
Benches, 159
Bersu, G., 6–8, 11, 16
Birds, in wall-painting, 144, Colour Pl. 4.3
Birrus Britannicus, 45, 203
Boats, 3
Bonus Eventus, worship of, 95
  in mosaic, 101, Pl. 3.14
Boon, G. C., 162
Borrow, George, 3
Boudicca, 200, 244
Bowen, H. C., 1–48, 177, 185, 192, 205, 215, 216
Bread, 20, 189
Brigantes, 187 (map)
  villas of, 210, 211 (map), 212, 213 (map)

Caesar, C. Julius, 4, 6, 21, 24, 29, 177, 183–4, 186, 196, 204
Calkin, J. B., 22
Cantiaci, villas of, 210, 211 (map), 212, 213 (map)
Caracalla (M. Aurelius Antoninus: Emperor), 184
Carausius, M. Aurelius Mausaeus, 202, 222
Carbon 14 dating, 221

Carts, 19
Casa, meaning of, 181
Caskets, 169
Cassivellaunus, 21, 188
Cato, M. Porcius, 12, 157–8, 159, 170, 179, 204
Cats, 45
Cattle, 20–21, 44–45, 47, 195; Pl. 1.2
  pre-Roman export of, 3, 186
Catuvellauni, 186, 187 (map)
  villas of, 210, 211 (map), 212, 213 (map)
Cauldrons, 158
Ceilings, painted, 148
Cellars, 16–17
Celtic art, 118–19, 165
'Celtic' fields, see Fields
Celtic kings and chieftains, wealth of, 9–10, 170
  society, 2–4, 182–5, 203–4
Centuriation, 31
Ceres, in mosaic, 82, 83, 92, 93, Pl. 3.17
  statue of, 154
Chairs and stools, 159–62
Chariots, 188
  in mosaic, 86, 87, 89 (ill.), 103, 106
Cheese, 20
Chests, 169
Chi-Rho symbol, in mosaic, 84, 87–88, 102, 109, 110, 118, Pl. 3.27, 3.29, Colour Pl. 3.2
  on wall plaster, 70, 150
Chickens, 21–22
Christ, head of, on mosaic pavement, 84, 87–88, 110, 118, Pl. 3.29, Colour Pl. 3.2
Christian symbols, in mosaic, 109–10, Pl. 3.27, 3.29, 3.30, Colour Pl. 3.2
  wall-paintings, 129, 141, 149
Christianity, 70, 84, 233

Christiansen, J., 127
Church, as property-owner, 208
Cincinnatus, T. Quinctius, 204
Circus scenes, in mosaic, 86
Cities, (Civitas Capitals) as centres of land settlement, 181
Claudius (Emperor), 186
Clientes, 4, 183
Coal, 33
Cobbett, W., 29
Cogidumnus, Ti. Claudius, 59, 74
Coinage, Celtic, 185–6, 187 (map), 209–10, 212
Coins, as dating evidence, 219–20, 234, 237, 248
Collingwood, R. G., 32, 176–7
Coloniae, as centres of land settlement, 180–1
Coloni, condition of, in late Empire, 214–15
Colours used in wall-paintings, 129
Columella, L. Junius Moderatus, 17, 40, 44, 174, 179–82, 197, 206
Columns, stone, 156–7
Combs, weaving, 13, 14 (ill.)
Constans (Emperor), 223
Constantine I (Emperor), 90, 115
Constitutio Antoniniana, 184–5
Continuity, problems of, 214–16, 221–37, 243–6, 249
Corder, P., 246–8
Corinian school of mosaic, 96 (map), 97–103, 108, 112–13, 115–16
Coritani, 186, 187 (map)
villas of, 210, 211 (map), 212, 213 (map)
Corn, consumption of, 12, 19, 197
exported from pre-Roman Britain, 3, 186–9
storage of, 2, 7, 11–13, 14 (ill.), 15–17, 31–32, 65, 69, 192

-drying ovens and kilns, 15–16, 19, 31, 42, 45–47, 56, 69, 233–4
Cornovii, 187 (map)
villas of, 210, 211 (map), 212, 213 (map)
Corridor houses, 53–59, 54 (plans), 57 (plans)
Corridors, social implications of, 50, 52, 205
Cottage houses, 52–53, 54 (plans)
Couches and beds, 158–9
Council for British Archaeology, 248–9
Courtyard houses, 59–64, 58 (plans), 61 (plan), 63 (plan)
Crawford, O. G. S., 30
Crops, variety of, 19, 45
Cupboards, 160 (ill.), 169, Pl. 4.30
Cupid and Psyche, in marble, 154
Cupid(s) in mosaic, 76–77, 82, 85, 87, 103, 109
Cupids, wall-painting from Herculaneum, 159, 160 (ill.)
Curiales, condition of in 3rd and 4th centuries, 207
Customs duties (*portoria*), 189

Days of the week, in mosaic, 83, Pl. 3.4
Deceangli, absence of villas in territory, 178, 210–13
Decianus Catus, 198
Decuriones, 10, 207–9
Deinarchos (poet), 93–94
Demetae, 187 (map)
villas of, 210, 211 (map)
Diana, in sculpture, 154–5
Dido and Aeneas, in mosaic, 117, Pl. 3.5, 3.6
Digest of Justinian, 177
Dio Cocceianus, Cassius, 185
Diocletian (Emperor), 214
Diodorus Siculus, 2, 3

Dionysus, *see* Bacchus

Dobunni, 186, 187 (map)
  villas of, 210, 211 (map), 212, 213 (map), 214

Dogs, 22
  export of, 3, 86, 186, 189

Dolphins, in mosaic, 86, 87, 109, 111–12

Drack, W., 152

Drying racks, 14 (ill.), 15

Dumnonii, 187 (map)
  absence of villas in territory, 178, 210–13

Durobrivan school of mosaic, 96 (map), 107–9, 115–16

Durnovarian school of mosaic, 96 (map), 109–13, 115–16

Durotriges, 186, 187 (map)
  villas of, 210, 211 (map), 212, 213 (map)

Edict of Diocletian on prices, 203

Equites in Celtic society, 4, 185

Europa and Bull, in mosaic, 83, 145, Pl. 3.7

Eusebius, 90

Evangelists, possible representation of, in mosaic, 88

Exports from pre-Roman Britain, 3, 186–9

Farming, 1–48, 51, 204, 215–16, 219

Farms, Iron Age, 1–48, 193 (map), 204, 215–16

Fields, 'Celtic', 18–19, 22–24, 26–28, 27 (plan), 29, 31, 34–35, 36 (plan), 41–44, 43 (plan), 219, Pl. 1.1
  'Celtic', related to villas, 24, 31, 42, 43 (plan)
  'Long', 26, 42
  'Strip', 18–19, 27 (ill.), 41–44

Fire, destruction of villas by, 224–7

Fish, in mosaic, 86
  in wall paintings, 144, 146

Flight of capital to Britain, 114, 208–9

Folding stools, 160–2, 161 (ill.)
  tripods, 162, 163 (ill.)

Footstools, 169

Fountains, 62

Fox, Sir Cyril, 186

Frere, S. S., 128, 234

Frisians, taxation of, 195

Fruit, 45

Fundus, meaning of, 177, 181

Furniture, 158–72

Ganymede, in mosaic, 83

Gardens, 45

Geese, 21

Gladiators, in mosaic, 85, 87

Glassware, imported, 186

Gnosticism, 84, 91

Goats, 45

Gold, pre-Roman export of, 3, 186, 189

Granaries, 2, 14 (fig.), 15, 31, 65, 69, 70

Gray, H. St George, 130

Greek, use of in Britain, 94

Gruel, 20

Gulioepius, dedication by, 155

Hadrian (Emperor), 199–200

Hamlets, 4, 203–4

Hares, 21

Haverfield, F., 176, 192

Hawkes, C. F. C., 25, 31

Hawkes, Mrs Sonia, 235

Helbaek, H., 16, 45

Hercules and Antaeus, in mosaic, 83
  and the Hydra, in mosaic, 83

Hides, pre-Roman export of, 3, 186

Highland and Lowland zones, 2–3, 186, 187 (map)
  Clearances, analogy of, 183
Hill-forts, Iron Age, 4ff., 25–26, 30–31, 184, 193 (map), 204
Honey, 19
Honorius (Emperor), 224
Horses, 44, 47
House-types, Iron Age, 2, 6 (plans), 7–11, 52
  Romano-British, 28, 49–70, 54 (plans), 57 (plans), 58 (plans), 61 (plan), 63 (plan), 66 (plans)
Human figures, in wall-paintings, 144–5, 150, Colour Pl. 4.4, 4.5
Hunting scenes, in mosaic, 86, 87, 109, 111

Iceni, 186, 187 (map)
  villas of, 210, 211 (map), 212, 213 (map)
Immigrant craftsmen, 170–1
Immigration in 4th century, 114, 208–9
Imperial estates, 33, 208, 221
Imports, 185–6
  pre-Roman, 185–6, 187 (map)
Inscriptions, 174
Irenaeus, St, 110
Irish evidence for the nature of Celtic society, 4, 182
Iron, pre-Roman export of, 3, 186, 189
  working, 24, 38
Ivory bracelets and necklaces, imported, 186

Jackson, K. H., 94
Johnson, Samuel, 185
Jones, A. H. M., 207
Jones, G. R., 203
Julia Velva, tomb of, 160, 164, Pl. 4.18

Julian (Emperor), 223

Kent, J. P. C., 234
Key, C. E., 134
Kilns, corn-drying, see Ovens
Kimmeridge shale, as material for furniture, 160, 165–8
Kirk, J. L., 246–8

Land, alienation of in 19th century, Africa, 182
Land clearance, Iron Age, 26
Landlords, 68, 183
Land tenure, 47, 182–4, 203–7
Latifundia, 180
Latin, use of in Britain, 94
Legions, supplies for, 195–8
Levi, D., 93
Lighting, effect of on colours, 172
Liversidge, Joan, 127–72, 182
Llys, 4, 7
Looms, 21
Loom-weights, 14 (ill.), 21
Luna, statuette of, 154, Pl. 4.12
Lycurgus and Ambrosia, in mosaic, 83, 92
Lysons, S., 61, 109, 130, 145, 153, –4

Machinery, use of, 40
McKenny Hughes, T., 219
Maenads, in mosaic, 85
  in wall-paintings, 144
Manning, W. H., 41
Manure, 17, 19, 21
Marble, as wall decoration, 153
Markets, 200
Mars, in mosaic, 83
Mars Lenus, dedication to, 209
Mattresses, 170
Medusa, in mosaic, 76, 83, 91, 130
Mellor, E., 139

Merchants, foreign, 200
Mercury, in mosaic, 83
　relief of, 154
Mertens, J., 40
Metals, pre-Roman export of, 3, 186, 189
Military equipment, Germanic, 235–6
　occupation of Britain, 189–98, 191 (map), 194 (map)
　rations, 201
Milk, 21
Mining, 28
Modius, meaning of, 196
Morley Hewitt, A. T., 168
Mosaicists, schools of, 95–113, 96 (map)
　use of pattern-books, 91, 95, 117
Mosaic pavements, 51, 71–125
　as indications of wealth, 72
　dating of, 82–95
　illustrations of, 89, 92, Pl. 3.1–3.32, Colour Pl. 3.1, 3.2
　inscriptions on, 94–95
　in villas, list and bibliography, 119–25
　motifs, 76–95
　number and distribution of, 71–74, 73 (map)
　prefabricated panels in, 110–11
　subjects and themes of, 82–95
Mosaics, wall, 153
Mother Goddesses, figurines of, 159–60, Pl. 4.16
　relief of, 154

Nash-Williams, V. E., 238–43
Nereids and Tritons, in mosaic, 85, Pl. 3.8
Neptune, in mosaic, 83, 86, 95, 99, 109, 112, Pl. 3.3, 3.11, 3.13, 3.15, 3.27
Nymphs, in mosaic, 85, Pl. 3.8, 3.19
　in wall-painting, 145, 149–50

Oats, 19
Oil, import of, 189
O'Neil, B. H. St J., 234
Oppida, Belgic, 184, 204
Opus sectile, 153
Ordovices, 187 (map)
　absence of villas in territory, 178, 210–13
Orpheus, in mosaic, 62, 84, 88–90, 91, 95, 97–102, 103, 105, 112, 116, 144, Pl. 3.10, 3.11, 3.12, 3.13, 3.16, 3.17
Ostorius Scapula, P., 186
Ovens and kilns, corn-drying, 15–16, 19, 31, 42, 45–47, 56, 69, 233–4
Ovid (P. Ovidius Naso), 91, 93
Oxen, 20–21, 44

Painted plaster, 127–53, 131 (ill.), 132 (ill.), 135 (ill.), 136 (ill.), 138 (ill.), 140 (ill.), 142 (ill.)
Palladius, Rutilius Taurus Aemilianus, 179
Parisi, 187 (map)
　villas of, 210, 211 (map), 212, 213 (map)
Pastoral farming, 20–21, 24, 28, 44–45, 51
Pattern-books, decorators', 151
　mosaicists', 91, 95–113, 117
Pay, military, 201
Payne, Mrs G., 133
Perseus, in mosaic, 83, 93–94
Petronius Arbiter, 180
Petuarian School of mosaicists, 96 (map), 102–7, 115–16
Pewter, manufacture of, 202
Piggott, S., 192, 197
Pigs, 45
Pillows, 170
Pipeclay figurines, 159–60

Pirates, 202
'Pit Alignments', 25
Pits, storage, 7, 11–13, 14 (ill.), 15–17, 31–32, 192
Pitt-Rivers, General A. H., 25, 33, 130, 219
Plautius, A., 186, 196
Pliny (C. Plinius Secundus, the Elder), 29, 40, 41, 179
Ploughs, 13, 14 (ill.), 18–19, 29, 39 (ill.), 40–44, 175; Pl. 1.2
Pomegranates, in mosaic, 109
Ponies, 21
Posidonius, 4, 20, 183
'Pot-boilers', 13
Potteries, Castor, 202, 208
Pottery, as dating evidence, 219–21, 235, 237–48
Pottery, imports of, 3–4, 186, 202, 235
Probus (Emperor), 203
Providentia, in mosaic, 84, Pl. 3.18

Querns, 13, 14 (ill.), 20, 47

Rabbits, not introduced until 12th century, 21
'Ranch Boundaries', 22–23
Rations, military, 195–7
Regnenses, villas of, 210, 211 (map), 212, 213 (map)
Richmond, Sir Ian, 49–70, 198
Rivet, A. L. F., 29, 173–216, 221
Roman army, supplies for, 28, 29
  military equipment, 30
  occupation, effects of, 28–32, 189–98, 221
  roads, 28, 34, 35, 37
Romulus, relief of, 155
Roofing stones, 47, Pl. 4.20
'Rounds' (small enclosures), 24
Rye, 19

Sacrovir, Julius, 181–2
Salt, 20
Salway, P., 37
Satyrs, in mosaics, 85
  in wall-paintings, 144
Saxon invasions and occupation, 214–16, 222, 235–7
  Shore defences, 222
Schools of wall-painters, 153
  of mosaicists, 95–113, 96 (map)
Sculpture, 153–5
Scythes, 38, 39 (ill.), 40, 44
Seasons, in mosaic, 85, 87, 93, 101, 102, 130, Pl. 3.3, 3.9, 3.16
Seed corn, 15, 196–7
Seneca, L. Annaeus, 200
Settlements, Iron Age, 5 (plans), 25–26, 35, Pl. 1.1
  Romano-British, 31ff., 36 (plan)
  Romano-British in Fenland, 29–30, 46 (ill.), Pl. 1.3
Severus (Emperor), 189, 201
Shears, 21
Sheep, 21, 214
Shelves, 169
Shepherds and nymphs, in mosaic, 85, Pl. 3.8
Sickles, 14 (ill.), 15, 38, 39 (ill.)
Sideboards, 168–9
Sidonius Apollinaris (C. Sollius Apoll-inaris Sidonius), 174
Silures, 187 (map)
  villas of, 210, 211 (map), 212, 213 (map)
Silver, pre-Roman export of, 3, 186,189
Skeletons, found in villas, 225, 233
Slaves, 3, 174, 189
Slave-chains, 184
Smith, D. J., 71–125, 133, 182, 203, 208
Spades, 38, 39 (ill.)
Spindle whorls, 13, 14 (ill.), 21

Spinning, 21
Sporting scenes, in mosaic, 85, 87
Spring, in mosaic, 85
Statues, 153–5
Stevens, C. E., 184
Stilicho, 223
Stools, 160–2
Storage jars, 13
  -pits, 7, 11–13, 14 (ill.), 15–17, 31–32, 192
Strabo, 2, 3, 20, 22, 186–9
Swoboda, K. M., 52, 55

Tables, 162–8, 164 (ill.), 166 (ill.), 167 (ill.), Pl. 4.21, 4.22, 4.23, 4.24, 4.25, 4.26, 4.27, 4.28, 4.29, 4.30
Tacitus, Cornelius, 2, 4, 10, 16, 45, 177, 188, 190, 195, 197, 244
Taeogtref, 7
Tapete Britannicum, 45, 203
Taxation, 184–5, 190–7, 199–200, 215–16
Tenants (*coloni*), 183, 203–7
Theodosius, Count, 223
Theseus and the Minotaur, in mosaic, 84
Thomas, A. C., 24
Threshing-floors, 69
Tiberius (Emperor), 190
Tierney, J. J., 2, 4
Tools, 18, 38, 39 (ill.), 219
Towels, 170
Towns, development of, 200, 204–5
Trade, 3, 185–9, 200
Tref, 7
Tribute, 190–7, 199–200, 215–16
Trimalchio, 180
Trinovantes, 187 (map)
  villas of, 210, 211 (map), 212, 213 (map)

Triptolemus, in mosaic, 83, 92, 93
Tritons, in mosaic, 85, 91, Pl. 3.8
Tugurium, meaning of, 181
Tyche, in mosaic, 85, 105, Pl. 3.19
Tyddyn, 7

Upper storeys, 50, 51

Vallus (reaping machine), 40 (ill.)
Varro, M. Terentius, 174, 179–82, 196
Varus, P. Quinctilius, 195
Vegetables, 44–45
Venus, in mosaic, 83, 90, 107, 118, Pl. 3.3, 3.5, 3.20, Colour Pl. 3.1
  statue of, 154, Pl. 4.14
Veranius, Q., 195
Vestorius Priscus, tomb of, 158
Vicesima hereditatum, 185
Victor, the Moor, tomb of, 170
Villa, meaning of word, 51, 175–82
Villas, attempted classification of, 210–14
  bath-houses, 51, 59, 62, 68–69, 86
  depicted in wall-paintings, 53, 146
  development of, 198–209
  distribution of, 51–52, 178 (map), 186, 209–14, 211 (map), 213 (map)
  end of, 214–16, 221–37, 229 (map), 230 (map)
  estates related to, 24, 59, 62, 70, 175, 203–8, 214–15
  excavation reports reassessed, 237–48
  fields related to, 24, 31, 42, 43 (plan); Pl. 2.1
  furniture and interior decoration, 127–72
  house types, 49–70
  mosaics in, 71–125
  outbuildings of, 68–70
  plans of, 49–70

social and economic aspects, 173–216

types of evidence for study, 217–21

wall-paintings in, 127–53

[For individual villas see names marked with an asterisk in Index of Places]

Villages, 4, 11, 32ff., 176

Virgil, 90–91, 117

line in wall-painting, 145

Virtus, in mosaic, 85

Visigoths, settled in Gaul, 224, 236

Wall-paintings, 33, 70, 127–72

Ward, John, 65

Ward-Perkins, J. B., 243–6

Warfare, intertribal, 188

Water-storage, 17

Weaving, 21, 203

combs, 21

Webster, G., 214, 217–49

Wells, 44

Welsh evidence for Celtic society, 2–4, 182, 203–4

Wheat, varieties of, 19

Wheeled ploughs, 18

Wheeler, Sir Mortimer, 24, 243

Wickerwork chairs, 159–60, 171

Windows, 56, 65, 69

Window glass, 33

Winds, in mosaic, 85, 91, 93, 109, 110, Pl. 3.28

Wine, import of, 4, 189, 200

Winged corridor houses, 53–59, 54 (plans), 57 (plans)

Wool, 21, 203, 214

Yields of crops, estimates of, 196–7